VERTICAL EMPIRE

VERTICAL EMPIRE

The General Resettlement of Indians in the Colonial Andes

Jeremy Ravi Mumford

DUKE UNIVERSITY PRESS   DURHAM AND LONDON   2012

© 2012 Duke University Press

All rights reserved

Printed in the United States of America on acid-free paper ∞

Designed by Heather Hensley

Typeset in Quadraat by Copperline Book Services, Inc.

Library of Congress Cataloging-in-Publication Data appear
on the last printed page of this book.

This book is dedicated to Sohini Ramachandran

A new world

CONTENTS

ACKNOWLEDGMENTS

I owe many people my gratitude. This book began at Yale, where I benefited from the guidance and savoir-faire of my advisor, Stuart Schwartz, and from the advice of teachers and colleagues. I wrote my dissertation alongside Martin Kenner, so that Andeans, Spaniards, and German-British bankers walked side by side. Those who taught me the most about the colonial Andes were Herbert Klein, Pedro Guibovich, and Rolena Adorno, who invited me to her home and introduced me to Guaman Poma and Cieza de León. President Howard Lamar explained much to me at Mory's. And the person who helped me begin my career as an investigator was Johnny Faragher, a true guide.

In Seville, I had the privilege of working at the Archivo General de Indias, and enjoyed the resources of the Escuela de Estudios Hispano-Americanos and its kind director Enriqueta Vila Vilar. While there I received help and advice from fellow researchers such as Tom Cummins, Gary Urton, Luis Miguel Glave, Kristin Huffine, the late Sabine MacCormack, Matt O'Hara, Peter Gose, Berta Ares, Chuck Walker, and especially David Cook and Sasha Cook. In Sucre, I enjoyed the richness of the Archivo Nacional de Bolivia, and the opportunity to discuss my work with Josep Barnadas, Carmen Beatriz Loza, Ximena Medinaceli, and Tristan Platt. In Cochabamba, I benefited from the erudition of scholar archivists at the Archivo Departamental de Cochabamba, especially Susy Portillo and Itala de Mamán, and the kindness of friends such as Nancy Arispe, Sister Aleksandra Sojka, and my Quechua teachers, especially Fritzy Zembrana.

At Brandeis University I enjoyed the mentorship of Silvia Arrom. In the Michigan Society of Fellows, I benefited from the guidance of several mentors, in particular Donald Lopez, Rebecca Scott, and Richard Turits, and colleagues including Katherine Ibbett, Hussein Fancy, Anna Guillemin, and Stella Nair. At the University of Mississippi, I received friendship and advice from Joe Ward, Douglass Sullivan-Gonzales, and Charles Eagles, among others.

For reading all or most of the manuscript, in its stages, I thank Silvia Arrom, David Cook, Alan Durston, Renzo Honores, Jane Mangan, David Mumford, Daniel Stolzenberg, the late Catherine Julien, and especially Ken Mills, Karen Spalding, and Sohini Ramachandran. For useful comments on specific chapters, I thank Karene Grad, Stella Nair, Kerstin Nowack, Claudia Brittenham, Kathryn Burns, John Charles, Kris Lane, Rolena Adorno, Steve Wernke, Susan Ramirez, Naoko Shibusawa, Vazira Zamindar, and Jim Muldoon. I thank Hanna Rose Shell for giving the book encouragement and a title. I also received helpful advice from Thomas Abercrombie, Alejandro Málaga Nuñez, Elizabeth Penry, James Scott, Ann Whiteman, Rafael Varón, José de la Puente, Rachel O'Toole, Ann Farnsworth, Sam Haselby, Gordon Wood, Amy Remensnyder, Sabine Hyland, Charles Lansing, Amy Kurtz (now Kurtz-Lansing), Gen Liang, and Bernard Bailyn.

I received research funding from a Fulbright-Hays Fellowship, a fellowship from the Howard Lamar Center for the Study of Frontiers and Borders, and a Charlotte W. Newcombe Doctoral Dissertation Fellowship. Erin Clermont copyedited the manuscript. Bill Nelson designed the maps. And I thank Zingerman's Deli in Ann Arbor, where I wrote much of this book upstairs by the window.

I have been nourished by the love of my parents David, Erika and Jenifer, my sister and brothers, their partners, my parents-in-law, my nephews, my flower girls Maya, Leela, and Irene, and most of all Sohini Ramachandran.

My trajectory has been indirect, and I had already begun a doctoral dissertation on nineteenth-century North American circuit-riders when I discovered the path to this book. I made the discovery in Rome, behind the church of Santa Maria sopra Minerva—built over a pagan temple, the Coricancha of the Old World—when a black cat looked into my face and led me through the back door into the cool, dark church. I am grateful for the guidance which that cat, along with my other counselors, gave me.

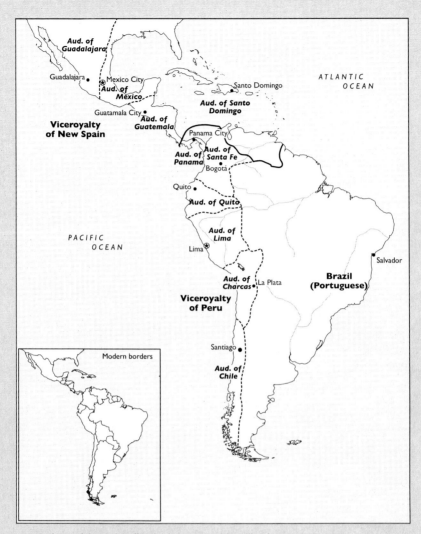

Map 1 Viceroyalties and Audiencias in 1570. Map by Bill Nelson.

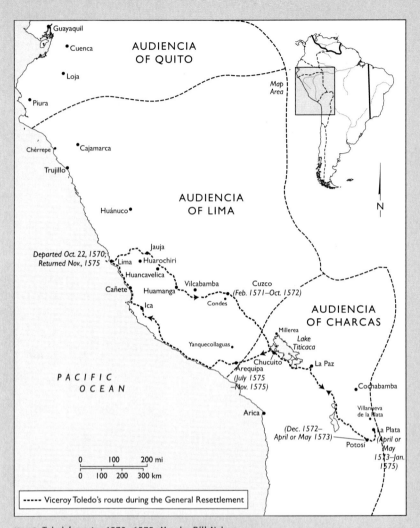

Map 2 Toledo's route, 1570–1575. Map by Bill Nelson.

INTRODUCTION

In 1569, the Spanish empire undertook something new in the history of European colonialism: forcing an entire conquered society to change its way of life overnight. The viceroy, don Francisco de Toledo, ordered the native people of the central Andes to abandon their homes and move to new towns founded after a Spanish model. The word for this process was *reducción*, from the Spanish verb *reducir*, meaning to reduce, subdue, persuade, or reorder. The viceroy's officials fanned out through the provinces with instructions to consolidate small settlements into larger ones, to lay out streets and house lots, and to force more than a million peasant farmers to relocate. The new towns, or *reducciones*, were to have a uniform, quadrilateral street grid surrounding a central plaza and church, governed by indigenous men holding Spanish municipal offices and titles. When they were done, the inspectors were to make their work permanent by destroying the old villages. This was the *Reducción General de Indios*—the General Resettlement of Indians.

It was not the first campaign of *reducción*. Spanish friars had already experimented with reorganizing Indian communities in the Caribbean and Mesoamerica. But in scope and organization, the Andean campaign surpassed all previous efforts and most later ones. Its ambition anticipated state projects of the twentieth century, from Tanzanian model villages to Soviet collectivization. With gridded streets, standardized institutions imposed from above, and vast population registers exposing individuals to the scrutiny of a distant monarch, the campaign foreshadowed the modern state.

How could a small group of colonizers, vastly outnumbered by indigenous people, accomplish something so violent and so profound? And what, exactly, did they have in mind? Surprisingly, historians have scarcely tried to answer these questions. Whether celebrating the General Resettlement's paternalism or decrying the destruction it wrought, scholars have acknowledged the campaign's importance while describing it only in general terms.

One reason for this neglect is the lack of sources: strikingly few have survived for such an important campaign by a government known for careful record-keeping. The officials who carried out the resettlement left little documentation of how they did so, and few observers described it in writing at the time. Some records shed light on the campaign—tribute documents, government financial accounts, judges' legal rulings—but the information they offer is scattered and hard to interpret. Historians have relied mainly on the orders and instructions for the Resettlement, which tell us more about what was supposed to happen than what actually happened. We know that the General Resettlement took place. Throughout Peru and Bolivia today, many of the oldest rural towns trace their origin to Toledo's campaign and preserve the checkerboard layout he demanded. But *how* and *why* it happened as it did—the contours and logic of this massive act of social engineering—have remained unclear.

In fact, the campaign succeeded by drawing on the organization of Andean communities, the power of the native lords, and the memory of the Incas. Paradoxically, the Resettlement's radical restructuring was designed to *preserve* certain aspects of indigenous culture, even while destroying others. There was much that Spaniards wanted to destroy, and much that they despised. Officials claimed that Andeans, "dispersed and separated in narrow valleys and ravines" on the steep mountain slopes, "live[d] bestially, [men] sleeping with their mothers and daughters," in wretched huts that "seem[ed] more for monkeys than for men"; until they were brought together in towns they could not be true Christians or, indeed, fully human.[1] The General Resettlement was designed to transform indigenous society—but not entirely. Even while laying out new streets and leadership positions, the *reducciones* were built on Andeans' existing institutions, which Spaniards believed were the creation of wise Inca kings. And, tacitly or explicitly, many of the old villages survived alongside the new towns. Entirely destroying those villages and institutions was not possible in any case, and the Resettlement relied on collaboration with native elites. But Spanish officials also knew that Andeans could not produce wealth, and therefore could not pay tribute, without their own institutions. Violent and exploitative, the General Resettlement of Indians was also recuperative, reflecting indigenous lords' cautious acquiescence and Spaniards' ethnographic inquiry into Andean society.

"Ethnography" is a frequent word in this book; I mean it in its most literal sense, as "writing about peoples." Early modern colonizers, while forcibly imposing Christianity and their own cultural norms, also practiced an open-ended study of conquered cultures, with roots in medieval travel writing, Christian apologetics, humanist philology, and the emerging science of government. Missionary priests studied indigenous cultures as an aid to evangelization, and the Spanish crown sent questionnaires to local officials on subjects such as native tribute systems. Those investigations shaped the General Resettlement of Indians.

Beginning soon after the Spanish conquest of the Inca empire in 1535, and its re-christening as the Viceroyalty of Peru, colonial officials inquired into how Andeans organized their societies and how those ways differed from their own. Their motivation was not a disinterested search for knowledge but a dilemma: the rich and populous land they had seized from the Incas was becoming poor and depopulated, threatening the supply of tribute and labor. Fascinated with the opulent, pagan Inca kings, Spaniards asked what the Incas had done right that they themselves were doing wrong. Spanish officials considered Andean labor a precious resource, renewable if carefully husbanded. They knew that one cause of the declining population was disease (without realizing that Europeans had introduced new diseases to the Americas). But they also suspected that they were undermining institutions that had promoted wealth in a challenging landscape.

What they learned was that the landscape of the Andes imposed its own rules on society. In an environment where no single place produced all the necessities of life, communities often controlled scattered settlements dedicated to producing specific things: llamas and alpacas on the high plateau, potatoes at a lower elevation, maize below that, vegetables and coca leaves in the hot lowlands. The vertical landscape encouraged a model of community that was not compact but a network of linked settlements. To function properly, these complex communities had to preserve tight internal organization and traditional leadership, even if that made them harder to control directly.

Curiosity did not mean sympathy: most colonists considered indigenous Americans radically inferior to themselves. Colonization was based on exploitation. Even the dedication of some Spanish friars to "protecting" Indians often disguised a desire to substitute their own control over Andeans for that of secular colonists. But regardless of their opinion of the Andean people they saw around them, Spaniards admired the accomplishments of the prehispanic Inca kings. To the extent that indigenous society functioned well, many Spaniards attributed it to the Incas, who they believed had designed institutions to maximize the environment's resources and compensate for their subjects' limitations.

Others, however, saw Andean communities as disorganized, deficient, and in need of rebuilding. Many Spaniards considered Christianity inseparable from a specific conception of community. For Spaniards, as for other Mediterranean peoples, the ideal community was the city, the classical *polis*, from which Spanish derived the word *policía*, a word that has no exact English equivalent. In its narrowest definition, *policía* referred to a town's clean and attractive appearance, but it could also encompass everything from the layout of the streets and the offices of municipal government to the virtue of the citizens. A common expression for what the Spanish hoped to bring to the Andes was *ley divina y policía humana*, divine law and human civilization.

These two colonial goals, cultural survival and cultural change, were not necessarily contradictory. Indeed, most officials believed that Andean society should be partly preserved and partly remade. The General Resettlement was designed to reconcile the two conflicting impulses: an ideology of civilizing Andeans, and an ethnographic tradition that warned officials to be careful about how they did so.

This book's argument builds on a half-century of work by ethnohistorians. In the 1960s and 1970s, the Romanian-American anthropologist John Murra rediscovered the same model of conquest-era Andean communities first described by early colonial Spanish writers. Murra worked with collaborators from South America, North America, and Europe. Combining document analysis, archaeology, human ecology, and anthropology—which combined to create the discipline of ethnohistory—they described a model in which Andean communities, prehispanic and colonial, maintained settlement enclaves at different elevations, and pooled the products of diverse ecological zones. Murra called this model the vertical archipelago.[2]

My project is different from that of the ethnohistorians. Murra's most important source was economic and census data from sixteenth-century *visitas*, which were inspections of Andean communities undertaken to assess their tribute obligations, rather than from more descriptive colonial accounts. His discovery was impressive precisely because he uncovered hidden patterns in raw data. In the quantitative records he used, the inspectors who recorded the information did not spell out its sociological implications: that was not the format of their reports. But the most insightful of the colonial officials understood those implications. Ethnohistorians have used those officials' writings as supplementary evidence, but have not pursued the significance of the fact that colonial experts anticipated their own findings. Their interest is in indigenous systems, mine in colonial ones.[3]

As a unified campaign, the General Resettlement of Indians took place in the Audiencias of Lima and Charcas, which map very roughly to the modern nations of Peru and Bolivia. This was the region Viceroy Toledo effectively controlled, although the viceroyalty of Peru was much larger, also including the Audiencias of Quito, Chile, New Granada, and Panama, and quasi-autonomous frontier districts such as Tucumán and Santa Cruz in the south and Popayán in the north. Each territory had separate administrative apparatuses for *gobierno*, government, and *justicia*, justice, or executive and judicial branches (although they did not correspond exactly to the modern categories). In each Audiencia the branches of gobierno and justicia were headed respectively by a governor and by a court, also called the Audiencia, which was composed of several judges, a president, and other officials. The line was not always sharp between the two branches: governors sometimes presided over judicial disputes, and Audiencias sometimes exercised executive powers, especially when the governor was absent. Conflicts between governors and Audiencias were chronic.[4]

Nominally, the viceroy was the supreme authority throughout the viceroyalty; in fact, not only did the Audiencias resist his control, but some territories had their own governors, which limited the viceroy's power even in the realm of gobierno. All territories, furthermore, corresponded directly with the king, who frequently disregarded his own viceroy. In New Granada, which had the title of a captaincy-general, the viceroy had little influence. Chile and Panama were more integrated into the viceroyalty, but they had their own governors; Toledo made little effort to exercise authority there except when physically present, as he was while passing through Panama on the way to Lima at the beginning of his term. It was only in the Audiencias of Lima, Charcas, and Quito, which covered the territory of the Inca empire and were the core provinces of the viceroyalty, that the viceroy had the title of governor. And even there his authority varied. In Lima, the capital of the viceroyalty, the viceroy was *ex officio* president of the Audiencia, and the members had little power to oppose him—although some did so when they could. The Audiencias of Charcas and Quito retained separate presidents, giving them a basis for defiance. Toledo spent significant time in the territory of the Charcas Audiencia, and was able to carry out the General Inspection (*Visita General*) and General Resettlement there. In Quito, though, the situation was different: the viceroy was far away, and the Audiencia had received a special privilege from the king to exercise powers of gobierno within its own jurisdiction during this period. Toledo had little leverage in Quito; he appointed a handful of inspectors there, but the Audiencia apparently took charge of resettlement efforts itself.[5]

This book, therefore, focuses on the Audiencias of Lima and Charcas, and especially on an area within it stretching from Lima and Jauja in the north (modern central Peru) to Potosí and La Plata in the south (modern central Bolivia). The best data from the General Resettlement survive from this region. This was the area where the vertical archipelago was most pronounced. The northern part of this zone had a highly irregular topography, in which people traditionally lived in small village on steep slopes, in close contact with settlements at various elevations; the southern part of it, the *altiplano* or high plateau, had larger settlements with substantial enclaves in distant valleys. This zone was the area in which the surviving Inca aristocracy in Cuzco negotiated with Toledo, and the refugee neo-Inca kings of Vilcabamba struggled for independence. It was the region of the great mines of Huancavelica and Potosí; these depended on the labor draft called the *mita*, which in turn depended on strong and self-sustaining Andean communities, so this was the region where Spanish authorities paid the most attention to Andean social structures. Finally, this was the area that Toledo toured personally while overseeing the General Resettlement.

Chapter Outline

Part 1 explores the ideological origins of the General Resettlement. It follows the parallel tracks along which Spaniards constructed an ethnographic vision of Andean community and an ideology of Indian resettlement. The first colonists were fascinated by the Incas' monumental stone cities, an infatuation which initiated a colonial ethnography of Andean space. But, as chapter 1 shows, the Inca cities were political and ceremonial centers, not spaces of household residence and trade as Mediterranean cities were. Chapter 2 shows the Spanish gradually turning their attention to the structure of community in the Andean highlands and the vertical networks that defined that community. Meanwhile, as discussed in chapter 3, colonists in the Caribbean and Mesoamerica began resettling Indians into centralized communities for the purpose of control and indoctrination; this social engineering was an innovation, unknown in medieval and early modern Europe. Colonial governors' efforts were scattershot, intermittent, and local, but established new patterns. Chapter 4 shows how the ideology of resettlement took root in Peru in the 1560s, in dialogue between Spanish officials and Andean ethnic lords, whom the Spanish called *caciques*.

Part 2, the central part of the book, examines the General Resettlement itself. It begins with the task force called the Junta Magna, which the king assembled at the Spanish court in 1568 to reassess colonial government. How did the Spanish crown decide to implement the first truly large-scale resettlement campaign, and to do so in the Andes, the region of the Americas where it was most challenging? Most scholars have attributed the decision to the Junta Magna. In fact, as chapter 5 shows, the Junta Magna considered elevating Indian resettlement to a high priority, but declined to do so. By default, the locus of decision making shifted to the colony itself. Chapter 6 shows how and why Toledo undertook the General Resettlement of Indians, a project that developed from earlier Spanish interventions but went far beyond them.

As resettler, Toledo reimagined himself as an heir to the Incas. He did not intend to destroy Andean culture, as scholars have often assumed, but to effect a combination of change and continuity. The key to that combination, explored in chapter 7, was his fascination with the conquered and dead Inca kings. He set out to prove that the Incas met Aristotle's definition of "tyrant," supplying a legal justification for the Spanish conquest. Yet, paradoxically, he believed the technologies of rule that Aristotle defined as tyrannical were what enabled the Incas to govern the Andes effectively, including designing the archipelago model of community. Toledo designed the General Resettlement of Indians in part to emulate the Incas' "tyrannical" legacy.

Chapter 8 addresses the most elusive question about Toledo's campaign:

What exactly happened on the ground? I approach the question through a series of case studies. The first uses accounts kept by an inspector and preserved in the Archivo General de Indias, in combination with the same inspector's report to the king, written (as he said) "with his hands in the dough." Another uses two lists of reducciones in a specific locality, reconstructing the logic by which the inspector assigned groups to reducciones. The third draws on archaeological research in the area of Collaguas to uncover the historical dynamic behind the locations chosen for two resettlements The fourth case study examines a lawsuit between neighboring indigenous communities, preserved in the Bolivian archives, which documents the decisions the inspectors made in that area. Cumulatively, the examples show how inspectors and caciques balanced resettlement with cultural survival.

Part 3 traces how the reducciones took root, gradually and incompletely, in Andean society. Chapter 9 describes the world the Resettlement created, drawing on archival evidence and on the vivid descriptions of the indigenous author don Felipe Guaman Poma de Ayala, while chapter 10 follows the reducciones up through today. In spite of Toledo's efforts to sideline the caciques, they remained for a long time the chief protagonists of indigenous politics, dominating the relationship between Andeans and the colonial state. The General Resettlement did not fully replace Andeans' previous villages, but supplemented them, while setting in place the structures of exploitation that constituted the mature colonial system in the Andes. The reducciones became something like what the Inca cities had been: ceremonial spaces for engagement between the local community and the state, where individual families had homes, but where they lived only part of the time. From the sixteenth century to the present, the ebb and flow between town and countryside has been a fundamental dynamic of Andean history.

The interpretation of the General Resettlement presented here is a new one. At one time scholars accepted what might be called the transparent model of the Resettlement: that Toledo had the straightforward goal of replacing Andean lifeways with Spanish ones; that reducciones laid out on a grid were a self-evident way to do this; and that his own reports are sufficient evidence of the Resettlement's methods and its success.[6] In recent decades, scholars have questioned or complicated each aspect of this model. Several have shown how complex was the seemingly simple urban grid, with a wealth of specific cultural resonances for both Spaniards and Andeans.[7] Others, re-examining Toledo's record, have shown that his thinking about Andean history was ambivalent and that he admired aspects of the Inca empire.[8] And studies of the General Resettlement in specific areas, although few, have shown that its success was variable, and often limited.[9] Some recent scholars have offered valuable brief discussions of the General Resettlement as a whole, unencumbered by the older model, though tending to address the Resettlement's long-term impact more than the campaign itself.[10] Most often, though, scholars critique some parts of the model while accepting others. Manfred Merluzzi's 2003 biography, *Politica e governo nel Nuovo Mondo: Francisco de Toledo, viceré del Perù*, offers a sophisticated reading of Toledo within a Foucauldian framework, but does not challenge the older depiction of him as a single-minded agent of cultural remaking. While scholars no longer accept the older model as a complete package, they have not presented a new synthesis. This book offers a coherent account of the General Resettlement by placing it in the context of developing New World imperialism and colonial ethnography. Indeed, it is impossible to understand the General Resettlement except through the lens of colonial ethnography.

In the General Resettlement, the twin impulses of ethnography and cultural remaking intersected with a new conception of government which was vertical, in more than one sense. Spaniards in Peru came to believe that the challenges of the Andean environment and its people necessitated a centralized, authoritarian government, and forms of social engineering unknown in Europe.[11] The vertical landscape, they believed, had created the vertical empire of the Incas. Some colonists argued that Inca rule, combining authoritarianism and surveillance with a specific, network-based form of community economy, should be the model for the Spanish in Peru. The General Resettlement of Indians, one of the earliest examples of large-scale state social engineering—in many ways a strikingly modern project—was informed by Spanish visions of a prehispanic empire.

If colonists were studying the Andean world, Andeans were studying the Spanish one. As subjects of the Incas, often in regions that fell to Inca rule less than a century before the Spanish arrived, they knew about cultural exchanges between conqueror and conquered. Andeans, especially caciques, sought ways to integrate themselves into the Spanish empire and build a future in it. Resettlement had the potential to do serious harm, but also to create a new and sustainable basis for Andean society and caciques' power. Andeans helped to shape the General Resettlement, but they did so from a position of weakness and in ways that appear only dimly in the documents. This book draws on both Spanish and Andean voices, but relies more on Spanish ones, partly because indigenous texts before 1580 are scarce, and partly because the book's focus is the theory and practice of imperial rule.[12] Colonial ethnography was not benign: it was motivated by the desire to exploit more efficiently, and it helped the conquerors to do so. In focusing on the colonists' curiosity about the Andes my aim is not to make ethnographic Spaniards into heroes, or to depict Andeans as objects rather than agents of their own history, but to portray the complexity of the imperial project.

The General Resettlement of Indians looks at first like a clear case of cultural remaking, even "ethnocide,"[13] but it was more complex than that. The campaign quietly embraced certain aspects of Andean culture, while loudly rejecting others. Spanish and indigenous officials, from the viceroy down, knew that Andeans could best support both themselves and their conquerors through their own methods. The result of the General Resettlement was a regime of local autonomy by peasant communities, closely watched and harshly exploited, but coping with that exploitation in ways they themselves constructed.

PART I **ETHNOGRAPHY**

1
—

THE CITIES

At the center of Cuzco, capital of the Inca empire, was Hawkaypata, "Terrace of Leisure," a plaza of about thirty thousand square meters. Its surface was a layer of fine sand carried by hand from the Pacific coast, in which were buried small figurines of gold, silver, and copper. Within it stood the ushnu, a gold-covered stone on a stepped platform, surrounded by a pool. Forming an almost continuous wall around the plaza, and rising high above it, were the palaces of the kings, living and dead. There were towers twenty-four meters tall, with most of that height in lofty thatched roofs, resting on wooden beams that projected as much as two meters past the external stone walls. Inca masons fit large stone blocks together without mortar, so closely, as Spanish observers noted, that a knife blade could not fit between them.[1]

Early in 1534 Francisco Pizarro and his companions witnessed the ceremonies by which a new Inca king received his office. For days Hawkaypata filled with singing, dancing and drinking from morning till night. The new king, one Spaniard wrote, brought "to the said fiestas all his dead grandfathers and relations . . . seated in their chairs, with much veneration and respect." Mummies of the dynasty's later kings, along with statues or objects representing the earliest members of the dynasty, sat under canopies in the plaza, surrounded by men and women who sang of the kings' exploits while living. A small fire burning in front of each dead king consumed the food he was given to eat. On the ushnu sat the living king along with a figure representing the Sun. Serving women carried jugs across the square to fill cups with chicha, or maize beer, "the dead toasting each other, and the dead the living, and the living the dead." So the Spaniards saw and recorded.[2]

Cajamarca

Cuzco was the greatest of the Inca cities, but not the only one. For the Spaniards who first glimpsed, then invaded, then conquered the Inca empire, Peru was a landscape of mountains and cities.[3] Following tentative explorations of the Pacific coast in the 1520s, Francisco Pizarro and 168 companions marched inland into the mountains in 1532, entering the previously unknown Inca empire as it endured the last stages of a civil war. The Incas, a relatively small ethnic group from the region of Cuzco, had conquered and built the New World's largest empire, called Tawantinsuyu, over little more than a century. On the death of the last king, two princes had fought each other to succeed him; the winner, Atahualpa, had conquered and captured his brother Huascar and was now consolidating his victory, vindicating the royal title, "The Only Inca."[4] The Spaniards set out to meet him. The earliest Spanish accounts of the conquest dwelt on the marvels they saw along the way: great herds of llamas, fine roads, monumental buildings, cities "made in the manner of those of Spain, and the streets well laid-out." Like other Mediterranean peoples, the Spanish considered cities a chief index of civilization.[5]

Andean cities were notable for their grid-like layout and large plazas. Francisco de Xérez, Pizarro's secretary, wrote that Cajamarca's plaza was larger than that of any city in Spain. We do not know exactly how large it was, but excavations in a comparable Inca regional center, Huánuco Pampa, reveal a rectangular plaza measuring about 350 × 550 meters.[6] Since Roman times, large plazas were one of the marks of a true city. The broad plaza of Cajamarca—gated and lined with stone houses, each two hundred paces wide, with running water—was something a Spaniard might admire.[7]

The conquerors certainly admired the Incas' imperial infrastructure. At the entrances to cities were officials who kept precise records of all cargo that entered and left. They noted that Inca roads were wide enough for six horses to ride abreast and were equipped at intervals with shade trees and piped-in water; in the uneven Andean landscape, the roads' engineering was impressive enough for a later Spanish author to compare them to the pyramids of Egypt.[8] At the end of every day's journey was a state-run house for travelers; over the rivers were bridges with officials to register wayfarers. The towns had enormous deposits of stored supplies—food, shoes, salt—for armies on the move. The Spaniards themselves relied on these supplies as they traveled. Xérez reported that when they had taken all they could (with Inca officials meticulously registering the seizures in their records), the storage deposits still appeared full, as if nothing had been taken. Inventories of stored goods were recorded in knots on cords called quipus.[9] The conquerors knew how to appreciate such efficiencies: Spanish armies in Italy, Germany, and the Netherlands were plagued by problems of logistics and supply.

When they reached Cajamarca, the Spaniards found it nearly empty; Atahualpa was camped some distance away with his army. Pizarro sent a few men and an interpreter with gifts. The Spaniards rode tensely through a silent, massed army to where Atahualpa was seated in the middle. Atahualpa maintained the posture considered appropriate to his office, eyes fixed on the ground, hearing the Spaniards without answering. Through interpreters, the Spaniards asked him to come the next day to return the visit. Atahualpa's passivity at this moment is a mystery. He apparently had little respect for their tiny contingent—one of his generals had described them to him as runaways and highwaymen—but in the moment he may have been intimidated by their horses (the first ever seen in the Andes), then felt it necessary to prove he did not fear the newcomers.[10]

In Cajamarca, the Spaniards prepared for Atahualpa's arrival. They hid cavalry in the large halls that lined the plaza and placed cannon on the ushnu in the plaza's center. When Atahualpa's litter and his guards entered the plaza, the Spanish friar Vicente de Valverde met him with a Christian book (some accounts say a Bible, others a breviary); Atahualpa glanced at the book and, according to most accounts, threw it on the ground. The friar ran back to his companions, shouting; guns blazed from the tower and horses leapt from darkened doors. The flat, enclosed plaza was ideal for artillery and horsemen. Within minutes, the Spaniards had killed thousands and imprisoned the king.

In captivity, Atahualpa agreed to pay Pizarro and his companions his ransom: a room filled with gold and another with silver.[11] He called in precious vessels and ornaments from the far-flung provinces; forges burned night and day in Cajamarca to melt and recast them into bars. The invaders had made free use of stored supplies even before reaching Cajamarca, and after taking the king prisoner they appropriated the full authority of Ata-

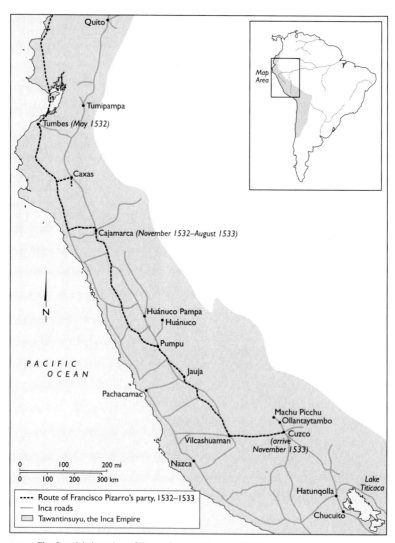

Map 3 The Spanish invasion of Tawantinsuyu. Map by Bill Nelson.

hualpa's command. One conquistador wrote that with the king a hostage, "a man can travel 500 leagues alone without anyone killing him—instead they give him everything he needs and carry him in a hammock." Kidnapping an Indian leader was a favorite strategy of Spanish invaders in the New World; by controlling a kingdom's head, the attacker could command its extensive body, at least for a while. The Spaniards, empire builders themselves, felt at home in the Inca empire and its cities.[12]

Cuzco

In August 1533 the Spaniards left Cajamarca, traveling the royal road to Cuzco. They had held Atahualpa hostage for eight months, receiving his ransom in stages, but finally garroted him in spite of their promises to restore him to power. In the Inca civil war before the Spaniards' arrival, Atahualpa's base of operation was the northern end of the empire, where he had been born (what is today Ecuador), while Huascar's was the southern Inca heartland around Cuzco. When the Spaniards arrived, Atahualpa had just conquered the Cuzco region and was consolidating his control there. The Spaniards' intervention reopened the contest and allowed both northern and southern armies to regroup under their generals, who waited to see what would happen next. Pizarro's ransom agreement with Atahualpa represented a de facto alliance between the Spanish and the northern army, which was tasked with delivering gold and silver to Cajamarca. In charge of the logistics, Atahualpa retained control over his chain of command; he took the opportunity to have Huascar, held captive at a distant location, quietly killed. But when Pizarro in his turn executed Atahualpa, it freed the Spaniards to make a new alliance with the dead Huascar's generals, joining forces against the northerners and opening the doors to the fabled city of Cuzco. A Cuzco prince named Manco Inca now claimed the royal office and joined the European invaders, welcoming their help in turning the tables against his northern enemies.[13] Manco Inca and Pizarro entered Cuzco at the head of an Andean army on November 15, one year to the day after their arrival in Cajamarca.

The urban splendor of Cuzco impressed Spaniards even more than what they had already seen.[14] The friar Valverde estimated the population at twenty thousand (archaeologists today estimate as many as forty thousand), and another Spaniard wrote that the city would be worthy of admiration in Spain for its stone buildings, solidly paved streets, and stone-lined sewage drains.[15] Next to the city stood a monumental stone complex named Sacsayhuaman, which the Spanish called a fortress but which was probably a religious center. In the city center were two linked central plazas, Hawkaypata and Kusipata.[16]

Most of the palaces lining Hawkaypata belonged to the dead kings, and housed their descendants, in royal kin-groups called *panacas*. Excluded from each king's panaca was whichever of his sons or brothers became the new king, who would build a new palace and found his own panaca. Each group of descendants cared for the mummy of its founder and administered the wealth he had owned in his lifetime. The most impressive palace was that of Huayna Capac, Atahualpa's and Manco Inca's father, the last uncontested king of Tawantinsuyu.[17] It was large enough to hold three thousand people, with a great red and white door, plastered and painted. In the compound surrounding it were an artificial pond and two tall, round towers facing the plaza. One Spaniard wrote that the higher tower was taller than any in Spain except for the great bell tower of Seville's cathedral.[18]

Early in 1534, unopposed by Manco Inca, Pizarro performed a ceremony to refound Cuzco as a Spanish municipality. He began by reminding the Spanish settlers that humans, "not being able to live separately, each man by himself," had founded towns and cities since the creation of the world. This being so, Pizarro declared:

> I found in this great city [ciudad] of Cuzco . . . a town [pueblo] of Spaniards . . . , finding it to be in the best region of the land, and as such the past lords made in it their seat . . . , populated it with the greatest nobles of their land, and built in this town rich buildings. . . . [Therefore] let the plaza of this town, which I found, be this [plaza] which was made by the natives, and let the house lots where the householders [vecinos] are to build their houses be laid out and arrayed all around it.[19]

Pizarro marked his symbolic possession of the spot by cutting a notch in the wooden picota, or pillar of justice, which the Spaniards erected in the sand of Hawkaypata, at a distance from the ushnu.[20] The act of foundation stated that the Spaniards would build themselves houses, but in fact they simply moved into the stone palaces already surrounding the plaza. Three days after the ceremony, Pizarro ordered his men not to alter these buildings in any way, since the Andean populace venerated the palaces and showing disrespect for them might cause a rebellion.[21]

A few months later, the newly established town council (cabildo) assigned house lots (solares) to the citizens. They assigned four lots to Pizarro, two or three to each of the other leaders, and a single lot each to the rest of the ninety-some founding Spanish householders. Leaders received lots fronting the plaza; the rest got ones farther back, in descending order of prestige as the distance from the plaza grew. The Spanish documents generally identified these solares by reference to streets and other Spanish lots, once again implying that Cuzco was an empty space being marked out by surveyors. But the council went on to note that "most of the lots . . . have been in the area already built by the native Indians," and that the existing "blocks and court-yards" had dimensions other than the prescribed ones for Spanish solares.[22] Therefore they resolved to fit the solares to the dimensions of the existing blocks "so that they make up in length what they lack in breadth in the same block" or in a neighboring block or space. If it was not possible to make up the square footage one way or another, the grantee would have to settle for the existing building as it was. Thus an imaginary map of Spanish solares was superimposed on a concrete map of Inca buildings; the flesh-and-blood Spaniards inhabited the latter.[23]

The conquerors shared the city uneasily with the Inca nobility and the new king whom they had helped bring to power. Manco Inca's name did not appear among the householders of Spanish Cuzco, nor did he receive a house lot when the cabildo distributed them. But he controlled an area of the city that the cabildo tacitly respected: the council described one of the assigned solares as adjoining "the new houses which the cacique [i.e., Manco Inca] is building," houses that they did not attempt to grant to Span-iards.[24] Since each Inca king traditionally built himself a new palace, Manco Inca had no personal claim on the splendid palaces that already filled Cuzco—but he may well have resented the Spaniards for seizing them.[25]

Yet the Cuzco aristocracy, associated with the panacas of the earlier kings, maintained a toehold in the old palaces. A Spaniard named Ulloa received title to "the courtyard where the *palla* of *teniente* Hernando de Soto lives." Ulloa had received a small part of a palace compound, of which the greater part was assigned to Hernando de Soto, one of Pizarro's principal lieutenants; Soto's mistress was living there, a *palla* (Inca princess) named Colla Quillor, whom the Spaniards called doña Leonor.[26] She was Huascar's daughter, who in the natural course of things would have lived in that very palace as a leading member of his panaca—an illustration of the ways that the earliest days of Spanish Cuzco were an uneasy compromise with the traditions of the Inca capital.[27] Such alliances offered advantages to both sides but only partial protection for the rights of Inca nobles. The cabildo instructed each householder to respect the tenancy of "native Indians who may be [living] in his *solar*," such as Colla Quillor.[28] But redefining Ande-ans' homes as Spaniards' property scarcely promoted comity between the two groups.

Cuzco's Spaniards pushed ever harder on their Andean neighbors, and their efforts to extend their control over the city finally precipitated a crisis. In April, 1536 two-and-a-half years after entering Cuzco at the Spaniards' side, Manco Inca slipped out of the city and organized the surviving Inca armies to lay siege to the occupied Inca capital. They burned the city's wood-and-thatch roofs with torches, a conflagration the Spaniards survived by huddling in the plaza. The few Spanish, along with non-Inca Andean soldiers (especially Cañaris, an ethnic group traditionally hostile to the Incas) and African slaves (recently transported from the Caribbean), fought daily against their besiegers in the smoking ruins. Andean soldiers used the tops of the stone walls of Cuzco's interconnecting courtyards, their roofs destroyed by fire, as a mazelike walkway into the heart of the city and fired stones from slings, out of reach of Spanish cavalry below. The Spaniards and their allies responded by pulling down parts of the walls at night, disassembling the city around them even as they took refuge in its center. They used the towers of Huayna Capac's palace to hold prisoners; in the raging fires of the siege, the towers' roofs took eight days to burn.[29]

At last, in mid-May, the Spaniards managed to seize the central tower of Sacsayhuaman, killing thousands of Andean soldiers and turning the tide of the war. Manco Inca lifted the siege. In time, he retreated along with many of his followers to the province of Vilcabamba, not far from Cuzco but rugged, heavily forested, and hard for Spanish horses to reach. There he reestablished a neo-Inca state, independent but a fragment of what it had been. Resistance to the Spanish continued, but never again came so close to victory.[30]

What had been the Incas' proudest city, shared by Spaniards and Andeans, was now a fire-blackened ruin.[31] Much of its Andean population gradually returned, a defeated caste who would now serve the conquerors. Leaving the king and his most committed generals and soldiers to their proud poverty in Vilcabamba, many Inca nobles likewise returned to Cuzco, offering submission in exchange for privileges. Along with the caciques (the non-Inca ethnic lords of the various provinces outside Cuzco) these nobles remained the ruling class of the indigenous society. Like Spanish nobles they were exempt from taxes, and the most powerful retained at least some of their lands and vassals. But the humblest Spaniard claimed the privilege of caste over the most exalted Andean lord: one was the conqueror, the other the conquered.

Cuzco's Spaniards created a more fully Spanish city. They rehabilitated the best-preserved buildings and took the stones of others for new construction. Built by Andean masons, the new houses showed features of indigenous design alongside Spanish ones, making Cuzco a metaphor in stone for the conquered empire. In 1540 Spanish Cuzco received from the king of Spain a coat of arms showing a castle, representing Sacsayhuaman, and eight Andean condors which perhaps, grimly, represented the carrion birds that devoured the native dead after the siege of Cuzco. Castles were a common element in European heraldry, typically symbolizing conquest. But the image on Cuzco's coat of arms referred not only to the Spanish castletakers but also to the Inca castlemakers, evoking the Incas' prowess as builders as well as the Spaniards' as conquerors.[32]

To Spaniards, the Incas' cities were their greatest achievement. Andean society had much that Spaniards admired, yet lacked things they saw as essential to civilization. The Inca empire was larger than many European kingdoms, but it lacked a European-style system of writing and any form of money.[33] It fielded large armies but had neither iron nor horses. Andeans produced an agricultural surplus without metal plows; they stored and distributed food, moving people and goods through some of the world's most difficult terrain, without wheeled vehicles or animals strong enough to carry a man's weight. (Llamas could carry goods but not people.) In later decades Spanish intellectuals debated how much value to place on Andean culture—and, by implication, what rights and consideration it deserved from the Spanish. The argument that indigenous Americans were "barbarians" of low capacity was a convenient axiom for many Spaniards. But a significant minority disagreed with this view, led by the Dominican friar Bartolomé de Las Casas, bishop of Chiapas and a royal advisor, who advocated for Native Americans' rights from 1514 till his death in 1564. Although he never visited Peru, he was to play a significant role in debates about how Spain should rule the Andes. In order to prove that Native Americans were not barbarians, he took as his main evidence the early accounts of cities such as Cuzco. Cities equaled civilization.[34]

Spanish and Inca Cities

What exactly were Cajamarca and Cuzco? Urbanism, in the sense of how people use densely built environments, takes diverse forms. As the invaders gradually came to understand, spaces in the Andes could look like spaces they knew from home yet be very different. For Spaniards, the essence of a community lay in its *vecinos*, its male householders or citizens.[35] Whether nobles or commoners, merchants or peasants, vecinos were property owners (those without property were defined as mere residents, *moradores*), with privileges such as grazing cattle on community land outside the town, the obligation to pay local taxes, and the right to hold civic office.[36] They were expected to reside permanently in town or village, even if they lived from agriculture: most landholding nobles were absentee landlords, and peasants typically lived in a village and walked each morning to their fields.[37] The Spanish municipality—aldea, villa or ciudad—was a legal entity, defined not by its size but by its status and privileges. An aldea might petition to be promoted to villa and a villa aspire to the status of ciudad. The words translate roughly to village, town, and city, but the translation can be misleading, since some villas were larger than some ciudades. What defined these legal categories was their relative prestige, and the extent of their power to impose legal jurisdiction over their territories. The picota, a pillar where miscreants were whipped or even executed, symbolized the community's aspirations for autonomy, peace and order, its right to back up its authority with force.[38]

The central figure of civic life was the alcalde, a distinctively Spanish official who combined administrative and judicial duties. In a typical municipality two alcaldes shared power with the representative of the lord or king, depending on whether the community lay in aristocratic or royal jurisdiction. The alcaldes presided over the cabildo, which was composed of regidores (councilmen), alguacil mayor (constable), escribano (scribe or notary), and lesser officials. Regidores often held their seats for life, especially in cities, having purchased them from the Crown, while alcaldes changed annually. The form of selection varied—alcaldes might be selected by the town council, nominated by the lord, chosen by lot, or elected by the citizens—but this office was never sold, given in perpetuity, or awarded to an outsider. The alcaldes' appointment involved rituals of civic participation by the vecinos, and, to the extent that local democracy existed in early modern Spain, it lay in this office. The humble aldea shared the same institutions of self-government, with annual selections of community officials, deliberations by a smaller version of the urban cabildo, and adjudication of crimes and disputes by the alcaldes. The institutional similarity between elite and peasant communities generated a literature of satire about rural bumpkins holding elevated-sounding titles. But it solidified a single model of the well-organized community.[39]

The early Spanish author Isidore of Seville wrote: "Inhabitants, not building stones, are called a city."[40] But building stones, too, were important. Urban spaces created the sensory experience of being a vecino: the view of a procession or an execution, the monumental facades of church and town hall, the sound of a town crier or church bell. One could tell the status of each householder by how close his house was to the plaza mayor. Early modern Spanish cities were densely built-up settlements, often walled, housing a large and diverse resident population. A city was a busy place, populated by nobles, landlords, merchants, lawyers, physicians, priests, artisans, petty traders, laborers, servants, slaves, and beggars. Churches were crowded with worship and socializing, plazas bustled with trade.[41]

Andean cities such as Cajamarca looked superficially familiar to the Spanish invaders. But they did not find families in the houses or market stalls in the plaza.[42] The cities had few men permanently residing there, but many women. Regarding the first highland city the Spaniards visited, Caxas, one account reported that "it was large, and in some very tall houses there was much maize, and shoes; others were full of wool, and more than five hundred women who did nothing else but make clothes and chicha for the soldiers."[43] These women were called aqlla, "chosen ones." They were celibate, their lives were tightly controlled, and their activities were considered sacred, so Spanish writers often compared them to nuns. But the early accounts made it clear that their primary role was economic: they produced much of what filled the state storage silos, especially clothing and maize beer, which they laboriously produced by chewing soaked kernels and allowing them to ferment.[44] As the Spanish advanced from city to city, they seized these women as servants and concubines, just as they took the stored supplies. As a conqueror later recalled, "We entered and the women, who were more than five hundred, were brought out to the plaza, and [our] captain gave many of them to the Spanish, and the Inca's captain [i.e., the resident state overseer] became very indignant."[45]

When Spaniards saw men in the cities, they were not permanent residents but soldiers of the armies passing through and the servants who attended them. Francisco Pizarro's brother Hernando stood on a hill outside one city and saw its central plaza entirely filled with men. He estimated the crowd as one hundred thousand men, all "Indians of service" [indios de servicio] called up to join an Inca army on the move.[46]

Another dimension to Andean cities subsequently emerged for the Spaniards: the cities were also places for ritual celebrations.[47] After the ambush at Cajamarca, when they held Atahualpa hostage, the Spaniards found the Inca cities quite hospitable. Hernando Pizarro discovered this while traveling during Atahualpa's captivity, accompanied by an Inca general in whose honor the people "were accustomed to celebrate fiestas."[48] Hernando reported: "In all these cities they held for us very great fiestas with performances and dancing."[49] The climax of this season of celebration was in Cuzco, after the Spanish and Manco Inca arrived there in November 1533. The Spaniards and the Cuzco Incas celebrated their victory over the northern armies with a month of fiestas in the great plaza of Cuzco, which probably represented Manco Inca's royal investiture. The Spaniards were impressed by the plaza's sewage system, two half-yard pipes that drained under paving stones to the river; Spanish sewage systems were generally more primitive. As one Spaniard wrote, "given the quantity that was drunk" during the celebrations, the torrent of urine that drained away from the plaza "is no marvel, although to see it is a marvel and a thing never before seen."[50]

Presiding over the festivities, and over the life of Cuzco, were the dead kings. The panacas—large households of nobles and servants—answered to the mummies and administered their wealth.[51] Speaking oracularly through their attendants, the dead made decisions and exercised authority. One Spaniard later wrote that Cuzco's lords lived a life of riotous indulgence under the mummies' slack hands, carrying the bodies among the palaces for visits and drinking, while attributing their desires to the mute cadavers they served. He recalled helping an indigenous officer in the Inca army arrange a marriage to a Cuzco noblewoman. He went to get permission from the woman's guardian, and until the last minute did not realize that the man he was visiting was dead. The Spaniard was shocked to find himself talking to a "bundle" (bulto, a wrapped object) in a litter, who—through the mouths of both a male and a female attendant—consented to the marriage.[52]

Cuzco, Huánuco Pampa, and Cajamarca were very different places from Seville and Madrid. Inside the Inca cities, the Spanish found stored goods in awe-inspiring quantities, industrial workshops staffed by women, feasts, and the drunken revelry of dead kings, but not the commerce that defined and dominated Spanish cities.[53] The massive and beautiful Inca complexes lacked an economy independent of the state, and seemed to have little permanent population besides state personnel and the retainers of governing elites. It is hard to know how many people lived in and around the Inca complexes, but to archaeologists they look more like political and ceremonial sites than residential centers. There had been large residential cities in the past, and that tradition survived in the Pacific coast kingdoms conquered only recently by the Incas. (We know little about the coastal cities, which collapsed soon after the Spanish invasion from the crushing impact of Old

World diseases, far more severe there than in the highlands). But the late prehispanic Andean highlands were a land of dispersed settlement punctuated by centers for ceremony, administration, and state production.[54]

Dispersed settlement was a natural response to the Andean landscape. On steep hillsides at high altitude, a walk of any length from home to field was a burden, and herding llamas and alpacas demanded even greater spreading out. During the war-torn era before the Inca empire emerged, highland regions had larger settlements for the sake of protection, but the peace brought by Inca rule allowed Andeans to spread out across the countryside.[55] Andean population was not low, in proportion to usable land. Although estimating contact-era populations is notoriously hard, most scholars believe that the highlands were relatively full of people, in many regions more so than today. But most Andeans did not travel from their fields and herds each night to sleep in a town or village, as Mediterranean peasants typically did.[56] The majority of people, an archaeologist writes, lived in small hamlets or "houses dispersed over the countryside in such a fashion that it would be difficult to call them villages."[57]

The urban sites that dotted the Andean highlands were for the most part Inca state complexes called tamp'u.[58] The Incas levied a labor draft called mit'a, which translates roughly to "turn-taking," through which each community contributed an annual quota of laborers. Detachments of workers trooped into the tamp'u with their caciques to be registered and sent to work on state farmlands, road building, or other projects.[59] One function of the tamp'u was to reward workers and their caciques with ritual hospitality on the plaza. Inca officials presented gifts infused with the prestige of the state: distinctive Inca textiles and vessels, feasts and drinking bouts with chicha made by the aqllas, and the aqllas themselves, whom governors periodically gave as wives to favored male subjects.[60] When archaeologists excavate these complexes, what they find most of are fragments of large ceramic vessels for chicha.[61] A large proportion of all young women and girls may have lived sequestered in these complexes, a counterpart to men called by the mit'a to work as food producers, haulers, and soldiers.[62] The aqllas' production enabled a fundamental Andean dynamic between king and people: the king rewarded the labor of his male subjects through the labor of his female subjects. The art historian Tom Cummins writes that "feasts on the plaza were the main forum where ideal social and political contracts were forged."[63]

European cities, too, were theaters for performance and ritual. Inca fiestas were not so different from the pageantry, devotion, and carnivals that took place on Spanish plazas.[64] European cities also housed the administrative machinery of secular and sacred government, as Inca cities did. Spaniards could recognize what the Incas accomplished through their cities, not to mention the Incas' superb infrastructure for production, storage, and communication. This recognition laid the groundwork for a long tradition of colonists admiring, even idealizing the Inca empire.

Yet, at the same time, Inca cities were stubbornly different from Spanish ones. They followed an old pattern in the central Andes: large and dense stone complexes which functioned as ceremonial centers, nodes of state power, and channels for tribute and labor. The Andes, in Spanish eyes, had no place for vecinos and policía.

This was what the General Resettlement of Indians would attempt to change. Thirty-five years after the conquest, viceroy Toledo would set out to do for the Andean people what Pizarro had done for the Spanish of Cuzco: found municipalities with plazas, churches, and uniform square blocks for a stable, permanent population. Through resettlement, the Spanish tried to impose the policía that the Inca kingdom, impressive though it was, had lacked. But the attempt only partly succeeded. To a remarkable extent, the reducciones resembled Inca cities: centers of sacred and secular government, of rituals on the plaza, of the flow of tribute and rotating labor from a population that spent much of its time outside the reducciones. Andean patterns survived, long after the Spanish climbed to the mountain kingdom, invaded its cities, and seized its king.

2

—

THE MOUNTAINS

In 1547, fifteen years after the bloody meeting in Cajamarca, licenciado Polo Ondegardo was serving the king as provisioner to a royal army camped in the province of Jauja, midway between Lima and Cuzco. They were awaiting dry weather to continue the campaign against Spanish rebels. In the wake of the conquest the Spanish conquerors had begun to fight among themselves, beginning a cycle of civil wars and rebellions against royal authority that continued, off and on, until 1554, even as more and more Spaniards arrived in Peru. (Among the first casualties was Francisco Pizarro, assassinated by his enemies in 1541.) To keep the soldiers fed and clothed during the long rainy season, Polo found that he was able to draw the supplies he needed from storage houses built by the Incas in Jauja, which he calculated held two million pounds of maize and dried potatoes. More than a decade after the Inca empire collapsed, the people of Jauja continued to harvest fields that had belonged to the Inca state and to deposit the produce in buildings set aside for it, as if "the time would come to give an account of it to the Inca."[1]

Andean society under Inca rule was an extraordinary machine for generating surplus production for its rulers. It did so in a harsh climate, without the benefit of a market economy anchored by urban capital. From the 1540s through the 1560s, some of the most intelligent colonists set out to learn what had made the Andes a rich land before the Spanish arrived, and why it was declining in wealth and population under their own rule. The continuing stockpiles in Jauja were the exception, not the rule, and even there the valley's population was falling. A growing number of Spaniards came to believe that they needed to understand pre-conquest social systems—systems which, they learned, were rooted in the mountainous landscape—to keep those systems working.

"Natives Exchanged and Passed from One Place to Another"

Early on, the conquerors were struck by how many Andeans seemed to be living away from home. Spaniards attributed this displacement to the chaos of war and conquest. But they soon learned that there existed a class of long-term sojourners, called *mitimas*, whom the Inca kings had uprooted from their ancestral homes and placed in distant locations. In doing so, the Spaniards came to believe, the Incas established connections between highlands and lowlands that created prosperity. The phenomenon of displacement, which at first seemed to be part of the problem of Andeans' declining wealth and population, was in fact part of the solution.

Spanish interest in how Andeans organized their communities was an outgrowth of the system of *encomienda*. The encomienda, a grant of Indian subjects to a Spanish overlord, was the key institution of early Spanish colonialism, the central structure connecting colonists and Indians, and the desire of every Spaniard. At the moment Columbus first looked at Caribbean Indians, he saw potential workers. He and succeeding governors granted individual Spanish settlers *repartimientos*, or "divisions" of Caribbean Indians, to pan for gold and work in the fields. As Spanish settlement moved to Mexico, Central America, and the Andes, the exploitation of Indian labor became somewhat less brutal and even took on a patina of idealism, as Spanish administrators tried to justify it. They called the system encomienda, or "trust," meaning that the king entrusted a repartimiento to a Spaniard (called an *encomendero*) who would exercise some of the king's duties toward his new indigenous subjects (above all, bringing them Christian doctrine) in exchange for collecting tribute and certain personal services. Tribute was not hard to collect: Indians in Mesoamerica and the Andes were peasant farmers long accustomed to supporting rulers with their labor and sweat. The encomienda system was a form of indirect rule, which freed Spaniards from most interaction with the Indian population but required attention to indigenous politics.[2]

Andean communities were organized in complex ways. The repartimientos in Peru were usually long-established communities, with caciques from lineages that predated not only the Spanish, but also the Incas. Outside their core territory (and sometimes even within it), the people of one repartimiento often lived interspersed with the people of others: a repartimiento was more a social and political unit than a territorial one. It was typically divided into upper and lower halves or *sayas*, which were called *hanansaya* (the upper half) and *hurinsaya* (the lower one); hanansaya exercised some degree of ascendancy over hurinsaya, the nature of which varied. The two sayas formed a unit jointly governed by the two caciques, with the Spanish calling the hanansaya cacique the *cacique principal*. The cacique of each saya himself had an assistant, whom the Spanish called the *segunda persona*, making a total of four caciques for the repartimiento as a whole.[3] The sayas were themselves subdivided into lineage groups called *ayllus*, often five each, making a total of ten in the community as a whole; the ayllus had their own leaders, whom the Spanish called *principales*. (In practice the situation was more complex than this idealized picture suggests; a repartimiento might actually have three sayas instead of two, and the number of component ayllus might vary.) Although the repartimiento possessed land, it was actually the ayllus who controlled the fields, periodically redistributing them among their members. Repartimientos and their component ayllus were not necessarily ancient: they sometimes melded or split, while the Incas, and later the Spaniards, sometimes reorganized them for administrative purposes. But they tended to recover their organic integrity quickly. Just as the ayllu considered itself a single lineage, the repartimiento had the qualities of a miniature ethnic group, often marked by specific clothing and hairstyles. Repartimientos were part of larger, nested groupings, which corresponded to Inca provinces and macroprovinces, with complex organization at every level.[4]

It was precisely because Andean society was so organized and disciplined that it was valuable to Spain. As early as 1533, a colonist in Panama requested a detachment of Andean laborers, noting that they were "a people of capacity" among whom "the common people [were] accustomed to serving the lords."[5] Through a cacique the Spanish could direct the labor of the whole group, learn its secrets, and siphon off its wealth. The cacique principal was responsible for everyone in his community and their behavior. The repartimientos did not function exactly like preconquest political units, nor was the amount of tribute necessarily the same as it had been: rather, the tribute was at first whatever the encomenderos could extort, and later what the Spanish governors decided the community could afford. But the same groups were paying the tribute as in Inca times, often in the same forms (labor, cloth, and agricultural products, although the Spanish gradually shifted the tribute to gold and silver), under the same caciques and local institutions. The encomendero did not try to take the cacique's place as local lord. Spanish law forbade it, and, more to the point, it would not have paid to do so. The encomendero's wealth lay in a preexisting, functioning machinery of local government. He might shake it to make it produce more, but he had no interest in dismantling it.[6]

The efficiency of the encomienda system meant that Spanish officials at first paid little attention to how and where Andeans lived. Beginning with Pizarro, Spanish officials took censuses to record the total population and number of tributaries in each repartimiento. Technically, tributaries were men between eighteen and fifty years old, but in most cases, the tribute-paying unit was the family: wife, husband, children, and elderly or incapacitated relatives who contributed what labor they could. Censuses counted, in effect, the number of households under each cacique's control. Spaniards were less interested in settlement patterns than in the flow of tribute.

Still, too much population dispersion could make encomiendas difficult to administer. If Spaniards could count on a cacique to collect tribute from all of his subjects and give most of it to his encomendero, it was irrelevant where they lived. But if the cacique could get his tribute assessment lowered by hiding some of his people (thus claiming a smaller tributary population), or if he himself lost control over distant subjects, that was a problem. Thus, while little interested in the pattern of settlement for its own sake, Pizarro and his lieutenants wanted to stop the disruption and dispersion of Andean communities.

The population was, indeed, highly dispersed. We know this from the rare censuses that did list people by village. A 1543 census in the north central Andes, in an area not far from Cajamarca, covered seventy-seven larger and smaller settlements (*pueblos* and *poblezuelos*); three had more than one hundred households each, but the median number was fifteen, and a third had fewer than ten households.[7] A 1549 census in the province of Huánuco found settlements with as few as five inhabitants and typically containing between fifteen and twenty-five households.[8] Diseases brought by the Spanish may have reduced these villages' population, but the general pattern of demographic dispersion was not new.[9]

Early on, Francisco Pizarro suspected the violence and chaos of the conquest had displaced Andeans from their homes and fields. Those who were or hoped to be encomenderos claimed that the encomienda system would improve the situation by giving them an interest in protecting their Andean subjects. Already in 1534 the cabildo of one newly founded Spanish city petitioned Pizarro to assign Andeans in encomienda, ostensibly for the Andeans' own protection.[10] The petitioners found a receptive audience in Pizarro, who assigned Andean communities to encomenderos as fast as he could, reserving the best for himself, his brothers, and the Crown. (Some of the largest repartimientos came to belong to the Crown, an important source for state revenue.) He ordered encomenderos to collect Andean runaways and restore them to their places of origin; he assumed that they had left because there was no one to defend them. Displaced Andean peasants, Pizarro believed, needed to be brought home.[11]

But as Pizarro pursued his project of distributing the people of Peru to Spanish masters, he encountered a complicating factor. Although many Andeans had recently been displaced by war, he came to realize that the displacement went deeper than that. He observed: "In the villages and settlements which the natives have made in the land, it has been seen and learned that in the time of the past lords the said natives had been exchanged and passed from one place to another and removed from their native place [naturaleza] to reside and settle in places marked out for them, with the result that . . . the natives who in their own language are mitimas . . . have long since converted the lands and towns where they live into their native place."[12]

According to Andeans the Spanish spoke with, the Incas had moved their subjects around the Andes like pieces on a chessboard. They resettled groups known for warfare, such as the Cañaris and Chachapoyas, to serve as military garrisons; they resettled groups skilled in pottery or metalworking, such as the Moche of the north coast, in the highlands to produce goods for the state. They resettled people to prevent or punish rebellions, to make land available for state use, and, most importantly, to give their subjects access to new lands. Once resettled, the mitimas did not always remain under their home cacique's political control, but they kept ties to their homeland, as well as its distinctive clothing and hairstyles, forming expatriate colonies within the Incas' diverse empire.[13] For the Spanish, the mitimas represented an alien institution: "natives . . . exchanged and passed from one place to another," in a web of ethnic enclaves created by the Inca empire as a kind of social engineering.[14]

Mitimas also posed an administrative problem: it was unclear to whom mitimas should pay tribute, the cacique and encomendero of the area where they lived or the cacique and encomendero of their community of origin. Pizarro might have solved this problem by eliminating the mitimas' separate status, either sending them home or integrating them into their local communities. Instead, he preserved their status as a legally recognized class, requiring them to remain where the Incas had placed them, even though he required all other Andeans to remain in their home villages. Whichever cacique had traditionally received their tribute under the Incas would continue to receive it under the Spanish, to the benefit of that cacique's encomendero. In a quest for order, Pizarro set up a double restriction on mobility: ordinary Andeans were forbidden to leave their places of origin, while mitimas were forbidden to return to them.[15]

These restrictions did not find favor at the Spanish court, where the king's administration upheld his Indian subjects' freedom of movement. In 1536 the Council of the Indies, the body tasked with advising the king on colonial matters, and the queen (who was ruling as regent while Charles V waged war in France) rejected Pizarro's order on the mitimas. She ordered that "if some of these who thus live outside their own towns wish to return to their lands you will make it possible for them to go freely and populate in the lands that they wish."[16] From this perspective, native Andeans had the same essential liberties as other Spanish subjects, including the right to move around. The queen's decree on Indian freedom did not necessarily have much effect in Peru, where colonists had already begun the practice of ignoring royal orders when they could get away with it, a practice reflected in the phrase *obedezco pero no cumplo*, "I obey but do not comply."[17] But, while asserting its subjects' freedom of movement, the Crown accepted Pizarro's decision on the mitimas' separate legal status.[18]

Pizarro and his successors institutionalized that status by writing it into encomienda grants, defining a repartimiento as a community of "Indians with their caciques, principales, Indians, mitimas and fields subject to them."[19] In 1549 when an encomendero took formal possession of his repartimiento, the local Spanish authorities placed in his hands the hands of three principales, one of them representing the mitimas.[20] Preserving the institution of mitimas made the system more complicated, but self-interest made the Spanish elite reluctant to tamper with the mitimas. Pizarro wanted to maintain the status quo, with Andeans following their old customs and paying their old tribute—for the Spaniards' benefit.[21]

To elucidate the situation, Pizarro ordered the first of what would become a basic institution of Andean administration: the *visita general*, or General

Inspection. The visita was a standard mechanism of Spanish government; it meant sending an outside official to ask questions, make judgments, and report back to the central authority. An inspector (*visitador*) might be sent to check on the priests in a diocese, the judges in a court, or the members of a council; he had broad powers to audit accounts, compile statistics, investigate corruption, and often to impose new rules and procedures. In the colonial context, officials ordered frequent visitas of individual districts and occasional visitas generales of a whole Audiencia or viceroyalty, to produce an up-to-date census and economic report for each repartimiento of Andeans and to set rates of tribute, as well as assess the performance of Spanish priests and encomenderos.[22] For the first General Inspection, Pizarro ordered the inspectors to establish mitimas' political affiliations. The question was, he knew, quite complex. Pizarro suggested saying a mass and praying God to "enlighten your understanding" before wading into this morass.[23]

The ambiguity of jurisdiction led to frequent lawsuits between encomenderos over mitimas' tribute. Following Pizarro's policy, Spanish judges usually upheld the rights of mitimas to their land and the right of their home communities to preserve jurisdiction over them (in which case it was the caciques who benefited, and consequently the Spanish, not the mitimas themselves). Despite clearly articulated and plausible arguments that some Spaniards made against the mitima system, judges continued to support it. One argument against the system was that the Incas had abused their power by planting mitima enclaves, unjustly taking the land from local inhabitants, and the mitimas should therefore be sent home. Another was that the mitimas, being rootless and mobile, indulged in vices and idolatry. Yet these arguments could not overcome the mitimas' ties to their home communities. One lawsuit illustrates the strength of the mitima system in Spanish courts. Around 1560 in the Chillón valley on the northern coast of Peru, local people and mitimas staked rival claims to the same land. The locals asserted that the Inca regime had installed this group of mitimas for a purpose calculated to offend Spanish judges: facilitating human sacrifice. These mitimas had guarded the processional route for an Inca procession which, allegedly, culminated in human sacrifice. Furthermore, the mitimas' own encomendero did not support them; the two communities' encomenderos had worked out a deal over their subjects' heads, whereby the locals would give the mitimas a herd of llamas in exchange for renouncing their claim. Yet even in the face of these facts, the judges ruled in favor of the mitimas, upholding an alien institution even when it conflicted with the logic of colonial law.[24]

Pizarro and his successors came to understand that mitimas were part of the basis of the Andean economy. All Spanish colonists, and especially the elite stratum of encomenderos and royal officials, knew that their fortunes were tied to those of the indigenous communities: Andeans' prosperity was the foundation of the viceroyalty. The Spaniards were beginning to understand the organization of Andean space.

A Mountain Sociology

For Spanish colonists Peru was, first and foremost, a mountain society. In Spain, mountains were not the center but the periphery: spaces of poverty and lawlessness. Fernand Braudel wrote of the Mediterranean world: "The mountains are as a rule a world apart from civilizations, which are an urban and lowland achievement. . . . [Civilizations] may spread over great distances in the horizontal plane but are powerless to move vertically when faced with an obstacle of a few hundred meters." In the Andes, the situation was exactly the reverse: the center of political power, wealth, and culture was in the highlands, and the Inca capital, Cuzco, was at 3,400 meters, higher than the peak of Mount Olympus in Greece. From the beginning, Spaniards had found Peru's bleak and cold highlands daunting. Pedro Sancho, one of Pizarro's companions, wrote: "All or most of the people . . . live on high hills and mountains" in which "settlements of Christians cannot be made." A Spanish governor wrote in 1551 that much of the country was "so high that it [was] in the middle region of the air," as if the country lay outside the terrestrial sphere, ascending toward the starry skies above. Yet somehow, the Incas had made their unpromising land rich. The question was how.[25]

Ethnography was a part of Spanish imperialism. Renaissance study of the classical world had promoted the idea that language, society, and culture formed an organic unity, alien to one's own but possible to understand. While many Spaniards had no curiosity about New World cultures, others saw concrete benefits in trying to understand those whom Spain had conquered. Priests brought humanistic methods to studying indigenous culture, on the premise that missionaries needed to know not just the language of those they wanted to convert but their history, myths, politics, and gods. Often, the motive for missionary curiosity was to understand pagan traditions in order to root them out more effectively: some colonial manuals for destroying Indian "idolatry" are priceless records of indigenous beliefs. But at times the fascination with Indian culture led to sympathy. Fray Bernardino de Sahagún, a Franciscan in Mexico, collaborated with young men from the native elite to compile a massive encyclopedia of Nahua life that extended to collections of jokes and proverbs. Royal officials, too, perceived the value of ethnographic knowledge. Beginning in the 1550s the Crown sent a series of questionnaires to the colonies to gather information about a wide range of subjects, beginning with geography and local resources, but including Indian history and society.[26]

In 1557, in response to one of these questionnaires, an official named Damián de la Bandera tried to explain the relationship between high and low altitudes in the central Andes. Describing the high-relief landscape of the highlands south of Jauja, he wrote: "It is a broken and cavernous land. The heights are a cold, bare, dry and sterile land; the lowlands, where there are rivers and ravines with water, are a temperate and fertile land . . . , [but much of it] an unhealthy land for the highland Indians." The people, consequently, built their villages halfway up the slopes, "where they enjoy the two extremes," the highlands for herding and the lowlands for planting. Bandera articulated a notion of ecological carrying capacity, asserting that the Andeans had filled every spot capable of supporting a community; though the villages were small, many could not support any more people than they already did.[27]

The Dominican friar Domingo de Santo Tomás analyzed the benefits that this high-relief region had for Andeans. Santo Tomás, who had come to Peru a decade before, was an intelligent observer of Andean culture. He visited the Spanish court as an advisor on native matters—he may in fact have drafted one of the ethnographic questionnaires issued by the Crown—published a Quechua grammar and dictionary, and received the posts of theology professor in Lima, Provincial of the Dominicans in Peru, and bishop of La Plata.[28] In a report to the king in 1550, he noted that within a relatively small area, warm river valleys and cold mountain plateaus produced different products: maize and vegetables below, potatoes and llama wool above. He made three observations about this situation. First, each zone was dependent on the other to meet its needs; second, each cacique controlled land and subjects in both zones; and third, when the political ties between the zones were severed, they stopped exchanging products. He noted that traditionally "all dealt together like brothers in their food and trading . . . ; since all was one and of one lord, they all had the enjoyment of it."[29] The same phenomenon of interconnectedness between highland and lowland operated on a larger scale, when mitimas shared their products with home communities, sometimes over distances of hundreds of kilometers.

Spanish observers gave the credit for this arrangement to the Incas. The Spanish were fascinated with the Inca infrastructure of roads, inns, messengers, and storage facilities.[30] They admired the system of mit'a (Hispanicized as mita), by which the Incas drafted Andean commoners' labor in periodic rotations to build and maintain that infrastructure; as one viceroy wrote, "it could not be ordered in any way better that the way the [Inca] lords had provided."[31] They were impressed by the rationality of a system that organized people into groups of ten, one hundred, one thousand, and ten thousand households, each under its own leader. Spanish writers also believed that the Incas reorganized small villages into larger settlements, choosing the best and healthiest locations and establishing the benefits of civic life.[32] The Incas, it seemed, were masters of both civil and social engineering.

By this logic, it was natural to conclude that the mitimas were another of the Incas' good ideas. As early as 1541 an ecclesiastical official named Luis de Morales wrote that the Incas, recognizing the natural poverty of the altiplano, selected a few families from each village as mitimas to colonize distant valleys and supply their highland homes with maize, coca, chile peppers, and other vegetables.[33] The bishop of La Plata wrote in 1552 that the Incas had established a tie between the coastal lowlands and the highland provinces so that the two regions could exchange the products they needed.[34] In 1551 the soldier, traveler, and author Pedro de Cieza de León described the Incas as "wise and foresighted" for sending highland mitimas to the lowlands, so that "even though in all the Collao [the altiplano region south of Cuzco] no maize is planted or harvested, the [caciques] do not lack for it . . . for they are always bringing in loads of maize, coca, fruits of all kinds, and a great deal of honey. . . . If it were not by this means, most of the peoples under [Inca] rule . . . would have lived in great necessity, as they did before they were conquered [by the Incas]."[35] Two officials stationed on the coast likewise wrote that the Incas had paired specific lowland and highland areas, recognizing that "each lacked what the other had," and divided tribute responsibilities between them.[36] Whereas in Europe a town or village was a nucleus surrounded by a single unified territory, many Andean communities were networks of scattered settlements intermingled with other communities, and the mitimas were key to this strategy. As these observers came to believe, mitimas represented a grand complementarity between highland and lowland that was the key to the Andean economy.

Modern scholars have confirmed much of this model, for which they have coined the term "vertical archipelago." But they differ on one main point: attributing the vertical archipelago to the Incas. It is now clear that long before the Incas, Andean communities founded satellite settlements, both near and far, to share products in a nonmarket economy. The Incas took advantage of this custom to legitimize their own practice of transplanting colonies of people from ethnic groups known for specific expertise, such as skilled weavers, goldworkers, or soldiers, to establish what amounted to state workshops and garrisons.[37] Modern scholars distinguish rigorously between pre-Inca and Inca enclaves, and sometimes restrict the word mitima to the latter. But they acknowledge that some settlements fulfilled both functions, serving the needs of their community and the needs of the state. Andeans themselves, and the early colonial officials who talked to them, thoroughly conflated the two categories of settlers, calling all of them mitimas. The prestige that the Incas enjoyed in colonial times, and the known value of the vertical economy, reinforced each other. Mitimas who wanted to stay where they were, or caciques who wanted to keep them there, drew on both sources of legitimacy.[38]

The most important of the colonial ethnographic officials was Polo Ondegardo. The son of a minor Inquisition official in Spain, he had earned a degree in law (that of licenciado) and come to Peru in 1544. When he arrived, Polo knew a great deal about Roman and canon law and nothing about the Andes, but he had a great curiosity for the world around him. During a long career as lawyer, government official, and entrepreneur, Polo won a reputation for shrewdness, the ability to choose the winning side in political crises, and a profound interest in native society. He served the king in arms against Spanish rebels more than once, receiving a wound in his leg that left him permanently lame. Adept at exploiting Andeans for his own business interests, and sympathetic to their aspirations only when it benefited either himself or the Crown, he was for a series of colonial governors the most reliable Andean expert.[39]

In 1548 as a reward for his service to the king, Polo was made encomendero of the repartimiento of El Paso in the Cochabamba valley. He never disguised his advocacy for the encomenderos' interests, but he believed that the best way to get rich from Andean peasants was by understanding and protecting their traditions. In 1561, having spent the better part of two decades in the colony, Polo replied to a request for information with a lengthy report for the Crown on the problem of how to govern the Indians of Peru. This was the first of two reports, written in 1561 and 1571, which are among the most valuable documents of Andean ethnohistory that survive.[40]

Polo argued that the vertical landscape of the Andes, where no place was self-sufficient, imposed a certain kind of mobility on society: "There are very few lands, or none in the highlands, where the Indians can avoid going to others for what they need." The Incas had created the system of mitimas to exploit the complementarity of high and low, and had set up a collective property regime in the communities to make it possible. Tampering with the system would mean "to take away their order, which they understand, without giving them any other." The population would dwindle and die.[41]

He praised the Inca empire for providing order in Andeans' lives and suggested that Spain should do the same. Asked how much tribute Andeans had paid the Incas, he replied that they had not paid in fixed sums but rather in their labor and time—virtually all of it. They possessed almost nothing of their own, but all their needs were provided for. The dominance of the Incas over their people was like nothing he had ever heard of in any other nation. Polo argued that freedom was less valuable to a kingdom than order, above all in the Andes where individuals had never managed their affairs for themselves. The Incas, he believed, had resettled Andeans into towns and villages, improved agriculture, and established the benefits of civilized life. The Incas had distributed labor in such an orderly way, he wrote, that "in my opinion it would be difficult to improve it, given their condition and customs."[42]

In the high, cold Andes, the challenge of climate required cooperation. To survive, highland communities kept mitimas in the lowlands and made frequent visits there for food they could not produce at home, especially when their own harvests failed, as they regularly did. The Incas, Polo believed, had established these systems and created these colonies in order to maintain the material basis of highland society: "If one thinks long about it, one will not find a better way or means" to sustain population in the highlands.[43]

Polo elaborated on Morales's arguments about the economic importance of mitimas in the distinctively challenging Andean landscape. A prominent example was the mitimas from the altiplano living in the valleys to the west, where the mountains fall to the Pacific coast. Although distant mitimas were typically included in encomienda grants, the first coastal encomenderos had established control over these enclaves. Once encomiendas were established—in this case dividing the highlanders in the east from their mitimas in the west—it was hard to change them.[44] But Polo made a persuasive case that this endangered the economic balance in the altiplano; by breaking the Incas' order, Spaniards were forcing Andeans to abandon the highlands. Beginning in the 1550s he advocated, with some success, that the viceroys intervene to reunite highland provinces with their lowland mitimas.[45]

To the Spanish, the highlands were the most important region of Andean settlement. This was not just because they had the densest indigenous population, and the traditional centers of Inca power, but also because they had the silver mines of Porco and Potosí. Already by the mid-sixteenth century, the silver that Andean laborers were extracting, for Spanish miners and on their own account, was becoming an important source of revenue: for Spanish miners, for the encomenderos who collected tribute from Andeans, and also for the Crown, which collected a 20 percent tax on all mining and siphoned off profits in various other ways. But the yield from the mines fluctuated alarmingly from one year to the next. There was much debate at court over how to stabilize it, and some argued for letting Andeans return to the labor systems of Inca times, dispensing with Spanish oversight, at least on mines belonging to the Crown.[46] As Polo, Santo Tomás, and a few others believed, the Inca kings had designed the structures of Andean prosperity, and it was in Spain's self-interest to promote those structures. Soon after the conquest, fray Vicente de Valverde, who had been made a bishop following his participation in the ambush of Atahualpa, called for allowing Andeans to raise their tribute payments "in their own manner."[47] If they prospered, according to their own proven methods, so would the Spanish.

3

THE GRID

In *Don Quixote* Cervantes tells of a village in which a regidor has lost an ass. As he stands disconsolate on the plaza, another regidor reports that he has just seen a lost donkey wandering outside the village, so the two stroll out to look for it. To draw it to them, they begin braying. Walking through the woods, they bray so well that they repeatedly mistake one another for the animal they are seeking, and they marvel and praise each other's gift for mimicking an ass. Sadly, they at last find the ass dead, killed by wolves; yet they agree the excursion has been worth it for the chance to test and share their abilities. As the story spreads, in the telling the braying regidores become even more exalted figures: the village's two alcaldes. But not everyone is impressed by the potentates' performance. In fact, outsiders mock them so mercilessly that all the men of the village march out with weapons, trumpets, and drums to wage war against the neighboring village. They carry a banner reading "No rebuznaron en balde / el uno y el otro alcalde": "They did not bray in vain, either the one or the other alcalde."

The story sketches an image of the rural community. Peasants do not live in scattered homesteads but in streets around a plaza. The village is a corporate entity, a little republic, ready to go to war with its neighbors like a kingdom. It boasts a full cabildo, including regidores and a pair of alcaldes; they may be bumpkins, willing to bray like an ass to recover an ass, but they hold the same titles as the city fathers of Seville or Valladolid. This was a model widely shared by Spaniards. The conquerors of Peru, while holding little respect for rustic people either at home or in the New World, had a clear vision of what peasant communities looked like.

Old World Conquest and Cultural Pluralism

Colonial ethnography argued that the Spanish would benefit from preserving Andeans' ways and traditions. As the decades went on, though, it ran up against a different idea: that the Spanish should remake Andean culture in their own image. In the context of previous Spanish history, this idea was a remarkable innovation. Spanish rulers had previously made little effort to dictate the settlement patterns and daily lives of those they conquered and ruled. But as they advanced from the Caribbean to Mexico and then Peru, Spaniards developed tools of ruling not yet known in Europe. They sought to impose a new way of organizing people in space, and a new ideology of civilizing subjects.

The sixteenth-century Spanish model of a king's or lord's relationship to his subjects remained a medieval one, consisting primarily of judging disputes and crimes while skimming off surplus production. As J. H. Parry wrote, "the principal task of government was considered to be that of adjudicating between competing interests, rather than that of deliberately planning and constructing a new society."[1] Lords and kings had no interest in closely managing peasants, whose tightly structured communities were organized to draw wealth from the soil; from a lord's perspective, it did not matter whether or not they built their houses on straight streets. A lord might invite peasants to settle on newly conquered territory, offering incentives such as free land, houses, and low taxes, but without tinkering with the structure of peasant communities. The point was to plant the seeds from which communities would grow, in an organic, self-managing process. This was not out of respect for peasants' ways of life: elites in Spain, as everywhere in Europe, despised those who sweated a living from the soil.[2] However, lords and kings felt no responsibility for changing their subjects' cultural habits; they benefited from leaving them as they were.

This hands-off policy even extended to the Muslims and Jews who came under Christian rule. Certainly, Christians agreed that it was extremely desirable for infidels to convert to Christianity. But, until the late 1400s, conquered people continued to live under their own local leaders and laws. *Mudejares*, or Muslims under Christian rule, retained not only their religion but also their laws and institutions "as was the custom in the former days of the Saracens." Mudejares in medieval Valencia continued to practice circumcision, possibly practiced polygamy, swore oaths on the Quran, heard public prayer and the call of the muezzin and used their own courts and coins. Their Christian lords generally left them alone as long as they paid tribute or rent. On the rare occasions when Christians forced Muslims to resettle, it was not in order to reorganize their communities but simply to take their land. In such cases, the lord directed the Muslims in a given place to move and found a new community, under their own leadership, "as befits their religion and their laws." More often, though, Christian kings and lords allowed Muslim peasants to stay where they were, living and farming according to their traditional ways. Muslim peasant subjects were a famously valuable commodity for a Spanish lord, since they were less able to resist his demands for tribute and service than Christian peasants. As the proverb went, "*Quien tiene moro tiene oro*"—he who has a Moor has gold. To the lucky possessors of such gold, meddling with the ways their subjects organized their villages made little sense. [3]

Although conquered Muslims and Jews were allowed to practice their own religion for most of the medieval period, Christian prejudice led to a gradually building oppression. Finally in 1492, the year Columbus crossed the Atlantic, Castile conquered the last Iberian Muslim kingdom, Granada. Breaking all precedents, Isabella and Ferdinand then forced Spanish Jews to convert to Christianity or leave the country, and they did the same to Muslims a few years later. But these brutal policies were different from cultural tutelage: Spanish rulers were not interested in how Jews and Muslims organized their communities, laid out their streets, or chose their municipal officials. Spain had more experience with unsettling its conquered subjects than with resettling them.

It was only in the later sixteenth century that this pattern changed. Unlike converted Jews, who in most respects assimilated to the majority population, converted Muslims (called *moriscos*) continued to live in their own communities, retaining their own traditions and often practicing Islam in secret.[4] The Spanish king and his advisors believed that religious orthodoxy was necessary for the security of the state, and the *moriscos'* cultural isolation appeared to be the main stumbling block to their becoming full Christians. In 1567 the crown ordered them to give up their Arabic names, their distinctive clothing, and their ritual baths. Moriscos had three years to learn the Castilian language; after that it would be a crime to speak Arabic.

In desperation, the *moriscos* of Granada revolted in 1570 and were crushed; as punishment, Philip II's government exiled them from Granada and resettled them in Castile's other provinces, assigning them by families to various towns and villages. A few decades later, the Spanish crown expelled the *moriscos* from Spain. The long tradition of cultural pluralism among conquered peoples within the Iberian peninsula was finally, definitively over.[5]

New World Conquest and Cultural Remaking

It was not in Granada that the new policy began, however, but in America. From the beginning, New World colonization included projects to change Indian culture and force them to resettle. In 1503 Isabella and Ferdinand ordered the founding of new villages for native people in the Caribbean, using a language that would be repeated with little variation for decades to come: "It is necessary that the Indians be assigned to towns in which they will live together, and that they not remain or wander separated from each other in the backcountry."[6]

Initially, this shift reflected the conditions of the Caribbean islands. Just as rulers' interests persuaded them to leave Spanish peasants alone, their interests here dictated the opposite. Taino Indians did not have as much experience as Spanish peasants in providing regular goods and labor to lords; also, the trauma of the Spanish conquest destroyed many of the Indians' community institutions. The original version of encomienda implanted in the Caribbean was a highly regimented regime of forced labor. (This was for nominally "free" Indians; Spaniards held others in out-and-out slavery, rationalized by having taken them prisoner in a "just" war.) To facilitate Spaniards' access to laborers, the Crown commanded the Indians' old villages to be destroyed and new ones built near Spanish settlements. They were to have four buildings, 15 × 30 feet in size, for every fifty families. The new rules for Indian life, going beyond what was necessary for labor recruitment, banned body painting, purges, and ritual baths, ordered Indians to wear clothes and sleep in Spanish-style beds, and demanded that some men in each village learn trades such as carpenter, blacksmith, or tailor.[7]

The Spanish crown wanted to preserve, discipline, and Christianize Indian labor. Spaniards were aware from early on that mass deaths of Caribbean Indians—from disease, famine, unbridled Spanish abuse, and native attempts to resist it—put their workforce at risk. Forced labor was deadly to Indians, as some Spaniards acknowledged. Yet regimenting it seemed to offer the hope of keeping people alive. Also, the pope had given the Spanish invasion of the New World his blessing in exchange for a promise to convert Indians to Christianity. Spanish officials, from the monarchs down, perceived a need to shape the behavior of their Indian subjects in ways that they had never tried to shape European peasants.

Hernán Cortés's lightning conquest of the Aztec empire in 1519 shifted the colonial center of gravity from the Caribbean, a region without cities, to Mesoamerica, the most urbanized part of the New World. Mexican cities resembled European ones, and Mesoamerican Indians, like Spanish peasants, had a long history of producing a surplus to support the elite; Spaniards simply took the place of the Aztecs (and other Mesoamerican rulers) as its recipients. Unlike in the Caribbean, Crown officials in Mexico did not at first call for Indian resettlement. Yet they urged other kinds of cultural change: while acknowledging that "the said Indians have the means and reason to live in a civilized and ordered manner in the towns they have," the Crown called on colonial officials to establish "good customs" and a "good order of living." The project of social engineering, born in the Caribbean, accompanied Spanish colonists to the mainland.[8]

The chief agents of change were the friars, members of Catholic religious orders to whom the Crown delegated much of its authority over its new Indian subjects. The friars (especially Franciscans) exercised influence in part by allying with caciques, heirs to the preconquest regional lords; with royal backing and the caciques' acquiescence, they introduced Spanish municipal offices into the city-states of central Mexico. Indian cities now had cabildos composed of alcaldes and regidores, elected by and from the Indian noble class, under a governor who was usually the cacique. As Charles Gibson wrote, "this rapid political Hispanicization is one of the impressive phenomena of colonial history, . . . the civil counterpart of Christianization." Indian nobles embraced the new offices as a way to legitimize their own status under colonialism.[9]

Christianity and cabildos went along with a specific vision of what a town should look like. In 1538, fifteen years after endorsing the Indians' existing towns as sufficient, the king wrote: "I have been informed that in order for our sacred Catholic faith to spread among the Indians . . . it would be necessary to instill in them human civilization [policía humana], so that this will be a path and means for knowing the divine, and for this, commands should be given for them to live together in good arrangement [concertadamente] in their streets and plazas."[10] The concept of policía linked religion, municipal government, and urban design into a single package. In spite of their initial perception that Mesoamerican towns in their existing forms were adequate for Christian civilization, royal officials began to call for redesigning the physical space of Indian communities. Gradually, friars pressed Indians to resettle in new towns.

The king did not spell out what it meant to live "in good arrangement in their streets and plazas," but the larger context of colonial Spanish urbanism offers clues. In sixteenth-century Spanish eyes, an ideal community was laid out on a *traza*, or urban grid, in which broad, straight streets crossed at right angles, centered on a large, symmetrical central plaza. This was not the norm in Spain itself, where a typical city had several small and irregularly shaped plazas facing neighborhood churches, and streets formed a tangle rather than a grid. Most cities in Spain had expanded gradually from small towns, or been founded by Muslims whose own urban traditions emphasized private interior spaces over public ones.[11] But in a widely shared vision of what a city should look like, the streets marked out regular, square blocks in parallel lines, and the plaza lay at the center. Spaniards were beginning to implement this vision in their own cities, to some extent in the mother country, but above all in the New World colonies. Santo Domingo, the first colonial city, was built on a semiregular grid, but Panama City and Vera Cruz in Mexico were each founded in 1519 on grids of identical square blocks, a checkerboard pattern which has been called the *traza americana*. One scholar has found that out of sixty sixteenth-century Spanish towns and cities whose original plan is known, forty had checkerboard grids.[12] Urban authorities required vecinos to maintain the grids: in Mexico City, as early as 1532, Hernán Cortés ordered a building's façade to be torn down because it broke the line of the street.[13] The grid was the characteristic form of sixteenth-century Spanish colonial urban design.

Paradoxically the gridded traza and large central plaza, which spoke to Spaniards' ideas about their own culture yet were rare in Spain, were prominent in at least some prehispanic cities in Mexico as in Peru.[14] The Mexico City grid that Cortés enforced followed the city blocks of Aztec Tenochtitlán, and the plaza mayor of Mexico City was built on Tenochtitlán's plaza. Its size was a point of pride in the colonial Mexican capital; one resident wrote in 1554 that the plaza was "the largest in either hemisphere, good lord—how flat and broad, how joyful! . . . If those porticos were removed it could hold an army."[15] The plaza mayor of colonial Cuzco, likewise, was simply the Incas' Hawkaypata under new management. Yet in Mexico, Peru, and elsewhere, Spaniards believed that grids and plazas symbolized Christian policía. Whether or not the king had the checkerboard grid in mind when he legislated for Indian communities in 1538, over time the Spanish insisted on it.

Scholars have debated the origins of the checkerboard traza and its sudden ubiquity in the sixteenth century. They once pointed to Philip II's "Ordenanzas de descubrimiento, población y pacificación de las Indias" of 1573, which mandated urban grids (among other things), but by then the traza americana was already well-established; the 1573 ordinances, which differed in certain details from colonial practice, had little direct impact. Some have seen the grid as a cultural inheritance with a precise genealogy, passing from ancient models through medieval gridded towns (rare in Spain, more common in France) to Spanish America; others have suggested that decisions made in the earliest colonial foundations set a precedent for later planners. Some emphasize the influence of Renaissance architectural treatises, others the example of indigenous cities, still others the simple practicality of laying out new settlements on a grid. What is clear is that colonial Spaniards saw the urban grid as expressing their civilization's most important values.[16]

The ideological meaning of grids is not obvious or universal; they are found in many societies in world history, with many functions. In and of itself, a grid signifies only the existence of institutions able to impose a preconceived pattern on a town. In the case of Anglo-American cities, some scholars have seen grids as implying democratic equality. But in the case of colonial Latin America, most have followed Henri Lefebvre's vision of the urban grid as a tool of hegemony and exploitation. It was certainly associated with conquest: the most prominent gridded city in Spain was Santa Fe, founded in 1491 as a base for the siege of Granada. But to colonists, the grid also symbolized civic and moral rectitude. In Spanish as well as Indian communities, grids communicated both regimentation and civilization. Valerie Fraser argues that the "uniformity, familiarity, [and] standardization" of Spanish architecture and urban design reflected colonists' "turn[ing] back to the fundamentals of their culture for guidance." This argument ignores the paradox that their most immediate examples of urban grids were those of indigenous civilizations. Still, Spaniards believed that rectilinear streets and plazas encapsulated the cultural values, the policía, that they carried with them to America.[17]

The ideal of policía was connected to a mid-sixteenth-century vision of Spanish and Indian populations as distinct polities, the "Republic of Spaniards" and the "Republic of Indians," which had the same land, faith, and king, but separate communities, languages, and traditions. In reality many Spaniards and Indians lived side by side, but the ideal of separation survived throughout the colonial period. It justified a network of self-contained Indian villages and towns, with native cabildos and Spanish priests, which were expected to display their policía in their houses and streets.[18]

Resettling Indians into a central location, known as *reducción* in Peru, was usually called *congregación* in Mexico and Guatemala. But the word *reducción* was also in use from the beginning, referring to the larger process of cultural transformation. The verb *reducir* was not synonymous with the English word "reduce," but reflected its Latin origins: the prefix *re-* added to the verb *ducire* meant "to lead back," restoring something to its previous state, to its component parts, or to a state of order. In early modern Spanish *reducir* could mean conquering an enemy, converting someone to Christianity, separating ore into its different minerals, summarizing an argument, or identifying the grammatical rules of a language.[19]

We do not know much about the earliest Indian resettlements in Mexico. Presumably, friars began by building churches in existing settlements and expanded their interventions as circumstances allowed. They might order buildings torn down to create a plaza in front of the church, or call for the straightening of streets. In time, they might pressure a community to move to another location or consolidate several villages into a single one. The focus on resettlement steadily increased, as indigenous deaths from Old World diseases left previously dense regions sparsely settled. At the same time, colonial rule was expanding to areas without urban traditions, especially mountainous parts of Mexico and Guatemala.[20]

Sixteenth-century sources refer to friar-led resettlement as commonplace, though the details are obscure. We have a report of a resettlement in 1526, but its date has been questioned. For that town, Acámbaro in Michoacán, Franciscan friars chose a large area of level ground near a river. First they erected a central cross, then laid out the traza: five streets in either direction, centered on a plaza. The town was divided in half between two local ethnic groups. Four hundred families each received a *solar* 150 feet wide (while twelve caciques received double), although the villagers did not build their houses until two years later. The residents brought in running water and established a cabildo. Other, smaller villages were founded outside among the fields.[21]

During the 1530s and 1540s, resettlement was a scattershot policy, an extension of friars' pastoral mission, mainly in a few areas such as Guatemala.[22] A 1546 council of bishops in Mexico City wrote that "to be truly Christian and civilized [políticos], as the rational men they are, it is necessary [for Indians] to be congregated and reduced into towns, and not to live scattered and dispersed in the mountains and wilderness."[23] The Mexican bishops were likely trying to shore up their control of the Indians. But their appeal, coming from a region that was highly urbanized at the time of conquest, impressed officials at court. In response, the emperor Charles V in 1549 established a new mandate for resettlement throughout the colonies. The new towns were to have cabildos, marketplaces, jails, and inns for travelers. The Indians were to be persuaded in "the most soft and loving way" to move to their new homes, and could choose the sites themselves. Ultimately, though, resettlement was to be compulsory.[24]

Don Luis de Velasco, Viceroy of Mexico from 1550 to 1564, undertook a general policy of congregación at the hands of the friars. Indian elites did not necessarily reject the policy; some found that assuming the role of alcaldes and regidores strengthened their status. Others, though, feared that it would undermine their communities' land base, and their own incomes.[25] Those being moved resisted it almost universally, as the friars acknowledged: "there is no sick person who does not find the taste of medicine unpleasant. . . . Among all these Indians there is not one who wishes to leave behind the hut passed on to him by his father, nor to abandon a pestilential ravine or to desert some inaccessible crags, for that is where the bones of his forefathers rest." Resettlement carried benefits for a few, heavy costs for most.[26]

During the fourteen years of Velasco's administration, friars in central Mexico, the Yucatan, and Guatemala made significant progress in rearranging local structures of government and the physical layout of villages and towns. But some officials, perhaps hostile to the friars for other reasons, complained that resettlement harmed Indian society, especially when it moved people away from their fields.[27] After Velasco's death in 1564, the colonial government removed the free hand he had given the friars, and resettlement efforts subsided for the rest of the sixteenth century. (A new cycle of resettlement in Mexico began in the first years of the seventeenth century.)[28]

Initially, the Mexican campaign found little echo in Peru. The law of 1549 was directed to all the territories, but its impact outside Mexico and Guatemala was small. The Audiencia of Lima responded by ordering Andeans in and around the capital city to establish concentrated settlements.[29] The Spanish court sent at least two reminders to Peru in the next two years, but little else was done.[30] A council of Peruvian bishops who assembled in Lima in 1551 ignored the resettlement policy on which their Mexican colleagues had placed so much emphasis. The bishops noted that "in this land the Indians are divided among many hamlets and it would be a great harm and burden if they had to assemble," even to hear mass together each week; instead of calling for resettlement, the Peruvian prelates ordered priests to base themselves in the larger villages while periodically visiting the small ones.[31] During years when rebellions and civil wars among the Peruvian encomenderos were a constant threat, neither secular administrators nor bishops were ready to take responsibility for reorganizing the Andean countryside.[32]

But the Peruvian colonial elite gradually came to embrace resettlement, at least in principle. By the 1560s, both sides—Spaniards who saw themselves as representing Andeans' interests as well as those who thought that the Crown coddled them—agreed on it. While some colonists believed resettlement would curb Andeans' allegedly lazy and vicious natures, others saw it as the necessary basis for Christian liberty. Decades after the invasion, the Spanish conquest of the Andes was in a sense unfinished: Spaniards ruled the land indirectly by controlling the indigenous elite, rather than directly by controlling the Andean masses. Many Andeans had probably never seen a Spaniard or heard the Castilian language. The indigenous masses and the colonial rulers remained invisible to each other. Resettlement promised to strengthen Spanish rule, while giving Andeans the incalculable benefits of Christianity and policía.[33]

The two viceroys who governed Peru between 1556 and 1564 both tried to resettle Andeans. Each ordered a General Inspection to collect information, set tribute levels, and found resettlements. Both failed, in whole or in part. Attempts at resettlement by the Marquis of Cañete (viceroy from 1556 to 1560) were halfhearted. Besides continuing the Audiencia's work in segregating Andeans living in Lima into a single neighborhood, he directed some of his officials to follow suit in other areas. Licenciado Polo Ondegardo, as governor in the city of Cuzco, established four urban neighborhoods (barrios) for Andeans, with Spanish-style municipal self-government in each. Another of Cañete's officials, Damián de la Bandera, produced two reports on rural resettlement projects. In one of them, in the Yucay valley outside Cuzco, he consolidated a scattered population into three towns or large villages, with populations ranging from 140 to 400 households. But another area yielded poorer results. In the rocky district surrounding Guamanga (modern Ayacucho), he found that consolidating villages was out of the question. The population was dispersed among 251 hamlets, each containing on average fewer than ninety households. With settlements in every possible spot, each filled to the capacity that local land and water resources could sustain, Bandera claimed that no location could fit even ten more people. It was a discouraging sign for resettlement in the Andean landscape.[34]

The Count of Nieva, Cañete's successor (1560–64), instructed his inspectors to found new towns for Andeans.[35] A few areas witnessed a significant degree of resettlement by the mid-1560s, especially the north coast of Peru, near Trujillo.[36] Overall, though, both viceroys' efforts came to little; according to a subsequent report by the archbishop of Lima, in most places resettlement remained a distant goal.[37] The Count of Nieva gradually came to the same conclusion that Damián de la Bandera had expressed: the mountainous landscape could not sustain larger settlements than it already had. Writing to the king in 1562, Nieva made an extraordinary argument: "The way the land is populated is the way the Incas settled and left it. One supposes—or at least suspects—that since their government in secular matters was as good as we understand it to be, they would have established larger settlements if it were possible." The Incas, in other words, had established the best settlement pattern possible; if villages were small, it was because larger ones were impossible. A developing set of ideas about the Andean landscape, the Andean people, and the wisdom of the Incas made resettlement seem ever further out of reach.[38]

Nieva also mentioned another barrier: the opposition of the caciques. Some had approached him "to discuss this article of resettling them to larger settlements, saying that this would do them harm."[39] Although virtually all colonial Spaniards agreed on the resettlement policy in principle (including the caciques' allies among the friars), virtually all Andean commoners and many Andean lords opposed it. As events would show, caciques were difficult for Spanish rulers to ignore.[40]

4

—

LORDS

In 1561 a group of caciques and principales from the Cuzco area offered to supply the king of Spain with money that his government, nearly bankrupt from wars in Europe, desperately needed: "They had learned that the King was constrained by necessity, and many of them were rich and powerful, and they wanted to give some *servicio* of money in order to supply part of his necessity and so he would not place them perpetually under their masters [the encomenderos]."[1] Their offer signaled a certain self-confidence, a level of comfort about the place they occupied in the Spanish empire and their ability to leverage it to obtain what they wanted. In exchange for the money, they asked the king to remove them from encomenderos' authority and confirm their status as independent lords of their Andean subjects. They knew that the king took such offers seriously.

The Spaniards were not the only colonial ethnographers. While the Spanish elite was trying to understand Andean culture, the Andean elite was working to understand Spanish culture. Royal governors wanted to preserve the wealth that the Incas had extracted from the Andean people and their caciques; the caciques wanted to preserve, under their new overlords, the status they had enjoyed under the Incas. Each side scrutinized the other, searching for the key to its problem.

One technique that the caciques learned was the system of *servicio* and *merced*. In offering money to Philip, the caciques invoked a widely shared understanding about the complementary roles of a Spanish king and his subjects: the subject offered a *servicio*, or service, and the king gave a *merced*, a reward. The servicio could take the form of actions—military or governmental service—or, simply, cash. The Cuzco caciques were one of several indigenous groups to offer Philip money between 1559 and 1562, and they did so in response to an earlier offer made collectively by Peru's encomenderos. The encomenderos were asking the king to make them permanent overlords of the caciques and their subjects; the caciques, in response, urged him to eliminate the encomenderos entirely. To obtain what they wanted the two groups engaged in an extraordinary bidding war, known to historians as the *perpetuity controversy*, in which each tried to buy the privilege of lordship from the king. King Philip, excited by the prospect, sent a commission to investigate the competing offers. In fact, and unfortunately for themselves, both groups were essentially bluffing: it is likely that neither side could pay anything close to what it offered, and the bidding war fizzled out. For the caciques, though, their participation in the controversy was an apprenticeship in playing the game of imperial politics and an introduction to the ways they later used the General Resettlement to their own advantage.[2]

The origins of the bidding war were in 1554 in the province of Jauja when Spaniards and Andeans fought side by side to defeat a Spaniard who had rebelled against the king—the most recent of the series of civil wars which had roiled the colony since its founding. Like most of the others, this one was a rebellion by certain encomenderos, and would-be encomenderos, against royal attempts to limit the power of their class. Others, however, remained loyal to the king. As the wet summer gave way to fall and winter the two sides skirmished and maneuvered against the rebel leader, Francisco Hernández Girón. The king's warriors, Spanish and Andean, wore down the rebels month by month, and at last defeated and captured Girón in the king's name.[3]

Prominent in the loyalist campaign were leaders of the province of Jauja, both caciques, such as don Gerónimo Guacrapaucar, and encomenderos, such as don Antonio de Ribera. Ribera, however, was not present at Girón's capture. He had already departed for Spain, where his fellow loyalist encomenderos had sent him as their representative to the Spanish court, to ask the king, ironically, for the same thing for which Girón had rebelled: more power for encomenderos.[4] Legally, an encomendero had no right over "his" Indians except to collect tribute, and most encomienda grants were limited to two lifetimes, that is, they would expire at the death of the original grantee's heir, giving the king the right to grant them to another person.[5] On behalf of his peers, Ribera asked for two things. First, for what was called perpetuity: the right to pass their titles to their descendants indefinitely. Second, for jurisdiction: the authority to appoint judges over their Andean subjects, as Spanish lords did over their Spanish subjects. These two rights, together, would make the encomenderos the permanent lords of the Andes.[6]

The encomenderos argued that enlarging their powers would be good for the colony. Peru was Spain's most turbulent possession. Every time a rebellion broke out, those who suppressed it received new or larger encomiendas, and rebels who switched to the king's side just in time earned rewards as well. In fact, the revolving door between rebellion and loyalty was a recognized incentive for rebellion. With no standing army except the encomenderos themselves, the Crown could not break the cycle. Perpetuity, the encomenderos argued, would give the colony's natural leaders—themselves—a stake in peace.[7] Don Antonio de Ribera was well qualified to discuss Peru's troubles: he himself had sided with the rebels in an earlier civil war, before proclaiming his loyalty and taking up arms against the current rebels.[8]

More important than such arguments, however, was the money the encomenderos offered. Ribera caught the king's attention with an extravagant proposal. In exchange for perpetuity and jurisdiction, the encomenderos of Peru would give the Crown a servicio of 7.6 million pesos—twice the national debt of the chronically cash-strapped monarchy. In Peru, a peso could buy a ham, or three pairs of rope sandals; in Spain, where money went farther, it could buy a third of a fine hunting falcon.[9]

The offer came at an opportune time. Charles V, who was both king of Spain (1516–55) and Holy Roman Emperor in Germany, was worn down by ruinously expensive wars. He was soon to abdicate the Spanish throne, which passed to his son, Philip II (1555–98), under the shadow of bankruptcy. Philip immediately placed the Peruvian proposal at the top of his agenda. He ordered the Council of the Indies to put all other business on hold until this was resolved.[10]

The proposed sale was the talk of the court. The royal financial advisors embraced it, but others resisted. The Council of the Indies feared that selling royal jurisdiction meant squandering a nonrenewable resource. And Bartolomé de Las Casas, who was currently one of the king's advisors, raised the subject of Indian rights. In the Americas, he argued, the king had gained a new continent of free Indian subjects; he had the duty to rule them well, not to sell them to Spanish adventurers. Las Casas urged Philip to delay the decision, calling it "the most difficult and of the greatest importance and risk . . . that any prince in the world . . . has ever debated or decided."[11] In a meeting on the subject, a bishop and an archbishop had to be physically restrained from hitting each other.[12]

Philip decided to compromise. He would sell the encomenderos half of what they wanted: perpetuity, but not legal jurisdiction. They would have to consent to part of the lordship they desired, not all of it. Since the original offer, seeking jurisdiction as well as perpetuity, was presumably no longer valid, he appointed a commission to go to Peru to negotiate the sale on these terms. But he ordered them to proceed cautiously and keep all options open.[13]

In 1559—five years after don Antonio de Ribera departed for Spain, and as the king was preparing to send commissioners to Peru—a group of caciques met to formulate a response. The caciques, representing seventeen repartimientos in the region of Lima, appointed two Spanish friars to represent them at the Spanish court, Las Casas and Domingo de Santo Tomás.[14] Speaking in the caciques' name, the friars offered the king one hundred thousand pesos more than whatever the encomenderos might bid, and a minimum of two million pesos if the encomenderos could not muster a bid for what the king was prepared to sell (i.e., perpetuity without jurisdiction). In exchange, the king would not appoint new encomenderos when the current ones died off, but would restore, under his own overlordship, "the old political order they had in the time of the Inca kings, because in this consists their entire conservation."[15]

Natural Lords

Who, exactly, were caciques? Although the caciques had served the Inca empire, as they did the Spanish, their authority was independent of it. The Andes were a patchwork of local ethnic groups, with their own histories and customs, and most had lived under Inca rule for less than a century before the Spanish arrived. Many cacique lineages were much older. The Incas depended on the local lords for the same reason the Spanish did later: to control their subjects and deliver tribute and labor. With the Spanish conquest the caciques exchanged one empire for another, and the difference, at least initially, may not have seemed very great to them.[16]

Each encomendero received tribute from one or more caciques. As overlord, the encomendero depended on the cacique for his power, but the cacique did not depend on the encomendero for his own. Many colonists despised caciques as scheming, treacherous, and even abusive to their own subjects, but the viceroyalty could not function without them.[17]

The caciques' identity was enigmatic. Spaniards accepted that legitimate hereditary rulers, whether Christian or non-Christian, were natural lords (señores naturales) with the right to maintain their position after conquest. There was some controversy whether New World caciques fell into this category, and the Crown debated whether caciques could carry the title of señor, but ruled in 1558 that they could.[18] Caciques certainly claimed this status, styling themselves (the words of a later petition) "like the dukes and counts and marquises in Spain."[19] And colonial Spaniards, while often abusing caciques in word and deed, called them by the honorific "don," which at this time only truly aristocratic Spaniards dared claim.[20] (Antonio de Ribera was a don, based on his high birth in Spain, but many encomenderos were not.) Militarily, politically, and economically, almost any encomendero was superior to almost any cacique, yet caciques had the greater right to be called lords.

If anyone understood the ambiguous position of the colonial cacique, it was don Gerónimo Guacrapaucar, cacique general of Luringuanca in the province of Jauja. Don Gerónimo came to power before the Spanish conquest and died some time after 1565, in one lifetime witnessing a whole era of transformation.[21] But to understand what the Spanish conquest meant to Guacrapaucar, we have to go further back, to the Inca conquest of Jauja and its Huanca people some seventy-five years before. Before the Incas came, the Huancas' world was a hard one. They lived on the mountain peaks, in the thin air at 3,800 meters a punishing climb from their fields lower down the slopes, in order to protect themselves from their enemies; the chiefdoms were perpetually at war. We can still see the remains of their walled villages, dense with small round houses high up on the mountaintops. Incas described the Huancas as savage warriors who stretched their enemies' skins for their battle drums.[22]

Inca conquest brought the Huancas both costs and rewards. It brought new labor demands and the burden of foreign rule, but also a peace which allowed them to move down from the peaks and spread out in the valleys.[23] The Incas retained some of the preexisting leaders as caciques to rule on their behalf, as they did throughout their empire, while bringing the caciques' sons home to educate in Cuzco. They modified Huanca customs they disapproved of, for instance pressing them to substitute deer skulls for dog skulls as musical instruments.[24] Excavating elite Huanca households, archaeologists map a slow spread of Inca architecture and implements, evidence that caciques were embracing Inca culture.[25]

The relationship between Inca kings and caciques drew on an Andean discourse of reciprocity, unequal but complementary, between ruler and ruled. At the local level, when commoners labored on a cacique's field, he reciprocated with a feast; its value was less than their labor, but its abundance and spectacle made up the difference. The Inca kings established a similar relationship, as we have seen, providing feasts and participatory rituals, an appearance of empire-sized "generosity," in exchange for their subjects' labor as mediated by the caciques. In the formation of the Inca empire, the caciques surrendered their preexisting authority to the king who then "generously" returned it to them, under Inca overlordship.[26] This resembled the encomenderos' relationship to the Spanish king. In their own eyes, the encomenderos had conquered Peru for their king (or, later, reconquered it from rebels), surrendering to him the lordship they had won with their own strength; it was his part of the bargain to give it back to them in the form of an encomienda. The Spanish economy of servicio and merced resembled a pattern Andeans already knew well.

The caciques, then, had a model for what it meant to be a conquered lord: collective defeat, personal advancement, and the seductive embrace of a powerful outside culture. One of don Gerónimo's ancestors, perhaps his grandfather, had surrendered to the conquering Incas. The Huancas served the Incas loyally, but chose the wrong side in the Inca civil war of the 1520s, siding with Huascar against Atahualpa and suffering serious reprisals.[27] So it was natural for them to cast their lot with the invading Spaniards. Soon after the Spanish arrived, a young cacique named Apu Manco Guacrapaucar was baptized don Gerónimo. He sent his sons to school with Spanish friars and raised them to serve their faraway Spanish king. He built a Christian church where he would one day be buried.[28]

One difference between the Inca conquest and the Spanish one was that the Incas brought peace, but the Spanish brought sickness and wars that never seemed to end. During don Gerónimo's long reign he watched his people die around him: he had fifty to sixty thousand subjects when he came to power, but a census soon after his death showed only a third of that number.[29] Some died from Spanish diseases, some fled Spanish demands, and others perished in Spanish wars, including the encomendero rebellions and a slow-burning war against the independent Inca princes in Vilcabamba.[30]

The Huancas embraced the Spanish cause from the beginning, and paid a heavy price for it. Don Gerónimo recalled that he was among the first to pay homage to Francisco Pizarro, giving the conqueror food, clothing, gold and silver, and Huanca men and women to serve him in future battles; more than seven hundred of this group never came home. They were not the last. Almost every time the king's captains marched between the mountains and the coast they marched through Jauja and conscripted Huanca servants and fighters. The capture of the rebel Girón in Jauja province was only the most recent. "In the encounter," Guacrapaucar reported laconically to the king, "some Indians died."[31]

Don Gerónimo, who had come to power as a Huanca and Inca lord, might now be described as a Huanca and Spanish lord. And when a Spanish lord performed a servicio for his king, sacrificing lives and treasure, he expected a merced.[32] Why should not don Gerónimo receive honor from his king, rather than subjection to an encomendero? The caciques' advocate Las Casas asserted: ". . . The natural lords of the Indians, their kings and caciques, should be restored to their old power, liberty and property . . . [and] the king of Castile should be recognized . . . as the supreme lord and as emperor over many kings . . . [subject to him] of their own will and not by violence or force." Out of love for their king, Las Casas predicted, the caciques would adopt his "just laws and commands" while keeping their own "reasonable ancient laws."[33]

The caciques who gathered in Lima in 1559, and in other regional assemblies throughout the country that soon followed their example, enacted Las Casas's theory in real politics. They called the bluff of a colonial class that needed them to control the indigenous masses, but was reluctant to legitimize their authority. They claimed a political role, not as conquered subjects, but as natural lords freely acknowledging their emperor. And they offered to pay for it.

But could the caciques—or the encomenderos—afford to pay the millions of pesos they offered? Many Spaniards doubted it.[34] Yet neither offer was implausible at the time. In the past, the caciques' power had created extravagant fortunes for a few encomenderos, and Pizarro's companions who plundered the Incas had won legendary wealth. Some said that more Inca gold remained hidden in places known only to the caciques. But the caches of Inca gold were mythical, the caciques had just endured two decades of exploitation, war, and disease, and the encomenderos possessed little beyond what they could extort from the caciques. Caciques were still able to raise money from their subjects' labor when necessary—to prosecute lawsuits in colonial courts, for instance, or send representatives to Spain—but not the enormous sums being tossed around on paper. The king, though, was willing to hope that both sides could back up their promises. He gave Santo Tomás permission to help organize the caciques and negotiate on their behalf in Peru.[35]

Manacancho

In 1561 the king's commissioners sailed for Peru, along with the friar Santo Tomás and the new viceroy, the Count of Nieva. Arriving in Lima, the commissioners issued a letter to the Spanish city and town councils of Peru, asking them to send representatives to the capital to discuss perpetuity. Since the town councils were dominated by encomenderos, this was to be an assembly of the encomendero class.[36]

As their representatives assembled in Lima, some time in the second half of 1561, a number of native leaders met in Cuzco to formulate their own response. It was this meeting that sent one of the caciques to speak to the city's governor, offering to send money to "supply [the king's] necessity."[37] The caciques gave power of attorney to two Inca princes, named don Juan Sona and don Alonso Sayri Topa, to offer up to four million pesos.[38] In Lima, the viceroy and commissioners were unsympathetic to such initiatives. They had an interest in closing the deal they were sent to negotiate, sympathized with the encomenderos, and saw any further interventions by friars and caciques as unwelcome if not subversive.[39] The viceroy and commissioners sent Gregorio González de Cuenca, an Audiencia judge, to suppress the caciques' antiperpetuity meetings in Cuzco by prosecuting their mestizo translator for fraud.[40]

The two representatives of the Cuzco caciques, undeterred by the commissioners' attacks, traveled through the southern Andes with Santo Tomás in 1562 and convened new assemblies to canvas caciques' views.[41] The commissioners sent licenciado Polo Ondegardo alongside them to give the caciques the other side of the story, asking them to support perpetuity; Polo, himself an encomendero, considered perpetuity of encomiendas perfectly compatible with his goal of preserving Andean institutions. But the caciques stood firm, in spite of pressure from their encomenderos.[42]

Santo Tomás wrote to a colleague that Polo "gives them to understand the great benefits that will come to them if they are perpetually under [the encomenderos], but with all that they say that they *manacancho* want perpetuity." Manacancho (or *mana kanchu*), in Quechua, means "it is not," "there is none," or, emphatically, "no."[43]

Some Spanish officials argued that friars such as Santo Tomás were manipulating caciques to magnify their own power. The friars certainly played a crucial role. While caciques' names appear on powers of attorney expressing their opposition to perpetuity and their willingness to pay to avert it, it was often friars who made arguments and offers in the caciques' names. Yet the caciques were not mere tools; it was they who organized the meetings, established a consensus, and named friars as their legal representatives, alongside Andeans such as the Inca princes. The assemblies of 1559–62 were the first supralocal native institutions formed since the Spanish conquest. They did not represent a return to Inca-era political institutions; a few Inca princes were involved in the movement, but no one suggested restoring the Inca dynasty. The caciques saw the encomenderos organizing themselves to seek benefits from the king, and they learned from it.

The caciques of Jauja took an active role in these assemblies. At one of the assemblies in 1562, over a third of the attendees (the largest single contingent) were under the authority of three Jauja caciques. Don Gerónimo Guacrapaucar sent one of his sons, don Carlos, to represent him.[44] But he sent another son, don Felipe, to Spain to plead his merits directly at the royal court. Like any Spanish lord, he submitted a record of his past *servicios* and asked for royal *mercedes*. It is likely that the courtiers had never encountered anyone quite like don Felipe—a cacique's son educated by Franciscan friars, who had helped capture the last Spanish rebel in Peru—and he must have made an impression. From the autumn of 1563 to the following spring, accompanying the king on his travels between Spanish cities, Felipe received from him more than ten different grants and privileges. They included a royal pension, a prohibition against Spanish cattle ranching in Jauja, a coat of arms (with three severed Inca heads representing his family's military service on the king's behalf), and the title of the province's paramount lord. Young don Felipe more than satisfied his father's hopes.[45]

The encomenderos' negotiations in Lima, meanwhile, had gone poorly. They wanted both perpetuity and jurisdiction, but the commissioners were only authorized to sell them perpetuity. And even if the commissioners could have given them everything they asked for, the encomenderos now offered to pay far less than what Ribera had at first proposed.[46]

Philip II never tried to collect from either side. Frustrated at the lack of a deal, he ordered the commissioners home.[47] The commissioners' final report proposed a compromise: selling a third of the encomiendas to their holders in perpetuity, selling a third to their caciques under royal jurisdiction (in both cases, at lower prices that reflected the two groups' actual resources), and keeping a third to give to new candidates for the period of one or two generations, as before.[48] Whatever weight the commissioners' suggestions might have had, however, vanished when they and the viceroy were unexpectedly caught in a corrupt influence-peddling scheme: embezzlement and graft were common in colonial administration.[49] The project of selling either perpetuity to encomenderos or independence to caciques, which had seemed to promise great things, had wound down to stalemate.

The governor who was sent to replace Nieva, Lope Garcia de Castro, was not an aristocrat like Cañete and Nieva but a *letrado*, a man from a modest background who made his career through university training and service in the royal bureaucracy. Castro came to Peru not as viceroy but as president of the Audiencia of Lima with the authority to govern its territory until the next viceroy was selected. Yet, during his five years of government before Toledo arrived, he formed ambitious plans.

Soon after arriving, Castro received disturbing news: a secret plot had come to light in Jauja. A local Spanish artisan named Felipe de Segovia wrote to the governor that he had discovered his Andean employee, a carpenter, plotting with other Andeans to rebel while the Spanish were celebrating Holy Week. The planned uprising was to stretch from Quito to Chile, including the Incas of Vilcabamba, and to target all Spaniards and Africans, leaving only mestizos and mulattoes unharmed. Castro immediately sent men to investigate; they uncovered a hidden cache of some seven hundred Spanish-style pikes, and they believed that more than two thousand others had been preemptively destroyed.[50] The hidden weapons seemed to prove the plot. Castro was all the more shocked by this treachery since (as he reported to the king), "the Indians of this valley are those who have served your Majesty better than any others."[51]

The valley's caciques, however, denied the plot. They claimed that they had had the pikes made as a *servicio* for the king, to be used as part of a planned campaign against Araucanian Indians on the Chilean frontier.[52] While historians have often concluded that the rebellion was real, the Jauja caciques were probably telling the truth. It is unlikely that they would have allied with the neo-Inca princes after years of fighting on the Spanish side; don Felipe's new coat of arms, after all, featured three severed Inca heads. Huanca Indians had manufactured pikes for the royal war against Girón,[53] and there is little reason to doubt that these new pikes were likewise intended for the king's service, which was the basis for the ambitions of men such as Guacrapaucar. Just like the encomenderos, they traded in the economy of servicio and merced.

But the colony's embattled and insecure state, which might have made a shipment of pikes a welcome gift for Castro, made them all the more menacing in the circumstances in which they were found. European pikes at the time were from ten- to twenty-feet long,[54] with a wooden shaft and iron point; fixed in the ground and pointing up at an angle, they could stop charging horses, which were the Spaniards' main military advantage over Andeans. Although a simple technology, the pike had had an enormous impact in medieval Europe, where cavalry had previously dominated foot soldiers, just as in the conquest of Peru. "In the eleventh century," historian William McNeill writes, "a few hundred Norman knights had been able to conquer and rule south Italy and Sicily," but in 1176 pikes deployed by northern Italian cities against a German army allowed foot soldiers to resist the onslaught of cavalry for the first time. Until the development of effective gunnery in the sixteenth century, pikes gave even poorly trained soldiers in Europe the possibility to resist attack.[55] And good guns were in short supply in Peru. Andean acculturation was beginning to reduce the military gap between Spaniards and Andeans.

Jauja was a center of acculturation. Many Huancas (including Segovia's servant) had learned trades in Spanish workshops, which is what made the mass production of pikes possible. Huanca hispanicization, which had assisted the loyalist defeat of Girón, now seemed to threaten the colonial state. It was the acculturation of the elite, more than of laborers, which most disturbed Castro. He ordered that henceforth native Andeans be forbidden to ride horses or use Spanish arms—skills that he acknowledged many had learned all too well.[56] The image of a cacique on horseback was a disturbing one for Spaniards, and the need to prohibit caciques from using horses and Spanish arms was a commonplace in colonial writing.[57]

Castro responded firmly to the apparent treason of the Huancas: ordering the arrest of Guacrapaucar's son don Carlos, he deputized the encomenderos of Jauja to disarm their own caciques. One of his deputies in the

Figure 4-1 Pikemen, anonymous woodcut, Augsburg, 1533. Courtesy of the Anne S. K. Brown Military Collection, Brown University Library

matter was don Antonio de Ribera, leader of the encomenderos' movement a decade before, who had started the perpetuity controversy with his phantom offer of 7.6 million pesos. Now, riding with thirty Spanish horsemen to take command of the valley from its native lords, Ribera might have reflected that he had won at last.[58]

Agents of the King

If Ribera thought so, he was mistaken. Even while Governor Castro was sending encomenderos to crack down on caciques, he was laying plans for a new class of royal officials who would finally end both sides' hopes for seigneurial rule. The Huancas' thwarted rebellion served as justification for appointing new, powerful rural governors, called *corregidores de indios*. This office had no precedent in the mother country. Spain and its colonies had royally appointed urban corregidores who governed alongside city councils; in Peru, they were sometimes called *corregidores de españoles*. But the corregidor de indios was something new. He had direct authority over a wide area of countryside and its Andean population, without anything equivalent to the city council that balanced the urban corregidor's power. The jurisdiction of the corregidor de indios was large, typically the territory of four or five repartimientos. The new officials promised a level of centralized royal control over the countryside well in advance of that exercised in Spain itself.[59]

A central aspect of the new system was resettlement into new towns. Castro, who blamed the ferment of the caciques partly on meddling priests, summoned the colony's bishops, theologians, and provincials of the religious orders, posing to them several questions about priests' behavior in Andean villages. He pressed the group for answers, even interrupting their private meeting to hector them. In the end the churchmen refused to answer his questions, instead telling him that they saw only one solution to Andeans' problems: reducción.[60]

Castro assigned the responsibility of resettlement to the new corregidores. (In what follows I will use corregidor to mean corregidor de indios.) But that was just one of their duties. Apart from carrying out a census, and imposing a new tax to pay his own salary, the corregidor was to police Andeans closely. For the reducciones, each corregidor was to seek locations with good climate and access to water and firewood. He had the option to settle a few Spaniards in the reducciones to set a good example for the villagers, and he would also appoint priests to say mass and root out idolatry. Traveling on a regular basis among the reducciones, he would watch the natives and prohibit them from having Spanish weapons, horses, or secret meetings; he would also keep accurate count of their numbers and economic resources and send the information every year to Lima. Finally, he would keep the caciques from abusing their subjects. The reducciones would govern themselves through Spanish municipal institutions, with indigenous alcaldes and cabildos, to be selected from the Andean commoners, not the caciques.[61]

For Jauja, in 1565 Castro appointed as corregidor Juan de Larréinaga.[62] Larréinaga was a Basque of obscure antecedents, inferior to an encomendero such as don Antonio de Ribera in social background, connections, and wealth.[63] Castro may have selected such men precisely because he thought they were easy to control. Yet in appointing him corregidor, Castro gave him nominal powers and responsibilities that dwarfed either Ribera's or Guacrapaucar's. A month after his appointment, Larréinaga designated sites for three new towns in Jauja and assigned priests to them. He chose locations at a distance from existing population centers, locating the town of Santa Fe de Jatunjauja half a league from an older settlement, the residence of don Gerónimo Guacrapaucar. Some Andeans, he reported, had complained that the old location was rocky and sloping; furthermore, the new site was farther from the people's graves and holy places, and thus would discourage idolatry. The town's name combined a Spanish and an Andean name, the Spanish part taken from the day he laid it out, July 3, the day of Santa Fe (Feast of the Holy Faith) in the Catholic calendar. The town had a picota in the plaza—the pillar of justice and symbol of civic independence—and a house for himself, the corregidor, adjoining the council building.[64]

Yet just six months later he was gone from his job, disconsolately seeking new opportunities in Lima. A Spanish priest appealed to Castro on his behalf: "for all that he has worked in this province and the great beginning he has given to what your Lordship assigned him, he should be compensated for a life which his unhappy fortune has made far from what it should be."[65]

While the precise nature of Larréinaga's unhappy fortune in unclear, his "great beginning" as corregidor was not all that it appeared: he failed to tame the power of the caciques. In fact, instead of appointing a commoner as alcalde for Guacrapaucar's community, he appointed Guacrapaucar himself. In spite of the affair of the pikes, don Gerónimo remained in charge of his repartimiento; although his son don Carlos languished in prison on the accusation of rebellion, don Gerónimo's power remained unchallenged. Appointing him alcalde overturned the purpose of Castro's project, but it was probably necessary for Larréinaga to establish himself at all. Even encomenderos such as Ribera, with greater personal resources and connections than Larréinaga had, did not try to deal with Andean peasants except through their caciques.

Caciques resisted the new institution of corregidor, but not that of cabildo. Throughout the province of Jauja, just as in Mexico, caciques and their relatives became the alcaldes and regidores, treating the new offices not as threats but as vehicles for their own ambitions. This is not surprising; in Spain, nobles and oligarchies tended to control the once-popular institutions of municipal self-government. Members of one indigenous cabildo near Jauja appealed to the king to grant them "the privileges and preeminences which such officials [i.e., town councilors] have" in Spain, including holding their office in perpetuity and being ranked as gentlemen (cavalleros).[66]

A corregidor in a neighboring province sent Castro a letter that encapsulated the gap between his responsibilities and his real power. Castro had ordered him to suspend his census in a part of his territory, since the Andeans had pleaded that the census was onerous and kept them from their work in the fields. Outraged, the corregidor replied that the work was all on his side, riding on rough, roadless country. The natives' complaint was doubly false. First, they had all their population records amply recorded on quipu knot records, so giving him the information would be no work at all. Second, the men left farm work to the women in any case, and spent their days "drinking with the caciques in the plaza, where they hold cabildo meetings every day of the world." Even before the corregidor's census and reducciones, the Andeans already had forms of political organization resembling what the Spaniards considered policía—they already had civic records on quipus, public life on the small plazas of preresettlement villages, and the sophistication to communicate effectively with the royal governor in Lima. But instead of mobilizing local civic organization against the caciques, the Crown's local official had to watch while the caciques used it against himself.[67]

Soon after their establishment, the Jauja town councils and caciques were asking Castro to abolish the office of corregidor. Elsewhere in the Andes, caciques' resistance began even earlier, continuing the spirit of activism that had developed during the perpetuity debates. Three months after the first appointments, a group of caciques from the highlands above Lima met to protest the new head tax that Castro had instituted to fund the corregidores' salaries. It was, they said, against both Spanish and Inca principles of government to impose a tax on subjects to pay for an administrator they did not want in the first place.[68]

This dramatic extension of royal power, the appointment of corregidores de indios, succeeded in uniting all the major factions of the Andean countryside—caciques, encomenderos, priests, the judges of other jurisdictions—against Castro.[69] With the help of a Spanish priest, caciques filed a lawsuit claiming that Castro's decision was illegal.[70] The archbishop of Lima criticized Castro for sending unknown and unreliable men to exercise vast powers.[71] The most vulnerable point of the policy was imposing a new tax to pay corregidores' salaries—in Spain it was the king who paid his magistrates, not the people.[72] Some accused Castro of creating the office of corregidor purely as a new source of income for his friends and supporters.[73] Finally, in February 1566 about eight months after appointing the corregidores, Castro backed down and repealed the salary provision, leaving it somewhat unclear how they would make a living.[74] But this did not end the popular dissatisfaction, as caciques and friars continued to assert that the new office was incompatible with Andeans' rights, and appealing to the king to treat them "with the [same] liberty and justice as the rest of [his] vassals."[75]

The controversy over the corregidores focused on the legitimacy of their office, rather than on the transformation Castro hoped they would effect in Andean society by creating reducciones with strong cabildos, independent of the caciques. This can been seen most clearly in the laws for one Andean region made on Castro's orders by Gregorio González de Cuenca. Castro sent Cuenca, the judge who had suppressed the caciques' antiperpetuity movement in Cuzco, to visit the coastal area north of Lima. Acting not as a corregidor but as an inspector, he carried out Castro's program by founding reducciones and passing laws. Cuenca ordered that each repartimiento consolidate its population into one principal reducción and several smaller dependent villages. The principal reducciones were to have cabildos with two alcaldes, four regidores, a special irrigation judge, and a notary. Cuenca set out rules for Andeans in extraordinary detail, such as a provision that parents of twins could pay lighter tribute for the first two years. Cuenca's local ordinances in the north coast region were the most exhaustive body of Indian legislation to emerge from Castro's government.[76]

It is unclear how much real impact Cuenca had: as an inspector, he did not stay long enough to see his laws implemented. The north coast had already experienced a severe demographic drop (much worse than in the highlands) and intensive integration into the colonial economy. Some caciques used Spanish titles and spoke Castilian; soon after Cuenca's visit, one cacique was producing wine from his own vineyards and bought a horse from the alcalde of a nearby Spanish town.[77] Falling population and acculturation had already stimulated the consolidation of many villages into a few, some of which had Spanish-style cabildos even before Cuenca arrived, and it is unlikely that they adopted all of Cuenca's elaborate new system.[78] Its broader impact was in setting a template for Toledo's later legislation, as Toledo himself acknowledged.

Outside of a few areas such as Jauja, there is little evidence of what Castro's corregidores actually did. But Castro did not abolish the office of corregidor, and under later viceroys these officials came to subordinate both encomenderos and caciques to themselves. Their territories, or *corregimientos*, became the provinces of Peru. But the evidence suggests that during Castro's years of administration, the widespread opposition of all classes largely stymied the corregidores' work. It is even unclear how many of them continued to hold the office for the rest of Castro's term, and whether Toledo later ratified Castro's system or recreated it from whole cloth.[79] Castro had overreached: as a commoner lacking the title of viceroy, he had less authority than a viceroy from the Spanish aristocracy, such as Toledo. And few reports document the creation of reducciones during this period. Andean resettlement, it seems, remained largely theoretical by the end of Castro's time in office.[80]

Natural Slaves

The most important advocate for resettlement and Andean cabildos in the 1560s was Juan de Matienzo, who in 1567 wrote a treatise titled "Government of Peru." Matienzo was a university-trained lawyer who had worked in one of Spain's highest courts, before being sent as a judge to the newly founded Charcas Audiencia in 1561, in the city of La Plata (contemporary Sucre, Bolivia). He advocated Andean resettlement almost from his arrival in Peru.[81] "Government of Peru" discussed a series of different topics and included a page of proposed laws following each chapter, many passing virtually unchanged into Toledo's program.[82]

Until Andeans lived in well-ordered towns, Matienzo wrote, they would not truly "be men"; he added, "it is unnecessary to give reasons for this beyond those which all the world knows." Matienzo, more than any earlier writer, focused on the reducciones' physical layout and even sketched a model street plan. His street plan specified towns of five hundred households, with square blocks surrounding a plaza. On the plaza there should be one block for the church. The second would house the Andean cabildo, and a municipal hospital (or, alternatively, the house of the cacique). The third was for the jail and the house of the corregidor de indios, and the fourth would contain an inn for traveling Spaniards. The native people would live in the blocks farther out from the plaza, each of which would be divided into four house lots. An ordinary household would have one or two house lots, while a noble would have two to four. (If as compact and ordered as Matienzo hoped, the reducción would not take up much space: five blocks out from the plaza would be the edge of town.) Each reducción was to have one or two alguaciles and two alcaldes ordinarios, who would judge minor disputes, recording the verdicts either on paper or in quipus, while larger cases would go to the cacique. Municipal offices would rotate among the prominent non-noble families in the reducción, which would diffuse norms of policía among the villagers, while Matienzo's proposals for Spanish-style household organization, with raised beds in separate rooms for parents, sons, and daughters, would inculcate modesty and virtue.[83]

Most of Matienzo's plans for the reducciones resembled Castro's and those Toledo would later make. But he had one unusual idea: to reinstate the Inca office of tocuirico, or overseer. Spanish officials would appoint to-cuiricos to govern jointly with caciques, choosing them from other regions and changing them each year. An Inca tool of central state oversight, this figure would be an indigenous version of Castro's corregidor de indios, an antidote to caciques' corruption and abuse.[84]

Matienzo despised the caciques and worried that they were learning too much from the Spanish. He endorsed the ban on caciques' access to horses and guns.[85] He was alarmed that some of them could ride and shoot better than many Spaniards, made excellent gunpowder, and even excelled in the juego de cañas, a Spanish game played on horseback: "The Indians of the kingdom are so skillful (hábiles) that there is nothing they are taught which they do not learn very well—as long as it is not something which requires prudence. . . . If this [prudence] were not lacking, they would not be among those who Aristotle says were born slaves by nature."[86] He referred here to a famous passage in Aristotle's Politics saying that some people are born to be slaves. In the 1530s a well-known scholar at the Spanish court had applied Aristotle's idea to Native Americans, and although the famous Las Casas loudly opposed it the idea had caught on.[87] In the context of Andean caciques, the allusion was significant. No one denied that caciques were natural lords, but if they were also natural slaves, their lordship must be of a peculiar kind. It was not the lordship for which the caciques had attempted to bid.

Even while finding Andeans and especially caciques "skillful," and able to learn anything they tried to, Matienzo judged that they lacked prudence and understanding. For him, in fact, Andean culture was one of drunken-ness, idolatry, incest, sodomy, and filth. Andeans' base nature, Matienzo believed, justified strict control by the Spanish: "I hold it no servitude to compel those who have such small understanding as these (whom Nature created to obey and serve) . . . to do that which is good for them, even though they desire something else." It was precisely for this reason that Matienzo called for bringing the caciques to heel, while reinstituting the Inca institu-tion of the strong, centrally appointed, Andean district governor. In spite of his contempt for Andean culture and tradition—or in another sense, pre-cisely because of it—he appreciated the Incas and believed Spain should learn from them.[88]

Like Matienzo, Castro drew examples from the Incas, noting that their powerful provincial officials suppressed possible uprisings such as the one in Jauja.[89] By combining corregidores with cabildos, composed of Andean commoners and independent of caciques, Castro hoped to replicate in Peru a phenomenon familiar from Spanish politics at home: an alliance between royal authority and local self-government, at the expense of the lords. In Spain, peasant villages routinely petitioned the king to remove them from aristocratic jurisdiction to his own direct rule, while at the same time promoting them to the status of villa, or self-governing town—in effect, confiscating the lord's power and dividing it between king and commoners.[90] In Peru, likewise, the corregidor was to select Andean municipal officials from the commoners, not the caciques. In emancipating Andeans from their caciques, Castro saw himself as their champion, offering them self-rule in the truest sense, even while strengthening the power of the king.

But even as Spaniards invoked interpretations of Andean history to undermine the caciques, some caciques invoked interpretations of Spanish culture to enhance their power, reinventing themselves in hybrid terms. Without abandoning traditional lordly practices and understandings, they collaborated actively and creatively with the colonial regime. Adopting and manipulating the Spanish system of servicio and merced, caciques attempted to become the dukes and counts of Peru.[91] Though their success was only partial, they showed themselves indispensible for Spanish rule in the Andes.

Increasingly, Spanish officials believed that effective colonial rule required Indian resettlement. This was established royal policy, though it was more theoretical than real.[92] Off and on, with varying degrees of commitment and success, colonial officials had tried to carry it out in the Caribbean, Mexico, and Guatemala, but Peru, Castile's most turbulent colony, was unusually resistant. While caciques in Jauja had shown that reducciones and cabildos could serve as a platform for their authority rather than challenging it, most caciques opposed resettlement aggressively. In Peru by the late 1560s, the resettlement of Andeans had a history, an ideology, and a record of failure.

PART II **RESETTLEMENT**

5

—

"THAT SO-QUALIFIED ASSEMBLY"

How did the Spanish imperial state resolve on universal forced resettlement and carry it out? Previous governors had attempted resettlement, but the vigor with which Toledo committed the state's energies to a campaign of sudden and uniform social transformation was new. And it went hand in hand with an aggressive package of reforms to the Church, secular government, the law and the economy. These various policies established a bright line in Andean history, separating before from after.

According to Toledo, he was implementing a package of reforms with which the king and his counselors had entrusted him. King Philip II appointed Toledo viceroy to Peru late in 1567 as part of a major overhaul of colonial policy. Following revelations of corruption and incompetence in colonial administration, Philip and his advisors assembled a committee of twenty-two men to address the problem, under the presidency of Diego de Espinosa, cardinal of Sigüenza, Spain's de facto prime minister and Toledo's patron. The committee, which later writers called the Junta Magna, included some of the most prominent figures at court: members of the key state councils, high aristocrats, learned friars, and royal secretaries. Apart from their own general experience in administration, the members had a library of reports on colonial affairs at their fingertips. The Junta Magna—"that so-qualified assembly," as Toledo called it—

met repeatedly over several months in 1568, with Peru's viceroy-elect in attendance, hashing out solutions to the problems of governing the Indies.[1]

The Junta Magna has a distinctly modern feeling: a group of experienced officials from different branches of the political elite summoned to discuss an important policy issue, gathering the most reliable information and recommendations from the field—the whole affair has the air of a government task force or blue-ribbon panel today. In *The Grand Strategy of Philip II*, Geoffrey Parker describes the Junta Magna as an example of Philip's "'global' strategic vision."[2] Nothing could be more natural—one might suppose—than to draw a direct line from that strategic vision to Toledo's social engineering in Peru. The two sides of the equation seem to fit together: at the center a consciousness of power, deployed through organized, consultative decision making; at the periphery an exercise of power, operating directly on the lives of subjects. Yet of the three major and controversial policies that Toledo carried out in Peru—personally leading a General Inspection, regularizing the forced labor draft, and carrying out universal resettlement—the Junta Magna did not unambiguously endorse a single one. While scholars have seen Toledo's project as a fairly straightforward implementation of decisions made by the king and his advisors, Toledo was in fact operating in a relative vacuum of central direction. The forces behind the General Resettlement of Indians were not "the state," but the viceroy and struggles on the ground, in Peru.[3]

By the late 1560s the viceroyalty of Peru was in crisis. Military threats from rebellious colonists as well as native leaders—declining population and wealth in the tribute-paying native communities—conflicts between friars and secular officials—the apparent exhaustion of previously rich mines—all of these had kept Spain's colonies in turmoil, but especially Peru, the jewel in her crown. Peru's silver mines were a major source for the Spanish national budget, but an unreliable one, their yield dropping periodically through political turmoil or failure of production. Peru's recent history illustrated both of these dangers: encomendero rebellions in the 1540s and 1550s had stopped the flow of silver, while by the late 1560s the mines' yield was tapering off.[4]

When, on top of everything else, a pattern of financial malfeasance was discovered in the Council of the Indies, the king ordered an official named Juan de Ovando to carry out a visita of the council. Ovando discovered a basic problem: "First, in the Council there is and can be no information about affairs in the Indies; . . . second, neither in the Council nor in the Indies is there information about the Laws and Ordinances by which all those states are ruled and governed." The response was the Junta Magna.[5]

The Junta Magna represented the ideas and experience of a rising group in court politics. The three men most responsible for the Junta Magna's work—Espinosa, Ovando, and Mateo Vázquez de Leca, the junta's secretary—had no direct colonial experience. They had made their careers as officials of the Spanish Inquisition and in the diocesan church establishment of Seville, the port city that controlled colonial commerce. By the end of the 1560s Cardinal Espinosa had become the most powerful figure in the government of Philip II. The circle of allies and followers Espinosa brought with him, including Ovando and Vázquez, belonged mostly to the letrado class: university-trained men of nonaristocratic origins, who worked in the interlocking bureaucracies of church and secular government. Philip II, himself at home in the world of official reports and secret correspondence, valued Espinosa and his associates for their efficiency, their religious zeal, and their relatively humble backgrounds, which made them all the more dependent on his favor. Espinosa, who was (among other things) inquisitor general, opposed liberal and humanistic currents at court and in the religious orders. Espinosa brought to the government a hard-edged style, like that of his protégé, don Francisco de Toledo.[6]

Born in 1515, Toledo was the fourth and last child of the Count of Oropesa, one of the most powerful magnates of Spain. Losing his mother soon after birth, he had grown up in the vicinity of the royal family: At age eight he joined the household of Eleanor of Austria, a sister of Emperor Charles V, and moved a few years later to that of Charles's wife, the Empress Isabella. He was twelve when Philip, Isabella's son and the future king of Spain, was born; if Toledo had been younger he might have grown up as a companion to the prince, which would have raised him to a much higher status as an adult. As an adolescent he began a military career in the service of Charles V and spent his twenties fighting in North Africa, the Low Countries, France, and Germany—a period of continuous war on many fronts, as Charles sought hegemony in Europe. In 1555, stalemated in his wars, the disappointed emperor divided his realms between his son Philip in Spain and his brother Ferdinand, who succeeded him as Holy Roman Emperor in Germany. Charles retired to a Spanish monastery, where he died three years later. Toledo had frequent contact with Charles during these final years: he and his older brother the Count of Oropesa hosted the emperor in one of the family palaces while his final residence was being prepared, and Toledo was present at his death in 1558.[7]

As a young man Toledo entered the Order of Alcántara, a quasi-monastic military order. The knights of such orders formed a special group within the nobility. Founded centuries earlier to advance the Crusades and the Iberian Reconquest, by the sixteenth century they concerned themselves primarily with their own lands, bylaws, rituals, and honors. The majority of members occupied purely honorary positions conferred by the Crown, but those in their upper tiers (often the younger sons of aristocratic families) held lucrative, though noninheritable, rent-paying estates; the orders controlled vast tracts throughout Spain and exercised jurisdiction over peasant villages on their land. When he became a knight of Alcántara, Toledo swore oaths of chastity, poverty, and obedience. Once meaningful, these oaths were by now symbolic: many knights of the orders were married and few if any were poor. But Toledo's oaths fit a somewhat monastic personality; in any case, he never married or founded a family line.[8]

As Charles's military plans wound down, Toledo threw himself into a career in his order. He advanced through its ranks and helped revise its statutes; his signature is on a great deal of the order's business correspondence. Alcántara was the least prestigious of Spain's three major military orders, far less so the famous Order of Santiago. But it was the ruling passion of Toledo's life, and the focus of his ambitions was to become *comendador mayor*, the order's highest official.[9]

Yet Toledo responded positively when, in the mid-1560s, Cardinal Espinosa drew him from comparative obscurity and began to make use of his considerable energy. Though born into a far more distinguished lineage than Espinosa's, Toledo addressed his patron with deference. During a tense period in Spanish church politics, the cardinal dispatched him as royal delegate to a church Provincial Council in the city of Toledo in 1565, where he kept a tight leash on the assembled bishops' deliberations. (Despite his name, don Francisco de Toledo had no direct family connection to the city; his appointment as delegate was a test of his abilities.) The king gave Toledo detailed instructions on guiding the bishops without offending their dignity, and Toledo wrote equally detailed reports back. Following his successful oversight of the council, Espinosa proposed Toledo as viceroy of Peru.[10]

Born into the world of the great territorial lords, and trained in the military orders' seigneurial privileges, Toledo knew more about ruling peasant farmers than his bureaucratic patron. Although the expanding powers of the Spanish monarchy had drained away much of the aristocracy's power, the orders and the titled lords retained some of their former quasi-governmental authority over the thousands of people who lived on their lands. Cardinal Espinosa and other high officials were primarily concerned about royal revenue and the Church; the question of how the Crown should rule Indians, fairly abstract to those at court, was of central importance to Toledo.[11]

He acquired a strong grasp of Andean policy debates, as well as the region's geography and economy, before leaving Spain. The Junta Magna had a library which included most reports on colonial affairs that Ovando had solicited from experts in both Spain and America. Toledo seems to have had access to many of the same documents historians today rely on: the writings of licenciado Polo Ondegardo, Juan de Matienzo, and many other observers; manuscript histories of both the Incas and the colony; and the correspondence of viceroys and governors previously sent to Peru.[12] Toledo made a number of suggestions to the Junta Magna, which included most of the policies he later put in practice, including his proposal to personally lead a General Inspection of the kingdom; he in fact proposed something very close to the route he later took through the central and south central Andes. The most important policy of all, to his mind, was a campaign for universal resettlement to transform Andeans "from savages to men and from barbarians to civilized people."[13]

The Junta Magna responded without enthusiasm. Toledo complained that the members paid little attention to the subject of governing Indians. He submitted a memorandum to the junta, requesting that it "open up slightly the subject of government and justice"; noting that the meetings were almost finished, he complained that his previous suggestions had been shelved unread.[14] The secretary Mateo Vázquez de Leca most likely had already drafted the junta's report to the king before Toledo submitted this memorandum. Vázquez did, however, add a postscript, entitled "Government," addressing Toledo's suggestions.[15] The postscript acknowledged that resettlement was a long-standing goal and agreed that Toledo should "exercise greatest diligence in this matter," while noting that the policy had so far failed because "the business [was] in itself so difficult, and in some places almost impossible." As for Toledo personally leading a General Inspection, the report noted arguments both for and against it: the viceroy would learn a great deal, but the tour would be expensive and his absence from Lima would cause problems. The report proposed leaving the decision in Toledo's hands.[16] Toledo's official instructions, drawn up following issuance of the Junta Magna's report and signed by the king, allotted only a brief section to Toledo's pet projects, duplicating the Junta Magna's lukewarm language.[17]

One reason that the Junta Magna was inclined to skirt "the subject of government and justice" was that the subject had become a delicate one. Pope Pius V (1566–72) had recently indicated that he was paying close attention to Spain's treatment of Indians, having received reports that the cruelty of Spanish colonists impeded their conversion to Christianity. He convened a meeting of his own to discuss establishing a permanent representative in Spanish America, who would reclaim for the pope some of the sweeping powers exercised by the king over the colonial church. Philip was alarmed by the pope's power play, but responded cautiously.[18]

Pope Pius's challenge was reminiscent of arguments made earlier by Bartolomé de Las Casas, who contended that colonial violence and exploitation was contrary to natural law. These views grew out of a long tradition of Christian thinking about natural law, in particular the rights that even pagans had to property and self-government.[19] In the 1550s Las Casas's ideas had enjoyed cautious support from some of Spain's most prominent theologians and bishops, and won fervent loyalty from a cadre of friars in Spain and the colonies. Charles V treated Las Casas with respect and honored him with a bishopric. Furthermore, the emperor assembled panels of lawyers and theologians to assess the justifications for Spanish conquest, and these panels sometimes criticized colonial policies, prompting legal reforms to protect Indian rights.[20]

In fact, Charles's interests were aligned with Las Casas's views. Charles V used the friar's indictment of encomenderos' cruelty to justify expanding his own authority.[21] By the 1560s, however, Las Casas's position was becoming ever more radical. He began to assert that the Crown could legitimize its overseas rule only by restoring all property stolen from Indians, withdrawing most colonists, and returning local authority to the heirs of the preconquest rulers—proposals which would have effectively ended Spain's New World empire.[22] Las Casas wore out his welcome at court, where the incoming king Philip had never shared his father's sympathy for the idealistic friar. But even after Las Casas's death in 1566 his teachings remained strong among some Spanish churchmen, especially Dominicans, and especially in

Peru.[23] A few of them brought their case to the pope, himself a Dominican friar, and warned that the "king's conscience" was at risk: in other words, due to Spanish mistreatment of Indians, His Highness was in danger of going to hell.[24]

The members of the Junta Magna knew of the radical claims being made against the Crown, and they intended to block the pope's challenge.[25] Although the Junta Magna superficially resembled the panels of jurists and theologians that had been called under Las Casas's inspiration, its purpose was opposite: to shunt aside ethical dilemmas and address practical problems.[26] Cardinal Espinosa was determined to reverse the pernicious effects of his fellow churchman Las Casas. Yet Philip, for all his dislike of Las Casas's disciples, could not simply dismiss or punish their views: Christian ideals were the Spanish empire's ideological basis. Furthermore, the friars were a crucial section of the colonial establishment, highly motivated, and energetic; if they became alienated, the king had a problem.[27]

In the light of these various challenges, the Junta Magna brainstormed policies that would promote royal power and revenue while denying the pope a pretext to intervene.[28] Its priorities are clearly indicated by the subjects of the four main sections of Vázquez's report: the church, royal finance, commerce, and encomienda inheritance. The Junta Magna's most important decision was to establish the Inquisition in the colonies, where it had not previously operated. The Inquisition's jurisdiction would extend to Spaniards, blacks, and mestizos but not to Indians, whom churchmen considered too new in the faith to be subject to that stern tribunal. But placing Inquisition courts and jails in the New World would show that Philip was exercising effective control over the church within his jurisdiction (which the papacy acknowledged was his right and duty, formally delegated to Castilian monarchs under the *patronato real*) so there was no need for the pope to send his own representative. The junta also proposed tightening royal control over the diocesan church hierarchy, improving the process of revenue gathering, and strengthening the monopolies of Seville's transatlantic merchants, reflecting Espinosa's history in church administration, royal finances, and the city of Seville. In these deliberations, Indian resettlement was little more than a distraction.[29]

Not that Philip II and Cardinal Espinosa were afraid of imposing cultural change on conquered people: shortly before the Junta Magna, Espinosa had ordered the moriscos of Granada to adopt the majority culture, a policy which failed disastrously in the morisco rebellion of 1570 and the deportation of the Granadan moriscos.[30] Imposing cultural change on indigenous Andeans, however, was not at the moment a major concern at court. What was urgent, though unwise to articulate clearly, was the question of forced labor. Over the previous thirty years Philip II and his father had mobilized theologians and friars to attack encomenderos' use of Indian labor, using a language of liberty and rights. The theology professors at the University of Salamanca, Spain's most prestigious university, had proved from the best authorities that it was forbidden to force Indians to work against their will, as the early encomenderos had done. But now the question was whether the king could appropriate for himself the labor he had kept from the encomenderos. The pope—along with Philip's own friars and theologians—was watching closely to see what he would do. Toledo was to systematize the Andean mita as an extraordinarily harsh and effective labor draft, for the benefit of Spanish colonists and the Crown. But no hint of that appeared either in the Junta Magna's report or in the king's instructions.[31]

Royal instructions to viceroys were extremely conservative documents, with long passages copied from one viceroy to the next, sometimes referring to people and circumstances many years out of date.[32] The first clause of the king's instructions to Toledo, an order to make Christianizing Andeans his first priority, shared its exact language with those of earlier and later viceroys.[33] Regarding the office of corregidor de indios, which Toledo was to expand significantly, the king's instructions to Philip directed Toledo to scale back the program, even though it had the clear potential to increase the Crown's power and income.[34] And the only reference to forced labor in Toledo's royal instructions was a twelve-year-old paragraph drafted to urge a previous viceroy to abolish forced labor imposed by encomenderos.[35] The language of royal instructions was not that of grand strategy but legal boilerplate; lawyers, after all, are notoriously loath to change a text that serves its purpose. Under papal scrutiny, and in the light of well-articulated theories of universal law prohibiting exploitation of Indians, Philip and his advisors may have consciously avoided leaving a paper trail on the question of forced labor. But a letter from Philip to Toledo insinuated, with a wink and a nudge, that the law was one thing, the needs of the Crown another: "Regardless that it is ordered that there be no force or compulsion against [the Indians], let them be attracted by all just means and reasons so that there is at all times the necessary number [of workers] in the mines."[36]

The same cautionary logic might apply to the question of resettlement. This did not occupy a major place in Toledo's orders, although a few weeks before signing Toledo's formal instructions, Philip re-issued an order he had sent to Lope García de Castro several years earlier, urging the policy.[37] While resettlement in itself was uncontroversial, carrying it out by *force* raised similar doubts to forced labor—and, significantly, concentrating Andeans into centralized locations would make forced labor more efficient. The pope, in a papal bull sent directly to Toledo as viceroy, endorsed resettlement only if it were carried out "with the gentleness that one would use with new plants."[38] But it was clear that Andean resettlement would not be a gentle process.

It is possible that the king personally ordered Toledo's aggressive program, either verbally or in documents that have not come to light.[39] But there is reason to doubt it. Toledo's letters to the king never mentioned any such understanding, but instead begged in vain for the king's approval.[40] One of the few pieces of evidence we have of Philip's response to the General Resettlement of Indians is a scribble he made on the margin of one of the viceroy's letters. The king wrote that, unless carried out carefully, resettlement might "be done for [the Indians'] good but redound to their detriment."[41] Even this note seems to have been only for the eyes of his advisors at court, not for the viceroy himself. Philip II was famous for postponing difficult decisions, and, when he made them, for communicating them ambiguously.[42]

Once in Peru, Toledo asserted that his controversial policies were at the orders of the Junta Magna and the king. But the viceroy was reduced to ventriloquizing his monarch. A viceroy was allowed to bring with him a number of blank sheets with the king's signature at the bottom, which allowed him to invoke royal authority for his own decisions in urgent cases (although the king might reverse these decisions later).[43] In Peru, Toledo drafted a document stating that the king had ordered the General Inspection on the advice of the Junta Magna, and warning all colonial officials to "keep and obey the provisions which our viceroy has given or will give for the above-mentioned purposes."[44] The document was signed "I, the king," although the king had never seen it. It was exactly the support for his policies that Toledo yearned for from Philip, but which he never received.[45]

The anxiety and secrecy in the Spanish court, at this crucial juncture, were not propitious for clearly articulating any policy innovations in governing Indians. The pope's challenge generated a climate of furtiveness in court. Toledo from an early point advocated much of what he ended up doing, but others' opinions are not clear. Ultimately, the responsibility of deciding that now was the time to resettle all native Andeans lay with the viceroy. The details of the policy's execution were negotiated on the ground, in Peru, by the viceroy, the colonists, and the Andean people.

6

—

THE VICEROY

Toledo arrived in Lima in late November, 1569, but not to stay. Like his predecessors, Toledo ordered a General Inspection, a *Visita General*, the most famous one in colonial times. Leaving Lima less than a year after his arrival from Spain, Toledo brought the entire viceregal court into the mountains for five years, making a slow tour through the central and southern highlands, with long stays in Cuzco, the southern cities of La Plata and Potosí, and Arequipa. While on the road Toledo checked up on his inspectors, pressed them to work faster, observed local conditions, directed military expeditions on the frontiers of the viceroyalty, and dictated volumes of laws and instructions as he went. The body of rules he established was less original than historians have sometimes considered it; there was little in it that earlier governors had not either ordered or proposed. But it had the originality of completeness. It governed Spanish and Andean community organization, crown participation in mining and the economy, and the administration of tribute and forced labor, and formed the framework for a colonial system that would last centuries. Underlying every other aspect of Toledo's program was his determination to reorganize Andean society.

Inspection and Resettlement

Toledo considered the General Inspection and General Resettlement his most important work as viceroy. In a voluminous series of reports to the court, he defended his decision to lead the Inspection in person. He argued that what best fitted him to make laws for Peru was his youthful experience accompanying Charles V on travels and campaigns throughout Europe, observing each country's nature and customs. In the alien world of the Andes—he observed that "the light of God must be very extraordinary and continuous to govern so extraordinary a world . . . impossible to understand by inference from other kingdoms"—direct experience was essential.[1]

Toledo spent the first eleven months after his arrival in Lima laying the groundwork for the Inspection, cajoling or bullying support from the colony's secular and ecclesiastical officials, and recruiting inspectors and advisors. He appointed at least forty-two inspectors[2]: three for the Audiencia of Quito, and the rest divided about equally between the Audiencias of Lima and Charcas.[3] (Quito was a special case, as discussed below.) On average, they were responsible for eleven repartimientos each.[4] Toledo gave them detailed instructions. Each inspector was to travel with a team: a *visitador eclesiástico* or ecclesiastical inspector, to investigate the performance of priests in the Andean communities; an *alguacil*, to enforce the inspector's decisions; an *escribano* or notary, to record and formalize the inspector's acts; and one or more *lenguas* or interpreters. The General Inspection would take the form of a party of traveling officials, whom the people of each repartimiento would have to feed during their time there. When they reached a given repartimiento, the inspector and his team would call together its caciques, tributaries, and the encomendero or his representative. The priest would say a mass and the inspector would address the people, promising that the results of the Inspection would improve their lives, above all by being "resettled in towns where they would live together and in company with one another, as Christians live."[5]

The inspector's next task was to record a census of the population, and persuade caciques not to conceal any of their subjects in order to lower the community's tribute burden. The inspector was to gather information on a wide range of topics including the lineages of the caciques, the local value of cloth, and mestizos who wore traditional Andean clothing and lived in the community, a possible bad influence. The inspector would recommend future tribute rates, rule on any pending litigation among the Andeans (the inspectors had the authority of judges for this), and decide among rival claimants to the title of *cacique principal*.[6] The inspector would appoint either the alguacil or the notary, theoretically with the community's consent, as the *curador* or *protector de indios*, the designated advocate for Indians' interests during the inspection.[7] Thomas Abercrombie writes: "[The] visita was anything but a noninvasive technique of observation. It was a slow-moving, highly disruptive social event, punctuated by a series of rituals. . . . Beginning with the usual census taking, which for the common Indian involved both trauma and endless boredom . . . [the General Inspection] aimed to reshape indigenous society utterly."[8]

The last subject of Toledo's instructions, which defined *how* indigenous society would be reshaped, was the Resettlement. The inspectors were to identify the best locations for new towns, with access to water, good local resources, and healthful breezes. Equally important, the towns should be as far as possible from Andeans' graves and *huacas*, where they might return to worship their idols. Ideally, a reducción should have about four hundred families, which was the number that a single priest could realistically tend; but if there was no spot to fit such a large settlement, the inspector could found two or three smaller ones close enough together to make up a single parish. Knowing that Andeans hated the Resettlement, Toledo told the inspector to identify the right number of reducciones and then quote an even lower number to the Andeans, from which he could bargain back to the number he wanted. Identical to one another in every way possible, the reducciones were to have straight streets laid out in a grid surrounding a square plaza, on which would be the church, council hall, jail, and the houses of the parish priest and jailer. Each house was to have separate bedrooms for males and females, and the beds should be raised from the ground. All houses were to open on the street, not onto one another, to minimize the danger that too much privacy would lead to idolatry, drunkenness, and illicit sexual intercourse.[9]

While still in Lima, during the cold and damp month of July, Toledo carried out a dress rehearsal for the reducciones by completing a walled settlement just outside the city for Andeans resident in Lima. Lope García de Castro had founded the settlement, and it is not clear how much was left to do to complete it when Toledo arrived—indeed, Andeans in the capital city had been theoretically centralized since at least 1550—but it served as a concrete and visible example of the new viceroy's project. The settlement called El Cercado (meaning "The Walled [Zone]"), had a more elaborate organization than earlier versions. It was divided into thirty-five square blocks, each with four solares, that were divided among the various repartimientos whose members were represented in Lima. The cabildo had a full complement of officials, chosen by the residents. El Cercado was designed to facilitate the exploitation of Andean laborers and segregate them from non-Andeans, while establishing a system of self-government within the settlement.[10]

Toledo left Lima at the end of October, 1570 following the old Inca road up the mountains over the Pariacaca pass, a road famous among Spaniards for its breathtaking heights. An earlier writer had marveled at Inca roads "laid through such bitter and frightful mountains that in some places in looking down one loses one's sight."[11] The road up from Lima was a shared reference point for Spaniards; it was the immigrant's gateway into a world different from anything in Spain. By the 1570s there were even specially prepared guidebooks for it.[12] But it was rare for a viceroy to travel that road, leaving Lima to see the mountain kingdom at first hand. Toledo traveled with scores of people—his entourage, the great majority of them men, included prominent colonists and officials, friars and Jesuits, Quechua interpreters, members of his household from Spain, Andean servants and porters—living at the expense of the communities through which they passed.[13]

In the provinces he passed through between Lima and Cuzco, Toledo could not resist the temptation to begin the resettlement process himself. He chose sites for the reducciones, with the advice of local caciques, and appointed men to see to the matter even before the inspector arrived. He wrote to the king: "Although the inspectors were given the order which they should follow for the resettlement of the natives, since it is a matter in which they [i.e., the Indians] have always shown great resistance and repugnance it was necessary for me to put my hand in it so that the inspectors find it easier . . . as a thing very necessary for the brevity of the General Inspection."[14] Brevity was the key word: Toledo was racing to accomplish a number of different tasks at once, as quickly as possible.

Toledo changed his mind repeatedly about who was to be responsible for seeing the reducciones through to completion. His initial instruction implied that the inspectors would oversee the process fairly closely, allowing Andeans a "brief period" to build the reducciones and move in, and punishing them if they did not do so. Toledo did not specify the length of the brief period, though he told the inspectors to take whatever time was necessary to complete their assigned tasks.[15] The problem was that the longer they took, the more money they would need in salary, and funding was scarce. It made sense to work fast.

Shortly before leaving Lima, Toledo revised the instructions, telling the inspectors to trace out the towns and leave them to the local priest and the Andean alcaldes to finish.[16] In Cuzco in 1571 he tried to hurry the inspectors along, telling them to choose the sites of the reducciones but to leave the rest to the encomenderos.[17] An instruction apparently written the following year told the inspectors to designate specific principales to oversee resettlement, under the authority, this time, of the cacique and the local priest. (If they had not finished it in the time called for, the cacique would be deposed and the principales exiled.)[18] An even later codicil to the instructions, written in Potosí in 1573, expressed Toledo's growing frustration: in spite of his previous orders, neither the encomenderos nor the caciques were carrying out the resettlement. The inspectors should therefore appoint special Spanish officials to oversee it, called "resettlers," *reducidores*, who would receive a salary out of the Andeans' tribute. There would be a *reducidor* for each province, who was responsible for completing the process in six months, receiving two pesos a day from the local people, plus his food. He was to take down Andeans' old houses as soon as the new ones were built, starting with the caciques, and to break any pots that they did not move immediately into their new homes.[19]

Infuriated by the slow pace, Toledo looked for someone to punish. He instructed the Lima Audiencia to make all the inspectors within the Lima district set benchmarks for finishing the Resettlement, threatening that the inspectors themselves, as well as the reducidores, would lose their salaries unless the work was completed on time.[20] A further instruction warned the inspectors to resist pressure from encomenderos as well as caciques to let resettlement slide.[21] In a speech to a group of caciques from the area between Cuzco and Arequipa, Toledo warned that if caciques did not wholeheartedly support the project, he would assume that their motivation was to practice idolatry in private—the main reason Andeans did not want to move, he believed.[22] Writing to the king at the end of 1574, Toledo complained that he had to oversee every detail of the Resettlement himself if he wanted it finished.[23]

Resettling Andean families meant unsettling property rights. The best land was often in valleys dominated by Spanish haciendas. Toledo instructed the inspectors to arrange for Andeans to trade fields they were leaving behind for new ones near the reducción, even if they belonged to a Spaniard.[24] This outraged the rural Spanish elite, and Toledo later specified that land given to Andeans should come, whenever possible, from other communities who were moving to their own reducciones.[25] But even if such land transfers were sometimes necessary, the viceroy wanted to keep them to a minimum, since Andeans' existing land base was what enabled them to pay their tribute. Still, it was never entirely clear what fields they would be allowed to keep, and Spanish landowners took advantage of the Resettlement to enlarge their holdings at Andeans' expense. When they swapped fields with Spaniards, Andeans often traded prime farmland for wasteland. On the other hand, inspectors were looking for land to sustain the new reducciones, and Spanish settlers sometimes lost good fields when they could not produce a solid legal title. Many rural Spaniards feared they had more to lose than to gain when Toledo's inspectors began nosing around.

Toledo was aware of a growing climate of opposition. Initially, most of it came from Andeans themselves, for whom forced resettlement meant losing their homes and disrupting their daily lives, losing easy access to their land or even the land itself. Soon after his arrival a group of caciques, repeating the strategy from the debate over perpetuity several years earlier, offered Toledo eight hundred thousand pesos to abandon the idea.[26] Our record of the offer comes not from the caciques themselves but from Toledo, who dismissed it peremptorily: "the very reasons which the Indians give for not being resettled are those that show that they should be, and much more so those that they do not say, which are to practice their idolatries and drunkenness . . . without witnesses in their hiding places." Toledo did not think it necessary to record the caciques' actual arguments.[27]

What disturbed Toledo far more was Spanish opposition. Initially, the great majority of Spanish colonists supported the Resettlement, at least in principle. The friars, and others who considered themselves sympathetic to Andeans' rights, thought that demographic concentration would make them safer from abusive authorities (both Spanish and Andean), more civilized, and more Christian.[28] Meanwhile, Spaniards who thought that the king coddled the Indians supported anything that would subject them to tighter control. Such writers vented their disgust at Andeans' bodies, homes, villages and culture:

> The settlements they have are ordinarily . . . very vile, low and tight, and so dirty that they never know what it is to sweep. . . . Where they eat, there they sleep and do everything else.[29] Their huts seem more for monkeys than for men. The solitude draws them [to their isolated settlements], as well as their bad inclination toward continual sacrifices to the devil, and to live bestially, sleeping with their mothers and daughters.[30]

Resettlement, discipline, and the supervision of priests seemed natural remedies for this state of affairs.

Some Spaniards, however, pointed out the hardship that forced resettlement would impose on Andeans, especially in an agriculturally challenging landscape. One official paraphrased their objections:

> It is a question in all these kingdoms, discussed by many, whether it is right that the Indians' pueblos be brought together and . . . large and civilized pueblos created. Those who say no, and that it would be a great irritation for the Indians . . . give as the principal reason the large quantity of Indians and that the land is thin in valleys and places to plant and harvest food, and that being as there are now [only] ten or twenty houses together . . . they are no more than the land can sustain.[31]

Toledo rejected this argument. The population had been higher under the Incas, so the current population was not the limit of what the landscape could sustain. But he recognized that it was difficult to confront Andean and Spanish opposition simultaneously. His convoluted syntax, piling one qualification on another, underlined the various different threats that the program seemed to face: "Even if your majesty had not ordered this point so earnestly, . . . even if I saw by experience some individual harm in exchange for the great and notable benefit that would follow, when by this cause a few of the natives died, . . . there would be no reason to stop carrying it out, even if they didn't want [to move]. . . . Those who remained [alive] and their descendants would be useful for the service of our lord and your majesty and their own good."[32]

Though Toledo implied that each of these problems was merely a possibility, each was in fact the simple truth: the king had not earnestly ordered it; it would indeed lead to widespread hardship and dispossession; the Andeans (legally, free vassals of the Crown) opposed it energetically; and, by disrupting the subsistence economy of a population already ravaged by disease and malnutrition, it would kill many people. The program's benefits, Toledo was certain, would offset all possible problems. But in defending the General Resettlement to the king he judged it necessary to play his trump card: the greatest benefit would come from "planting them near the labors of the mines."[33]

By early 1572, however, people whose views the viceroy could not afford to ignore were complaining directly to the king. The archbishop of Lima, the colony's highest ecclesiastical authority, offered a bleak assessment of the viceroy's performance, warning that overfast and incompetent execution of the Resettlement would require the process to be repeated at a later date, "with more labors and harm to the Indians."[34] Caciques continued to express their alarm; one wrote to the king: "we have been abused by the imposition of these resettlements and our Indians have fled because they were forced to abandon their houses and their lands against their will."[35] One Spaniard wrote that the General Resettlement would lead to an Andean rebellion, adding that if the king had searched for a viceroy who would destroy the colony, he could not have found anyone better than Toledo.[36]

Equally alarming were the judicial complaints that began to pour in against his program. The judicial system was the one part of colonial administration unambiguously outside the viceroy's control and was therefore a key channel for opposition. Although Toledo was *de oficio* president of the Lima Audiencia, he spent much of the General Inspection in the jurisdiction of the Charcas Audiencia, with the result that he faced more effective opposition from Lima; its judges demanded that his inspectors submit cash bonds as insurance against possible judicial complaints, a requirement Toledo found outrageous.[37] The judges, in defense, complained to the king that the campaign was disastrous and the inspectors corrupt.[38] The Audiencia later claimed to have received more than five hundred complaints and wrote that those involved in the campaign included mestizos, mulattoes, and even known criminals, men whose ears had been cut off in their earlier careers as punishment for crimes.[39] The Lima judges warned that the Resettlement would lead to "the perdition and decline of this kingdom."[40] As for the Quito Audiencia, it seems to have entirely and successfully defied Toledo's authority.[41]

Toledo suspected, rightly, that Spanish complaints were often self-interested.[42] Apart from the General Resettlement's danger for Spaniards who occupied land without legal title, some worried about its effect on the labor market, since it threatened to take Andean laborers away from Spanish workshops, farms, or ranches.[43] Some laborers worked for wages while others were held in quasi-servitude as *yanaconas*. To blunt employers' objections, Toledo guaranteed that yanaconas and Andeans working in cities would be registered where they currently were.[44]

The General Resettlement also threatened encomenderos, who were few but powerful. Although they could not yet know just how fully the new order of Andean society would marginalize them, they resented any outside meddling. And they knew that in the short term, at least, the Resettlement would be expensive to them. Lacking royal approval to pay for the campaign out of state funds, Toledo told inspectors to fund their salaries out of the fines they would levy, primarily on Spaniards who had abused Andeans in one way or another. Most such fines were for a specific infraction: the failure of encomenderos to provide religious instruction to Andeans. Each encomendero, in exchange for his tribute, hired a priest to bring them the blessings of Christianity. But many had not done so, either from negligence or due to the shortage of priests; in other cases, the priests had neglected their work, spending long periods in the city. From Andeans' point of view, this was the least of their problems; those whose encomenderos neglected the duty of evangelization may well have been grateful for it. But Toledo ordered his inspectors to levy heavy fines on the negligent encomenderos for defrauding their charges of Christian doctrine. The money, naturally, went not to the "victims" but to the costs of the General Resettlement.[45]

A potentially even more lucrative source of funding was Andeans' tribute. In various earlier laws encouraging resettlement, Spanish monarchs had ordered that Indian tribute be remitted during the time it took to build the reducciones.[46] In practice, it was too dangerous to take away all of the encomenderos' income, but Toledo ordered the inspectors to embargo one third of the tribute during the period of the Resettlement. The king's intention had apparently been to relieve Indians from a double burden of having to pay while being forced to move, but Toledo earmarked the tribute for the Resettlement's costs; Andean tributaries paid no less than before.[47] In the city of La Plata in 1574, Toledo called a meeting of the judges of the Audiencia of Charcas along with many of the colony's Christian prelates, to confirm that it was the encomenderos' responsibility to pay for the Resettlement with fines and tribute. The assembled leaders, though many were connected to encomendero interests themselves, grudgingly agreed to his questions.[48]

The most controversial issue Toledo raised was the question of corregidores de indios. When Lope García de Castro created the office, it had provoked bitter criticism in the Audiencia of Lima and the Charcas judges had blocked it entirely in their jurisdiction. The king himself had told Toledo to appoint corregidores only where absolutely necessary.[49] But Toledo had decided that these officials were essential for preserving the reducciones once they were established, and for extending effective royal control into the countryside. The corregidores threatened the encomenderos' influence over Andean communities, and also, since they had the power to act as judges, threatened the income of urban lawyers to whom Andeans brought their lawsuits.[50] Juan de Matienzo, one of the judges on the Audiencia, argued on Toledo's behalf that, once the Andeans had moved to the reducciones, corregidores were probably necessary to keep them there, while the failure of the General Resettlement would lead to a "worse calamity to the Indians than before, and contempt for those who govern them." A half-finished Resettlement would leave the situation worse than it was before. In Toledo's intimidating presence, most of the Charcas judges accepted the corregidores.[51]

Later, however, with Toledo on his way back to Lima, the Charcas Audiencia's president sent the king a harsh indictment of how he was executing the General Resettlement: "The Indians . . . were not so tormented or afflicted with all the past turmoil and wars, because the persecution of these inspectors and reducidores has lasted more than four years; they eat at the Indians' cost, with the many people and horses that each one has brought, and have resettled [the Indians] many times, moving them from one place to another and burning their houses." The forced moves and removes had separated Andean communities from their lands and thrown them into chaos: "The worst has been that many or most of the reducciones and villages . . . are very far from the fields and lands where they harvest their food, and to go and cultivate them they have to wade through dangerously fast rivers . . . and the Indians walk around as if shocked and astonished."[52]

For all the Spanish resistance Toledo encountered, in the end the most stubborn obstacle was the Andeans themselves. Commoners and caciques alike delayed complying with the inspectors' orders. By early 1575 Toledo faced the fact that the Resettlement was nowhere near complete: Andeans had begun building most of the reducciones, but had finished and moved into only a few of them. Andeans' poverty, and the difficulty of obtaining building materials, slowed things down. Based on reports from his inspectors, he estimated that it would take at least two to three more years to complete the job. The General Resettlement was proving far more difficult than he had anticipated.[53]

The Republic of Indians

Toledo did, however, transform space that Andean society occupied. On the most basic level, he established the corregimiento—the jurisdiction of the corregidor de indios—as the rural province, the unit through which colonial governments administered territory and through which Andeans and Spaniards perceived it. It is not clear exactly how and when the boundaries of these provincial units were formalized. Before Toledo, colonists divided up the rural landscape not by territorial boundaries but by the names of Andean ethnic groups. The corregimientos preserved this tradition in that most were named after the same ethnic groups, although they sometimes combined two ethnic groups in one corregimiento (for instance Canas y Canches), or divided an ethnic group in half. But the corregimientos had fixed boundaries, where ethnic groups had sometimes been intermingled. In any case, the corregimiento became part of the system of nested territories in the colony: first, the viceroyalty; within that, the Audiencia; within that, the jurisdiction of the Spanish city, such as Cuzco or La Paz; within that, the corregimiento; within that, the repartimiento; and within that, the reducción. Below the level of the Spanish city, nearly all jurisdictional units were defined by and named after their component Andean groups. In spite of Spaniards who lived or traveled there, the countryside was indigenous space.

Fiscally, Toledo incorporated the Andean community into the royal budget. In Toledo's system, instead of dealing directly with the community, the encomendero, cacique, and priest received their income from the state. The cacique delivered the community's tribute to the corregidor, who then paid about 35 percent of it in salaries to priests and caciques, and 65 percent to the encomendero.[54] (In Crown encomiendas, this went to the king.) The encomendero thus exchanged overlordship for a mere pension, which he sometimes had to share with others: the viceroy might assign a fixed sum, called a *situación*, to be deducted from the encomendero's tribute for the benefit of another individual. As Andean populations continued to fall, and arrears piled up unpaid, viceroys would periodically order new inspections (*revisitas*) and revise the tribute requirement, lowering the encomenderos' expected income; even so, their actual receipts seldom matched those promised. Legally, the encomenderos could no longer ride armed into the villages and squeeze the Andeans for more, as they might have done before. And the priests and even the caciques had no right to receive any goods or services beyond those specified by law. (In fact, though, priests and caciques were better able to extort extra services than encomenderos: negotiation and intimidation remained at the priests' disposal, and caciques retained a legitimacy quite independent of the viceroy.[55])

Among Toledo's most consequential acts was to formalize the mita. Spaniards had embraced this Inca institution from the beginning. The communities that had sent laborers to staff the Inca *tampu* had continued to do so in many places, keeping what Spaniards called *tambos* running to provide cheap lodging, food, forage, and often (illicitly, whether motivated by payments or threats) the labor of porters and prostitutes to Spanish travelers.[56] Spanish governors had also called on caciques to provide a quota of laborers to serve other colonists. The beneficiaries of the labor—often builders constructing houses in Spanish cities, or mine operators—would pay a relatively small wage, set by law, usually to the cacique rather than to the laborers. Toledo confirmed and extended this system, assigning each community a number of laborers to work at the tambos and in the cities, and especially in the mines. In the region of Guamanga in the central highlands of the Lima Audiencia, Toledo assigned laborers, or mitayos, to work in the mercury mines of Huancavelica (mercury was used in refining silver), and in the highland provinces south of Cuzco he assigned mitayos to the infamous silver mines of Potosí. For Toledo, the mita was part of his efforts to organize Andean labor in general. A number of his laws were dedicated to stabilizing working conditions for Andeans, and ending the most abusive practices, such as unpaid freight carrying or long service in the disease-ridden coca fields. Colonists were outraged at what they took to be his protective attitude to Andeans, but these reforms made the exploitation of Andean labor sustainable in the long term.[57]

A key part of his efforts to turn the Andean population into a disciplined workforce was asserting stronger control over the caciques. Previously, the words that Spaniards translated as cacique—*kuraka* in Quechua, other words in Aymara and other languages—represented the top layer of a broadly defined noble class, in which various lineages formed a pool of candidates for positions of authority. The office of cacique principal, the head of the community, was hereditary (although it sometimes passed from brother to brother, or nephew to uncle, instead of father to son). Henceforth, the viceroy had the right to appoint any cacique principal, as Toledo believed the Incas had done.[58] In actual fact, the office remained loosely hereditary. Toledo and succeeding viceroys found that a cacique needed legitimacy in the eyes of his community in order to raise tribute effectively. Still, Spanish officials did have some leverage. Since there was no fixed traditional rule of inheritance, upon a cacique's death rival candidates often presented themselves. The local corregidor and priest often took advantage of the uncertainty to put their own preferred candidates in office.[59]

As he neared the end of his long circle through the central Andes, while staying in Arequipa in late 1575, Toledo announced a body of legislation for reducciones, extending general principles he had laid out in his instructions to the inspectors.[60] The reducciones were to have the same system of self-government as a Spanish village: a parallel system of an annually rotating council of commoners and a hereditary lord. The cabildo comprised two alcaldes, four regidores, an alguacil, and several lesser officials. The alcaldes would hear disputes in the council house and visit the jail once a week. Just as in a Spanish village, New Year's Day saw a formal ceremony in which the alcaldes surrendered their ceremonial staffs of office to their replacements. Caciques and principales were barred from municipal offices.[61] Toledo likewise included no significant role in the town government for the priest. The system was not democratic: the alcaldes and regidores chose their own successors each year, who then selected the lower officials. But, composed of commoners rotating out of office each year, the cabildo represented a principle of popular self-rule within the "Republic of Indians."

If the cabildo's main responsibility was the internal administration of the community, the cacique was its liaison with the larger colonial world. The cacique gathered tribute, and unlike other Andeans was permitted to own a horse in order to collect it from outlying communities. He had the responsibility of maintaining the roads and tambos and filling the mita. The cacique was not, however, permitted to do most of the other activities of the colonial elite: to ride in a litter, wear fine Spanish clothes, keep African servants, or give banquets for Spanish guests. As caciques had traditionally done, he was permitted to manage the collective working of community land, including hosting feasts with a ration of one azumbre (about two liters) of chicha per person. And the cacique was responsible for making sure that the Andean population stayed in the reducciones.

Toledo ordered every community to employ a fully literate notary to record municipal laws, accounts, and personal wills. Toledo admonished the villagers to treat the notary with respect. He was to have a writing table and a locked office; the community would supply him with a ream of paper a year and a supply of pens, along with a knife to keep them sharp. Municipal documents were to be stored in a strongbox with three keys belonging to the notary, one of the alcaldes, and the alguacil, all of whom would need to be present to open it. (This system was traditional in Spanish communities.) All information previously recorded on quipus was to be copied to paper documents, which Toledo considered "more certain and durable." The new Andean communities, like Spanish ones, were to be built on a foundation of laws and documents.[62]

Toledo hoped to transform Andean culture by banning customs he considered sinful or unclean. People were to sleep on raised beds, not the ground, and follow detailed rules of personal grooming for church festivals. Toledo prohibited not only pagan rituals, dances, and songs but even personal names derived from the natural world, such as Amaru ("snake") or Waman ("falcon"), which smacked of idolatry. Instead of carrying infants in slings under their clothes, directly against their skin, mothers were to carry them in their arms or on their backs. Toledo instituted a stern control over alcohol, ordering that all chicha and even the cups to drink it (called *queros*, they were important objects in Andean tradition), be guarded and doled out sparingly. He not only banned adultery and fornication, but forbade unmarried women to live with male relatives, which he feared might lead to incest.

In public as in private life, Toledo wanted to establish discipline in the reducciones. A curfew, beginning two hours after nightfall, was to be announced by fifteen minutes of bell ringing. The alguacil would then make his rounds, locking up anyone found in the street. Offenses great and small earned fines, head shaving, whipping, banishment, or public exposure at the picota in the plaza. Perhaps most important, Andeans were to attend church in the reducción. For families who had to absent themselves from the reducción to tend to distant fields or herds, he required the husband and the wife to come to the reducción on alternate Sundays; for shepherds who tended flocks on far slopes many days walk from town, he required them to come to mass at least twice a year. Any Andean, woman or man, who identified another Andean living outside the reducciones and off the tribute rolls, could claim him or her as a servant for life. And Toledo gave individual Spaniards licenses to seize Andeans who had escaped the reducciones, on the same terms, up to a certain number. Toledo was willing to turn the Andean countryside into a place of radical insecurity for unattached individuals, in order to establish the reducciones as safe havens from that insecurity.[63]

7

—

TYRANTS

Don Francisco de Toledo was a creative and a destructive figure. An aristocrat trained to command, decisive, and willing to confront challengers with violence, he made enemies but also had a gift for mobilizing the talents of subordinates. He dictated whole books of legislation, defining norms as if on a blank slate. He established new institutions in the colonial church, bringing with him Peru's first Jesuits and Inquisitors. He waged two wars, defeating the neo-Incas of Vilcabamba but losing his war against the Chiriguanos of the eastern Andes. He was determined to bend the colonial and above all the Andean population to his will, as if thrusting the viceroyalty into a forge and hammering it out anew. Two prominent scholars of the last century called Toledo, respectively, "the supreme organizer of Peru" and Peru's "great tyrant."[1]

As it happens, the concept of tyranny profoundly interested Toledo himself. But in his view, it was the long-dead Inca kings who were the tyrants. He devoted considerable energy to proving what might seem, by 1569, a moot point: that the Spanish conquest was legitimate because the Incas had met the definition of tyranny in European law. With Las Casas dead, the legality of the conquest was no longer an urgent concern in Madrid, but Toledo brought it back into discussion. He set out to prove it empirically, through historical research, and he considered the demonstration an important part of his work. For a busy viceroy, Toledo was surprisingly invested in interpretations of the past.[2] Scholars have credited him with creating a "Toledan school" of historiography, which shifted the portrayal of the Inca dynasty 180 degrees, from very positive to very negative.[3]

Recent scholarship has complicated our picture of Viceroy Toledo. Skeptical of claims that he was either a great tyrant or a supreme organizer, scholars have shown that much of his program of reform was neither original to him nor fully successful in his time. A few have also noted that he treated some Inca practices as useful models. The historian David Brading writes, "In many ways, the Toledan project for Peru created what can only be called a successor-state to the Incas, with key institutions modeled on native practice." But historians have not examined the contradiction this presents: on the one hand, Toledo's vituperation against the Incas, on the other, his desire to emulate them.[4]

The explanation is not mere cynicism or hypocrisy, but a peculiar conjunction of Spanish ideas about tyranny and about the Andes. Some elements in the legal and philosophical theory of tyranny matched techniques of rule that Spaniards saw as both characteristic of the Incas and necessary for ruling Andeans: social control and surveillance, the equalization and atomization of subjects, public construction projects that kept Andeans always at work, and, above all, the social engineering that led to population movements. Toledo's indignation toward the Incas was inseparable from admiration. The General Resettlement represented Toledo's attempt to emulate the Incas' "tyrannical" legacy.

The Viceroy's Incas

As Toledo's entourage traveled through the Andes, he ordered a judicial inquiry into Inca and pre-Inca government by his personal secretary, Alvaro Ruiz de Navamuel, and his highest judicial official, Dr. Gabriel de Loarte. Along with a group of Andean and mestizo interpreters, they recorded testimony from Andean witnesses in several provinces. Since Navamuel was Toledo's scribe and notary, the inquiry competed with other important business: a surviving note explains that the interpreter had not brought any historical witnesses that day, so Navamuel was taking advantage of a free moment to draft a report to the king. There is no better illustration of the inquiry's importance to the viceroy than the time and effort invested in it.[5]

The inquiry was not an open-ended investigation but a polemical exercise designed to support the rights of the king. Toledo wanted to rebut Las Casas's claim that Spanish kings could govern Peru only as overlords of its indigenous hereditary rulers. Las Casas had died in 1566, and though a faction of friars remained loyal to his principles, few people at court still took them seriously. But Toledo considered them an urgent threat. (He had been alerted to their harmful consequences, he said, during the Junta Magna.[6]) To disprove Las Casas's argument, Toledo asserted three claims: the Inca regime met a legal definition of tyranny and was therefore illegitimate; before the Incas there had been no real government at all; and the Incas had created the position of cacique as an appointive office, not a hereditary one, so the caciques were illegitimate as well, and presented no threat to Spanish rights. These three proofs, he believed, would demolish any legal challenge to Spanish rule in Peru.

"Tyrant" in Toledo's time was a technical term within the discourses of law, philosophy, and theology. The most important source was Aristotle's Politics, rediscovered in the West and translated into Latin around 1260, a millennium and a half after its composition. Just a few years after its translation, Thomas Aquinas drew heavily on the Politics for his treatise De regno, which in turn influenced Spanish neo-Scholastic theologians in the sixteenth century. Aristotle's discussion also influenced the Siete Partidas, the medieval Castilian law code that remained in force in sixteenth-century Castile and its colonies.[7] Aristotle taught that tyranny was a distinct form of government, sharply distinguished from legitimate kingship, that it was the worst form of government, and that tyrants could legally be deposed by their subjects.[8] A ruler who came to power illegally was a tyrant, but so was one who did so legally and then ruled for his own rather than his subjects' benefit.[9] The Siete Partidas, compiled soon after the discovery of the Politics, offered a definition drawn directly from Aristotle: " 'Tyrant' means a lord who has taken power in a kingdom or land by force, by deceit, or by betrayal. And their nature is such that after they have taken power in the land they prefer to act for their own benefit (although it may be harmful to the country) than for the common benefit of all."[10]

A number of specific behaviors characterized tyrants. They undermined education in order to keep their subjects ignorant; they reduced their subjects to an equal level of poverty; they prohibited the private and public associations that create social bonds; they kept their subjects busy with endless public works and unceasing warfare. In the words of the Siete Partidas: "They used their power always against the people, in three kinds of artfulness. The first is, that such ones always strive to make those in their power foolish and fearful, because when they are so, they would not dare to rise against them, or oppose their will. The second is, that the people have animosity among themselves, so that they distrust each other. . . . The third is, that they strive to make them poor, and to put them to such great works that they can never finish them. . . . And above all, tyrants always strove to ruin the powerful and kill the wise . . . and they ever seek to know what is said or done in the land."[11] The definition of tyranny in the Siete Partidas, in other words, was more specific than the vague connotations we associate with the word. The modern conception that is closest to this conception tyranny is totalitarianism.

Even before Toledo, the word tyrant was part of the lexicon of polemic in colonial Peru. It was the most common epithet for the rebels in the civil wars of the 1530s to 1550s, since they had tried to take power from the king "by force, by deceit, or by betrayal." Critics of the Spanish conquest such as Las Casas applied the term to the conquistadors who had unjustly deposed Peru's legitimate monarchs, the Incas. Defenders of the conquest turned the charge of tyranny around to call the Incas and caciques tyrants. Toledo and his advisors were familiar with this debate—Toledo mentioned it even before leaving Spain—but were the first to develop the claim of Inca tyranny in any depth.[12]

The most profound exposition of Toledo's views about Inca tyranny came in a report he commissioned from one of his advisors, the Dominican fray García de Toledo.[13] Fray García, a cousin of the viceroy who had accompanied him from Spain, completed the assignment in early 1571. He argued that the Inca kings met every requirement for the definition of tyrant. Invoking the principle that a regime is legitimate only through the tacit consent of the governed, he asserted that the Incas had founded their state by fraud, claiming to be the children of the Sun, and expanded it by brutal conquest. He acknowledged that an ill-founded regime could legitimate itself through good rule and the passage of time.[14] But the Incas had not satisfied the requirements for this process, fray García believed. First, though their rule in Cuzco went back a millennium (as he mistakenly believed), the expansion of most of their empire was comparatively recent. Second, their misrule was so brutal that it would have made them tyrants even if their origins had been legitimate. The Incas took everything from their subjects: property, labor, even free will, and periodically murdered them in great numbers. Under these conditions, not only a thousand but even a hundred thousand years would be insufficient to make them legitimate. Fray García concluded smugly: "One marvels at the ignorance of these [Incas], who in almost a thousand years since they began to tyrannize did not learn the trick of being legitimate lords. One marvels also at the wisdom of God, in knowing how to keep these kingdoms . . . without legitimate title." Without title, that is, until the Spaniards arrived, sent by God to take their rightful place.[15]

Such were the law and the facts that Toledo wanted to establish. In the legal procedure of the period, testimony had a highly structured format: a judge or litigant would prepare in advance a written list of questions, the *interrogatorio*, to be presented to all witnesses. His interrogatorio asked witnesses to confirm that the Incas had seized territories without being freely chosen as rulers either by the people or by a preexisting legitimate ruler. In the words of the *Siete Partidas*, they seized power "by force, by deceit, or by betrayal." Toledo's men also asked questions designed to show that the Incas had levied an extraordinarily high tax in goods and labor. This would demonstrate that they "they prefer to act for their own benefit (although it may be harmful to the country) than for the common benefit of all," again in the words of *Siete Partidas*. The *interrogatorio*, Toledo hoped, would expose the Incas' illegitimacy as a regime that had expanded by cruel conquest and which local people had never accepted. The top of the page read: "This is the testimony and proof that by order of his Excellency was made of the origin and descent of the tyranny of the Incas of this kingdom and of the true fact of how before and after this tyranny there were no natural lords in this land."[16]

The witnesses formally consented to the terms of each question. Yet they stubbornly insisted on adding details that complicated the picture, even as Toledo's team adjusted the interrogatorio to make the questions even more leading. The witnesses described the Incas as magnanimous and generous in victory, undermining Toledo's claim of Inca tyranny, and as planting deep roots in local institutions and in people's hearts and minds.

In June 1571, after arriving in Cuzco, Toledo's team prepared a new interrogatorio. This questionnaire abruptly changed its emphasis to the *benefits* of Inca rule. Was it true, Navamuel and Loarte asked, that the Incas kept their subjects constantly working and that this was the "best way of governing them"? Was it, in fact, Andeans' natural condition to be lazy if they were not kept working? And did they need a strong ruler to make decisions on their behalf?[17]

This time, the response was gratifying. The interrogators assembled men from both the Inca aristocracy and non-Inca indigenous elites. The witnesses—who were now being questioned in groups, which drastically reduced the detail and spontaneity of the answers—endorsed Toledo's description of their subjects. "They said, each for himself and all together, that they know for a very certain thing that the Indians of this kingdom are a people of such small understanding that they need a guardian [curador] to govern them," even in private decisions. Like children, Andean commoners did not know their own best interests.[18] Like the previous interrogatorio, this one emphasized the Incas' extreme power over their subjects, but it now seemed to be a necessary response to Andeans' weakness. The purpose of the inquiry was still to support Spanish rights, but the Incas had taken on a new role. They were still tyrants but they also provided, somehow, a legitimate precedent for the Spanish.

Toledo never abandoned the claim that the Inca regime was illegitimate. He was infuriated by a published history of the Spanish conquest, Diego Fernández de Palencia's *Primera y segunda parte de la historia del Peru* (Seville, 1571), which contained some positive comments about the Incas. Such an account, Toledo complained to the king, "affirm[s] false principles about the Incas' deeds, which greatly prejudice your Majesty's rights in these kingdoms." Since Las Casas's falsehoods had been discredited, he continued, similar ideas could hardly be tolerated in a lesser writer. The book was subsequently banned.[19] Other writers learned the lesson: one historian adjusted the text of his book between the 1555 and 1577 editions to add a line asserting that the Incas were illegitimate tyrants.[20]

Disgusted by the existing literature, Toledo decided to produce his own history of the Incas. He assigned the task to a member of his entourage, Pedro Sarmiento de Gamboa, who conducted interviews with the Inca aristocracy in Cuzco and cast the results in the form of a chronicle confirming Toledo's theories. Sarmiento was a picaresque figure, an intrepid naval explorer as well as an amateur magician who got into trouble with the Church for possessing love amulets and mystic Chaldean rings.[21] Embracing his patron's agenda, Sarmiento repeated each part of the argument that fray García de Toledo had drafted a year earlier (which he clearly had read), even seeming to suggest that God had arranged Francisco de Toledo's appointment as viceroy primarily to rebut Las Casas's claims. The Incas, Sarmiento concluded, had conquered and ruled their empire tyrannically, and the caciques were equally illegitimate. The Spanish crown's rights were unchallengeable.[22] Sarmiento ended the book with a Latin poem addressed to subversive theologians and carping friars:

Go away, know-it-alls, there is no place for you here!
For our king possesses the Indians rightfully.[23]

For all this, Sarmiento's chronicle is not merely the polemical exercise that scholars have considered it. Throughout the book Sarmiento showed that he admired the Incas' achievements, which for him were inseparable from their tyranny. Nearly all scholars who have written about Sarmiento's book ignore the strong appeal that the Incas' tyrannical accomplishments held for Toledo's chronicler.[24]

Though returning to the concept of tyranny and its proofs in almost every chapter, Sarmiento associated tyranny with a level of state achievement similar to that found in earlier, pro-Inca chroniclers such as Cieza de León and Las Casas. Much of Sarmiento's book centers on the ninth and tenth kings in the dynasty, Atahualpa's great-grandfather and grandfather, Pachacuti Inca Yupanqui and Topa Inca Yupanqui, who had transformed a small state in the valley of Cuzco into an empire. He summed up Pachacuti's reign with a reference to Aristotle's definition of tyranny: "All of the laws that he made for the people were directed to tyranny and individual self-interest."[25] But what laws and actions did Sarmiento attribute to him? Pachacuti expanded the city of Cuzco with open areas and monumental buildings; he built canals and terraces to open up new farmland in conquered provinces; he built a network of roads and inns throughout the empire.[26] Pachacuti's "self-interest," for Sarmiento, was of the enlightened kind.

The evidence of tyranny that Sarmiento invoked most regularly throughout the book was the Inca subjects' frequent rebellions, which showed nonconsent to Inca rule. But from the moment early in his narrative when a young Inca prince kills some rebels with a toy ball, Sarmiento's emphasis was less on rebellion than on the Incas' ability to defeat it.[27] Sarmiento sometimes seemed to forget which side he was on. Of Topa Inca, he wrote: "He was liberal, forgiving in peace and cruel in war and punishment, a favorer of the poor, spirited and a man of much industry, a builder. He was the greatest tyrant of all the Incas."[28] The tyrant had become, it appears, a model for kings.

More to the point, he was a model for viceroys. Many of Pachacuti's and Topa Inca's deeds, in Sarmiento's telling, anticipated Toledo's. They toured the realm, dictating laws while gathering information about each province.[29] They established norms for the organization of local communities. They inquired into everything, from the sources of gold, silver, and jewels—a concern shared, to say the least, by the Spanish—to the history of the land, which they preserved in an authoritative chronicle on painted boards.[30] Their curiosity extended to the sea, where they sent boats and discovered the Solomon Islands; Sarmiento took the opportunity to remind the king that he himself, as a naval explorer, had rediscovered the same islands. Sarmiento even used the Spanish term *visita general* for the Incas' tours of inspection.[31] One of Pachacuti's goals was to forestall rebellions by moving populations around. He told his officials to visit all the provinces and return with three-dimensional clay models of the landscape with its fortresses and people. Then he knocked down the models of the fortresses he wanted destroyed and moved the clay figures representing the people to the models of other provinces. Pachacuti's inspectors—exemplars of the efficient and universal authority to which Toledo aspired—departed to carry out his will.[32]

This extraordinary act of social engineering, rearranging his subjects like pieces on a game board, was how, Sarmiento believed, Pachacuti created the mitimas. Sarmiento portrayed this institution as the apogee of the great king's surveillance and control, "the greatest tyranny he committed, although colored with a kind of generosity." The "generosity" was in granting the mitimas lands confiscated from the provinces they were relocated to; at the same time, the Incas enlisted mitimas as spies to report on suspicious behavior among the local people.[33]

Topa Inca, Sarmiento wrote, added another kind of population movement to his father's policies: he concentrated his subjects into new towns, like Spanish reducciones. The chief inspector (*visitador general*) whom Topa Inca appointed "resettled many of the Indians into towns and houses [who had] previously lived in caves and mountains and riverbanks, each by himself."[34] Sarmiento was not the only colonial writer to make this assertion. Polo Ondegardo wrote that, after the Incas conquered a new province, "the first thing they did was to resettle the Indians into towns and order them to live in community, because up until then [the Indians] lived very much divided and separated."[35] The assertion that the Incas founded reducciones raised the question why Andeans no longer lived in concentrated settlements; Sarmiento may have believed that Topa Inca's campaign was simply incomplete, or that the population later reverted to its pre-Inca dispersion. In any case, Sarmiento described considerable overlap between Inca tyranny and Toledo's goals.

One conclusion that follows from this account of Inca reducciones is that population consolidation was consistent with the system of mitima enclaves that the Incas also created. The General Resettlement, following the Inca model, would combine an aggressive policy of resettlement with an attempt to preserve the mitima system and the vertical archipelago.

Toledo sent Sarmiento's manuscript to the king, along with a set of paintings he had had made by Andean artists. Three of them displayed royal portraits and the fourth an annotated genealogy of the Inca dynasty; Toledo also included a group of Inca royal objects. Both paintings and objects are lost, and though we do not know exactly what the paintings looked like, Toledo described them as illustrating "the policía that [the Incas] attained in their time, in costumes, and instruments of war, and the religious worship of their idolatries." He suggested that the paintings could hang in the king's wardrobe, to "entertain and amaze whatever prince might come to [His] Majesty's court," and also suggested having them copied as tapestries. (King Philip hung them in the palace alongside portraits by Titian.) By creating a graphic record of the Inca kings and queens, along with a historical chronicle of their reigns, Toledo portrayed them as a royal dynasty analogous to a European one—exactly contrary to the argument of Inca illegitimacy that Toledo articulated in words.[36]

Sarmiento based the book largely on interviews with the Inca elite in Cuzco, and after he finished it, in March 1572, Toledo held a public reading to solicit a notarized endorsement from the assembled Incas. The Inca lords' participation in Sarmiento's project cast them as privileged validators of the Inca past. Not surprisingly, some of them complained to Toledo about calling the Inca kings tyrants. The word tyrant was associated with the reviled perpetrators of the encomenderos' rebellions, and rebels' severed heads were still on display in the plazas of Spanish cities. Toledo, framing his discussion with the colonial Inca lords as an amusing anecdote (una cosa de harto donaire), told the king that it was "no small trick to undeceive them." Although he described the conversation lightheartedly, Toledo's determination to "undeceive" the Inca lords of their ambitions within the colonial order was deadly serious.[37]

Cuzco's Inca nobles were right to worry about the word tyrant. They were committed to their accommodation with the colonial system, which previous Spanish governors had nurtured with recognition and rewards. The most important Inca princes and princesses held encomiendas, many owned estates, and a large segment of the Inca ethnic group were exempt from tribute and labor demands.[38] Even Titu Cusi, leader of the neo-Incas of Vilcabamba, had finally agreed to incorporate his state into Spanish Peru in exchange for an honorable peace and a pension. The agreement was finalized shortly before Toledo's appointment, and the king instructed him to carry it out. But Toledo hated dealing with indigenous leaders on a diplomatic basis. Instead, he attacked first the independent Incas of Vilcabamba, then the Inca elite of Cuzco—for Toledo, the last dregs of a tyrannical dynasty.[39]

The Vilcabamba war began when Titu Cusi died unexpectedly and the resulting political turmoil led to the murder of several Spaniards in Vilcabamba. This provocation was a welcome development for Toledo, who had already been preparing for war. He sent an expedition to Vilcabamba that overran the settlement and brought Titu Cusi's successor, Tupac Amaru, back in chains to Cuzco, where Toledo had him tried and beheaded on the city plaza.

Toledo had made no secret of his wish to destroy the Vilcabamba state, but his attack on Cuzco's Inca elite, immediately afterward, was unexpected. The Cuzco Incas had cooperated with Toledo and supported the war on Vilcabamba.[40] But their position was less secure than it appeared. On the false accusation of having conspired with the lords of Vilcabamba, Toledo placed the most powerful Cuzco Incas on trial, then exiled them to Lima, Panama, and elsewhere. Many died in prison or en route.[41]

Toledo contemplated extending this banishment to the whole Inca population of Cuzco. He imagined it as a variation of the Incas' own institution of mitimas: "Let [the same thing be done to them], because of their crime, that the Incas did with these natives every day to secure their tyranny, which was to make them mitimas . . . to divide and scatter [the Incas] in the lower provinces where they are abhorred . . . so that this race (semilla) of Incas may be consumed in this kingdom." Although not ultimately carrying it out, Toledo imagined this retribution as poetic justice, turning the tyrants' own tyranny against them.[42]

What was distinctive about Inca government, in Spaniards' eyes, was its totalizing quality. In authoritative works such Aristotle's *Politics*, the jurist Bartolus's *De tyrannia*, and Gregorio López's sixteenth-century commentary on the *Siete Partidas*, tyranny meant surveillance and control, a climate of fear, the destruction of civil society, social leveling via the immiseration of subjects, and a state monopoly on their energies, intended less for productive purposes than to prevent all individual initiative.[43] Toledo and his advisors identified precisely these behaviors in the Inca regime. The Incas' goal was national wealth and individual impoverishment. The Incas claimed as their "tribute," wrote fray García, neither more nor less than the entirety of their subjects' labor and property, "the greatest tribute that ever a tyrant levied."[44] The subject was, in a sense, the slave of the state. Even the most intimate decisions were under royal control: one's marriage choice, children's education, and religion. The Inca kings "took away the liberty of souls to select a faith," the Dominican recorded primly. The Incas channeled their subjects' energies and productive surplus into endless wars and unnecessary labors. And all for no other reason than to prevent rebellion.

But these tyrannical forms of rule were closely tied to the Incas' most admired achievements. Toledo wrote about how they had invented work projects to keep their subjects busy: "When there were no useful things [to do], they made them work in useless things, such as directing rivers in one direction or another, and making very long walls from one place to another along the roads and stone steps, which were not necessary; this they did because it seemed to them very desirable to keep them always occupied."[45] Yet nearly all Spanish writers praised the Incas' civil engineering. Their monumental buildings, walls, roads, agricultural terraces, and canals reminded Spaniards of classical civilizations; Cieza de León compared Inca roads to Roman roads and Egyptian pyramids. The ambiguity of monumental building projects, to be sure, was an old problem for political theorists: explaining how tyrants engrossed their subjects' energies with public works, Aristotle himself had cited the Egyptian pyramids. The *Siete Partidas* said that tyrants "put [their subjects] to such great deeds (*grandes fechos*) that they can never finish them." For all that, no one stopped praising "great deeds." Pyramids may have signified tyranny, but they still took the breath away. The same logic applied to the Incas' never-ending wars, for which Spaniards compared them to Romans. If the Incas' monuments and wars made them tyrants, they were in good company.[46]

The Incas' social engineering, like their civil engineering, appeared as both admirable and tyrannical. As one Spanish witness testified to Toledo's investigators, "When an Indian was most secure in his house, [the Incas] moved him from his homeland by force and placed him in another, very far away." Since the mitimas then became royal dependents, living on land seized from the local population, they also reflected the classical tyrant's strategy of playing factions off against one another. Yet some Spanish officials considered the mitima system one of the Incas' most beneficial policies.[47] Yet another diagnostic of tyranny was surveillance, what the *Siete*

Partidas called the tyrant's need "to know what is said or what is done in the land." But even Sarmiento, with his constant references to tyranny, made no pretense of criticizing Inca surveillance methods, the source of their exceptional knowledge of their subjects. Toledo, after all, premised his own administration on information gathering.[48]

There is, of course, no necessary contradiction in praising and blaming similar practices in different contexts. There could be good surveillance and bad surveillance, good building projects and bad ones, just and unjust resettlement campaigns. Still, Inca tyranny and Inca achievement were difficult to separate. The Inca regime, as Sarmiento and Toledo understood it, was one of surveillance, central control, and leveling. Inca tyranny meant an infrastructure of communication: roads, way stations, and message carriers. It meant an efficient organization of communal labor for large projects, whether for agriculture, road building or war. It also meant reducing subjects to atomized, interchangeable units, without individual property or initiative, whose energies belonged to the collectivity. To Toledo, as to many Spaniards, this totalizing government came to seem appropriate both to the challenges of the Andean landscape and to the character of Andean people.[49]

In his letter to the king presenting the results of his Inca inquiry, Toledo showed how the Incas' policies fit the canonical definition of tyrants; then, without noting the irony, he went on to urge Philip II to practice similar policies. The Incas had tyrannically established the caciques as their fully dependent agents in the communities; the Spanish should do the same. Furthermore, it was the king's duty to prevent Andeans from being idle, which could only be harmful, given their weak nature. "Although they contradict it and it seems contrary to their freedom," the king should "occupy them in things that would be good for them."[50] They were like children: "It is shown that these natives . . . need a caretaker [curador] for the serious matters they encounter, of their souls as well as of their property."[51] Fray García's concern about Andeans' right to choose their own faith was irrelevant in this context.

A few months later a letter from Toledo to an ally at court raised the stakes. He began by asserting that the Incas had learned their techniques of rule from the devil, who had correctly assessed the Andean character, observing that they were weak and could best be ruled by fear. Yet Toledo asserted that Spain likewise needed to "understand the nature of this people and that they need to fear in order to be governed."[52] In urging imitation not only of the Incas but of the devil himself, Toledo was placing the Spanish king in dubious company; what they had in common, as he saw it, was a realistic understanding of the Andean people.

The introduction that Toledo wrote for the *tasa* (the document laying out the tribute due from every repartimiento), which was his most formal statement of policy about ruling Andeans, distilled his ambivalence about the Inca legacy. Gesturing yet again toward the classic elements of tyranny, he noted that the Incas had prevented their subjects from initiating their own work or owning property. Yet Inca tyranny had the virtue of "not allowing them to be idle . . . and keeping track of the life of each individual." If the Spanish had followed their example in this, the viceroy speculated, the Andean population would have prospered instead of declining.[53]

To understand the paradox of how Inca precedents could be satanic and useful at the same time, it is helpful to return to Aristotle's discussion of tyranny. Aristotle wrote that barbarians' legitimate kings resembled tyrants, which reflected barbarians' slavish character.[54] In this light Andeans, too, were suited for tyrannical rule. It did not make the Incas legitimate, but it allowed their legitimate Spanish successors to learn some lessons from them. Some Mexican colonists felt the same way about the Aztecs. During the 1570s, contemporaneously with Toledo's tenure in Peru, the Mexican archbishop Pedro de Moya y Contreras made a point remarkably similar to Toledo's, praising the "time of Moctezuma, who ordered his governors . . . to keep track individually of the occupation of each person, compelling them to work."[55] It was precisely those Spaniards most contemptuous of the Indians they saw around them who most extravagantly praised prehispanic Indian kings' severe justice.

Descriptions of Aztec surveillance and control, however, never reached the extremes of the colonists' visions of the Incas. In trying to establish that the Incas were tyrants, Toledo and his advisors painted a picture of an extraordinary state, one unknown in European politics, though reminiscent of classical empires such as that of Herodotus's Persians, and foreshadowed in the utopias of Plato and Thomas More. It was not just that Spaniards attributed the whole existing order of Andean society—the settlements, roads, social groupings, religious practices, and methods of record keeping—to Inca initiative. Those pagan kings' command of society extended from the most intimate level (marriage choices, rites of passages, and agricultural calendar) to the most grand (large-scale movements of people and goods from one end of the far-flung empire to the other). With these methods the Incas had wrung prosperity from an unforgiving landscape, stored surpluses for lean years, and sustained a higher Andean population than that which now languished and declined under Spanish rule. They had successfully managed the affairs of a people too weak and foolish to manage their own. The Incas, in other words, had understood and mastered the Andes, both people and place. It would have been hard not to admire such a regime, and Toledo was willing to imitate it.

"Preserving for the Indians Their Laws"

Toledo's intention of inheriting the Incas' "tyranny" was part of a broader program of preserving Andean systems as the best method through which Spaniards could rule them, even within the context of the General Resettlement. And the key Andean institution was that of the mitimas. It seemingly conflicted with the guiding principles of his reforms. By living in one place but remaining members of a distant repartimiento, mitimas undermined the countability and accountability of the native population. Furthermore, Toledo claimed that establishing the mitima class was an act of Inca tyranny and that most Andeans who moved around were vagabonds. Not unreasonably, scholars have concluded that Toledo wanted to destroy the archipelago model of community and the institution of mitimas, forcing them to return home or sever ties with their home communities.[56] In fact, Toledo protected the mitimas' special status, because he saw it as necessary.

Toledo instructed his inspectors to "keep the custom of the time of the Incas and restore [to the mitimas] whatever has been taken from them."[57] He warned that the caciques of each locality would try to exploit the mitimas who lived among them, or to expand their own jurisdiction over them; in spite of this pressure, the ties of loyalty connecting mitimas with their home caciques should be preserved. Home caciques could register distant subjects in the inspectors' census, even without calling them home to be counted in person.[58] The inspectors should found satellite villages away from the main one, for those who tended fields and herds away from their home communities.[59] Toledo was aware of the importance of Andeans' access to lands they owned at a distance from their new residences, and instructed his inspectors to maintain that access. How well this instruction was followed is another question, which will be considered in the next chapter. But it is clear that from the beginning of the General Resettlement, Toledo went out of his way to preserve Andean enclaves.[60]

The explanation for Toledo's policy is not a general respect for freedom of movement. He had no sympathy for Andeans who were not mitimas but simply chose to live away from their homes. Those who had been in their current residence for ten years were to enroll as tribute-paying members of the community where they currently lived; the rest were to return to their original home. Toledo meant to curb spontaneous migration, while preserving the mitimas who allowed native communities to stay economically viable.[61]

In other contexts, too, Toledo instructed his inspectors to protect the "order and custom of the time of the Inca." Reflecting Spanish admiration for the Incas' infrastructure, Toledo was keen to preserve Inca systems for maintaining roads, bridges, tambos, and deposits for harvest surpluses. He told the inspectors to investigate Inca-era traditions for apportioning communal lands and irrigation water to see whether those, too, should be preserved. The viceroy wanted to preserve preconquest norms for designating craft specialists and for growing unusual crops such as cotton.[62] He urged the king, repeatedly and in the face of repeated dismissals, to move the Spanish viceregal capital to the Incas' city, Cuzco.[63]

Toledo's rules for Andean communities preserved many features of what he understood to be Inca law (although many of these practices were in fact much older than the Incas). Within the reducciones Toledo preserved the prehispanic system of ranked sayas in many highland communities, not only in those that had such a tradition already, but strikingly, in many that were assembled from unrelated small groups, where the sayas were wholly artificial.[64] Toledo applied this conservatism even to small details of the Andean labor system. For laborers in the hot and humid coca fields, he restored the Inca rule that no highlander could stay there for more than twenty-four days, to protect them from diseases.[65] He even called for preserving a civic custom of traditional Andean villages: public meals held by caciques in the plaza for the benefit of the poor.[66] Given Toledo's commitment to transforming Andean communities, it is striking to see him calling for the protection of old community norms that were vulnerable to being lost.

How Toledo learned about traditional Andean culture and the need to preserve it is not entirely clear. He had learned a lot about the Andes while still in Spain, and had access to reports that discussed mitimas. He was probably not the sole author of his instructions to the inspectors, written soon after his arrival, but rather collaborated with knowledgeable officials such as Gregorio González de Cuenca and the archbishop of Lima, fray Gerónimo de Loayza.[67] Loayza, a longtime proponent of resettlement,[68] had a good grasp of the indigenous Andean economy and the role of mitimas, having led a systematic revision of the tribute scales two decades earlier, in collaboration with licenciado Polo Ondegardo.[69] An ally of Las Casas, Loayza was to become a harsh critic of the viceroy. Yet during his early months in Peru Toledo sought the advice of Loayza and others, making a serious effort to learn from their years of experience in the Andes.[70]

Beginning in 1571, Toledo's most important advisor on indigenous society was Polo de Ondegardo. One of the key sources scholars today rely on for Andean ethnohistory is a report Polo drafted for Toledo, entitled "Account of the Arguments Regarding the Notable Harm that Results from Not Preserving for the Indians their Laws." Like his contemporaries, Polo attributed the laws of the Andes to the wisdom of the Incas. He particularly admired their meticulous and exhaustive records—keeping count of current population, the sizes of the llama herds, and yields of agriculture. No other indigenous regime, Polo believed, had ruled so well or instilled such good customs in those it conquered.[71]

The Incas' exceptional qualities, Polo believed, stemmed in part from their mountainous environment. Their "most harsh and strong" land (along with their "better shrewdness and greater intelligence") instilled in the Incas a "much better order in what touches human life than all the others." Counterintuitively, a harsh landscape produced a wealthier society than a fertile one did: the altiplano forced its people to develop their own resources and build networks of exchange.[72] Polo made the case to Toledo that Peru's distinctive landscape meant it should be ruled differently from other countries. Even Mexico, though mountainous, was flat compared to Peru, and Mexican Indians inhabited a landscape of town and countryside, much like Europeans. In the unrelentingly vertical landscape of Peru, people lived by necessity in dispersed and often shifting settlements.

In his 1571 report Polo developed an argument he had made a decade earlier. He argued that the Incas' wisest policy was to establish the form that many Andean communities took: dispersed, with pockets of land and population in both highland and lowland. "If one thinks long about it," Polo wrote in 1561, "one will not find a better way or means" to promote a dense and stable population in the mountainous Andean environment.[73] Noting that an earlier governor had followed his advice in reuniting the highland province of Chucuito with its western lowland colonies, he pressed Toledo to do the same.[74]

In 1575 Toledo followed licenciado Polo's principles in a situation that closely concerned Polo himself.[75] The context was a long-running dispute between the highland repartimientos of Carangas province and their mitimas in the valley of Cochabamba, where Polo held an encomienda. Some time in the early sixteenth century, the Inca king Huayna Capac had established a large agricultural complex in Cochabamba, with highland workers rotating through the valley to do mit'a labor, as well as a smaller, permanent enclave of highland colonists in the valley. After the Spanish conquest, the rotating laborers stopped coming but there continued to be long-term highland residents in Cochabamba, who called themselves mitimas; they included those placed there by Huayna Capac, and possibly others who had lived there earlier and supplied food to highland relatives. In the early colonial period, as we have seen, the distinction blurred between mitimas sent by the Inca state for its own purposes and archipelago colonists sent by their home communities: all formed a single group who called themselves mitimas. But in Cochabamba, while recognizing their historic ties to highland communities, they wanted to be liberated from the highlanders' demands for labor and tribute. The highlanders appealed to the Spanish to enforce their control over the mitimas and their ownership of the land the mitimas occupied.

The inspectors of Carangas and Cochabamba, in an effort to resolve the dispute, submitted recommendations to Toledo. Each inspector took the side of the province that he himself was visiting; each, after all, was getting his information from that side and had an interest in maximizing the tribute it could afford to pay. The inspector in Carangas, Francisco de Saavedra Ulloa, argued in favor of the highlanders on the basis of the vertical archipelago: he asserted that they needed access to lowland produce because Carangas was a "very sterile land." He wrote that, due to the mitimas' de facto secession from the highlands, six hundred people were forced to travel from Carangas to Cochabamba for three or four months a year in order to trade for maize. He urged Toledo to establish a special reducción for these seasonal migrants in Cochabamba and give them possession of the lands Carangas had once possessed, which the mitimas claimed. The inspector in Cochabamba, Diego Núñez de Bazán, argued in favor of the mitimas, on the basis not of ecology but of history and property rights. He asserted that the land in Cochabamba had belonged to the Inca kings, not to the highland communities, even though Huayna Capac placed highland workers on it. Núñez contended that after the Spanish conquest, the land in question had passed into the ownership of the Spanish king, who should rightfully give it to the families currently living and farming there—that is, the mitimas—and affiliate them with the Cochabamba repartimientos.

Having read the two recommendations, Toledo issued his decision in favor of Carangas.[76] He concluded that the highlanders had an economic need and customary right to their fields in Cochabamba, which would therefore belong to them until a competent judge ruled otherwise. He also recognized the highland caciques' right to the mitimas' allegiance. The mitimas should be enrolled in the highland repartimientos, and give tribute and labor to their homelands. He reassigned one group of 114 mitima families in Cochabamba, who had assimilated themselves to Polo's repartimiento, making them members of the repartimiento of Paria in Carangas. In doing so, he turned Polo own arguments against him, removing tribute-paying families from his jurisdiction. But what he took from Polo with one hand he gave back with the other: he assigned him a pension (situación) from the repartimiento of Paria equivalent to the tribute of those 114 families.[77] As encomendero, Polo's continued to hold a financial claim over the mitimas who labored side by side with the people of his own repartimiento, but that claim was tied into the larger, organic structure of the vertical archipelago.

Toledo's intervention in the case of the mitimas of Cochabamba was typical of his approach. His intention was never to destroy Andean culture and impose a new culture from scratch, after a model imported from Spain. Rather, he designed the General Resettlement to achieve a much more ambiguous combination of change and continuity. Toledo loudly called for transforming the Andean way of organizing space, in the broad outlines, while quietly preserving it in the details.

Viceroy Toledo, soon after arriving in the area immediately above Lima to the east, summoned the province's caciques and resident Spaniards and ordered them to draw up maps so he could get a head start on the General Resettlement: "I commanded them to make paintings and descriptions of the pueblos that existed in each repartimiento and where it would be possible to resettle them, and having seen these, with the agreement of all, they were resettled in the locations and places that seemed most appropriate."[78] Toledo's use of maps to plan reducciones (though it is not clear whether he or his inspectors did this in other parts of the Andes) looks ahead to the Crown's attempts to gather a registry of maps of its colonial and peninsular territories in the 1580s.[79] But it also looks backward, to Pachacuti. Sarmiento recorded that Pachacuti directed his inspectors to bring him scale models of the various provinces, on which he moved populations around, in the process creating the mitimas. The resemblance between Toledo and Pachacuti, their shared determination to master space, is striking.[80]

Toledo did not need the Incas' example to make maps or to magnify state power: he brought with him from Spain a deep confidence in his own ability to understand and shape his viceroyalty. Yet the General Resettlement was enough to challenge any viceroy's confidence. Though Indian resettlement was not new, no one had ever attempted it in the rapid, uniform, and centralized manner that Toledo did in the Andes. During the months that he began to put it into effect, he indulged a remarkable preoccupation with the ways and deeds of his pagan predecessors. Toledo's inquiry was motivated by anger at what he considered the Incas' wickedness and at the dangerous naïveté of his own countrymen who idealized them. Yet the picture that it led to was a paradoxical one, simultaneously condemning and admiring. Toledo's obsessive investigation into Inca "tyranny" was inseparable from his own exploration of new forms of state control. His disgust and admiration infused the General Resettlement of Indians.

8

—

ON THE GROUND

Under Viceroy Toledo's authority, more than a million people were assigned to live in about six hundred reducciones. Toledo called universal forced resettlement "the first and most important part" of his work as viceroy. And from our perspective today, it is natural to see it as the most significant of his many projects, the one that changed the face of the land. Yet it left the fewest records. It is easy to read Toledo's laws and instructions, and his opponents' criticism of them, as if they were the history of the resettlement campaign. In fact, though, Toledo's laws are the record of his intentions and his opponents' criticism the record of their opposition. The lack of sources remains a serious problem, but scattered documents shine a spotlight on how, in a handful of places, the inspectors carried out the Resettlement.[1]

Choosing a Location

The location of a reducción was vitally important to its inhabitants. Toledo's emphasis on choosing sites with good climates implied a preference for valleys over high and arid places, since early modern Europeans thought that temperate air kept people healthy.[2] On the other hand, since Spaniards also believed that Andeans' constitutions were weak and that moving from one altitude to another was dangerous to them, Toledo told inspectors to avoid moving people to a different climate.[3] Actual practices depended on the region. In the area south of Lake Titicaca, reducciones were founded disproportionately on the altiplano, which was flat and accessible to the Spanish. Existing villages there were larger than in other parts of the Andes, making it unnecessary to concentrate the population further. [4] On the other hand, in the more irregular landscape of central Peru, studies suggest that the Resettlement moved people to lower altitudes, making communities more accessible to Spaniards on horseback and bringing Andean labor closer to Spanish settlers. [5]

In most cases the record is silent about who chose a reducción's location, and how. Most inspectors probably spent little time on it: as we will see, they had other priorities. They may have made decisions based on a superficial tour of the area, or accommodated Spaniards who wanted to move Andeans away from land the Spaniards desired. But caciques also played a role in the decision: Toledo had instructed inspectors to consult caciques, and inspectors found their work difficult without some cooperation from them. Caciques presumably steered inspectors toward sites with an adequate agricultural base. Occasional evidence survives of a cacique negotiating with an inspector or even with Toledo himself about the site for a reducción. [6]

A reducción was sometimes near one of the existing villages from which its population was drawn: today, in rural and undeveloped areas, a reducción may be a few minutes walk from the ruins of a prereducción village. This was not Toledo's intention; he scolded his inspectors for letting Andeans stay near their old homes, "where they have their idolatries and the graves of their ancestors." [7] On the other hand, he told the king that in the best sites, where reducciones were to be built, there were probably Christian churches already standing; Spanish friars had often chosen to build their churches in existing villages. [8] In any case, caciques often succeeded in placing reducciones near their own homes. [9] In some cases a lesser cacique or principal displaced the repartimiento's cacique general as the inspector's main collaborator, and used the reducción's location to strengthen his own power base. [10] But if a reducción was founded close to one village, it was far from many more: separating people from their homes and fields was inevitable. In spite of local input, sites were often bad ones, without easy access to water and arable land. [11]

One subject of negotiation when founding reducciones was the fate of mitimas. As we have seen, encomienda grants typically respected the principle by which mitimas could remain in distant locations while remaining in the jurisdiction of their home cacique. Toledo's instructions had implied that this should remain the case. Inspectors were inconsistent on the subject. Their first impulse was often to order mitimas either to return home or to attach themselves to the communities where they were living, but inspectors also knew that some communities depended on produce from their mitima colonies. In one place, the inspector initially ordered mitimas to return home, then relented and assigned them a block of houses in a reducción in the district where they lived.[12] In another, the inspector founded a special reducción for members of a repartimiento living in a valley two weeks away by llama train.[13] When inspectors did order Andeans to abandon distant settlements, they promised that the community's property there would remain inviolate—a promise often betrayed.[14]

Another issue was what to do when repartimientos' core territories overlapped. Apart from mitimas at distant locations, people of different repartimientos often lived intermixed within their home territories: in the Andes, community was defined by kinship and political authority, not territory. For the inspectors, there were two approaches to such intermixed repartimientos: to insist that all residents of a reducción be members of the same repartimiento, or allow members of different repartimientos to share the same reducción. The first strategy would make sense from the point of view of the state. Since the repartimiento was the unit that paid tribute and contributed mita laborers, homogeneous reducciones were simpler to administer. But the second strategy, creating mixed reducciones, allowed people to remain near their previous homes and minimized the shock of the Resettlement. Some inspectors were determined to homogenize the reducciones, others more willing to found mixed reducciones.

Ultimately, repartimiento and reducción were two separate systems for categorizing people, which did not map onto each other perfectly. The repartimiento was a unit of kinship and allegiance, while the reducción was a place of residence. Each had its own authorities: the repartimiento had its cacique and the reducción had its alcaldes. Yet the two were yoked together; among other things, the tribute Andeans gave through their caciques and repartimientos paid the salaries of the reducción priests. The uneven fit between the repartimientos and the reducciones made the Resettlement and its aftermath complicated.

Moromoro

In 1576 after the campaign was finished, Toledo ordered his accountants to present documentation from the General Inspection of the money received, spent, and deposited in the king's treasury; these financial accounts survive in the Archivo General de Indias in Seville.[15] The inspectors had generated an income in the course of their work, from fines and fees, but remitted little money to the Crown. Toledo had decided at the beginning that, since the king had not given any instructions on financing the General Inspection (and in fact never formally approved it), the inspectors would earn their own salaries and expenses in the field, as well as paying part of their expenses from tribute given by the communities being resettled.[16] Through these records of income and expenditure, we can identify the paid participants in the Inspection and the periods of time for which they were paid. Most of the accounts are brief, but the fullest ones trace a weak outline of the General Inspection through the money that flowed through it.

The members of an inspection team were the secular inspector, ecclesiastical inspector, alguacil, and notary. A few accounts also recorded expenses for a reducidor, a Spaniard charged with facilitating resettlement. We know little about these figures, whose appointment Toledo did not formally endorse until 1573.[17] In addition to salaries, one account includes eight pesos for a local map commissioned from a mestizo painter; another, ominously, records ten pesos spent for some iron shackles. Overall, the accounts suggest that the inspectors' primary work was collecting various fines from local Spaniards (and some Andeans) to pay their own salaries, and assembling the censuses that they would bring back to the viceroy. The primary members of the team typically collected salaries for six months to a year's work, while the translators (almost always Andean or mestizo) generally earned no more than one or two months' pay, which suggests that the inspectors were spending more time with local Spaniards than with Andeans. They invested little time or money in resettlement.[18]

One of the most complete sets of accounts is that of Juan de Matienzo, who served as inspector in the district around the city of La Plata, where he was a judge in the Audiencia of Charcas. He also sent a letter to the king in the middle of his work, written, as he said, "with his hands in the dough."[19] Matienzo paid himself a salary for about eight months of work and, judging by the dates of the fines he levied, most of his activity was during August to October of two successive years, 1572 and 1573. Taking the salaries of the officials as a fraction of Matienzo's (1,777 *pesos ensayados*), the ecclesiastical inspector received 31 percent of Matienzo's salary, the alguacil 28 percent, the notary 25 percent, the two interpreters 9 percent and 4 percent respectively, and two reducidores 6 percent each, while an Andean man received 1 percent, or fifty *pesos corrientes*, for carrying dispatches to the viceroy.[20]

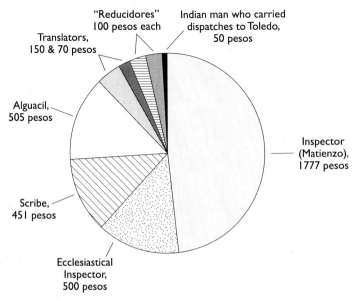

Figure 8-1 Salaries of Juan de Matienzo's inspection team. All sums are in pesos ensayados. For my calculations, here and throughout, I rely on Luengo Múñoz, "Sumaria noción de las monedas de Castilla e Indias en el siglo XVI," who defines pesos ensayados as equivalent to 425 maravedís (until 1592 when silver was devalued and the peso ensayado was reset to 450 maravedís) and pesos corrientes as 8 reales or 272 maravedís. All salaries were calculated in pesos ensayados except that given to the Andean man who carried dispatches, which was 50 pesos corrientes, equivalent to 30 pesos ensayados.

(Apart from their pay, the team received food from the communities it visited; the interpreters, for instance, were supposed to receive a llama a week for meat.[21]) Matienzo collected fines and fees from lawsuits over which he presided as judge, as well as fining encomenderos for infractions such as failure to make priests available to Andeans.[22]

As he collected them, Matienzo earmarked most of the fines for his team's salaries. He seems to have paid the lesser officials (interpreters, reducidores, messengers) right away, but the others could not collect their salaries until those paying the fines had exhausted their judicial appeals. (The Audiencia, which heard the appeals, often decided in favor of the defendant, to the inspectors' frustration.) Toledo's opponents, in fact, argued that "to pay their expenses it is necessary to find infractions and to seek out such old ones that it looks very bad to bring them up."[23] In Matienzo's case, operational costs ate up nearly all of the team's income from fines: he spent over seven thousand pesos in expenses and salaries, and forwarded only 150 pesos to the king.[24]

In his report to the king, Matienzo described founding three reducciones. One of these was Villanueva de la Plata, in which he settled all of the roughly two hundred households of the repartimiento of Moromoro. (In time the reducción came to be called Moromoro, the name of the repartimiento, rather than Villanueva.) The reducción's 1,182 inhabitants were drawn from eleven small villages over an area of twenty-five leagues. These villages would have had an average population of just over one hundred people each, although their actual size must have varied.[25]

How did the inspector choose the reducción site? Matienzo wrote that some of Moromoro's eleven villages were high and cold, others low and hot; he chose the new town's location as being that of an already-existing settlement called Moroto, in a good climate, close to Andeans' fields, and close to the tambo that they served. All the local Andeans and Spaniards unanimously urged this location, he said. It is possible that the village already in that spot served as a political or population center to the other ten.[26]

But Matienzo did not simply designate the preexisting village of Moroto as the reducción of Villanueva: he claimed to have laid out a new street plan around a central plaza, with 150-foot-square blocks and 14-foot-wide streets. (Was Moroto dismantled to build Villanueva on the same spot, or was Villanueva built nearby? It is unclear.) He appointed a native cabildo and assigned buildings to serve as church, council house, school, inn, and jail.

Matienzo departed from the norm in one respect: he appointed a Spanish couple to live in the town "so that the Indians would learn the good customs of the Spanish." This was a recommendation that Matienzo had previously advocated but that Toledo had declined to adopt, instead preserving the traditional rule that priests were the only non-Andeans permitted to reside in indigenous communities.[27] That Matienzo followed it anyway suggests the relative autonomy with which inspectors worked.

Revealingly, however, Matienzo ended his report on this reducción by complaining that at the last minute he had lost control of the process. A local friar, a licentious Augustinian, had become enraged when Matienzo removed the stocks in which he used to punish the villagers when they disobeyed him. The friar had gone on to convince Matienzo's colleagues on the Charcas Audiencia to overturn many of his decisions, and convinced the local people, Matienzo wrote, that "he would get everything I had done revoked, which he said and did in order to recover his authority with the Indians." Matienzo's work now stood in jeopardy.[28] The case was not unique. Matienzo complained that another reducción he founded was in danger because a Spaniard claimed to own the land where it was located and had filed an appeal.[29]

Matienzo's struggles make it clear that even the most motivated and well-connected inspector, operating in his own backyard, could not control the process of creating reducciones as fully as Toledo's instructions implied. In Moromoro, Matienzo initiated a process of creating a new municipal entity out of an old one. But once he had laid out the plaza and streets, other actors intervened. The new towns came into existence as a result of the General Inspection, but in a more chaotic and undocumented process than Toledo had contemplated. Full control was illusory.

Chérrepe

In the 1970s, in the Peruvian national archives, the historian Susan Ramírez found a rare and revealing document: an *auto de reducción*, or act of resettlement, in which one of Toledo's inspectors issued specific orders for founding reducciones in the repartimiento of Chérrepe. I do not know of any other auto de reducción that has been found.[30] The absence is all the more striking given the full documentation that often survives of the founding and early communal life of Spanish towns. Founding a town involved civic rituals—taking possession of the site, laying out the plaza, church, town hall and streets, assigning house lots, constituting the town council—each of which was documented and notarized. Paper records of civic ritual constituted what Ángel Rama called the "lettered city," so important in Hispanic culture, yet few such records survive for reducciones de indios.[31]

The population of repartimiento Chérrepe, about nine hundred people, had been living in three settlements: the village of Chérrepe, a small hamlet named Noquique, and a group of households near a house of Spanish friars named Nuestra Señora de Guadalupe. The inspector, Juan de Hoces, decided to dissolve Noquique and concentrate the whole population into the other two settlements, rebuilding both according to Toledo's norms with central plazas, gridded streets, and civic buildings. He ordered the people to build their new homes within twelve days, promising to remit part of their tribute if they completed construction in that time and to destroy their existing houses if they did not. The document provides fine-grained information about the resettlement process.

The two reducciones, Chérrepe and Guadalupe, were not equal. Both would have civic buildings such as a school and a house for storing chicha, but only Chérrepe, where the cacique lived, was to have two important buildings mandated in Toledo's instructions: an inn for traveling Spaniards and a cabildo hall.[32] Lacking a cabildo of its own, Guadalupe would be a dependency of Chérrepe, which would be the *cabecera* or head town. Hoces was continuing the tradition Cuenca had established in the north coast, and that likely preceded him, of cabeceras and satellite villages.[33] This is significant because Toledo's instructions implied that all reducciones were self-governing. But the Chérrepe document suggests that it may have been common, in repartimientos with more than one reducción, for only one to have a cabildo—a scenario that is otherwise invisible in the early documentation of the Resettlement.[34]

Although the auto gives us an unusual amount of information about the process, it does not say how many people had to relocate or how far. Chérrepe already existed as a village, although its homes were scattered and needed to be brought closer together and organized in a grid; the houses near the convent, on the other hand, had no central nucleus, so that the reducción had to be built from scratch.[35] Those living in Noquique—10 to 15 percent of the repartimiento's population—had to move a considerable distance to settle in one of the two reducciones.[36] Hoces claimed that Noquique's location was swampy and unhealthy, that it was close to mountains, which were worshipped as huacas, and that people from this and another repartimiento visited it to practice idolatrous rites.[37] But he had preserved the existing location of the village of Chérrepe, he wrote, at the request of its residents. The auto portrayed Hoces as responsive to Andeans' needs and working to minimize the pain of resettlement.

Ramírez, however, advanced an alternative account. She noted that Noquique's land, which occupied higher ground than the other two sites, later became a Spanish hacienda. Hoces, who was the corregidor of a nearby Spanish town, knew the area well. His claim that Noquique's population was small, which could no longer have been verified after the Resettlement, may have been false. And his concern that Noquique's proximity to mountain huacas promoted idolatry is dubious, since Andeans worshipped mountain gods from distant as well as nearby places. More relevant, probably, was the quality of the land: Noquique's higher elevation made it more fertile than the arid coastal soil which was shaded much of the year by ocean mist. Ramírez hypothesized that reducciones in the north coast region were systematically designed to free up desirable land for Spaniards.[38]

Even if Hoces robbed the repartimiento of fertile land, he had no desire to undermine its ethnic leadership. Indeed, he programmed the repartimiento's existing power structure into the organization of the reducciones. This explains his decision, otherwise mysterious, to exchange families between Chérrepe and Guadalupe in order to segregate them by occupation. The repartimiento was divided between farmers and fishermen who lived intermingled in each of the three existing settlements, Chérrepe, Guadalupe, and Noquique. Hoces ordered that all fishermen settle in Chérrepe and all farmers in Guadalupe. His intention was probably to simplify lines of authority within the repartimiento. Hoces entrusted the Resettlement, in part, to two principales, "one of them lord of Indian fishermen and the other of farmers."[39] The phrase suggests that the repartimiento contained twin moieties, occupationally defined, sharing a single cacique but each with its own lesser leader.

The population exchange between Chérrepe and Guadalupe established a one-to-one correspondence between reducción and occupation. This would make it easier for traditional leaders to maintain their authority within the reducciones. The cacique oversaw both groups but lived in Chérrepe. Since tribute and mita laborers were collected by ayllus, channeled upward by the principales to the cacique, this organization would make that process easier. Hoces separated previously intermingled populations in order to create homogeneous, governable towns.

In founding Chérrepe's reducciones, Hoces relied not only on the hereditary Andean authorities but also on the encomendero, whose local representative Hoces instructed to oversee the construction. This was a departure from the spirit of Toledo's project, which aimed to marginalize encomenderos. Rather than establishing new forms of authority in the repartimiento, Hoces relied on traditional authorities: cacique, principales, and encomendero. By separating previously intermingled populations, Hoces disrupted older systems. But he simultaneously aligned the reducciones with the existing power structure, reinforcing tradition in one way even while undermining it in another.

Condes

An equally useful document of the General Resettlement survives from the region of Condesuyos, to the southwest of Cuzco: not an auto de reducción, but an unusually detailed inspector's report. Most inspectors probably submitted reports showing not only census information for the repartimientos they inspected, but also the names of reducciones they founded and the number of people from each repartimiento they assigned to each reducción. In the great majority of cases, however, that information has been lost; we have only the names of the reducciones and the gross census numbers for each repartimiento.[40] For Condesuyos, though, the original report survives from the ecclesiastical inspector, Luis Mexía; the anthropologist Catherine Julien has published a valuable study of this document.[41]

Although the report is unusual, the region of Condesuyos was not particularly so. Its financial accounts look similar to those in other places.[42] The accounts register income and expenditure over an eighteen-month period from 1571 to 1572, and show an income of about 6000 pesos. This came from eighteen large fines on encomenderos for failure to provide priests to Andean communities, plus five small ones on other Spaniards for mistreating Andeans. Only two percent of this income went to the king; the rest went to expenses and salaries. No reducidor was listed, and the budget for interpreting was minimal (two translators earned 150 and 75 pesos, respectively). Mexía held all three offices of ecclesiastical inspector, alguacil, and protector de indios. But without a staff or a recorded budget, he registered the Resettlement as a completed job in this territory.

The report does not tell us everything we would like to know about the process of resettling. It does not, for instance, say whether Mexía chose the reducciones' locations and organized them by himself, or in collaboration with others. Nor does it say whether the local people had already built and settled the towns by the time he prepared the list. It does, however, offer insight into how he (or his collaborators) planned the towns.

The reducciones founded by Mexía varied greatly in size. Although the mean population of 420 tributaries was close to Toledo's recommendation of 400, the reducciones varied from 80 to 800 tributaries, and fewer than half fell in the middle range between 300 and 500. This wide variation belies the image of cookie-cutter standardization that one might infer from Toledo's instructions, and suggests that Mexía responded to local conditions.[43]

The organization of Mexía's reducciones was the opposite of those in Chérrepe: instead of having clean lines of authority and jurisdiction, the Resettlement in Condesuyos mixed them bewilderingly, dividing repartimientos among reducciones and reducciones among repartimientos. An example illustrates how complex this was. In the district of Condes—one of several in the area Mexía inspected within Condesuyos—the people of eight repartimientos

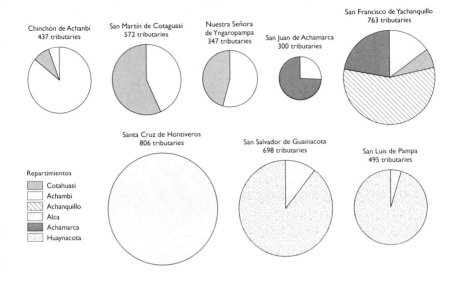

Figure 8-2 Distribution of repartimientos among eight reducciones

were divided among sixteen reducciones. For each repartimiento, there was one town that shared its name; this was probably the residence of its cacique and the center for tribute collection, analogous to the reducción of Chérrepe in the repartimiento of Chérrepe. In sharp contrast to Chérrepe, though, most of the towns in Condes had mixed populations. The repartimientos of Achambi and Cotahuasi had three towns between them: Achambi provided the large majority of one town, while they shared the two others in roughly equal portions. They also made up a fifth of another town, Achanquillo, the rest of which was divided between the repartimientos of Achanquillo and Achamarca. The repartimiento of Alca had a large town entirely to itself, while contributing a small amount to the population of three others. And the people of repartimiento Chilpacas lived in three small villages, each of which was listed as an annex (anejo) of another town. (See figure 8-2.)

Why did Mexía create reducciones that straddled and overlapped the repartimientos with no clean fit? And why did the reducciones vary so greatly in size? He probably designed the reducciones to minimize disruption to the existing pattern of settlement, so that people would not have to walk far to reach their old fields. Since each rural neighborhood varied in its population and had residents from several repartimientos, so did the town Mexía founded there. The reducciones preserved the complexity of local society.[44]

Yanquecollaguas

The previous case studies discussed specific documents—financial accounts, a letter to the king, an auto de reducción, and an inspector's report—which shed light on the Resettlement process. This case study examines the use of archaeology to reconstruct that process in Yanquecollaguas, one of several large and prosperous repartimientos of the Collagua people in the Colca valley. The case study draws primarily on the work of anthropologist Steven Wernke, combining the tools of archaeological surveys, computer-based mapping, place names and oral history, along with early colonial documents. His work, in turn, builds on a long-term, multidisciplinary study of the Colca valley by Peruvian and foreign scholars.[45] One of Toledo's inspectors, Lope de Suazo, consolidated the repartimiento of Yanquecollaguas into two reducciones. But Suazo's intervention was just one more in a series of stages through which the community passed: pre-Inca, Inca, early colonial, and, finally, the General Resettlement.

Both before and after the Incas conquered them, the Collaguas lived in small, dispersed settlements. In Yanquecollaguas the Incas did not carry out any comprehensive resettlement policy, such as Sarmiento was later to attribute to them. But the Incas put their mark on the larger Collagua settlements, in which two characteristic features of Inca architecture appear at this point: central plazas and long gabled buildings adjoining them, which archaeologists call *kallankas*: small versions of the halls lining the plaza at Cajamarca, from which Pizarro's men ambushed Atahualpa. The Incas also founded a new state complex, called Yanque, in a previously empty location. As with other complexes founded by the Incas, its primary purposes seem to have been administration, production, storage, and ritual, rather than a population center.[46]

The next stage of Yanquecollaguas settlement was under the influence of Spanish Franciscans. In the early years after the Spanish conquest, with the permission of the newly appointed encomenderos, Franciscans entered the valley. Small, rustic Christian chapels appeared on the Inca plazas of Collagua villages, incongruously facing the Incas' kallankas.[47] A little later, in the 1560s, as the local Franciscans grew in numbers and self-confidence, they constructed two larger buildings: a convent in the Inca complex Yanque, and a church in a previously unoccupied site called Coporaque.[48]

By the time Toledo's inspector Lope de Suazo reached Yanquecollaguas, then, its settlement pattern had already passed through several changes. The Incas and the Franciscans had each added their own characteristic structures to existing villages, and each had established a new center on empty land: Yanque, founded by the Incas on the south side of the Colca River, and Coporaque, founded by the Franciscans on the north. Suazo, by contrast, did not choose any new sites, but instead turned Yanque and Coporaque into the repartimiento's two reducciones. He ordered the population to abandon their small villages, which had remained occupied during the pre-Inca, Inca, and Franciscan periods, and move to Yanque and Coporaque.

The logic behind the choice of reducción sites is one of the most elusive aspects of the Resettlement. In the case of Coporaque, Wernke brought together archaeology, documents, and information gathered from modern residents to show that the town's location—chosen as the site for a church by Franciscans, established as a reducción by Suazo—reflected an understanding of the area's settlement and land tenure patterns.

Wernke started with a census of the Hanansaya segment of Coporaque, made about forty years after the Resettlement.[49] For each tributary, the census listed both his ayllu and the parcels of land he owned, which were identified by the names of the larger fields in which they were located.[50] The colonial documents did not indicate where these were on a map, but by speaking to farmers Wernke collected the names of fields and other landmarks; he found that about twenty percent of the toponyms listed in the colonial census were still in use almost four centuries later.[51] Wernke mapped the landholdings from the census that he was able to identify. The ayllus' lands were intermingled, but he used statistical methods to assign a central point to each ayllu's cluster of land parcels. In most cases those central points were close to small archaeological sites, suggesting that the colonial ayllus were centered on specific pre-Resettlement villages.[52] The ayllus fell into two groups, divided by a pair of ravines, one of which passed through the town of Coporaque and descended to the Colca River. Each ayllu had property on only one side of the ravines. Some of the ayllus had names containing the Aymara words for "right" and "left," which were located on opposite sides of the ravines and corresponded to the right and left sides for someone looking down from the top of the slope. It appeared that Coporaque Hanansaya, one of the community's two sayas or moieties, was itself divided into a right-hand and a left-hand moiety.

This analysis shed light on the significance of Coporaque's location, which the Franciscans chose in the 1560s for the site of a church, and Suazo ratified in the 1570s as a reducción. Taking into account both the fields' locations and the shape of the terrain, Wernke used a computer model to estimate the time it took to walk to each field from the town. He found that Coporaque, while located between the fields of the two moieties, was closer to those of the right-hand moiety–the side associated in Aymara thought with masculinity, higher elevation, and prestige. This was significant, since one of the costs of resettlement was having to walk long distances every day over steep and uneven terrain. Coporaque's location in the center of the community minimized this cost overall, but favored the higher-ranking part of the community. It is clear that the reducción's location was not a capricious decision by inspector but reflected negotiation between Spaniards and Andeans and an understanding of the local community.[53]

We have no direct evidence of when or how people were forced to move to Coporaque. But at some point they did move. In the 1970s Alejandro Málaga Medina found a list of pre-Resettlement hamlets, dating from 1574; in the 1980s the geographer John Treacy found that sixteen out of seventeen names of the pre-Resettlement hamlets were now names for irrigation canals, which extended 2.5 kilometers from Coporaque. Nine of these canals had intact ruins of abandoned settlements, with anywhere from two to more than twenty houses. The most intact ruins were on the canals further away from Coporaque, suggesting that nearer hamlets may have been dismantled to build houses in the reducción. The more distant hamlets survived undismantled, and villagers may have used them occasionally or continuously.[54]

In 1977 the historian Noble David Cook recorded a story from Yanque-collaguas's other reducción, Yanque: a family named Choquehuanca invited another named Checa to live with them. The Checas came, bringing their most important religious image and installing it in the Choquehuancas' church, but the image was homesick and vanished from the church, turning up back home. The Checas fetched it again but it returned, three times. Finally, stained with tears of blood, the image was permanently lodged in a chapel halfway between the communities. Cook identified the names Checa and Choquehuancas in seventeenth-century parish registers as prominent families in Yanque's two moieties. The lower moiety, that of the Checas, was apparently resettled to Yanque from a spot some distance away, where it still has land today. This story, as Cook points out, encodes a memory of loss, and a successful act of state coercion.[55]

Millerea

One of the richest sources for Andean history is litigation. Native communities regularly filed suits in colonial courts, and there are thousands of files from such lawsuits in Spanish and South American archives. Since the General Resettlement affected land access, later land disputes occasionally include information about the campaign. A major source of contention was the rights of mitimas: Toledo's inspectors sometimes sent them home, sometimes forced them to integrate into the local community, and sometimes allowed them to remain in their current liminal status, even when that undermined the reducción system.

A lawsuit in the Bolivian national archives documents the confusion of one of Toledo's inspectors in dealing with mitimas. In this case the inspector initially ordered them to return to their ancestral home. But their cacique complained that this would mean losing the mitimas' lands. So the inspector relented and allowed them to remain, on the condition that they live and go to church in the nearest newly founded reducción, where he assigned them their own block of houses.[56]

Another lawsuit treats the problem of mitimas in a more extended way. It illustrates the ambiguities of the way Spanish bureaucrats dealt with Andean social geography, which in this case allowed the status quo to continue—even if against the officials' own better judgment.[57] The story begins before the Spanish conquest. The Incas founded a settlement called Millerea, on the shore of Lake Titicaca, where artisans made pots, cloth, and ritual feather garments for the state. The colony had one thousand families from ten communities, seven of them in a neighboring region.[58] The Incas gave the mitimas extensive lands, which represented a loss to the local caciques since the colonists remained members of their home communities.

At the time of the Spanish conquest, a witness later testified, an Inca official passed through Millerea and told the colonists: "brothers, the time of the Inca is over and you may each return to your own land."[59] The mitimas followed his advice and the village was abandoned. But at some point during the 1550s or 1560s a few of them came back, and again began making pots from the local clay deposits. They claimed to be working to help their home communities pay their tribute; the local caciques, however, accused them of coming for no other reason than to escape Spanish priests, get drunk, and worship idols.[60]

This was the situation when Toledo's inspectors came through in 1572. Millerea fell in the jurisdiction of one inspector, while the mitimas' home region, now within the province of Omasuyo, belonged to a different one. In a move that hardly seems in the spirit of the Resettlement campaign, the mitimas approached each inspector separately and managed to get houses assigned to them in both the nearby reducción of Guancané and in the distant reducciones in their home communities, allowing them the freedom to move back and forth. Yet the mitimas neglected to take up residency in either town, and instead stayed right where they were in Millerea—a hamlet that according to the Resettlement program was no longer supposed to exist. The outcome was thus an unplanned ratification of the status quo, in complete defiance of the new system of reducciones.

It led to decades of litigation, because the local caciques in Guancané wanted the mitimas' land. They argued before a series of Spanish judges that the Incas had tyrannically seized Guancané land to create Millerea: Spanish justice should reverse that tyranny once and for all and send the mitimas home. But a succession of judges rejected these arguments, upholding the rights of the mitimas to stay where they were, as long as they were rooted in a reducción. They tried a series of solutions: ordering the mitimas to live part of each year in their Omasuyo reducciones, or to live in Guancané and commute three days a week to Millerea. But without dismantling the Millerea settlement, these halfway measures had little chance of success. Caciques in Guancané continued to complain that the mitimas were living in muddy Millerea, drinking chicha and making pots, in happy ignorance of both divine law and human civilization. The upshot of the litigation was to preserve the status quo and the system of mitima enclaves, at the expense of the Resettlement regime.

The Millerea lawsuit offers a firsthand view of Toledo's inspectors organizing reducciones from the perspective of some native people they intended to settle there. It makes clear that the inspectors of these two provinces did indeed preside over laying out reducciones and decided who would live where. On the other hand, it portrays the General Resettlement as just one episode in a longer narrative of upheaval, a series of forced and spontaneous migrations. The Resettlement campaign made demands on the potters of Millerea that were real, but negotiable; it changed the pre-existing pattern of settlement and mobility, but did not sweep it entirely away.

Toledo Goes Home

Toledo returned to Lima in November 1575, five years after he had left. From that point on he directed his attention to subjects such as regulations for the city of Lima and political infighting. He waged bitter power struggles with institutions he himself had brought to Peru, including the Jesuits and the Inquisition. Then, in 1578 the English pirate Francis Drake attacked Lima's port and withdrew in a watery trail of destruction. Toledo came up with some creative approaches to the problem: he recruited another Englishman, a pirate already languishing in the Inquisition jail, to direct the manufacture of cannons, and he drafted Andeans from the highlands to come and help build them. He sent Pedro Sarmiento de Gamboa by ship south to the Straits of Magellan to intercept Drake, who he believed would return by that route for a second attack. Drake, however, returned to England and Sarmiento continued on to Spain. (Sarmiento did catch up with an English pirate eventually, being captured at sea by Sir Walter Raleigh in 1586 and held prisoner in England for a year, but he never realized his literary ambitions: King Philip filed his Inca history in the royal archives, and it was not published until 1906.) Beset by pirates and Jesuits, Toledo had no more time for either Inca history or Andean resettlement.[61]

He grew disillusioned. For someone so domineering, Viceroy Toledo was surprisingly eager to give up power: soon after his arrival in Peru he had begun asking Philip to bring him back to Spain. He faced more challenges than he expected; he responded furiously to them, but his unpopularity depressed him. His health declined sharply, and in 1578 he sent the king sworn statements attesting to his gout and to symptoms that sound like malaria. This may have begun during his visit to the eastern Bolivian jungle in 1574, when his military campaign against the Chiriguano Indians ended in a humiliating defeat, and his underlings carried the sick viceroy back up the mountains in a basket, while his Chiriguano opponents shouted after him that he was "an old woman." In any case he had always understood his administration as a drastic but temporary intervention to fix a broken colony. He yearned to return to Spain as, at long last, comendador mayor of the Order of Alcántara.[62]

But his reputation at court was now reaching its nadir. Cardinal Espinosa had died in 1572. In 1578 the Council of the Indies sent the king a list of Toledo's major and minor failures, and the king requested suggestions for possible successors; in 1580 Philip appointed don Martín Enríquez de

Almansa to replace him. Toledo left Lima even before Enríquez arrived, in order to catch the next fleet leaving for Spain. In court, his debriefing was brief. The king did not appoint Toledo comendador mayor or, indeed, give him any significant reward, as previous governors had received. Toledo returned home to one of the family estates and died soon after. Some later writers claimed that Philip was offended because Toledo, a mere viceroy, put to death Tupac Amaru, a king like Philip himself. This story is likely apocryphal. But don Francisco de Toledo, student and connoisseur of tyranny, had a way of making himself disliked.[63]

Indian Resettlement in the Rest of the Viceroyalty of Peru

The General Resettlement of Indians, as organized and led by Viceroy Toledo, was mainly limited to the Audiencias of Lima and Charcas. It had some impact in the Audiencia of Quito, but that impact is not clearly visible in the record. There had been earlier resettlement efforts there: for part of the 1560s it was under the authority of a royal inspector named Salazar de Villasante who claimed to have personally laid out two reducciones near the city of Quito, with 400 and 500 households respectively, which he named after himself and the viceroy. They were characterized by so much policía, he boasted, that Indians in other areas voluntarily imitated his model. He asserted that the towns not only civilized the local people and provided eggs and garden vegetables for Quito, but also offered the Spanish a destination for holiday tourism: "The locations are so pleasant [frescos] that the people of the city go with their wives on holidays to have dinner or lunch."[64]

The Audiencia of Quito traditionally exercised a significant degree of autonomy from the viceroy. Toledo, when he began his own campaign, appointed at least five inspectors for that territory (three original ones, and two replacements), but the Quito judges sent him, for his perusal, a copy of a royal order granting them governmental as well as judicial powers, independent of the viceroy. In any case, that he appointed so few inspectors for such a large area suggests that Toledo did not expect to accomplish much there. Quito's repartimientos were not included in the final records (the tasa) of the General Inspection, at least in the surviving versions.[65]

However, we have records of resettlements by two of the inspectors Toledo appointed. Not coincidentally, they were both judges on the Quito Audiencia, and likely operated without much oversight from him; as Audiencia judges, they were expected to conduct periodic inspections of their territory in any case. One of them, the licenciado Francisco de Cárdenas, sent a representative in his place who founded reducciones in the provinces of Riobamba, Chimbo, Ambato, and Latacunga, between Quito city and the border of the Lima Audiencia. The other, Dr. Pedro de Hinojosa, founded reducciones in Otavalo.[66] At least one reducción was founded in the mid-1570s in the vicinity of Quito.[67] Perhaps in a gesture of autonomy, in 1572 the bishops of the Audiencia called for reducciones while making no reference to Toledo's campaign.[68]

We also have scattered documentation of resettlement efforts in Pasto and Popayán, border provinces between Quito and New Granada. The Audiencia of New Granada sent inspectors to resettle Indians in Popayán in the late 1560s, but they were largely unable to overcome the resistance of encomenderos. The first effective resettlements were in 1585, when the governor of the province personally carried out an inspection; documentation survives for eight reducciones in the area of Cartago, but only one of them was actually completed at the time. Overall, the Popayán reducciones of the 1580s were relatively few. Being built on steep slopes and hilltops, as Indian villages had traditionally been there, they were probably simply refoundations of existing villages.[69] From Pasto, meanwhile, we have a 1571 report from an inspector named García de Valverde. Sent to carry out resettlement, he did little: most people already lived in concentrated villages, he reported, so out of the seventy villages he visited he relocated only fifteen.[70]

The archbishop of Bogotá in New Granada, fray Luis Zapata de Cárdenas, had been in Peru during the General Resettlement and was impressed by Toledo's work; in early 1575 he called a meeting in Bogotá with Audiencia judges and others to discuss a plan for Indian resettlement.[71] It is not clear what immediate effect that had, but we have a report from 1599 in which an inspector founded the reducción of Guachetá in the province of Santa Fe, specifying the size of the plaza, the width of the streets, and the residences of the Indian authorities in it. The town was composed of several caciques and their subjects; each cacique maintained his authority over his own subjects in the town.[72] Another report, from 1586, documents a Spanish judge founding a town for people of the Muchuchiz ethnic group, who were divided among three repartimientos; it was still populated in 1602, but had to be laid out again in 1619.[73] The process was intermittent.

In the territories south and east of Charcas—Chile, Tucumán, and Santa Cruz—colonial settlement and control was still in its early stages. Chile, at the southern tip of the viceroyalty, was a place of chronic war between Spaniards and Araucanian Indians since its founding; royal control over even colonized Indian communities was tenuous. There was a resettlement campaign there following the General Resettlement, and modeled on it, but it apparently had little success.[74] Scholars who have studied Indian reducciones in those territories have focused primarily on their later history, with little information about the circumstances of their founding; this reflects the limitations of the available evidence.[75]

The creation of reducciones in other parts of the viceroyalty of Peru was influenced by the General Resettlement of Indians, but was largely independent of it. Much of the work was carried out after the General Resettlement, just as similar projects of resettlement and re-resettlement continued place in Peru and throughout Spanish America through the following centuries.

Toledo's inspectors began the process of resettlement but did not complete it. Evidence survives from many places of inspectors situating reducciones, naming them, presiding over laying out streets, even assigning house lots to families. Some inspectors did only that, no doubt, or less. Others supervised the building of a church, cabildo, and houses. But only the most conscientious inspectors stayed to confirm that people actually moved into their new houses. There is one thing that virtually no documents mention the inspectors doing: destroying the old villages, as Toledo ordered.[76]

It was not in the inspectors' interest to intervene too aggressively in Andean settlement patterns. For the long term, they wanted to maximize tribute, and therefore had a stake in communities' economic viability. Even for the short term, being aggressive about resettlement offered the inspector more cost than benefit. He had limited time, money, and influence for persuading Spanish and Andean authorities to help with his various projects, of which others were more important to his success as an inspector. It was absolutely necessary to present Toledo a completed census, and judicial work provided a payoff in fines and fees, but the time spent on founding reducciones offered no immediate reward. Although universal forced re-settlement might seem, to a modern observer, to be among the most important of Toledo's projects—indeed, it seemed that way to Toledo as well—the incentive structure he set up for the General Inspection left it for last.

Some inspectors later wrote about what they had accomplished in the General Resettlement, especially those who later served as corregidores of the territories they had inspected. In a letter to the king in 1575, Juan Maldonado Buendía bragged about his success in consolidating 226 hamlets into twenty-two reducciones in the province of Colesuyo.[77] In the 1580s Pedro Mercado de Peñalosa, inspector and later corregidor of Pacajes, included some information about the Resettlement in a report on his province, submitted in reply to a government questionnaire.[78] What is surprising, however, is how little many of the inspectors had to say about their work. In later years some of them submitted *probanzas de méritos*, testimonial records which elite Spaniards routinely submitted to the Crown, detailing their past services, in hopes of reward. While describing in loving detail the supplicants' military service to the king, most of their probanzas either ignored their role in the General Resettlement entirely, or mentioned it only in passing. These inspectors, apparently, did not consider their work in the General Resettlement something to boast about.[79] Unlike the corregidores Maldonado Buendía and Mercado de Peñalosa, who had the opportunity to oversee the later development of the reducciones, most inspectors probably finished the inspection before the process of actual resettlement had gone far.

Building the reducciones was a slow process. In a lawsuit from 1586, a cacique in the region of Cochabamba described a site, designated by the inspector for a reducción, on which only two or three houses had so far been built.[80] A priest complained in 1588 that "many of the towns have yet to be resettled, and many churches are yet to be built."[81] In 1600 an official of the Franciscan order wrote that in one reducción, which had been founded in a good site outside of Lima, "some houses [were] finished, others half-built, and others just begun," while Andeans continued to live "in the old hamlets and gullies, in clusters of houses (*caseríos*) so wretched that it [was] impossible to enter them."[82]

But the powerful figures of Andean society—caciques, Spanish priests, and corregidores—had incentives to continue settling the reducciones. The priests, naturally, wanted to keep their flocks where they could see them, and the corregidores wanted to know where tribute-payers could be found. The caciques had an interest in having a physical point at which to channel the flow of tribute up from the local people and to channel state authority down upon them. Still, no one had any interest in imprisoning Andeans in the reducciones. Access to land and flocks was essential to the community. The caciques, furthermore, wanted to be able to move people in and out, in order to keep the exact number of their subjects secret if possible. And it was wise for the corregidores to give Andeans some latitude in managing their own lives and communities, as Toledo and his advisors understood. Even priests may have been willing to accord Andeans some privacy. Constant confrontation was exhausting for any priest: if Andeans had spaces outside the reducción for agricultural rituals the Spanish defined as idolatrous, it would be easier for them to follow the priest's guidance while inside it.

Over time, most of the reducciones became established. During their early years, some reducciones became the only or primary homes of their designated residents, while others functioned more as administrative and religious centers than as demographic ones. Regardless of how much of it Toledo's inspectors personally oversaw, the reducciones were remembered as his creation, which obscures their slow growth and the patterns of population movement that characterized Andean society before, during, and after Toledo's campaign. The creation of the reducciones was gradual, ebbing and flowing, never complete.

PART III **AFTER**

9

IN AND OUT OF THE REDUCCIONES

Over time, the reducciones took root. But what struck many observers at the time was their failure. In *El primer nueva corónica y buen gobierno*, "The First New Chronicle and Good Government," a study of Andeans' history and current state written four decades after the General Resettlement, don Felipe Guaman Poma de Ayala described the reducciones as places of corruption, abuse, and flight. Addressing himself rhetorically to King Philip III, he asked: "How could your majesty expect Indians not to leave?"[1]

The *Nueva corónica*, completed in 1615 or 1616, is the most extraordinary document of colonial Peru. It is a twelve-hundred-page handwritten book, richly illustrated with drawings and anecdotes. The author, Guaman Poma, was an Andean man born in central Peru into a noble but not particularly distinguished family, who possessed a basic Spanish education and a deep knowledge of his own country. He traveled, worked as an assistant to Spanish priests, and pursued long, ultimately fruitless lawsuits over land and titles that he believed were his by right. In his old age, frustrated by both Spanish and Andean authorities, Guaman Poma sat down to distill his experience into a book. He dedicated it to the king, calling on him to reform colonial rule and honor Spain's own Christian ideals. An ethnographer in the same way as Polo Ondegardo, he sought to make sense of the Andean world in Spanish terms and the Spanish world in Andean ones, on the premise that both sides would benefit from the understanding. In his travels Guaman Poma stayed in or passed through many reducciones, and his book is full of anecdotes about everyday life, conveyed in loose but vivid Spanish sprinkled with Quechua. His experience was probably limited to the area between Guamanga, Cuzco, and Lima, but records from other regions confirm his observations.[2]

Guaman Poma agreed wholeheartedly with the principle of the Resettlement, and the picture of the orderly and disciplined society that should result from it. But he was unhappy with almost every aspect of its execution. His frustration began with the reducciones' locations: "Some [were] in good places," he wrote, "some in bad places, as luck fell." He attributed the selection of sites variously to Toledo's inspectors, to local corregidores, to priests, or to Toledo himself, but he claimed that interested parties had influenced Spanish officials' decisions with bribes as high as five hundred pesos. The reducciones were often far from Andeans' fields, and located in unhealthy places. The result was disastrous: "The Indians of this kingdom are dying out . . . because they left towns in sites . . . chosen by their principales, wise men, doctors, licenciados[3] and philosophers, and approved by the first Incas, with climate, lands and water to multiply the people." They exchanged these well-chosen spots, he wrote, for places with damp and unhealthy soil, stench, and pestilence.[4]

We know from the archives that Andean residents, in the years after the Resettlement, often complained about reducciones' unhealthy locations. Occasionally they got permission to move. In 1583 a cacique complained that his people's reducción on the outskirts of La Paz was built on such a steep slope that people and livestock were falling to their death at night. The corregidor came to an agreement with the city's cabildo to give them another spot—quite a small one—on public land outside the city. But the city's attorney went to court to reverse the decision and send the Andeans back to the mountainside. He argued that the new settlement was blocking the main entrance to the city, while also making the contradictory claim that the Andeans wanted the spot for its isolation, since their real motive was to practice idolatry in secret. He succeeded in getting them turned out of their new houses and the doors locked to keep them from returning; the land was then put up for auction.[5]

Worse than the new towns' unhealthy locations, Guaman Poma made clear, was separation from the fields that people depended on for their livelihood. A corregidor in central Peru wrote in 1586: "They always complain, saying that they have their fields . . . in their old town, and that going to farm them gives them a lot of work."[6] Though communities that lost fields were supposed to receive equivalent ones near the reducciones, truly equitable land swaps were rare. Sometimes the land was claimed by Spaniards who refused to give it up; at other times the community needed its old lands to preserve the archipelago economy. Even where a trade was possible, many resisted leaving their land. A *chacara*, for Andeans, was a group of fields with a name, a history, and a host of associations; today, in some parts of the Andes, a chacara may carry the same name it had almost five hundred years ago.[7] Land was owned collectively by ayllus, but individuals might have deep ties to specific fields. For those being resettled, exchanging a field for a new and unknown one might be like trading one's own child for someone else's. Guaman Poma described families torn from their *querencia*, an evocative Spanish word meaning the home to which one longs to return.[8]

When Andeans could not or would not trade away their old fields, they continued to own them by law. But Spanish farmers everywhere saw the General Resettlement as an opportunity to expand their landholding at Andeans' expense. The cabildos of Spanish towns had the right to grant empty land to individuals, so Spaniards would identify an Andean community's field that was temporarily lying fallow and claim that it was virgin soil that had never been farmed. Andeans were not shy about fighting for their rights by hiring lawyers and going to court. One cacique from the Audiencia of Quito went to Spain and returned with an order to Spaniards who had seized part of his community's land to return it.[9] Most did not have to go that far: judges in Peru gave Andeans similar documents. But Spanish landowners hired their own lawyers. They argued that Andeans had more than enough land near their reducción, and used their distant fields for idolatry and drunkenness. If Andeans persuaded one Spanish judge, their opponents persuaded another, and—in a system of competing jurisdictions and multiple appeals—lawsuits dragged on for years.

One example from the archives, out of many, illustrates the conflict the Resettlement brought. In a warm valley in the region of Potosí, before the General Resettlement, the people of Macha farmed corn, cotton, chile peppers, and vegetables—crucial for nutrition to a people who lived largely on high-altitude potatoes and other tubers—and even had a church that a priest occasionally visited to say Mass. Toledo's inspector guaranteed their property rights, permitting them to go to the valley every October from their reducción five leagues away, living there for the time they needed for planting. In the years after the General Resettlement, a Spaniard named Alonso Díaz decided to establish a livestock ranch there. The Machas sued, with the help of the local *protector de indios*, and the two sides fought on the ground as well. Díaz, with his servants, burned the Machas' houses and beat those he found there; the Machas, in turn, attacked him in his house with knives and stones. The final outcome of the case is unclear. But it was dangerous for Andeans to defend their rights against Spaniards by force, and few were as intrepid as the Machas in doing so.[10]

In the wake of the Resettlement, Spaniards found the opportunities to seize Andean land hard to resist. Native communities often owned what seemed to be more land than they really needed, partly because they traditionally rotated fields and allowed land to lie fallow for several years between cultivation. At the same time, the population of many repartimientos had fallen, so that they did not in fact need all the land they owned. But the land was Andeans' most precious possession, and they hoped and expected to regain the population they had once had. In the meantime, they found it hard to hold onto land unless physically occupying it. Some groups adopted the strategy of farming at least a portion of each chacara all the time.[11] Others rented their land to Spanish farmers, although that, too, had a tendency to turn into permanent ownership by the renter. Still others cut their losses by selling the land outright. The colonial government had made such sales illegal without special permission, to protect the land base of a people presumed to be, like children, unable to make important decisions by themselves. But fraudulent sales were common, and Spanish buyers sometimes bribed encomenderos to facilitate them.[12]

The Andean Cabildos

If the General Resettlement came at a terrible cost in loss of homes and land, it carried the promise of strengthening the Republic of Indians through the institutions of municipal self-government. Guaman Poma cared deeply about these institutions. He devoted a section of his book to describing the reducciones' indigenous officials, drawing each one in a full-length portrait with his appropriate clothing: alcalde, regidor, alguacil, notary, and town crier (*pregonero*), as well as parallel officials for the parish church.[13] Guaman Poma told a story about the bumps on the road to establishing the cabildo as an institution. He wrote that the men who became the first alcaldes were young and inexperienced, while mature and respected men became town

Figure 9-1 The alcalde. Guaman Poma, *El primer nueva corónica y buen gobierno*, 808. Courtesy of the Royal Library, Copenhagen, Denmark

Figure 9-3 The notary. Guaman Poma, *El primer nueva corónica y buen gobierno*, 828. Courtesy of the Royal Library, Copenhagen, Denmark

Figure 9-2 The regidor. Guaman Poma, *El primer nueva corónica y buen gobierno*, 814. Courtesy of the Royal Library, Copenhagen, Denmark

criers, whose job included carrying out punishments at the picota in the plaza. But the alcaldes soon proved so incompetent that the older men, although they occupied a lower position in the hierarchy, mocked and then whipped them. The Spanish inspectors who chose the first alcaldes apparently made poor choices, but the indigenous system of authority within the communities was able to adjust for mistakes, making the cabildo viable.[14]

How did the new cabildos take root in indigenous society? The office of alcalde was essentially a judicial one, but we have little evidence of the judicial functions of alcaldes in Andean towns. Virtually no such internal records have survived from colonial indigenous communities in the Andes (in contrast to Mesoamerica, where Indian municipalities kept abundant records in native languages written in the Roman alphabet). Their judicial proceedings were seldom committed to writing. One case that survives from the Cochabamba valley shows that at least in some places the alcalde-based judicial system functioned as the viceroy had intended. Early in 1580 a man affiliated with another reducción appeared before the alcalde of Sipesipe, to complain about a Sipesipe man. Sixteen llamas had been stolen from the complainant, Martin Pongo, while he was traveling; a few months later Pongo identified three of the llamas in the possession of one Esteban Calla. Calla responded that he had bought the animals in good faith from some Andeans from the north. The Sipesipe alcalde, don Martin Poma, ordered the three llamas in the defendant's possession restored to Pongo at once, but gave Calla one year to try to find the people he claimed to have bought them from. The alcalde was not literate enough to sign his name. But he rendered a judgment that gave something to both sides, and was willing to rule in favor of a member of another jurisdiction against a member of his own. In some places, at least, the Hispanic office of alcalde functioned exactly as it was supposed to.[15]

But Andean cabildos appear less often in colonial censuses and litigation than caciques and principales. In one case from 1617, a cacique spoke for the community, while an alcalde appeared as his Spanish translator.[16] It was the repartimiento and its component ayllus, not the reducción, that owned land, paid tribute, and provided laborers for the mita. The low profile of cabildos is not just the bias of the Spanish archives: even Guaman Poma, writing from within Andean society, wrote more often about caciques and principales than alcaldes and regidores.[17]

Corruption

Justice and good government were Guaman Poma's paramount concerns. The reducciones were good communities when they functioned as intended, he believed, but they seldom did. In his anecdotes of reducción life, the keynote is corruption, of Spaniards and Andeans alike. The corregidores seized all opportunities for bribery and extortion. Guaman Poma described a corregidor who had an alcalde beaten because two eggs were missing from the food allowance he had demanded. The corregidores did not really want the cabildos to function as they were supposed to; above all they feared Andean officials' right, and responsibility, to work within the system for better treatment. The example of corruption was set from the top; everyone else followed suit.[18]

Worst of all was the corruption of the Spanish priests. A devout Christian, Guaman Poma reserved his bitterest words for them because he expected the most from them: time and again he returned to their avarice, wrath, and lust. They gambled and dueled, extorted gifts from their parishioners, and even falsified Andeans' wills to get their property. Toledo had told priests to educate Andean boys in their homes; the priests instead took young women, ostensibly for Christian training, in fact to form a captive workforce and a harem of concubines. Some women they kept to scratch their bellies, Guaman Poma wrote, and others to rub them. The priests' women bore them an ever-growing multitude of illegitimate children.[19]

The priests managed to pervert even the municipal rituals of the reducciones, which Guaman Poma prized. The alguaciles were supposed to make their rounds through the streets at night to make sure nothing untoward was happening. But priests would take this duty on themselves, enter women's houses, and pull off their blankets to gaze at their "shameful parts." They manipulated the election of Andean officials, elevating their concubines' fathers and brothers, and said that being a priest's mistress was more honorable than being the legitimate wife of an Andean man. The priests' sexual abuse of native women epitomized everything that was wrong with the reducciones.[20]

Guaman Poma noted that a corrupt priest's worst fear, like the corregidor's, was that Andean town self-government would function well enough to register complaints against him. If Andeans complained, he would take revenge by ordering them to say all the prayers and whipping them if they made a single mistake. Or he would falsely accuse them of idolatry, a se-

Figure 9-4 Spanish corregidor punishing an Andean petitioner. Guaman Poma, *El primer nueva corónica y buen gobierno*, 498. Courtesy of the Royal Library, Copenhagen, Denmark

rious charge that effectively trumped their complaints against him. (The record shows reducción priests doing just that; paradoxically, one of our best records of Andean mythology resulted from a reducción priest's effort to counter his parishioners' complaint against his corruption by documenting their "idolatry."[21]) The priests' fear of justice led them to betray what for Guaman Poma was one of the great promises of the reducciones: education. Bad priests didn't want Andeans to learn to speak or read Spanish; one priest favored a schoolmaster who collected a salary of eighty pesos plus board while refusing to do any teaching. Another priest, arriving at his new parish, asked to see the legal papers preserved in the reducción; seeing their quantity, he quit the job on the spot.[22]

Corrupt priests were right to fear the consequences of Andean literacy: numerous surviving Andean complaints confirm Guaman Poma's reports. Among many other examples, caciques of Chucuito province sent a detailed complaint to the Charcas Audiencia in 1592, listing nearly every one of the

Figure 9-5 Spanish priest forcing an Andean woman to labor for him. Guaman Poma, *El primer nueva corónica y buen gobierno*, 659. Courtesy of the Royal Library, Copenhagen, Denmark

problems that Guaman Poma identified. "It is a shame to see the way he lives," the petitioners wrote of one priest. But it is not clear that the petition had any result, although someone at the Audiencia notated in the margin that the bishop should be informed.[23]

Spaniards had no monopoly on corruption: the ranks of the caciques and cabildos had more than their share of scoundrels. Many of the caciques, indeed, were false ones, commoners whom a priest or corregidor had managed to install as caciques, and their behavior reflected their origins. Guaman Poma recalled one cacique who had previously made his living as a highway robber in Chile. The alcaldes followed the priests' example in keeping young women as servants and mistresses. Another reducción official, Guaman Poma recalled, seized a lamb from a girl who was bringing it to pay for a mass for her deceased father. Even ordinary Andeans, so often the victims of abuse, were not always innocent. Taking their example from the worst of the Spanish, Guaman Poma wrote, many Andeans had become avaricious, lazy, violent, and treacherous. The problem was not the corruption of any one class, but of the whole society.[24]

For Guaman Poma, the reducciones should have allowed Andean society to flourish on its own, protected from bad outside influences, and drawing the best from both Spanish and indigenous cultures. Although he did not use the term, he embraced the idea of the "two republics": for him Spaniards and Andeans formed two nations, under the same king and church but with separate leaders and customs, separate histories and traditions. Guaman Poma praised Toledo's order banning any non-Andean, except the priest, from the reducciones: Spaniards, Africans, mulattos, and even mestizos were forbidden to live there, though they could stay briefly while traveling through. The Republic of Indians could function properly only if its leaders, both caciques and alcaldes, were legitimate and honored. But he complained that Spanish officials undercut caciques' authority by alternately abusing Andean commoners and promoting them over the heads of their rightful lords, the caciques. Various non-Andeans found their way into the lives of the reducciones, with mestizos assuming the offices of alcalde and even cacique.[25]

Guaman Poma described complex factional battles in the reducciones, with ill-intentioned Andeans and Spaniards making common cause against the innocent. One priest managed to elevate the father of his Andean mistress to both cacique and alcalde—two offices Toledo commanded never to be held by the same person—turning a blind eye to the man's cruelty and debauchery. One day the cacique-alcalde, don Hernando, went too far: in a fit of rage against an Andean woman who had offended him, he beat her to death. The Spanish corregidor commissioned an Andean official to prosecute don Hernando, having him whipped and expelled, but the priest was able to have the corregidor's Andean representative fired and punished. Don Hernando was out of the picture, but the priest had no shortage of corrupt allies to take his place.[26]

Guaman Poma recounted episodes of ill treatment, both serious and petty, which had affected him. In 1608 he was visiting the reducción of Llallcaya. He had with him a jar of orange-flavored butter or lard (manteca de agua de azahar)—his ideal of separateness did not extend to forgoing the luxuries of colonial life—and he asked don Pedro Taypi Marca, a principal in the town, to store it for him. Taypi Marca agreed, but then turned around and presented it to the corregidor as a gift from himself, to Guaman Poma's fury. The anecdote points to several aspects of life in one reducción. Llallcaya was not an isolated, self-contained town but one where visitors came and went and Spanish and Andean authorities interacted with one another informally as well as formally. It was natural for Guaman Poma, as an elite Andean staying there temporarily, to establish a friendly relationship with Llallcaya's native authorities. But Taypi Marca did not hesitate to betray the trust of a fellow Andean noble in order to curry favor with the Spanish.[27]

The reducciones even failed to promote Christianity among the Andeans, in Guaman Poma's view. The priests, while wielding the threat of denunciation against their parishioners, in general turned a blind eye to idolatry out of laziness. Caciques used church holidays as cover for resuming pre-Christian rites, with drinking, dances, and idol worship in the very plaza of the reducción. Far from stopping this, one priest invited young women to do their pagan dances in his own home, and actively encouraged drunkenness, believing that by indulging them he benefited himself: his parishioners would not hold him to a higher standard than he held them. Many a Spaniard, in fact, enjoyed Andeans' idolatrous dances for his own entertainment: Guaman Poma told of an encomendero who encouraged the tributaries to welcome him into their pueblos with singing and dancing, carrying him in on a litter as if he were an Inca king. Pagan rituals flourished in the reducciones, ostensibly the centers of Christian evangelization.[28]

Flight

The biggest problem, for the long-term survival of the reducciones, was that much of their population was simply not in them. There were many reasons for being away from one's reducción: some people escaped, some were forced out, and some were absent for perfectly legitimate reasons. Andeans had the right to farm distant fields that their community still possessed, although priests sometimes tried to stop them or demanded a bribe to allow it. As for leaving the reducción to perform the mita in Spanish cities, tambos, or mines—the poisonous mercury mines of Huancavelica or the oppressive silver mines of Potosí—they had no choice.[29]

Typically the whole family went to the site of mita service, the men doing the service itself and women and children working in the market or elsewhere to support the family. One abuse of which Guaman Poma complained was when a Spanish priest forced the wives and children of departing men (whether they were going to the mita or to distant fields) to remain at home, ostensibly to preserve the integrity of the reducción, but actually so that he could install them in his own house and make his own use of them. When all the family members did leave together, their neighbors sometimes took advantage of their absence to enter their home and steal their property. The mita was supposed to draw a small part of the community for a portion of each year, but many (especially those who served in the mines) never returned: having finished their service they put their experience to work for a higher wage as free laborers, while at home their fields had been neglected and their property despoiled. Guaman Poma wanted safeguards for those traveling outside the reducción, not only as a matter of justice but also for the survival of the community.[30]

Given the corruption and abuse in the reducciones, Guaman Poma sympathized with many who left. Others, though, abandoned their reducciones to live as vagabonds and thieves, and Guaman Poma called on the authorities to force them to return. Spanish law theoretically allowed the king's subjects to travel freely, but Guaman Poma endorsed Toledo's restrictions on the free movement of Andean tributaries. Indeed, Guaman Poma would have liked to apply the same restrictions to swaggering Spaniards who wandered the countryside. The Incas, he wrote, had required travelers to obtain permits and to wear special badges on their chest; Toledo's rules were in the same spirit, and Guaman Poma praised Toledo for restoring the Inca system. Mobility was fundamental to Andean society and economy, but Guaman Poma believed it should be tightly controlled.[31]

Sometimes priests or caciques colluded in Andeans' absence from the reducciones. One priest closed the church and told his parishioners to leave the reducción—many were all too happy to do so—so that a visiting church inspector would find no one to question about his behavior.[32] Caciques, meanwhile, kept some of their subjects outside their reducciones. A Spaniard writing in 1589 described caciques keeping women in the prereducción hamlets and off the tribute rolls, to make maize beer for them. This was a return to a prehispanic model of leadership, where Inca kings and Andean lords controlled the labor of unmarried women to produce maize beer and cloth, which they then distributed to their followers in a display of ritual generosity. Most perversely, the priests who drafted women's labor for their own purposes in a sense cast themselves as prehispanic lords as well.[33]

Keeping people hidden allowed caciques to minimize the community's tribute quota. Toledo had authorized certain Spaniards to seize nonenrolled Andeans as their own laborers or servants, or yanaconas. But Spaniards sometimes kidnapped orphans or other unprotected villagers instead. Guaman Poma was outraged at the way Toledo's orders were abused to force the king's Andean subjects, including those who were temporarily and legitimately absent from their reducción, into virtual slavery. We know of Spaniards in the 1580s and 1590s forcing Andeans into service on haciendas, claiming (sometimes falsely) that they were not enrolled in a reducción.[34] Living or even traveling outside the reducciones could be dangerous: an Andean could never take his or her freedom for granted. Between all these factors, Guaman Poma complained, the reducciones were fast emptying out.[35]

While he wanted to protect Andeans outside the reducciones from being seized by Spaniards, Guaman Poma was committed to repopulating the towns, by force if necessary. Referring to one reducción whose tribute-paying population had dropped to fewer than fifteen households, he recommended paying non-Andeans one peso a head to bring them back by coercion. Some Spanish officials had made efforts to force people to return to their reducciones, and Guaman Poma praised Viceroy don Fernando de Torres y Portugal (1585–1590) for this. On the other hand, he perceived that some campaigns were counterproductive, cruel, and dangerous. He mentioned an official appointed in 1609 to bring the Andeans of one region back to their reducciones, who burned the homes where they were currently living—something that Toledo's own inspectors seem to have done seldom. In this case, Guaman Poma observed, Andeans were thriving and multiplying outside the reducciones; when they were forced back, they began to die.[36]

As an alternative to forcing everyone into the reducciones, Guaman Poma advocated a policy that many colonial officials came to accept: permitting the existence of annex villages (anejos) outside the reducción but in its orbit. The practice, which was the norm in Mexico, had begun in the General Resettlement itself, where inspectors sometimes founded smaller reducciones as lesser dependencies of larger ones, called cabeceras. Likewise, after the Resettlement, many people settled in villages half a day's or a day's walk from the reducción where they were enrolled, near herds or fields the community owned, and away from the worst abuses. These villages might be reconstituted pre-Resettlement hamlets, or newly founded ones. But if their residents continued to answer to their cacique and pay tribute, the Spanish should acknowledge their settlements as legitimate annexes, Guaman Poma believed. It was foolish for Spanish authorities to run the risk of chasing them away entirely by closing down their villages.[37]

Guaman Poma argued that priests should travel among the annexes, saying Mass in each one. But priests often resisted doing so. In 1582 the people living in an annex of Huarochirí said they were willing to return to the reducción church on Sundays and holidays, but asked to be excused from attendance on Wednesdays and Fridays (days the priest demanded their presence). The archbishop of Lima supported their request, but the priest opposed it stubbornly. By 1616 they had built their own chapel, with an image of Saint Francis, to bolster their claim that they were not trying to avoid Christian worship, but the reducción priest confiscated the statue.[38] Guaman Poma recognized that priests such as this were undermining the reducción system rather than strengthening it.

Guaman Poma was not the only one to consider the General Resettlement a failure: a number of Spanish officials made the same judgment. Some complained about how Toledo had carried out the campaign. His successor, Martín Enríquez de Almansa, described widespread unhappiness among relocated Andeans and wrote that "it could not be otherwise, given that the affair was so hurried," while the president of the Audiencia of Charcas wrote that Toledo had only begun the job.[39] In the mid-1580s, several corregidores in the Audiencias of Lima and Charcas described the reducciones as largely empty.[40] The official historian of the Spanish court believed that even those who were living in the reducciones were there against their will.[41] In 1604 the viceroy then in office offered a particularly harsh appraisal: "The reducciones that señor don Francisco de Toledo made are somewhat ruined, in the upper provinces, on account of many Indians dying and others who have fled in order to avoid the mitas . . . and [on account of] the vexations and bad treatment they receive from their corregidores and Christian ministers . . . and from the caciques, who are those who treat them the worst."[42] Everyone with any authority in the reducciones, it seems, was mistreating the villagers and driving them away. Many opted out of the new order, voting with their feet against the Resettlement.

10

—

FOUR HUNDRED YEARS

The reducciones survived—many or most are standing to-day—but they were at no point the only places where in-digenous Andeans lived. Settlement patterns varied greatly between periods and regions, and the historical data are spotty: "In some cases," or variations on the phrase, will ap-pear frequently in this chapter. Throughout colonial history, most Andeans were affiliated with a particular reducción. This might house a majority of the affiliated population, it might be all but empty, or it might acquire a population of Spaniards and mestizos along with Andean residents. The reducciones, whatever their population, contained the par-ish churches, the cabildos, and the homes of the caciques. Many of those who lived outside came in for occasions such as church festivals and the installation of the new year's ca-bildo, sleeping in houses that stood empty most of the year. In such cases the reducción could be called a ritual center, like the Incas' stone complexes. Whether full or empty, the reducciones exercised authority over most of the surround-ing rural population. The General Resettlement, one scholar has written, gave "a definitive form to the political and ad-ministrative structure of the Indian communities"—the political framework in which the history of the Republic of Indians unfolded over the next four hundred years.[1]

A major problem Andean communities faced was holding onto land and people at a distance from the reducciones. Co-lonial pressures worked to break up the vertical archipelago, through the usurpation of Spanish haciendas as well as by lawsuits and rivalries among Andeans themselves. But Andean communities fought hard and often successfully to hold onto their lands, both near and far. The General Resettlement itself laid some groundwork for this. It was the beginning of what scholars call the "colonial pact": the unstated agreement that the indigenous population would provide tribute and labor in exchange for some amount of land and autonomy. The pact enabled the vertical archipelago to survive here and there, especially in the regions south of Cuzco: communities continued to control distant landholdings and settlement enclaves, and people moved back and forth between them. The survival of the archipelago depended partly on the acquiescence of the Spanish authorities, partly on Andeans' own determination.[2]

Staying or Leaving

Most reducciones were fully populated immediately after the General Resettlement, but two decades or so later, officials began to complain that their inhabitants were returning to their previous homes or simply moving away, just as Guaman Poma said.[3] Many did not cut ties: Whether they lived an hour, a day, or several days' journey from the reducción, they remained comuneros, full members of the community with its rights and duties, including tribute and mita labor. Others, however, opted out of both the rights and responsibilities of membership and became forasteros, living as permanent outsiders in other Andean communities, or yanaconas, dependent laborers in Spanish haciendas or small-manufacturing workshops. Indeed, the fact that seventeenth-century censuses recorded continuous population decline was in part because many Andeans evaded censuses by staying away from the reducciones. By the late seventeenth century, in some regions these groups amounted to more than half of the native population.[4]

There were solid reasons to trade the status of comunero for that of forastero. For many, as Guaman Poma made clear, the burdens of tribute and mita simply outweighed the benefits of land and kinship networks. Natural disasters added to colonial demands, driving desperate people to seek survival where they could. The quarter century immediately following the General Resettlement was an unusually bad period of epidemics (made worse by concentrating people in reducciones), poor harvests, famine, El Niño floods, and two major volcano eruptions.[5] At the same time, Andeans left home for the same reasons as people everywhere: to marry, to escape trouble or the law, to seek opportunity or adventure. The more people left, the greater the burden on those who remained, who were forced to divide fixed tribute and labor quotas among a dwindling population, creating a vicious cycle of desperation and flight. Repartimientos fell into arrears with their tribute, and corregidores sometimes jailed caciques to try to extract from them what they could not pay. Flight from reducciones was most common where the colonial burdens were heaviest, and especially in the provinces from which the Potosí mita was drawn (primarily the highland provinces from Cuzco south), where the reducciones lost 60 percent of their population in the seventeenth century.[6] New censuses, carried out piecemeal as the situation in one repartimiento or another became critical, lowered quotas to reflect the falling population, but the remedy lagged behind the problem.

But leaving one community seldom led to full integration into another. Forasteros who married into a community usually lost rights to land in their old home without gaining them in the new one; instead, they lived as renters or paid laborers for the comuneros, often bequeathing their marginal status to their children and grandchildren. These people were free from most community obligations and often invisible to census takers and tribute collectors—Spanish officials struggled, with intermittent success, to track and tax them—but their status was precarious. Over the course of generations, forasteros achieved intermediate degrees of community membership, but new forasteros arrived faster than the old ones assimilated. The Republic of Indians became two tiered, with a nucleus of comuneros (themselves often living outside the reducción, but tied to it) inexorably shedding population into a periphery of forasteros.[7]

Other forasteros worked for wages in Spanish cities such as Lima, Quito, Arequipa, and La Paz, or mining towns such as Huancavelica, Oruro, and above all Potosí, the largest center of colonial mining, and for a while one of the world's largest and richest cities. In these places many Andeans already served Spanish masters as mitayos; others were there to earn money toward their home communities' tribute payments. When mitayo families completed their terms of service, they had a choice between returning home and continuing to pay tribute or staying where they were and selling their experience and skills on the labor market; many chose the latter.[8]

Yanaconas, unlike forasteros, were not free agents. They were bound laborers for Spanish enterprises: commercial farms, ranches, or workshops called *obrajes*, which produced cloth or other products. In areas of fertile land, commercial farms (called by the Quechua word *chacaras* or, later, haciendas) encroached on more and more of the Andeans' lands, through legal maneuvers or by force; by the eighteenth century they were crowding the free communities into marginal land, especially in what is now southern Ecuador and northern Peru. As with forasteros, Spanish officials went to great trouble to track and tax yanaconas; typically, their Spanish employers paid some quantity of tribute on their behalf.[9] The laborers were organized into corporate communities, as in the reducciones, and even had a limited degree of self-government, but they were considerably less free than either comuneros or forasteros. Some Andeans were coerced into indentured labor, but others may have chosen the relative security it offered over the open-ended demands placed on comuneros and the uncertain life of forasteros. Ann Wightman interprets flight from the reducciones as resistance to colonialism, the refusal to participate in an oppressive system. The bitter irony was that many migrants escaped mita and tribute only to ensnare themselves in the peonage of the haciendas, or the poverty of a rootless underclass. But to many, the reducciones represented little more than exploitation. Their residents preferred to live, in a literal sense, off the grid.[10]

Another refuge for those who left reducciones was the jungle of the upper Amazon, a region close to Andean population centers but outside Spanish control. Colonial administrators believed this was a major problem, but little direct evidence of it has come to scholars' attention. The alienation and hostility highland Andeans felt for Amazonian Indians, whom they perceived as savage and dangerous—of whom some groups, indeed, raided Andean communities in the colonial period—made this an unlikely destination for large numbers. But it likely attracted some for whom other options were even less appealing.[11]

A major theme of official discourse in seventeenth-century Peru, which Karen Spalding calls "a leitmotiv of official correspondence," was the need for a new resettlement campaign to restore Toledo's reducciones to full strength.[12] Beginning with a 1604 treatise by the friar Miguel de Monsalve entitled "Universal Resettlement of All Peru," royal advisors searched for solutions.[13] Numerous local campaigns were launched to force Andean people back to the reducciones, whether at the initiative of a regional inspector, a local corregidor, or a cacique, as well as larger campaigns in 1598, 1613, and 1622. Each was effective for a while, until the reducciones' residents migrated away once more. Among the officials, a sense of futility gradually settled in.[14]

A problem with the project of restoring the reducciones' population was that it conflicted with the interests of powerful Spaniards: many of the Andeans whom officials and caciques wanted to bring back were either yanaconas or wage laborers for Spanish employers—some of whom were themselves priests or corregidores.[15] The archbishop of Lima complained to the king in 1626 that colonists who employed Andeans would file legal appeals alleging reasons not to carry out resettlement, resulting in judicial orders to investigate the situation and take testimony, "which is the way here when one desires to do nothing."[16] The opponents of resettlement were willing to say openly that it was "a joke and served no purpose but to rob people [i.e., Spanish employers of Andean laborers] of their wealth."[17] The Spanish imperial administration was conservative, preferring to postpone decisive action in the face of conflicting claims. Seventeenth-century viceroys found their plans for aggressive and systematic resettlement campaigns blocked by royal orders.[18]

Another strategy for dealing with the reducciones' failure, as Guaman Poma suggested, was to legalize new villages and designate them as annexes of the original reducciones.[19] A writer in the Audiencia of Charcas in 1639 reported that 130 reducciones were surrounded by 470 annexes, each with fifty to one hundred families.[20] In Huarochirí, near Lima, seventeen reducciones founded in the General Resettlement had become forty-nine villages and towns by the mid-eighteenth century.[21] In some cases the reducción itself was empty, leaving only its ring of satellite villages, like a Pacific atoll.

Granting recognition to annexes, for the colonial authorities, had the benefit of keeping their residents within the orbit of church and state, but true stabilization was an ever-receding goal. In the early seventeenth century, Spanish officials recognized the annex of Soquicancha, fifteen miles from the reducción of Urutambo—only to find that the people of Soquicancha were spending much of their time at their coca fields at yet another site. The annex had generated its own annexes: the dynamic of Andean society was stubbornly centrifugal.[22]

Other reducciones did, in time, become towns.[23] Those that retained a substantial Andean population tended to be in the same ecological zones that they had been before. For highland areas, that meant where villagers had access to different microclimates, as the royal cosmographer and historian Juan López de Velasco noted: "The settlements which are populated are those in the midpoint between high and low in the mountains, more cold than hot, where they can take advantage of both extremes, the cold for herding and hunting, the hot for planting."[24] In the north coast of Peru, on the other hand, Toledo's inspectors had founded some reducciones on coastal floodplains that local people knew were not safe; a flood in 1578 killed thousands and erased reducciones entirely.[25]

While the reducciones' Andean population declined, many of them came to house non-Andeans: Spaniards, Afro-Andeans, and especially mestizos.[26] Apart from priests, non-Andeans were forbidden to live in Indian communities, not just in the Andes but in most parts of Spanish America. The Spanish crown frequently reiterated the law of caste segregation throughout the colonial period and included it in the authoritative legal code for Spanish America issued in 1680.[27]

Enforcement, however, was intermittent and ineffectual. Since there was little day-to-day government control in rural life, efforts to enforce policy took the form of after-the-fact expulsions of non-Andeans who had settled in reducciones. Viceroys or provincial governors would occasionally undertake systematic purges of illegal residents in a larger area's towns and villages, sometimes founding new towns to house the expelled people. But if it was hard to force Andeans to relocate against their will, it was even harder to force Spaniards. Officials typically interpreted the segregation laws nonliterally, so as to allow non-Andeans with good morals or long residence to remain where they were. Often the extent of the segregation laws' enforcement was simply to register and license non-Andeans living in the reducciones.[28]

When corregidores expelled non-Andeans from Andean towns, it was usually in response to specific complaints against individuals. A cacique or commoner would register a complaint with the local corregidor de indios against a resident Spaniard or mestizo, citing the principle of segregation in combination with other charges, such as land usurpation, violence, or concubinage with Andean women. In 1643 the Inquisition initiated bigamy proceedings against a Spaniard who had married a cacique's daughter in one reducción and a cacique's niece in another; the sentence against him was dissolution of the second marriage and temporary banishment from the reducción where he was currently living, a fairly mild punishment.[29] Exactly how many non-Andeans corregidores expelled is impossible to know, since few local judicial records survive except those appealed by one side or the other to a higher court. In these as in other kinds of disputes, Andean plaintiffs often complained that corregidores protected abusive resident Spaniards who were their allies or business partners. Furthermore, the machinery of the law was slow and inefficient. Someone who had received an order of expulsion could take advantage of a long sequence of judicial appeals, and when local officials moved on to their next jobs, older cases were often forgotten. At the same time, it is likely that many non-Andeans spent years in reducciones without incident, as long as they maintained acceptable relations with their Andean neighbors and the provincial Spanish authorities.[30]

With the passage of time, Spaniards entrenched themselves as a dominant minority or even a majority in many reducciones. By the seventeenth century, the reducción of Charazani in the corregimiento of Larecaja had a Spanish population determined to expand its landholdings into the Andean hamlets outside the town.[31] In 1790 Cabanaconde Anansaya in the southern part of the Lima Audiencia was almost one-quarter Spanish and mestizo.[32] Lambayeque, on Peru's north coast, had two cabildos, an Andean one and a Spanish one, a situation for which Spaniards in an increasing number of reducciones petitioned.[33] On the other hand, some reducciones remained exclusively Andean but became ever smaller and poorer, crowded by Spanish haciendas growing up around them.

The repartimientos lost more and more of their best land to Spaniards, through a variety of causes. Sometimes Spaniards purchased land from caciques, in spite of laws making Andean land theoretically inalienable; the cacique might be corrupt, or might be forced to do so to pay community debts, and colonial authorities could be persuaded to look the other way. Just as often, Spaniards simply seized land to which they had no legal title. Royal officials periodically visited areas to check land titles and confiscate land from those who held it illegally; yet they generally allowed hacienda-owners to regularize a faulty or nonexistent title by paying a fee to the Crown, confirming rather than redressing land theft.[34]

Alongside Spanish landowners, Spanish priests and corregidores exercised power over Andean communities—indeed, they were often land-owners themselves—and used their influence over reducción politics to enrich themselves. In addition to the everyday extortion chronicled by Guaman Poma, they were able to force caciques to draw on Andean labor for their fields or to carry their produce to market in mule trains. They also manipulated reducción and repartimiento finances, using Andean communities' assets as lending banks to fund their own and their friends' commercial enterprises.[35] Not all Spanish officials were cruel or abusive, but using their positions for enrichment was a recognized part of their job, and why they had paid and maneuvered to get it.[36] As for encomenderos, the General Resettlement had reduced them to pensioners with little political authority, but those who had established themselves as landowners continued to prosper through Andean labor.

Caciques and Comuneros

If rural Spaniards enriched themselves through Andean labor, the most powerful figures within the Republic of Indians after the Resettlement as before it were the caciques. Karen Spalding has called sixteenth-century caciques the "cutting edge" of colonialism, in that they represented the empire to the Andeans and the Andeans to the empire. They became rich by channeling indigenous labor into the colonial economy, making deals with Spanish landowners, priests, and corregidores. But to retain their authority the caciques had to satisfy both their own subjects and the Spanish overlords, a difficult balancing act. Pointing out that Toledo wanted to limit the caciques' power by turning them into salaried tax collectors, Spalding has shown that this responsibility actually increased their power, making them crucial intermediaries between Andeans and colonial state, with the open-ended powers that role required. In practice the General Resettlement supported caciques rather than undermining them.[37]

Caciques, while embracing some aspects of hispanic culture, played a key role in preserving Andean culture. A continuing source of their legitimacy with their own people was their role in preserving the worship of huacas and reconciling it with Christianity. No matter how convinced Andeans may have been of Christian truth, farmers in a challenging environment were unlikely to surrender long-standing rituals that protected people and crops and maintained a link to the past. Before the Spanish invasion, caciques had led rituals; after it, their role was indispensable in hiding "idolatry" from priests and corregidores, while mediating between factions within the community that differed over how to balance the two traditions.[38]

Surprisingly, syncretistic worship may have strengthened the reducciones rather then weakening them. Toledo's inspectors had tried to separate Andeans from the graves of their ancestors, to whom they looked for help and protection; Andeans answered this challenge, in parts of the archdiocese of Lima, by secretly reburying preconquest mummified bodies within the churches (Christian bodies were normally buried under the church floor), or exhuming those recently buried within the church to carry out pre-Christian rituals. Even for those who did not live in them, the reducciones could form a symbolic community center, fitting in with the older Andean idea that a community is centered on its graves.[39] This was not the only way in which the structure of the reducciones resonated with older Andean ideas of sacred space. The grid of the reducciones, often visible from a mountain pass as a visitor approached the town, evoked the messages in stone of Inca complexes and the geometric aesthetic of the Andes.[40] The grid organized blocks of houses into symmetrical groups centered on the plaza, enabling villagers to mark in space the patterns of two, four, or ten community segments which continued to mark their relations in ritual ways.[41] Even the early modern Spanish practice of defining a village's land by ritually walking along a sequence of boundary points (mojones), practiced in reducciones, continued long-standing Andean devotional practices of walking lines connecting the sacred sites of a community's shared identity.[42]

Reducción priests, as a rule, found it in their interest not to know about the Andean rituals taking place just out of sight, if they wanted a smooth relationship with their parishioners.[43] But in the first half of the seventeenth century, Lima church authorities organized a series of campaigns for "extirpation of idolatry." Once they left Lima they found huacas—from figurines to mummies to mountains revered as ancestors—almost everywhere they looked. They punished and destroyed wherever they could, but the problem was too large; campaigns against idolatry petered out, not because they had succeeded, but because the church concluded that it was better to let sleeping dogs lie.[44] One result, however, is that urban Spaniards in the colonial period never came to see the countryside as a domesticated and controlled space: it remained an alien one.[45] The population of Andeans working for Spaniards in cities, haciendas, and workshops grew, as did the Hispanicized mestizo population, but the free Andean population, paying tribute and labor and answering to caciques, priests, and corregidores in the reducciones, largely preserved its autonomy.

Still, Andean community structures were far from static. The system of nested groupings—ayllu, saya, repartimiento, and ethnic group—survived while changing. Ayllus shrank, vanished or merged due to reducciones' depopulation, while new ones sometimes appeared. The ayllus survived as census units, but the saya (the binary division within the community) took on some of their functions and became the group within which people were expected to choose their spouses. (Of course, endogamy was never absolute, and many married outside their communities.) Regional ethnic groups became less important in linking the people of various repartimientos. And reducciones gradually began to rival repartimientos as the primary focus of social identification.[46]

During the seventeenth and eighteenth centuries, caciques remained the chief authorities within indigenous society, directing tribute and labor from the comuneros to privileged Spaniards.[47] But as caciques strengthened their ties to the colonial state, often intermarrying with Spanish creoles, their ties to their Andean subjects weakened. And corregidores and priests were able to meddle in cacique successions, forcing their own candidates into the office after the previous cacique died. Beginning in the Audiencia of Quito in the seventeenth century, and in the southern provinces in the eighteenth century, many mestizos and even Spaniards came to occupy the office of cacique. Caciques, as a class, gradually lost legitimacy with their subjects.[48]

Meanwhile, a new democratic current became visible in the Republic of Indians, centered in the reducciones and the annexes. Denouncing corrupt caciques as "tyrants"—the formulation beloved by Toledo finally becoming current among Andeans themselves—the common people of the reducciones pushed back against them, regularly suing to have caciques replaced by more legitimate and honest candidates.[49] In 1774, enraged by their cacique's continuing depredations, the comuneros of a town called Condocondo stabbed and bludgeoned him to death. By the late eighteenth century, it was the reducción and its institutions that had become—literally, for this unfortunate cacique—Andean society's "cutting edge."[50]

The bloodshed in Condocondo was not unique: in the eighteenth century indigenous rebellions rocked the central and southern Andes. Ultimately unsuccessful, the uprisings represented the grievances of the Andean populace; with some exceptions, the targets were caciques as well as Spanish officials. Yet the Spanish government blamed the caciques: whether they had colluded with the comuneros or simply been too weak to prevent the rebellions, they were no longer serving the Crown effectively. The Spanish government phased out the office of cacique principal; with some exceptions, the cacique lineages, which had been the center of the Republic of Indians throughout the colonial period, were forgotten by the twentieth century.[51] In their fight against the caciques, the comuneros won.[52]

Policía, the Spanish vision of civic life, also won. The militant comuneros transferred their loyalty from the cacique to the community itself; the alcaldes and other municipal officials, who had long stood in the caciques' shadow, were now the main authorities. Community identity was as important in the annexes as in the reducciones. The inhabitants of the annexes took seriously their responsibility to visit the reducción and participate in its rituals of church and government,[53] but those in the larger and more distant ones aspired to secede from the reducción and establish their villages as fully independent municipalities, with their own churches and cabildos. By the eighteenth century, the Andean populace had internalized the Hispanic values and institutions of civic life—exactly what the General Resettlement had set out to accomplish.

Hispanic values and institutions, however, hybridized with indigenous Andean ones. The clearest example of this hybridization was the system of *cargos*, or municipal offices. Alongside secular offices such as the alcalde, the parish church had its own offices, especially for those who volunteered to pay the cost of saint's day celebrations; at some point, probably in the eighteenth century, the two sets of cargos combined into a single, ascending series. The offices were not separate and free-standing but steps on a ladder, from the most lowly to the most prestigious and demanding. The cargos were occupied not by men alone but by married couples, the traditional social unit in Andean society. Couples would advance up the cargo ladder as their status, wealth, and seniority grew. They were not generally elected to these offices—indeed, formal election had never been common in appointment to cabildo offices—but recruited by the town elders and the priest, and drawn from the community's component ayllus on a rotating basis. The principle that each ayllu contributed labor in sequence was an ancient one in Andean society. In the government of Andean towns, Hispanic systems thus merged with indigenous ones.[54]

New Republics

The end of colonialism—the end of the viceroyalty of Peru in 1824, and the birth of modern Peru, Bolivia, and Ecuador—brought new forces into play. Many of the leaders of the fight for independence were Enlightenment liberals who opposed not only colonialism but also the whole system of ideas behind it, including the idea of separate "republics" of Spaniards and Andeans. Independence, they assumed, would mean the end of racial distinctions in the law, erasing the special status of Andeans, and destroying cultural traditions the reformers saw as backward. "The Constitution of the Republic," Simón Bolívar decreed, "does not recognize inequality between Citizens."[55] The reformers wanted to end the colonial pact in which

Andeans accepted the burdens of tribute and mita in exchange for collective self-rule and the guarantee of their lands.[56]

But the new nations' policies toward their Andean majorities were far less coherent than Bolívar's pronouncement promised. The creole elites who controlled the governments were eager to end Andeans' legal protections and get their land for themselves, but less willing to dispense with indigenous tribute and forced labor. Laws frequently changed and were often reversed, but states at various times preserved tribute and labor requirements by formal reinstatement, illegal collection, or disguised forms, even through the late nineteenth century, within a system that had supposedly abolished racial laws. Still, the overall trend was toward unitary citizenship and the end of both formal race-based disabilities and collective land rights.

In the years after independence, the new republics were strapped for cash, and quickly reinstated Andean tribute requirements. Through the second half of the nineteenth century, between 20 and 50 percent of Bolivian state revenue came from Andean tribute.[57] But as the republics' economies grew, they developed new tax bases that made tribute less necessary, and all three nations abolished it between the 1850s and 1870s.[58] The recruitment of forced labor, too, seemed increasingly anachronistic, when wealthy employers were able to recruit ill-paid native workers on the free labor market. Still, as late as the 1860s and 1870s, the president of Ecuador organized forced Andean labor at the national level to build the country's first modern road network—an efficient reinvention of the colonial mita.[59]

The most damaging consequence of independence was the chipping away at collective land rights. Here, too, change was slow; Andean tribute, after all, was impossible without a basis in property. But legislators considered the principle of unalienable collective property archaic, and passed various laws to end it. Though couched in the rhetoric of emancipation, such laws had the effect of transferring Andean wealth to non-Andeans. Legal "reforms" sometimes divided Andean land among its individual occupiers but required them to pay a high fee to register their land titles, forcing them to lose their land by default; at other times they simply declared indigenous communal land to be state property, then sold it to hacienda owners from under its occupants' feet. Land that had remained in Andean hands throughout the colonial era was suddenly up for grabs: in Bolivia, native communities lost half of their land between 1880 and 1930.[60]

Andeans fought back aggressively. In some cases they pressed state officials to accept tribute they were not obligated to pay, hoping to reestablish the colonial pact. More often, they met attempted seizures with riot and rebellion. The late nineteenth and early twentieth centuries were one of the most violent periods in a history of exploitation that had never been free of violence. In a few regions, such as northern Potosí, ayllu structures and the vertical archipelago survived both nineteenth-century land privatization and twentieth-century revolutions. But the overall trend was toward Andeans' loss of land and autonomy.[61]

By the early twentieth century, more and more reducciones had become the preserve of non-Andean outsiders—called *mistis* (from the word mestizo) or *notables*—who controlled the town's economy, owned the best lands, and often seized control of the cabildo. Native people in many parts of the Andes suffered under a virtual racial caste system. Andeans living in the reducción, though they might still be the majority of its population, were a subservient class. A typical pattern was that mistis dominated the town center and its cabildo, and Andeans were organized into distinct neighborhoods within the town, each with its own alcalde.[62] The majority of the Andean population, as before, lived outside the reducciones as dependent laborers on haciendas or obrajes, in cities, or in free communities that had begun as annexes but now had their own cabildos and municipal life. Pushed to the margins of the ever-growing haciendas, Andeans who still lived in free communities farmed the least fertile land, rocky and steep, while hiring themselves out as laborers at harvest time. Free Andean villages had a variety of relationships with the now-Spanish-dominated reducciones, where mistis did everything possible to control Andeans, appoint their leaders, and draft them as workers.[63]

A few of the mistis living in the reducciones were rich landowners who exercised direct power over their Andean tenants. They received quasi-feudal services from their tenants, including the humiliating requirement to work periodically as household servants, called *pongos*. In Cabanaconde in the first half of the twentieth century, five wealthy families dominated the town, and its cabildo; one was remembered in the 1980s as swaggering with a whip in his hand, extorting labor for his fields.[64] But most mistis were not rich landowners: they owned a little land, which they hired Andean laborers to farm, but they worked in the town as small merchants, teachers, or government officeholders. Mistis dominated Andeans as landlords or creditors, but also through more subtle methods: a native couple might ask a misti couple to be godparents to their child, agreeing to sell agricultural products exclusively to them as godparents and undertake a variety of chores and services in exchange for a vague promise of protection.[65] Mistis sometimes approximated a closed caste, intermarrying from generation to generation and enforcing a rigorous line between themselves and their fellow townspeople. But the line was not as impermeable as it seemed. Mistis generally spoke Quechua or Aymara as well as Spanish, and were familiar with traditional Andean culture. Mistis who lost their fortunes might slip into the ranks of the comuneros, and comuneros who left town and returned rich might earn a place among the mistis.[66]

The population of the towns founded as reducciones varied considerably in the mid-twentieth century. In Chucuito in the 1940s, the old reducción had a population of 554 Andeans and ninety-eight mestizos, as well as Andean comuneros living in fourteen outlying settlements. Yura in the 1970s had only about one hundred people, half Andean and half mestizo, while more than four thousand Andeans lived in more than a hundred hamlets nearby. One reducción near Cuzco, assigned a population of two thousand in the General Resettlement, was almost deserted by 1980, although a significant population lived in nine small communities in a circle around it. Of the land this reducción had controlled in 1571, roughly half now belonged to the outlying communities and half to private owners and haciendas. In 1982 the geographers Daniel Gade and Mario Escobar reported that, out of 199 reducciones in the Cuzco region, 70 percent survived but contained less than 30 percent of the population assigned to them in the General Resettlement.[67]

The twentieth century saw a major mobilization of rural Andeans, as protests and uprisings evolved into broad-based movements in alliance with urban populism. As in the nineteenth century, government policy on the status and rights of indigenous communities in Bolivia, Peru, and Ecuador changed repeatedly, but the overall trend was now toward recognizing Andeans' basic civil rights and their right to some degree of collective self-determination. Unlike in previous eras, some educated Spanish-speakers started to associate their national identity with the history and culture of the indigenous majority, in a period when racial exploitation was coming under challenge throughout the world. The most important development was land reform in Bolivia in the 1950s and Peru in the 1960s, which broke up many of the haciendas and returned land to Andeans. Influenced by the international Left, Andean Indians began to define themselves not by ethnicity or culture but by class, organizing as peasants (*campesinos*) in labor unions (*sindicatos*). (Certain sectors of non-rural labor, especially mining in Bolivia, were heavily Andean and their labor unions allied with the peasant unions.) Often brutally suppressed, these movements also achieved a great deal, most notably the 1952 revolution in Bolivia. But to a lesser or greater extent, the class-based sindicatos were built on an ethnic foundation, and were a vehicle for the old forms of community organization and leadership. The leadership of sindicatos was analogous to and in some places continuous with that of the colonial towns and their component ayllus, a fusion of prehispanic, Catholic, Mediterranean municipal, and labor-union structures.[68]

The last thirty years of the twentieth century saw a new development: political parties, especially in Ecuador and Bolivia, that explicitly defined themselves as representing ethnic Andeans. Various factors contributed to the timing of this shift from class-based to ethnic mobilization. One was the simultaneous failure of international communism and mid-twentieth-century models for economic development in the Third World. Another factor was a new interest in multiculturalism and in indigenous identity politics all over the world. New movements found their target in the neoliberal economic policies that international banks were pressing developing countries to adopt. Whereas early and mid-twentieth-century reform movements had drawn on liberal rights and principles, the opposition to neoliberalism—like the opposition to the predatory and hypocritical liberalism of nineteenth-century states—led to recovering communitarian principles reminiscent of the colonial pact. Instead of individual rights and the free market, this opposition invoked communal ownership and inalienability of land. Instead of a universal and homogenizing citizenship, it invoked the Republic of Indians as a state within a state, subject to a separate legal regime, and itself composed of corporate collectivities.[69] Some indigenous groups in Bolivia have even drawn on the work of ethnohistorians to reconstruct prehispanic community institutions such as the ayllu.[70]

Andean political movements gained power in the 1990s. In Ecuador, a massive uprising of Indian communities in 1990 (both Andean highlanders and Amazonian Indians) forced the government to jettison proposed neoliberal reforms. A new Ecuadorian constitution in 1998 defined the nation as "pluricultural and multiethnic," established bilingual education, made Indians' communal lands indivisible and inalienable, and ended with a phrase popularly believed to have been the motto of the Inca empire: "Ama quilla, ama llulla, ama shua," or "Do not be lazy, do not lie, do not steal."

In Bolivia, the neoliberal presidential candidate of the governing party re-cruited an indigenous leader as vice-presidential candidate in 1992. And in 2006, an Andean candidate was at last elected as president of Bolivia: Evo Morales, who built his political career as leader of the coca-growers union and proudly asserted his roots in both Quechua and Aymara communi-ties. Morales governed with the support of highland Indian organizations, which in Bolivia are often called simply *los movimientos sociales* ("the social movements"), and which played a major role in drafting a new Bolivian constitution, approved in 2009.[71] Peru, unlike Ecuador and Bolivia, did not generate a powerful ethnic political movement; still, voters in 2001 chose as president Alejandro Toledo (served 2001–2006), an Andean man who had worked shining shoes as a boy—before going on to earn a doctorate in economics in the United States. His presidential inauguration, marked by a ceremony with chicha and coca leaves at the Inca ruins of Machu Picchu, was a sight most Peruvians would have had trouble imagining even twenty years earlier.[72]

Indigenous parties exercised much of their force at the local level, again most impressively in Bolivia and Ecuador. In the 1990s, more than five hun-dred Bolivian Indians were elected to municipal cabildos and almost one hundred were elected as alcaldes. Most were in small towns founded as re-ducciones de indios, but now inhabited primarily by mestizos, while Ande-ans lived in the surrounding countryside. The cabildo represented both the town and its rural surroundings, but mestizos had long since taken control of it. The Andeans were now, in a sense, taking it back, and reinstating the colonial reducción: the town as the center not of Andean residence but of Andean local government.[73]

In a study of municipal governments controlled by ethnic Indian par-ties in Ecuador and Bolivia, political scientist Donna Lee Van Cott found that certain aspects of governance resembled much older Andean govern-ing styles. As with any local government a main preoccupation of these municipal governments was raising money for public works, but they also called on the Andean citizens to carry out building, road, and irrigation maintenance. This collective form of public works, resembling the mita, had been mobilized coercively by non-Andean republican governments; however, governments led by Indian ethnic parties were able to do so more effectively and with much more perceived legitimacy. Another traditionally Andean aspect of governance was the principle of rotation in office. In various parts of highland Bolivia, ethnic parties required candidates for office to agree to resign halfway through their terms—for instance, two-and-a-half years into a five-year term—in favor of another candidate elected as an alternate. The old reducción of Jesús de Machaca divided its twenty-four constituent ayllus into five groups, with the understanding that the offices of alcalde and regidor would rotate regularly among them. The requirement that officeholders serve short terms had its roots, of course, in the Hispanic requirement that each alcalde serve for one year and then pass the staff of office to a new officeholder. But the idea that an office should rotate in a fixed sequence among ayllus had roots in prehispanic community organization: the "turn-taking" that is implied in the term mita. Both principles of governance represented the resurgence of very old community traditions.[74]

Though embattled, much of traditional Andean culture survives into the twenty-first century. Significant proportions of the central Andean nations speak Quechua or Aymara, wear traditional clothing identified with their regions, and (though it is less common) include indigenous rituals in Christian devotion, honoring features of the landscape such as mountains and making sacrifices of llamas, guinea pigs, and coca leaves. Villages often have collective ownership of at least part of their land, determining who can inherit it and how it is cultivated. Some villages retain relatively strong institutions with roots in those implanted by Toledo, though in different forms. The cabildo, the heart of Toledo's model of Andean local self-government, is widely perceived as an age-old aspect of Andean community. Like the Western-style bowler hats that many Aymara women wear, the Spanish title of alcalde and the alcalde's staff of justice seem to non-Indian Peruvians, Bolivians, and Ecuadorians to be signs of Indian ethnicity—even as this ethnicity has become ever more fluid, with people moving back and forth between Andean and mestizo identities.[75]

The reducciones throughout their history have been subject to alternating centrifugal and centripetal pressures that increased and decreased their resident population. Since the middle of the twentieth century, the centrifugal pressures have been strongest, and the old reducciones (along with their accumulated annexes) are even less important as actual demographic centers than before, even if they retain the loyalty of the people who have left them. Great numbers of the Andean rural population have moved to a handful of cities: Quito and Guayaquil in Ecuador, La Paz and Cochabamba in Bolivia, and Lima, Peru's capital, now one of the world's largest cities.

All of these cities came to be ringed by new towns, *pueblos jóvenes*, springing up to house immigrants from the countryside, straining the environmental limits of the area.[76]

Other people have migrated abroad, to the United States, Spain, and other countries.[77] A family today might have siblings in Lima, Los Angeles, Barcelona, and Brazil, all in regular contact, all rooted in a Peruvian highland town founded in the General Resettlement. Those who can, return on July 28 for Peruvian Independence Day, opening padlocked, empty houses on the one weekend a year when the quiet town fills up. Or a family might live together in a working-class neighborhood in Cochabamba, a brother driving a taxi and a sister selling inexpensive Chinese-made clothing in a market stall, but return for the festival of the reducción's patron saint, to see their grandmother and drink pueblo chicha, which all agree is better than the chicha sold in the city.

In their 1993 film *The Transnational Fiesta*, Paul Gelles and Wilton Martínez documented residents of the reducción town of Cabanaconde, Peru, who celebrated their patron saint's holiday simultaneously in the United States and Peru. In a book published in 2000, Gelles described a series of conversations with a Cabanaconde couple who lived in the United States but kept their roots in Cabanaconde. He talked to them first in Cabanaconde, where they wore traditional Andean clothes, then again in Cambridge, Massachusetts, where he shared Korean food and Mexican beer with them, and finally in Los Angeles, California, where he accompanied their children to the Universal Studios theme park. A family whose home remained the volcano-filled landscape of the Andes now traveled through imaginary volcanoes, in a ride based on the Hollywood film *Back to the Future*.[78]

Transnational family networks are hardly unique to Andeans. With modern methods of travel and communication, people all over the world have been able to preserve family ties across oceans, send money from high-wage countries to relatives in low-wage ones, hold dual citizenship, or maintain homes in two continents at once. For Andeans, though, the new pattern is continuous with the older one of the vertical archipelago. In the case of Cabanaconde, as in many others, the reducción survives as a community after more than four centuries, one that organizes but does not circumscribe its population.

Don Quixote de la Mancha, since he had no money to pay his squire Sancho Panza, paid him with promises. One day, he said, he would make Sancho the governor of an island, which he expected some monarch to reward him with for his noble deeds. Panza, an impoverished peasant in a remote, arid village, knew the real world's limitations. He was usually skeptical of Quixote's fantasies, and would have scorned as impossible an offer to make him alcalde of his own village. Yet the prospect of a far-off island offered him a larger vision of who he might be. Panza agreed to serve Quixote for free, assuring him: "I have taken my own pulse and find myself in good health for ruling kingdoms and governing islands. . . . Be it ever so big, I feel in myself the strength to know how to govern it just as well as anyone else in the world who has governed islands."[1] Miguel de Cervantes wrote Don Quixote a little over a century after Spaniards first set foot on the islands of the Caribbean. Cervantes, who himself hoped for a government position in Upper Peru, may have used Panza's delusions of grandeur to satirize the new ambitions for what a state could do and be—for what governing might accomplish—that New World empire inspired in Old World hearts.[2]

The General Resettlement was no delusion, but to a modern reader Viceroy don Francisco de Toledo can appear quixotic. While visiting the shores of Lake Titicaca during the General Inspection, he was informed that the people of the province spoke two different languages: the women spoke Puquina and the men Aymara. He ordered that everyone in the province, women and men, learn the Inca language of Quechua within six months.[3] The episode presents, in miniature, the same hubris that characterized the General Resettlement of Indians. What made Toledo think that a ruler could make a people change their language, let alone their entire mode of living, overnight? His patron, Cardinal Espinosa, had made the same demand of the *moriscos* of Granada just six years earlier, without providing an institutional framework to execute it, and the attempt had failed disastrously. Modern states have been able to force the majority's language onto a minority over the course of a generation or two, but only through expensive, laborious methods such as compulsory boarding schools.[4] Before crossing the Atlantic at age fifty-four, don Francisco had held high positions in the Order of Alcántara; many were calling for reform of the military orders, but he hatched no grand schemes there. Yet in Peru he embraced a concept of state power emanating irresistibly from a single point.[5] In the Andes, where the viceregal government had always interacted with Andeans through layers of middlemen, Toledo tried to establish a new and unmediated relationship between state and society. This model of rule, and the ambition of the General Resettlement of Indians, feel remarkably modern. The General Resettlement anticipated what political scientist James Scott, in his book *Seeing Like a State: How Certain Schemes to Improve the Human Condition Have Failed*, calls "authoritarian high modernism." It is worth examining the comparison in some detail.

Scott discusses an East African government campaign from the 1970s that was strikingly similar to the General Resettlement. Julius Nyerere, first president of independent Tanzania, decided to consolidate scattered settlements into larger villages easily accessible by road. Nyerere wanted to bring the people schools, clean water, electricity, up-to-date agricultural techniques, and cooperative farms. He and his officials had an aversion to everything they considered "backward": not only rural ignorance and unsanitary conditions but also practices that city dwellers found disorderly, such as small and informal settlements or mixing different crops in a single field. "For Nyerere," Scott writes, "village living, development services, communal agriculture, and mechanization were a single indissoluble package," one that promised a better life for rural people.[6]

In 1973 after plans to convince peasants to cooperate voluntarily had failed, President Nyerere decided to use force. Assisted by the army, officials would indoctrinate peasants about the need for a new village, choose, inspect, and demarcate a site for it, train village officials, and then move the residents to their new home. The pace was fast: officials sometimes had just one day to lay out the new village. The peasants' houses were light and relatively easy to take apart, transport by truck, and reassemble, but if they refused to do so soldiers sometimes burned their houses. In 1976 Nyerere reported success in moving 70 percent of the population to new villages. But the villages were often in poorly chosen sites, far from water and firewood, and without sufficient nearby arable land, forcing villagers to walk long distances to their fields. Crowded conditions led to outbreaks of human and livestock diseases; many people left the villages. In each stage and in its consequences, the Tanzanian campaign recalls the General Resettlement of Indians four hundred years earlier.[7]

It is not that the idea of resettling rural people into larger towns or villages had gone away in the meantime; it was an aspect of numerous government reform programs over the centuries. In fact, British colonial administrators in what would become independent Tanzania had pursued a similar policy of rural resettlement, for the same reasons as Nyerere (and Toledo): a more productive, more enlightened, and more governable population. But they never did so with the determination and uncompromising uniformity that characterized Nyerere's and Toledo's campaigns, and they had not had much success. Nyerere's regime, of course, was different from Toledo's. Spanish colonial rulers, though not without a certain idealism, perceived an unbridgeable gap between themselves and those they ruled, and their goal was to extract resources from Indians to send across the ocean; Tanzania's postcolonial government, on the other hand, was born in the intoxicating spirit of liberation and equality. But for all the distance between sixteenth-century Peru and twentieth-century Tanzania, the two resettlement campaigns were remarkably similar.

As an example of high modernism, Scott places the Tanzanian case alongside others, including the forced collectivization of Soviet farmers in the 1920s and the construction of Brazil's new capital city, Brasilia, in the 1950s. Soviet collectivization was designed to destroy farmers' ability to resist the government or withhold their crops from state confiscation, but also sprang from Marxist ideas about how a good society should work. Brasilia was a massive city built for an elite class of civil servants, designed to regulate every detail of their lives. Though the various projects differed in their goals and in the people targeted, all reflected a belief that the government should take extreme measures to track, plan, and—in theory—improve people's lives. The high modernist vision had three elements. The first was a system of tight social discipline, in which aspects of private as well as public life were specified in advance by central planners, and linked to the structure of the new communities as part of an integrated overall design. Second, what Scott calls "legibility": organizing people into units that could be observed, counted, and categorized. Third, a neoclassical aesthetic that emphasized straight lines and uniform architectural elements, arranged to separate functions hierarchically in space. These various elements were seen as a single policy that would transform virtually every element of traditional society into a modern form. The violence of the transformation, state actors believed, was painful but necessary to create a better society.

Each project failed in its emancipatory goals. Planners were ignorant of local conditions; indeed, the insistence on uniformity made local conditions irrelevant. The straight lines of the new settlements imposed a purely visual order that in fact undermined functional order, by ignoring the shape of the landscape. (Visual order is deceptive, as Scott points out: the arrangement of organs in the human body, or the parts in a car engine, appears disorderly but is functionally efficient.) Insofar as the new systems were viable at all, it was due to popular evasion. In the Soviet collective farms, people survived through "improvisations, gray markets, bartering, and ingenuity." In Brasilia, various unplanned settlements grew up on the periphery of the planned city and came to house a majority of the population, similar to the annexes of the reducciones. In Tanzania, farmers resisted communal farming and preserved traditional methods wherever possible. In each case, Scott argues, the survival of the transformed society depended on "an unofficial reality—a 'dark twin'—that [arose] to perform many of the various needs that the planned institution fail[ed] to fulfill." The only way in which the projects truly succeeded was in controlling the population and extracting resources. In the case of Soviet collectivization this came "at a massive cost in stagnation, waste, demoralization and ecological failure." Much the same could be said of the General Resettlement of Indians.[8]

Of course, the agent of the General Resettlement was not "the state." The decentralized sixteenth-century Spanish monarchy had nothing close to the personnel, revenue, or institutions on which a modern government depends.[9] But even on Soviet collective farms, it was not a monolithic state that acted on people's lives, but individuals who worked for and were part of political institutions, making decisions and implementing those of others.

As a construct, not a reality, the idea of the state—in the sense of a territorial government that is unitary and sovereign—is useful for thinking about the General Resettlement of the sixteenth century, which indeed was the era when the modern idea of the state first appeared.

In Michel Foucault's influential formulation, the nature of European governments began to change in the sixteenth century, when the Reformation and Counter-Reformation coincided with the development of newly powerful monarchies.[10] Two previously independent models of authority came together in the period: the ancient pastoral model of the Church, where the priest kept track of each member of his flock, and an invigorated body of thinking about how a sovereign monarch should marshal national resources. The merging of sacred and secular models of authority resulted in a simultaneous attention to the individual subject and to the collectivity, a form of government that Foucault called "both individualizing and totalitarian." It was the first step in the long development of a theory of the state for which Foucault coined the term *governmentality*, in which the governor's role shifted from a passive act of administering justice to an active project of social engineering. He connected this shift to a new body of laws that appeared the sixteenth and early seventeenth centuries to regulate the everyday habits of individuals, called *Policey* or *Polizei* in German and *police* in French.[11] Their Castilian cognate, although Foucault did not mention it, was *policía*. The early modern Spanish monarchy, which commentators have sometimes portrayed as backward, experimented quite early with new conceptions of governmentality.[12]

The authoritarian high modernism James Scott observes was the culmination of one strand of governmentality, in which the idea of an all-seeing state with full responsibility for citizens' lives led to some of the worst crimes of the twentieth century.[13] But well before these ideas matured in Europe, Viceroy Toledo carried them to its furthest periphery through the universal censuses of the General Inspection and the aggressive social engineering of the General Resettlement. In the name of divine law and human civilization, the General Resettlement of Indians pioneered a conception of state power that was remarkably—and from the perspective of individuals' freedom and dignity, chillingly—ahead of its time.[14]

For Toledo, however, this style of government was not new but old: he believed he was restoring policies that the Incas had devised long before Spaniards arrived, which would have been bizarre and wrong in Europe but were necessary in Peru. The Incas (as Toledo imagined them) practiced what Scott would call high modernism and that Toledo, following Aristotle, called "tyranny." But it was a tyranny appropriate to the challenges of the Andes. Just as the language Toledo chose to impose on Aymara- and Puquina-speakers was not Spanish but Quechua, the Inca imperial tongue, he saw the General Resettlement as a way of applying Andean solutions to Andean problems. For Toledo and his companions, the reducciones' tyranny was not radical but recuperative—not alien aggression but local tradition.

These claims were racist and self-serving. The idea that Andeans were weak, and that Spaniards should follow the example of prehispanic rulers who tracked them closely and governed with a strong hand, had roots in a European image of "servile" barbarian societies.[15] What was distinctive here was the other side of the Spaniards' ethnographic vision, and the other part of what Toledo wanted to restore and preserve: the vertical archipelago. When the Spaniards first arrived in Peru, what had most impressed them was the Inca infrastructure—cities, roads, stockpiles of goods, travelers' inns—but by the 1550s, most of this had been destroyed. The most perceptive colonists refocused their attention on another kind of infrastructure: the system of interregional mobility, exchange, and settlement enclaves linking different altitudes and climate zones with which Andeans made the most of a mountain landscape. Scholars today call this system the vertical archipelago, while sixteenth-century Spaniards invoked it when they described the people called mitimas, whom they recognized as necessary for Andean prosperity.

Sixteenth-century Spaniards thus had two images of Andean culture: authoritarianism and the archipelago. They were struck, on the one hand, by the extraordinary power of the Incas, and on the other by a model of community in which nodes of a network shared resources and labor across great distances. For early colonial administrators, the two were linked, each supporting the other. Early modern Europeans tended to assume that societies' organizing structures did not evolve organically, but were the creation of lawgivers.[16] As a watch implies a watchmaker, so the complex organization of the Andean community seemed impossible to Spaniards without Inca authority and planning. To have created a social structure so complex and effective, the Incas must have combined a level of state authority and knowledge seldom seen elsewhere—so colonial observers reasoned. In the Spanish imagination, Inca cities, Inca communication networks, and Inca mitimas were an integrated infrastructure that had maintained a prosperous society in the Andean landscape. This vision found its way into the General

Resettlement through the advice of Toledo's most trusted advisors, Toledo's instructions to the inspectors, and the inspectors' decisions on the ground. For Toledo and his circle—in spite of their determination to impose divine law and human civilization on the Andes—the vertical archipelago, in all its apparent disorder, was the Incas' valuable legacy.

The continuing necessity of the archipelago networks implied the continuing necessity of the caciques, and a degree of indirect rule. The reducciones were supposed to expose individual families directly to colonial rule for the first time, but in fact altered the chain of command fairly little at the local level. Periodic censuses kept track of Andean tributaries by name, yet people paid tribute collectively through their ayllus and repartimientos in ways largely opaque to colonial officials. Colonial officials assessed tribute according to the number of tributaries, but in practice each tributary did not always pay a fixed amount; instead, caciques and principales apportioned tribute according to their own judgment, collected it as best they could and made up the difference from community funds. The governable unit remained the community, not the individual. Toledo yearned to reduce the caciques to salaried appointees, but he and his immediate successors intervened rarely in cacique successions, knowing that caciques needed legitimacy in the eyes of their subjects to do their job. Just as the annex villages were necessary for the functioning of the reducciones, the caciques' authority was necessary for the authority of the state.

The balance of direct and indirect rule created by the General Resettlement has affinities to modern colonialism. Scholars of nineteenth- and twentieth-century colonial Africa and Asia have traditionally seen an evolution toward governmentality. According to this account, early administrators in British and French colonies governed through indigenous rulers, preserved traditional laws, and raised revenue through collective taxes—the trappings of indirect rule—while later administrators introduced censuses, direct taxes, and local personnel to regulate people's lives—the trappings of governmentality.[17] But recent scholarship has shown that the reality was messier: apparently traditional institutions lasted almost to the end of colonialism in the mid-twentieth century, coexisting with apparently modern ones. As Frederick Cooper points out, "colonial states did not necessarily want or need to see individual subjects in relation to the state . . . , [when those subjects] belonged in tribes and could be governed through the collectivity." Such collectivities, although opaque to the state, had the benefit of producing revenue and maintaining order with relatively little effort on the rulers' part.[18]

At the center of these modern colonial projects, as in their early modern analogues, was ethnography. In modern colonialism, empire builders have called into service a kind of ethnographic inquiry that was more formal and self-conscious than anything in the sixteenth century: the academic discipline of anthropology was, in a sense, born in the colonies. But, as in earlier periods, the motive behind colonial ethnography was practical. Nicholas Dirks writes of "early colonial efforts to know India well enough to profit by it, [bringing] together many strands of scientific curiosity, missionary frustration, Orientalist fascination, and administrative concerns with property and taxation"—a picture much like sixteenth-century Peru. British officials studied the Indian caste system, for instance, as part of the censuses by which they practiced an ever closer surveillance over the lives of their subjects. Colonial ethnography, according to this view, was a tool for governmentality, a means to make subjects legible and therefore governable.[19]

At the same time, colonial ethnography could be a tool for indirect rule, an imperial strategy diametrically opposed to governmentality. As Karuna Mantena shows in her 2010 study, *Alibis of Empire*, the British in late-nineteenth-century India drew on ethnography to preserve precolonial laws, institutions, and dynasties. Traditionally, the justification for empire had been bringing Christian civilization to benighted peoples. Britain implicitly promised Indians that, after defeating and humiliating them for its own commercial benefit, it would confer on them the opportunities of modernity and (eventually) civil liberties within the British Empire. But the failed anti-colonial Rebellion of 1857, which seemed to Britons an act of bewildering ingratitude, suggested that India was culturally unequipped for modernity. Their response was to change their strategy and the justification for empire, appealing to what Mantena calls "culturalist alibis," or ethnographic claims that England should postpone modern rights and freedoms out of respect for Indian culture. Freedom was all well and good, but not for *them*, not yet—better to rule them through their own self-regulating systems. Imposing British freedoms on Indians, policymakers claimed, would dissolve organic communities and leave a discontented, atomized mass. In this analysis, the purpose of ethnography was not governmentality (i.e., tracking and guiding individual subjects), but indirect rule—as Polo

Ondegardo put it, "preserving for the Indians" (in his case the "Indians" of Peru) "their laws."[20]

Neither indirect rule nor governmentality offers a complete picture of modern colonialism, any more than of the early modern kind. Within the context of partial indirect rule, and respect for indigenous customs, the British greatly extended their overall control of the Indian subcontinent and its people in the late nineteenth and early twentieth centuries. Britain oscillated between impulses toward governmentality and indirect rule, combining them in complex ways—just as Toledo had done in Peru.[21] In the various British colonies, as well as French and German ones, these two impulses stood in dynamic tension.[22] Writing about colonial Africa, John Comaroff describes a combination of apparently traditional and apparently modern forms of governance that was "unsystematic, murky, [and] incoherent."[23]

Modern colonizers probably did not study the example of Spanish Peru, centuries earlier, but the parallels are striking. It would be a mistake to equate early modern Spain with modern France and Britain. Spanish colonial ethnography was far less formal and self-conscious than the modern kind, and the ways Spaniards used it to preserve indigenous institutions were more conflicted and incomplete.[24] The results, though, were similar: an unsystematic combination of governmentality and indirect rule that created an equilibrium between exploitation and survival. In this, as in much else, the General Resettlement of Indians established patterns that reappeared in future colonial enterprises.[25]

Up until now scholars have generally interpreted the General Resettlement of Indians as a frontal attack on Andean culture, which survived, to the extent it did, through Andeans' determined resistance. This interpretation is not wholly wrong: Andeans resisted, and their culture evolved and survived. And it is true that virtually all Spanish colonial officials, including Toledo, believed that Andean culture was in certain respects deeply flawed and in need of correction. They designed the General Resettlement to extend Christian institutions in the Andean countryside, to create more compact and uniform towns, and to restrict Andeans' freedom—goals that undermined the communities' archipelago landholdings. But destroying the archipelago was not the intention; the program's architects, on the contrary, wanted to preserve that system. The Resettlement campaign was designed to have it both ways.

The General Resettlement of Indians was, among other things, a human catastrophe. The surveillance and population registers of the reducciones underlay a brutal extraction of labor and tribute. Widespread flight from the reducciones made the burden worse for those who stayed, while those who left often exchanged one form of oppression for another, on Spanish haciendas. Throughout the Andes the vertical archipelago declined, as communities were separated from mitimas and their lands, and in some places it vanished altogether. The reducciones supported a regime of racial exploitation, and stripped away part of the cultural inheritance connecting Andeans with their past.

In spite of all this, Andeans in many places asserted ownership over their own lives and communities. Many lived outside the reducciones away from priests' prying eyes, and held onto their traditions and religious devotions within a colonized culture. They preserved their archipelago landholdings where they could, enabling communities to survive and cohere. To achieve this survival, Andean caciques and comuneros fought Spanish officials at all levels, openly or secretly. Paradoxically, though, some of the decisions made in the General Resettlement set the groundwork for cultural survival. Ultimately, Andean agency was more important than colonial policies in the survival of Andean culture, but the policies framed the arena in which Andeans struggled for it.

Both sides of the General Resettlement, aggressive cultural remaking and ethnographic cultural preservation, offer new perspectives on early modern colonialism. The extraordinary scale, aggression, and ambition of the Resettlement foreshadowed at a remarkably early date the state projects of the twentieth century. And Spanish officials' self-interested ethnography anticipated modern anthropology. Just as scholars have seen eighteenth-century Creole politics as a laboratory for nationalism, so the sixteenth-century Spanish colonies were a place for re-imagining the nature of government.[26] And the Spanish image of the Inca empire was a tablet on which to sketch such possibilities.

The audacity of Toledo's ambition—the confidence with which he set out to remake a large settled society at the levels of individual conscience, daily practice, village structure, provincial leadership, and interregional labor flow, simultaneously in every place and at every scale—has obscured the preservationist aspects of his project. He and the colonizers of his generation wanted to remake indigenous culture after a Spanish model, but at the same time to preserve cultural systems that generated wealth for

Spain. While often hidden within a discourse of cultural remaking, the ethnographic project was ultimately what made colonialism pay for the colonizers.

If the colonists were ethnographers, so were Andeans. They were able to withstand the violence of forced resettlement precisely because mobility and multiple residences were already part of Andean culture, dictated by history and ecology; some Andean peoples, moreover, had experienced re-settlement at the hands of the Inca state. But another way Andeans navigated Toledo's campaign was by understanding the colonial state. Toledo hoped that the reducciones would control the caciques; instead, the caciques con-trolled the reducciones. The Spanish, even while making allowances for the mitima system, intended reducciones to be the exclusive places of residence for most Andeans. Instead, the reducción was one among several homes for many Andeans. It was the place through which they enacted their relation-ship with the government, much like the Inca stone complexes Pizarro and his companions had marveled at when they first climbed the Andes. The reducciones added another layer to a complex web of settlement—a web that Spaniards glimpsed and that Andeans defended fiercely—rather than displacing or destroying it.

APPENDIX

1. The Tasa of the General Inspection

Of the documents that the General Inspection generated, the most important one from Toledo's point of view was the tasa or tribute scale, which Toledo finalized in 1575 based on the inspectors' reports. It documented a population of roughly 1.4 million in 839 reducciones and approximately 450 repartimientos,[1] in the Audiencias of Lima and Charcas (not the Audiencia of Quito). There probably once existed a complete text of the tasa for the Audiencias of Lima and Charcas, which Noble David Cook estimated would have extended to between six and twelve thousand manuscript folios.[2] This complete documentation survives for only a handful of repartimientos (see below). For each repartimiento (assuming that the fullest information we have for some repartimientos originally existed for all of them), the tasa would have contained the following information:

The name of the inspector.

The name of the repartimiento and its encomendero or encomenderos.

Population numbers for each repartimiento, including five numbers: tributaries (i.e., men between the ages of 18 and 50); older men and invalids exempt from tribute; boys; women and girls; total population. (In some cases it also broke this down by categories within the repartimiento, especially Aymaras versus Urus, or other demographic information such as the numbers of tribute-exempt ethnic Incas living there.)

The tribute due from the repartimiento, in specie and kind, and the amount this came to per tributary.

The names of the caciques.

The sums paid out of this tribute for caciques, priests, and *de-*

fensores / protectores, and the gifts and services they could legitimately demand in addition.

The number and names of the reducciones to which the repartimiento's people had been assigned.

The number of pre-Resettlement hamlets in which that repartimiento's people had been settled, and their area, given in leagues. (This number is hard to interpret; see below.)

Various requirements about the records the Andean communities should keep and how they should manage their finances.

Finally, a notarized document from February 1575 stating that the information in the tasa was read aloud to the treasury officials and (via a translator) to the caciques.

The tasa may also have included the names of the Spanish cities and towns, the titles and salaries of their officials, the names of the corregimientos de indios, and the salaries of their corregidores. (This information was included in one of the reports drawn from the tasa, but it may not have been in the original manuscript of the tasa itself.)

The inspectors also submitted censuses (padrones), with names of all tributaries, which were not included in the tasa itself, but which often survive in cases where they were entered into later litigation. They group families by repartimiento, parcialidad (i.e., saya) and ayllu, not by reducción. In other words, they record the ethnic and political structure of Andean society rather than the changes introduced by the General Resettlement. This is logical: the main purpose of the censuses was to determine the tribute and labor that Andeans would render to the Spanish, and tribute and labor were allocated by repartimientos, parcialidades, and ayllus. The two systems for organizing population did not align cleanly with each other; on the contrary, many reducciones contained people from several repartimientos, while the people of a given repartimiento or ayllu were typically divided among several reducciones. For the purpose of managing tribute collection, it was more useful to count people by ayllu and repartimiento than by reducción. From the perspective of the censuses, therefore, the General Resettlement is almost invisible.[3]

We have three manuscript versions of the tasa (all now published) each of which extracts some part of the information given in the complete version for each repartimiento; the three versions vary both in the geographical area they cover and in the categories of information they contain. They are described below.

The complete tasa information survives, as far as I know, only for the following repartimientos:

Aullagas and Uruquillas (except for the first folios which are missing), in the AGI Contaduría 1786 manuscript, published in Cook, ed., *Tasa de la visita general de Francisco de Toledo*, 5–11.

Condes de Araute, in the Biblioteca Nacional del Perú (see Cook, ed., *Tasa de la visita general*, xvi).

Sipesipe, Macha, Chaqui, Bisisa/Caissa, Tacobamba, Colo/Caquina/Picachuri, Quillacas/Asanaques, in the Buenos Aires tasa (published in Salles and Noejovich, eds., *La Visita General*). The Sipesipe information is also published in Romero, "Libro de la visita general del virrey don Francisco de Toledo, 1570–1575," 204–16.

1. Cristóbal de Miranda, "Relación de los Corregimientos y otros officios que se proveen en los reynos e provincias del Piru, en el distrito e gobernación del visorrey dellos," Lima, 8 Feb. 1583. AGI. Published in *Gobernantes*, 9:128–230; Maúrtua, ed., *Juicio de límites entre el Perú y Bolivia*, 1:153–280.

   Geographic extent: territories of La Plata, La Paz, Cuzco, Arequipa, Guamanga, Lima, Huánuco, Trujillo, Piura, and Chachapoyas.

   Information given: titles and salaries (and sometimes names of incumbents) for municipal offices in Spanish ciudades and villas; salaries of corregidores de indios in each corregimiento; names and populations (tributaries and total) of the repartimientos in each corregimiento; name of encomendero for each repartimiento; number and names of reducciones in each repartimiento.

   Notes: This is not, strictly speaking, a tasa, since it does not provide amounts of tribute, but its information is drawn from the original complete tasa.

2. "Repartimientos de indios hecho en el año de 1582, en varias ciudades y distritos." AGI Contaduría 1786. Published in Cook, ed., *Tasa de la visita general*.

   Geographic extent: Territories of La Plata, La Paz, Cuzco, Arequipa, and Guamanga.

   Information given: for each repartimiento, census data (broken down into the four categories of tribute-paying men, old men, boys, and women of all ages); the tribute due each year in cash and commodities; the salaries to be paid out of this to priests, caciques, and other officials; and the names of the encomenderos who were to receive the balance of the tribute.

3. "Yndice del Reparttimientto de tazas de las provincias conttenidas en este Libro hechas en tempo del Exmo señor Don Francisco de Toledo, Virrey que fue de esttos Reynos." AGNA Sala 9—17-2-5, "Lib. de Retazas Libradas por el Ex. S.r. Toledo, 1785." Published in Salles and Noejovich, eds., *La Visita General*.

   Geographic extent: Territories of La Plata and La Paz.

   Information given: all the information given in the other two versions, as well as the name of the inspector for each repartimiento, the number of villages the repartimiento had before the resettlement, and the size of the area containing those villages, in leagues.

   The size of the area is given in units of distance, making it hard to interpret. We learn, for instance, that the repartimiento of Aullagas and Uruquillas, with 1,371 tributaries resettled into three reducciones, "was before settled in 19 pueblos and a district of 20 leagues." Twenty leagues might be the circumference or diameter of the district, but is most likely the length of the curving path the inspector took to pass through the district while visiting it.

For the first five repartimientos, it gives what appears to be the complete original text of the tasa, signed by Francisco de Toledo on 6 Feb. 1575. This includes, along with the previous information, the names of all the caciques in each repartimiento; and a detailed list of commodities, services and exemptions each will receive, by virtue of his office, in addition to his salary.

2. The Population of the Reducciones

Toledo wanted to make the reducciones as large and uniform as circumstances would allow. He thought that each town should have about four hundred tributaries, or roughly two thousand people, although he was willing to accept two or three smaller towns that were close enough together to form a single parish with this population. He recognized that reducción size would be the outcome of a process of bargaining between the inspector and the cacique, and he instructed the inspectors to start by bidding low, telling the cacique that he would have to concentrate his people into an even smaller number of towns than the inspector was ultimately willing to accept.[4] How large were the reducciones, and how much did their size vary?

In rough numbers, the tasas document a total population of 1.4 million, divided into 440 repartimientos, 840 reducciones, and 270,000 tributaries (a number that corresponds, roughly, to households). Dividing the number of tributaries by the number of reducciones gives a mean population of 320 per reducción—rather less than Toledo's goal of 400, but not radically so. This raw average, however, gives no picture of the range of variation, or even (since a few high or low numbers can throw off the average) of how close the mean was to the typical case.

The challenge in analyzing settlement size is that in most cases we know the population of the repartimiento but not that of the reducciones. As figure appendix-1 illustrates, there were four ways repartimientos and reducciones could map onto each other. The entire repartimiento might be assigned to a single reducción containing no one from other repartimientos (A); several small repartimientos might be consolidated into a single reducción (B); a repartimiento might be divided into several reducciones (C); or several repartimientos might share several reducciones between them (D).

Cases A and B can be called whole-repartimiento towns, and since we know the populations of the repartimientos we also know the populations of the reducciones. Cases C and D can be called partial-repartimiento towns and mixed-repartimiento towns, respectively. In the great majority of such cases we do not know the population of these reducciones, but in a handful of cases that information is available.

There were about 200 whole-repartimiento towns: almost half of the total number of repartimientos, a quarter of the total number of reducciones, and almost a third of the total resettled population. A study of their populations, as reported in the tasas, shows a wide distribution of size. They range from 25 to more than 2000 tributaries, with a median population of about 300 hundred tributaries and a widely dispersed distribution. (Again, the number of tributar-

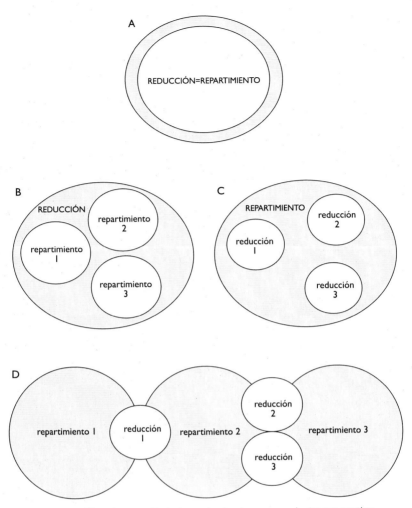

Figure Appendix-1 Ways that repartimientos and reducciones mapped onto one another

ies is a rough proxy for the number of households.) Reflective of this dispersion, almost 40 percent of the whole-repartimiento towns were either small (fewer than 150 tributaries) or large (more than 800). (See graph A in figure appendix-2.) As shown in the histograms in figure appendix-2 (graph B) and figure appendix-3, beginning at 100 tributaries, the greatest number of reducciones falls into the lower end of the range, but the number of reducciones declines gradually and relatively evenly up to about 1000 tributaries, with a handful of reducciones significantly larger than that. The distribution has a fairly long tail. This analysis applies only to the whole-repartimiento towns, which were not necessarily representative of the rest, but the relatively large proportion of the population assigned to them suggests the wide variety of Andeans' experience of the General Resettlement.[5]

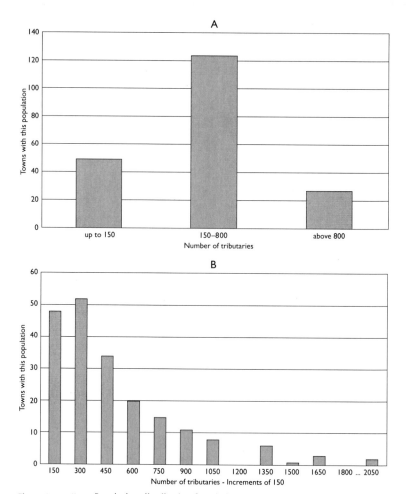

Figure Appendix-2 Population distribution for whole-repartimiento towns

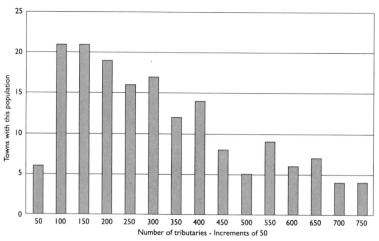

Figure Appendix-3 Population distribution for whole-repartimiento towns with 750 or fewer tributaries (numbers given are upper limits in increments of 50)

The wide variation in size among the whole-repartimiento towns reflects the wide variation of the repartimientos themselves. Repartimientos had been defined in the conquest era as autonomous political communities whose leaders could reliably deliver annual tribute to the Spanish. Virtually all repartimientos had shrunk in size during the two generations since the conquest, from disease, violence, and social chaos, although some remained large: those in Toledo's time ranged from twenty to 5,300 tributaries. The Spanish overlords had often brokered the consolidation of two or more declining repartimientos. Toledo's inspectors' willingness to combine two or more small repartimientos into a single town represented a continuation of this process (although the groups sometimes retained their separate leaders within the same town). The town of San Salvador de Ayapata, for instance, contained three small repartimientos, all of them with fewer than seventy-five tributaries, along with several dozen other families whom the inspector identified as belonging to "various encomenderos." In the adjoining province, the town of San Pablo de Cacha merged a tiny repartimiento of forty tributaries with an average-size one with ten times that number. But in other cases the inspector was willing to establish a single-repartimiento town with a small population, as in the case of Sonche, near the north coast, with forty-two tributaries, or Icho Guanaco, in the central sierra, with sixty-three. These repartimientos may not have been located near others with which they could conveniently combine.

The twenty-seven large whole-repartimiento towns—those with a population of more than eight hundred tributaries—present a different case. In any of them, the inspector could have created two reducciones with the officially recommended population of four hundred tributaries each. Given the challenge inspectors faced in forcing people to relocate against their will, these reducciones probably represent preexisting concentrations of settlement. Many of these large reducciones were located in the Aymara-speaking altiplano of the southern sierra, where Spanish observers had previously commented on the existence of large settlements, contradicting the Spanish stereotype of highly dispersed Andean settlement. Wealthy and powerful repartimientos such as Sacaca, near Potosí, Machaca la Grande, in the province of Pacajes, and Copacabana, on the south shore of Lake Titicaca, were settled into single reducciones with populations in excess of one thousand tributaries. These large towns (large by the standards of the early colonial Andes) thus reflected a cultural norm very specific to one part of the Aymara-speaking altiplano. Other large reducciones did not fit this pattern. The town of La Chimba was composed of almost two thousand Andean tributaries from various different, unnamed repartimientos. It was located near the Spanish city of Arequipa, and housed Andeans who worked there.

In any case, reducciones that were larger than the norm were preferable to the viceroy than small ones. In the interest of surveillance and evangelization by Spanish priests, and of tracking people for tribute and labor service, the more concentrated the population, the better. But the largest of the whole-repartimiento towns, like the smallest ones, make it clear that much of the diversity of settlement size that existed before the General Resettlement continued after it.

While we know the population of whole-repartimiento towns for all the regions documented in the tasas, we know the population of partial- and mixed-repartimiento towns in only a few cases. One example is in the reducciones of Condes, discussed in chapter 8. Another example is a group of reducciones in the jurisdiction of La Plata, for which the Buenos Aires tasa (as described above, and for reasons that are unclear) provides the exact population. These reducciones show several distribution patterns (see table 1). The repartimientos of Yamparaes, Tacobamba, and Bisisa were divided into pairs of reducciones with roughly similar populations. Macha had three reducciones with similar populations and one, in a warm valley, that was smaller. The combined population of Quillacas and Asanaques was divided into towns in a stepwise distribution, with approximately 40 percent, 30 percent, 20 percent and 10 percent of the total population, respectively. And Chaqui was mainly concentrated into one reducción along with a tiny satellite community.

In the partial-repartimiento towns of La Plata, as in the whole-repartimiento towns, the diversity of patterns underscores the diversity of experience within the resettlement process. The General Resettlement campaign did not impose a uniform structure on Andean society.

3. The Question of Secret Viceregal Instructions

Did Toledo carry secret instructions from the king, and if so, what were they? In a note to Philip II of 17 December 1572, the king's secretary Mateo Vázquez referred obliquely to secret dispatches, which he had drafted for Toledo ("los despachos secretos que llevó, escritos de mi letra"), but it is unclear what these were.[6] Maria-José Rodríguez Salgado, in a discussion of viceroys and governors in the Hapsburgs' European territories, writes that they received both a public and a secret set of instructions, the public one being a generic grant of royal authority and the secret one containing more substantive directions.[7] But if Toledo carried any documents explicitly designated as secret instructions, they have not come to light. Without clear citation, Demetrio Ramos Pérez suggests that Toledo carried secret instructions related to the need to restrict colonists' trade for the benefit of Seville merchants, which would be unpopular in Peru.[8] On the other hand, one contemporary source implied that Toledo kept all his instructions secret except those related to the Inquisition and the reorganization of the viceroy's judicial powers.[9]

Catherine Julien has inventoried two files in the Archivo General de Indias (AGI Lima 578, libro 2, and AGI Indiferente 2859, no. 2) that contain copies of royal orders intrusted to Toledo.[10] They fall into three groups:

1. *Títulos* and related documents. Toledo carried titles formally investing him as viceroy and Audiencia president, papers authorizing him to award encomiendas, pardon criminals, collect his salary, etc.[11]
2. *Instrucciones*. Each was a single lengthy document with various subheadings, one on secular and the other on church matters: "Instrucion" and "Doctrina y gobierno eclesiastico."[12]

TABLE 1 Partial-repartimiento towns in jurisdiction of La Plata

Corregimiento	Repartmiento	Reducciones	Tributaries	Percentage	Folio
Amparaes	Yamparaes	Yotaca	266	47	135v
		Quillaquilla	300	53	
Paria	Quillacas/ Asanques	Oropesa de Quillaca	1,000	40	116v
		San Juan del Pedroso	700	28	
		San Pedro de Condocondo	500	20	
		San Lucas de Pabacollo	300	12	
Chayanta	Macha	Alcazar de Poata	579	30	95v
		Santa Fe de Chayrapacta	536	28	
		Magdalena de Aymaya	483	25	
		S. Marcos de Miraflores de Yaure	309	16	
Porco	Chaqui	Sarandieta	506	96	96r
		Curi	23	4	
Porco	Tacobamba	San Pedro de Tacobamba	394	58	96v
		Santa Ana de Potobamba	286	42	
Porco	Bisisa	Nuestra Señora de la Concepción	520	56	96v
		Nuestra Señora de la Incarnación	402	44	

Source: AGNA tasa. Note that the populations of repartimientos do not always agree perfectly among the tasas. Furthermore, the reducción populations do not always add up to the population given for the repartimiento, because some families lived in the reducciones of other repartimientos.

3. *Reales cédulas / reales provisiones*. Toledo also carried forty-eight other laws on specific subjects, mostly brief, addressed to him, to one of the Audiencias, or to other officials.[13]

Except for the *títulos*, there was probably no mechanism forcing the viceroy to show *any* document to anybody. Discretion was expected from viceroys: once in Peru, when Toledo received laws from court that he judged would be dangerous to implement, he wrote to the king to protest them, and kept them secret in the meantime.[14] And there is no indication that Toledo was expected to make his *Instrucciones* public. Toledo's "secret" instructions may simply have been those sections of the "Instrucion" that he chose to keep private either temporarily or permanently.

NOTES

Introduction

1 Matienzo, *Gobierno del Perú*, 48: "apartados y escondidos en huaycos y quebradas . . . ni pueden ser dotrinado ni ser hombres perpetuamente, no estando juntos en pueblos"; BPR, II/2846, N. 12, "Memorial dado por el racionero Villarreal al virrey Toledo" [c. 1570], f. 304v; "una casilla que mas parece de monejos que de hombres, . . . vivir vestialmente, durmiendo con su madre e hijas."

2 Murra, "El control vertical de un máximo de pisos ecológicos en la economía de las sociedades andinas," in *Formaciones económicas*, 59–115. Scholars have seen the archipelago model most clearly in the regions surrounding and south of Lake Titicaca, while some scholars glimpsed it in one form or another in many other parts of the Andes. Van Buren, "Rethinking the Vertical Archipelago"; Goldstein, "Communities without Borders"; Angelis-Harmening, 'Cada uno tiene en la puna su gente.'

3 Murra did, however, observe that this was significant: "We note that the earliest sixteenth-century observers reached certain conclusions which have been confirmed by modern scholarship": "Andean Societies Before 1532," 61. Beginning in the 1980s, Murra became interested in early colonial ethnographic officials, although he published fairly little on the subject. See Murra, "Nos Hazen Mucha Ventaja" and "Le débat sur l'avenir des Andes en 1562."

4 Haring, *The Spanish Empire in America*, 83–88; Eagle, "Beard-Pulling and Furniture-Rearranging." The composition of the Audiencias varied between jurisdictions and over time, but each normally had several judges, called *oidores*, a president, an *alcalde de crimen* (criminal judge) and one or more *fiscales*

(crown attorneys). Haring, *The Spanish Empire*, 120. The governor, whether it was the viceroy or someone else, usually had the additional title of captain-general, or supreme military authority. The viceroy had the power to decide whether a problem was a matter of gobierno or justicia, and Toledo used this power aggressively against the Audiencias. Fray Rodrigo de Loaysa wrote in 1586: "Don Francisco de Toledo jamás tuvo paz con ninguna audiencia." Ibid., 87.

5 Ibid., 83–88. Toledo noted to the king that the Quito Audiencia had a *real cédula* granting the Audiencia president powers of gobierno, that Chile was likewise resisting his authority, and that his own papers did not grant him formal jurisdiction over Tucumán or Santa Cruz, frontier territories connected to Charcas. Toledo to king, Cuzco, 1 March 1572, in *Gobernantes*, 4:48–208, see 191–92.

6 This is the argument, or rather the underlying assumption, of Toledo's two major twentieth-century biographies: Levillier, *Don Francisco de Toledo, Supremo Organizador del Perú*, and Zimmerman, *Francisco de Toledo, Fifth Viceroy of Peru, 1569–1581*.

7 Fraser, *The Architecture of Conquest*; Durston, "Un régimen urbanístico en la América hispana colonial"; Cummins, "Forms of Andean Colonial Towns, Free Will, and Marriage."

8 Spalding, *Huarochirí*, 212–14; Brading, *The First America*, 138; Coello de la Rosa, "Discourse and Political Culture in the Formation of the Peruvian Reducciones in the Spanish Colonial Empire (1533–1592)"; Colajanni, "El Virrey Francisco de Toledo como 'primer antropólogo aplicado' de la edad moderna"; Cook and Cook, *People of the Volcano*, chap. 4; Julien, "History and Art in Translation"; Merluzzi, *Politica e governo nel Nuovo Mondo*, 101–15.

9 Alejandro Málaga Medina, while using primarily the same legislative sources Levillier had used, showed some of the ambiguity of the campaign's success: "Las reducciones en el virreinato del Perú" and *Reducciones toledanas en Arequipa*. Major steps forward were Saignes, "Las etnías de Charcas frente al sistema colonial," 72; Cañedo-Argüelles, "Las reducciones indígenas en el sur andino"; Jurado, "Las reducciones toledanas a pueblos de indios"; Río, *Etnicidad, territorialidad y colonialismo en los Andes*; Wernke, "Negotiating Community and Landscape in the Peruvian Andes."

10 Durston, "El proceso reduccional en el sur andino"; Huertas Vallejo, "El proceso de concentración social en el espacio andino"; Cook and Cook, *People of the Volcano*, chap. 4; Gose, *Invaders as Ancestors*, chap. 4.

11 This kind of social engineering had precedents in other parts of the world, as well as in the ancient Mediterranean, but not in medieval or early modern Europe.

12 Scholars have done impressive work in reconstructing Andean mentalities in the seventeenth century, though indigenous voices are more elusive during the middle decades of the sixteenth century. A key seventeenth-century source, discussed in chap. 9, is don Felipe Guaman Poma de Ayala's *Primer nueva corónica y buen gobierno* (1615–1616); see Adorno, "Guaman Poma de Ayala," in Pillsbury,

ed., *Guide to Documentary Sources*, 2:255–68. On the Huarochirí manuscript, see Frank Salomon's bibliography in ibid., 2:296–303. On the church as a forum for Spanish-Andean encounter, through pastoral relationships as well as extirpation campaigns, see Mills, *Idolatry and Its Enemies*; Durston, *Pastoral Quechua*; Charles, *Allies at Odds*. Early Quechua-language documents produced by Andeans are rare but exist: see Durston, "Native-Language Literacy in Colonial Peru."

13 Yaranga Valderrama, "Las 'reducciones,' uno de los instrumentos del etnocidio."

1. The Cities

1 Twenty-four meters is equivalent to an eight-story building today. Protzen and Rowe, "Hawkaypata"; Bauer, *Ancient Cuzco*, 3. There does not seem to be definite consensus on the dimensions of Hawkaypata; Protzen and Rowe, "Hawkaypata," 239, measures it as 190 x 210 meters, or 39,990 square meters; Moore, "The Archaeology of Plazas and the Proxemics of Ritual," 797, as 190 x 165 meters, or 31,350 square meters.

2 Estete, "Noticia del Perú" [1540s]: "trayendo a las dichas fiestas todos sus agüelos y deudos muertos . . . sentados en sus sillas, y con mucha veneración y respeto," 54–55. Pizarro, "Relación del descubrimiento y conquista de los reinos del Perú" [1571]: "convidándose unos muertos a otros, y los muertos a los vivos y los vivos a los muertos," 67. See also Polo Ondegardo. "Relación de los fundamentos acerca del notable daño que resulta de no guardar a los indios sus fueros," 97; Zuidema, "El ushnu"; Gose, "Oracles, Divine Kingship, and Political Representation in the Inka State"; Cummins, *Toasts with the Inca*, 104.

3 What follows is a narrative of the conquest as interpreted by the conquerors in its immediate aftermath, drawn from the earliest accounts: Miguel de Estete, "La relación del viaje que hizo el señor capitán Hernando Pizarro" [1533]; letter from Hernando Pizarro to the Audiencia de Santo Domingo, Puerto de la Yaguana, 23 Nov. 1533, in Urteaga, ed., *Informaciones sobre el antiguo Perú*, 167–80; Xérez, *Verdadera relación de la conquista del Perú* [1534]; the anonymous account from 1534 usually attributed to Cristóbal de Mena, in Pogo, ed., "The Anonymous 'La Conquista del Perú' (Seville, April 1534) and the Libro Vltimo del Svmmario delle Indie Occidentali (Venice, October 1534)"; Ruiz de Arce, "Una nueva relación de la conquista" [1543]; and the "Noticia del Perú" traditionally but not definitely attributed to Miguel de Estete (see Pease, *Las crónicas y los Andes*, 18–19), probably from the 1540s.

4 In Quechua, *Sapa Inka*. Tawantinsuyu was a multiethnic empire; the Incas, along with other ethnic groups from the Cuzco area who were called "Incas-by-privilege," ruled through the local ethnic lords of the conquered provinces.

5 Miguel de Estete described the Inca settlement of Jauja as "hecho a la manera de los de España, y las calles bien trazadas": "La relación del viaje que hizo el señor Capitán Hernando Pizarro," 144.

6 Morris and Thompson, *Huánuco Pampa*, 58. Huánuco Pampa's plaza (about two hundred thousand square meters) was considerably larger than Cuzco's twin plazas (approximately twenty thousand and thirty thousand square meters), perhaps because it was built later; it was comparable to that of other provincial complexes such as Pumpu. Moore, "The Archaeology of Plazas," 797. Its dimensions were 547 x 370 meters, the size of thirty-eight American football fields (which are 49 x 110 meters), but somewhat smaller than Tiananmen Square in Beijing (880 x 500 meters).

7 Escobar, *The Plaza Mayor and the Shaping of Baroque Madrid.* See Zucker, *Town and Square*, chap. 4; Low, *On the Plaza*, chap. 4; MacCormack, *On the Wings of Time*, 117–21.

8 Xérez, *Verdadera relación de la conquista del Perú*, 87; Cieza de León, *Crónica del Perú. Segunda Parte*, 185 (chap. 64). See MacCormack, *On the Wings of Time*, chap. 1.

9 Hernando Pizarro to Audiencia de Santo Domingo, 23 Nov. 1533, in Urteaga, ed., *Informaciones sobre el antiguo Perú*, 175.

10 "Quitas pumarrangra que dice gentes sin señor derramadas y salteadores," Betanzos, *Suma y narración de los Incas*, 264. For the Quechua phrase, González Holguín's 1604 Quechua dictionary offers "Qquita. Cimarron huydor" and "Pumaranra.Salteador de caminos dado a robar o matar": *Vocabulario de la lengua general de todo el Perú llamada Lengua Qquichua o del Inca*, 310, 295. Gonzalo Lamana offers a rich reading of Atahualpa's encounter with the Spaniards in *Domination without Dominance*, chap. 1.

11 About the exact ransom demand (how many rooms, up to what height?), as with other details in the story, there is slight disagreement in the documents, which this brief account omits.

12 Gaspar de Gárate to his father, Cajamarca, 20 July 1533, in Lockhart, *The Men of Cajamarca*, 461–63: "puede ir un hombre solo quinientas, sin que le maten, sino que antes le den todo lo que ha menester para su persona, y le lleven a cuestas en una hamaca. . . ."

13 Following Atahualpa's murder a different Cuzco prince, Topa Hualpa, had briefly collaborated with the Spaniards and claimed the title of king; he died under suspicious circumstances and Manco Inca took his place.

14 Gasparini and Margolies, *Arquitectura Inka*, 59, 186–98.

15 Bauer, *Ancient Cuzco*, 3. Figure of forty thousand from Protzen and Rowe, "Hawkaypata."

16 Hemming, *The Conquest of the Incas*, 197; Protzen and Rowe, "Hawkaypata"; Dean, "Creating a Ruin in Colonial Cusco."

17 My descriptions of Cuzco's palaces are drawn mainly from Bauer, *Ancient Cuzco*, 121–29, who in turn draws much of the information in this passage from Garcilaso de la Vega.

18 Bauer, *Ancient Cuzco*, 128, citing Garcilaso. This Inca tower was called Sondorhuasi; Seville's bell tower is the famous Giralda.

19 Acta de la fundación española del Cuzco, Cuzco, 23 March 1534, in Pizarro, *Testimonio*, 163–67:

"[yo fundo] en esta gran ciudad del Cuzco cabecera de toda la tierra . . . un pueblo despanoles poblado de los xpnos . . . hallando estar este asiento en la mejor comarca de la tierra y como en tal los senores passados hizieron en el su asiento y morada y le ennoblecieron y poblaron de los mas nobles de su tierra y hizieron en este pueblo ricos edeficios . . . y que la plaça deste pueblo que hago sea esta que estava hecha de los naturales y los solares donde an de hedificar sus casas los vezinos sean traçados y dados al derredor della . . . " 163–64.

20 Ibid., 165.

21 "Ordenanzas para los vecinos del Cuzco y trato de los naturales," Cuzco, 26 March 1534, ibid., 149–51.

22 The phrase "blocks and courtyards" (*cuadras y corrales*) referred to the characteristic Andean architectural trope of one-room buildings linked by shared walls to form semienclosed courtyards or *kanchas*.

23 Resolution by Cuzco cabildo, 29 Oct. 1534, printed in Romero, "La fundación española del Cuzco":

La mayor parte de los solares . . . ha sido en lo edificado que los indios naturales tenían antes de agora, en lo que hay muchas cuadras y corrales que tienen [more or less than 200'] . . . que se cumpla en largo lo que faltare en ancho en la misma cuadra si lo tuviere y si no, en otro o en calles de las que se hubieren de deshacer . . . y donde no se puediere hacer que se le dé y senale la tal cuadra o corral por un solar entero aunque tenga 30 o 40 pies menos de los 200 de ancho y largo . . . ," 151–52.

24 Ibid., "las casas nuevas que hace el cacique," 146.

25 MacCormack, "History, Historical Record, and Ceremonial Action," 343.

26 Ibid., 343 and 359n; Cuzco cabildo, 29 Oct. 1534, in Romero, "La fundación española," 148.

27 Bauer, *Ancient Cuzco*, 125–26.

28 Cuzco cabildo, 29 Oct. 1534, in Romero, "La fundación española," 152.

29 Urteaga, ed., *Relación del sitio del Cusco* [1539], 14–15, 24. See Hemming, *Conquest of the Incas*, 193–202; Himmerich y Valencia, "The 1536 Siege of Cuzco."

30 Manco Inca's state in the valley of Vilcabamba survived into the 1570s, as discussed in later chapters.

31 Valverde to king, 20 March 1539, in *Colección de documentos inéditos*, first series, 3:92–137, see 94.

32 Dean, "Creating a Ruin," 166; Cummins, *Toasts with the Inca*, 276. On Inca-to-colonial architectural continuity, see Nair, "Witnessing the In-visibility of Inca Architecture in Colonial Peru."

33 Absence of literacy: Andeans' quipus or knotted strings were a system of quantitative recordkeeping, though they had some capacity (still poorly understood) to record non-numerical information; see Urton, *Signs of the Inka Khipu*. Absence of money: La Lone, "The Inca as a Nonmarket Economy."

34 Las Casas, *Apologética Historia Sumaria*, Book III, chaps. 46–58, in *Obras escogidas*, vols. 3–4. He emphasized Cuzco and Tenochtitlán.

35 The following description of early modern Hispanic political culture represents

an ideal type. A community's organization varied according to its legal status (ciudad, villa or aldea), as well as differing local traditions, but most conformed to the broad outlines of this description or aspired to do so. There were also differences between communities under the direct authority of the Crown and those under the jurisdiction of a lord. Lucid overviews of the meaning of *vecindad* are found in Nader, *Liberty in Absolutist Spain*, introduction and chap. 1; Carzolio, "En los orígenes de la ciudadanía en Castilla"; Herzog, *Defining Nations*, chap. 2. For municipal self-government under seigneurial jurisdiction, see Guilarte, *El régimen señorial en el siglo XVI*, chap. 4. Tamar Herzog argues that the idea that the vecinos were a corporate community constituting a municipality was created in the era of the Reconquest: "Early Modern Spanish Citizenship in the Old and the New World," 207–8.

36 Carzolio, "En los orígenes de la ciudadanía en Castilla," 659; Herzog, *Defining Nations*, chap. 2. Immigrants to a community might become vecinos by their neighbors' tacit recognization or by formally petitioning to do so. Whether *hidalgos* were required to pay local taxes was a matter of negotiation. Being a vecino was a patriarchal status, but vecinos' wives and children shared their rights and status. In general, vecinos were expected to be married, and in a sense the holder of citizenship was not the man but the couple. Self-supporting widows were sometimes counted as vecinos in their own right. See Nader, *Liberty in Absolutist Spain*, 32–33.

37 Herzog, "Early Modern Spanish Citizenship," 208–9. The Castilian crown devoted considerable attention to forcing the New World settler elite to live in the towns of which they were vecinos, rather than in the countryside; this is the subject of many of the laws found in Konetzke, ed., *Colección de documentos para la historia de la formación social de Hispanoamérica (1493–1810)*, vol. 1.

38 Nader, *Liberty in Absolutist Spain*, chap. 1. When the Crown granted judicial authority in a given town to a lord, the grant authorized him to erect a picota (also called *rollo*). Picotas in Spain were often at the entrance to a town, in Spanish America on the plaza mayor; they could be quite elaborate, and cabildos sometimes maintained a special budget for their upkeep. Quirós, *La picota*, 46; Guilarte, *El régimen señorial*, 128.

39 Ots Capdequí, "Apuntes para la historia del Municipio hispano-americano durante el período colonial"; Vassberg, *Land and Society in Golden-Age Castile*. Satires on rural alcaldes include Cervantes's "La elección de los alcaldes de Daganzo" in *Entremeses*, 103–126, and *Don Quixote II*, 25. Medieval Spanish Christians adapted the word alcalde from Arabic, and may have conflated the Arabic titles of qadi (judge) and qa'id (governor): Harvey, *Islamic Spain, 1250–1500*, 127. See also Graubart, "De qadis y caciques."

40 "Civitas autem no saxa, sed habitatores vocantur." Isidore of Seville, *Etymologiae* 9:4, cited in Kostof, *The City Shaped*, 9.

41 Fraser, *The Architecture of Conquest*, 147; Nader, *Liberty in Absolutist Spain*; Escobar, *The Plaza Mayor*.

42 Pogo, "The Anonymous 'La Conquista'": "llegando al pueblo . . . hallamos la mayor parte de la gente escondida . . . ," 228. On the controversy over the existence of commerce under the Incas, see note 53 below.

43 Ibid.: "pueblo que era grande: y en vnas casas muy altas hallaron mucho mayz: y calçado, otras estauan llenas de lana y mas de 500 mugeres que no hazia otra cosa sino ropas y vino de mayz para la gente de guerra," 224.

44 The earliest Spanish description of the aqlla is Hernando Pizarro's letter of 1533, which contains all the elements in this description. Hernando Pizarro to Audiencia de Santo Domingo, 23 Nov. 1533, in Urteaga, ed., Informaciones, 175.

45 Diego de Trujillo, "Relación del descubrimiento del reino del Perú" [1571], in Xérez, Verdadera relación de la conquista del Perú, 191–205: "entramos y se sacaron las mujeres a la plaza, que eran más de quinientas, y el capitán dio muchas de ellas a los españoles, el capitán del Inca se ensorberbeció mucho," 199. See Gose, "The State as a Chosen Woman"; Graubart, "Indecent Living."

46 The plaza was so filled with men that at his distance he could only make out a "black mass, which we thought was something burnt." Hernando Pizarro to Audiencia de Santo Domingo, 23 Nov. 1533, in Urteaga, ed., Informaciones, 179: "un gran bulto negro, que pensamos ser cosa quemada." In a separate report, his companion Miguel de Estete also estimated that there were one hundred thousand men in the plaza: "La relación del viaje," 144. The number, however, may have been an overestimate.

47 On the material culture of Inca feasts, see Cummins, Toasts with the Inca, chap. 2; Bray, "Inka Pottery as Culinary Equipment."

48 Estete, "La relación del viaje": "hicieron gran fiesta por respecto del capitán Hernando Pizarro, y también por que venía con él Chilicuchima a quien solían hacer fiestas," 144–45.

49 Hernando Pizarro to Audiencia de Santo Domingo, 23 Nov. 1533, in Urteaga, Informaciones: "En todos estos pueblos nos hicieron muy grandes fiestas de danças e bayles," 175. Danza generally implied dancing as performance, baile, dancing as recreation, a distinction implicit in the respective definitions in Covarrubias, Tesoro de la lengua castellana o española.

50 [Estete], "Noticia del Perú": "según la cantidad de lo que bebían, y la gente que lo bebía, no es de maravillar, aunque verlo es maravilla y cosa nunca vista," 55.

51 Throughout the Andes, political structures formed from lineage groups centered around the revered bodies of ancestors: Isbell, Mummies and Mortuary Monuments. Whether panacas were in fact descended from the kings with whom they were associated as ancestors is unclear: Sherbondy, "Panaca Lands."

52 Pedro Pizarro, "Relación," 43. The bulto may have been the huauqui or statue of a dead king, rather than his mallqui, or embalmed body; either could represent the man, depending on the situation. See Gose, "Oracles."

53 Some have argued that Inca cities did have barter-based commerce, pointing to a statement by Miguel de Estete that Inca Jauja's "markets and streets were so full of people," but neither he nor any other witness refers to actual buying

and selling, a subject that filled the first descriptions of Mesoamerican cities. By "market" (*mercado*) Estete may have simply meant the plaza itself, a common Spanish synechdoche. Estete, "La relación del viaje," 144.

54 While the coast had large cities in the pre-Inca era, there is some evidence that coastal cities' resident population had declined by the Inca period: von Hagen and Morris, *Cities of the Ancient Andes*, 139–60.

However, characterizing any urban complex (highland or lowland) as an exclusively ceremonial center is hazardous. Further excavation can reveal more homes than previously thought, and it is difficult to estimate any settlement's population at a given time through archaeological evidence alone: see the essays in Billman and Feinman, eds., *Settlement Pattern Studies in the Americas*. I am not suggesting that Inca cities were never residential centers, but that their other functions were more prominent.

55 Earle et al., "Changing Settlement Patterns in the Upper Mantaro Valley, Peru"; Hyslop, *Inka Settlement Planning*, 292.

56 Vassberg, *Land and Society in Golden-Age Castile*, chap. 1

57 Hyslop, *Inka Settlement Planning*, 292. In a few highland regions outside the Inca heartland, settlement was more concentrated in large villages.

58 This interpretation of Inca state settlements owes largely to Craig Morris and John Murra. See Murra, "Cloth and Its Functions in the Inca State"; Morris and Thompson, *Huánuco Pampa*; Morris, "The Infrastructure of Inka Control in the Peruvian Central Highlands"; Morris, "Storage, Supply, and Redistribution in the Economy of the Inka State."

59 Later, in the colonial period, the word *tamp'u* was Hispanicized as *tambo* and referred to travelers' inns. Since the Spanish invaders described small lodging stations in the Inca empire, as well as Inca towns or cities, scholars have traditionally assumed that the Inca term *tamp'u* referred to the small lodging stations, not the cities. But many scholars now believe that the distinction between the two kinds of places was blurry, that all served some combination of Inca provincial needs (local administration, production, storage, lodging and feasting), and that all state complexes, small or large, may have fallen into the single category of tamp'u. See Hyslop, *The Inka Road System*, 275–93; D'Altroy, *The Incas*, 237–38.

60 Murra, "The Economic Organization of the Inka State," chap. 6; Murra, "Cloth and Its Functions"; Gose, "The State as a Chosen Woman," 86–88.

61 Bray, "Inka Pottery as Culinary Equipment."

62 Polo Ondegardo, "Informe . . . al Licenciado Briviesca de Muñatones sobre la perpetuidad de las encomiendas en el Perú," 139.

63 Cummins, *Toasts with the Inca*, 44.

64 Escobar, *The Plaza Mayor*, 176 and passim.

2. The Mountains

1 "Creyendo que avia de venyr tiempo en que diesen quenta dello al ynga." Polo Ondegardo, "Relación de los fundamentos acerca del notable daño que resulta de no guardar a los indios sus fueros," 41. Polo fed the king's soldiers (who were fighting against the rebel Gonzalo Pizarro, one of Francisco's brothers) from these storage deposits for seven weeks, and counted fifteen thousand fanegas in them. A fanega of flour was about 130 pounds in these years, meaning the stored grain would be nearly 2 million pounds.

2 Zavala, La encomienda indiana.

3 In Spanish documents it is sometimes unclear, though, whether the hanansaya cacique's segunda persona is the hurinsaya cacique or the secondary leader of hanansaya: Rostworowski and Morris, "The Fourfold Domain," 785. On communities' dualistic organization see Rostworowski, Estructuras andinas del poder; Cook and Cook, People of the Volcano, 21–23. Sayas were similar to moieties, although they did not entirely fit the classic definition, especially sayas in large political entities. The colonizers referred to sayas by the Spanish term parcialidad.

4 Rostworowski and Morris, "The Fourfold Domain"; Cook and Cook, People of the Volcano, 18–23, 105–10.

5 Licenciado Gaspar de Espinoza to the emperor, Panama, 10 Oct. 1533, in Porras Barrenechea, ed., Cartas del Perú, 66–75: "son acostumbrados a servir la gente común a los señores," 73.

6 Trelles, Lucas Martínez Vegazo, chap. 7; Stern, Peru's Indian Peoples and the Challenge of Spanish Conquest, chap. 2; Río, Etnicidad, territorialidad y colonialismo en los Andes, chap. 2, pt. 2.

7 Cook, "La visita de los Conchucos por Cristóbal Ponce de León, 1543." Some of what this inspector counted as villages actually consisted of two or more neighboring settlements, making the population per settlement even smaller.

8 Espinoza Soriano, "Ichoc-Huánuco y el senorío del curaca huanca en el Reino de Huánuco," 23.

9 "Virgin soil" epidemics devastated the Peruvian coast in the first decades after contact, as they did other lowland regions, but penetrated more slowly into the highlands. See Cook, Demographic Collapse.

10 Jauja cabildo to Francisco Pizarro, Jauja, 27 June 1534, in Colección de documentos inéditos, first series, 10:293–302.

11 AGI Lima 565 L2, ff 234r–v, Real Cédula "sobre cierta ordenança que el gobernador hizo para q los espanoles bolviesen los yndios a sus pueblos," Valladolid, 20 Nov. 1536, citing a previous undated ordenanza given by Pizarro.

12 AGI Lima 565 L2, ff 224r–225r, Real Cédula "sobre el residir de los indios en sus tierras," Valladolid, 3 Nov. 1536, incorporating a previous undated ordenanza of Pizarro: "por las poblaciones y asientos que en la tierra los naturales tienen hechos se ha visto y sabido que en tiempo de los senores pasados los dichos naturales avian sido trocados y pasados de unas partes a otras y sacados de sus

naturalezas para que residiesen y poblasen alli do les avia sido senalado de la qual orden resulto que . . . los dhos naturales que en lengua suya son mytimaes y por diurturnidad y luengos tiempos tienen convertida en naturaleza las tierras y pueblos en que biven. . . ."

13 Recent scholarship on Inca mitimas is large; see D'Altroy, "Remaking the Social Landscape"; Lorandi and Rodríguez, "Yanas y mitimaes."

14 Cieza de León, *Crónica del Perú, Primera Parte*, caps. 53, 57, 74, 92–93. Spaniards might have known about military colonization in ancient empires (and even in the contemporary Ottoman empire as a means of rewarding soldiers and securing border zones), but no Old World state practiced as varied and sweeping internal resettlement as the Incas. In the medieval Iberian *reconquista*, Christians settled on land conquered from Muslim kingdoms, but by their own choice, not state fiat.

15 AGI Lima 565 L2, ff 224r–225r.

16 Ibid., ff 224v–225r: "si algunos destos que ansi biven fuera de sus pueblos se quisieren bolver a sus tierras provereys como lo [225r] dexan yr libremente y poblar en las tierras que ellos quisyere. . . ."

17 Haring, *The Spanish Empire in America*, 114.

18 This principle was confirmed by Real Cédula in 1539. See Puente Brunke, *Encomienda y encomenderos en el Perú*, 174.

19 Many of the earliest encomienda grants do not mention mitimas: grant for Canta and Lima to Nicolas de Ribera el mozo, Jauja, 1 Sept. 1534, in Rostworowski, *Señoríos indígenas de Lima y Canta*, 197–216; grant for Cajamarca to Melchor Verdugo, Trujillo, 5 March 1535, in AGI Escribanía 500B, first document, ff 4–5. Pizarro did, however, know something about mitimas as early as mid-1534, and explicitly included them in some grants. Grant for Chincha to Hernando Pizarro, tambo de Pachacamac, 5 Aug. 1534, cited in Rostworowski, *Doña Francisca Pizarro*, 21; grant for Cabanas to Cristóbal Pérez and Juan de Arbes, Cuzco, 1 June 1535, cited in Cook and Cook, *People of the Volcano*, 31. The provision became routine; see, for example, encomienda grant to Pedro and Francisco de Isasaga, Cuzco, 31 Aug. 1548, in Barnadas, *Charcas*, 562–64.

20 AGI Justicia 656, N 1, R 1, pieza 1, ff 13–15. *Posesión* of repartimiento Caquingora, La Paz, 29 Dec. 1549. The document is slightly ambiguous but this is the most plausible reading. The other two principales likely represented the repartimiento's two sayas.

21 Susan Ramírez argues that Pizarro in fact undermined community integrity, writing that he, "out of ignorance or arrogance, often split the original polities into as many as four encomiendas": *The World Upside Down*, 156. Pizarro was arrogant but not entirely ignorant about Andean society. Pressure from encomienda seekers forced him and later governors to divide Andean communities into the smallest units possible, but Pizarro typically incorporated mitimas into encomienda grants in order to keep Andean communities viable for the purpose of tribute.

22 Guevara Gil and Salomon, "A 'Personal Visit' "; Sánchez Bella, *Las visitas gene-rales en la América española*; Cook, "Visitas, Censuses," in Pillsbury, *Guide to Documentary Sources*, 1:129–43.

23 To give an example of the complexity, Pizarro's inspector in Cajamarca counted six local caciques and their subjects, as well as thirteen different groups of mitimas, some from the coast and some from other parts of the highlands. Of these thirteen groups, he determined that four had severed all ties to their home caciques and should pay tribute to the Cajamarca encomendero, whereas the other nine answered to distant caciques and were not to be included in the Cajamarca census. Cristóbal de Barrientos, "Visita de las siete guarangas de la provincia de Caxamarca," Chiquelete, 24 Aug. 1540, in Espinoza Soriano, "El primer informe etnológico sobre Cajamarca, año de 1540," 38–39.

24 "Juicio por tierras de coca en Quivi entre los Canta y los Chaclla, dos etnías instaladas en el valle del Chillón, 1558–1567," discussed in Rostworowski, *Etnía y sociedad*, 176–87. The procession was the *capacocha*.

25 Braudel, *The Mediterranean and the Mediterranean World in the Age of Philip II*, 1:34; Sancho, *An Account of the Conquest of Peru*, 147, 149–50; Gasca, *Descripción del Perú*, 17. Mount Olympus in Greece is about 2,900 meters high.

26 Brading, *The First America*, 119–26; MacCormack, *On the Wings of Time*, chaps. 1–2; Barrera-Osorio, *Experiencing Nature*, chap. 4. Royal questionnaires from 1553 and 1559, part of a continuing project that led to the Relaciones Geográficas de Indias, had a major impact in promoting colonial ethnography: Escobedo Mansilla, "Pervivencias prehispánicas en el derecho criollo peruano," 132. As early as 1551 the Crown sent to Peru a request for information about the history of the caciques: Real Cédula, 21 Jan. 1551, in ANB, Reales Cédulas 8.

27 Damián de la Bandera, "Relacion general de la disposición y calidad de la provincia de Guamanga," Guamanga, 26 Aug. 1557, in Jiménez de la Espada, ed., *Relaciones geográficas de Indias*, 1:176–80: "Es tierra doblada y cavernosa: lo alto es tierra fría, pelada, seca y estéril; lo bajo, donde hay ríos e quebradas de agua, es tierra templada y fértil . . . tierra mal sana para los indios serranos . . . ," 176.

28 Vargas, *Fray Domingo de Santo Tomás*; Murra, "Le débat sur l'avenir des Andes en 1562," 627.

29 Santo Tomás to king, Lima, 1 July 1550, in Lissón Chaves, ed. *La iglesia de España en el Perú*, 1:195–96: "tratavanse todos y comunicabanse como hermanos en las comidas y contrataciones, . . . y como hera todo uno y de un señor gozaban todos dello."

30 See, for instance, the anonymous 1551 report in Rowe, ed., "Un memorial del gobierno de los Incas del ano 1551"; Cieza, *Crónica del Perú, Segunda Parte*, 40.

31 Vaca de Castro, "Ordenanzas de tambos" [1543]: "no se podría ordenar en otra manera mejor de como los dichos señores lo tenian proveido," 455.

32 Cieza, *Crónica del Perú*, 71; Polo Ondegardo, "Informe . . . al Licenciado Briviesca de Muñatones sobre la perpetuidad de las encomiendas en el Perú," " 133. Be-

tanzos's and Zárate's comments on this are discussed in Fraser, *The Architecture of Conquest*, 23–24.

33 "Relación que dio el provisor Luis de Morales sobre las cosas que debían proveerse para las provincias del Perú," in Lissón Chaves, *La iglesia*, 1:48–93, see 78.

34 AGI Charcas 135, no. 1 bis, "Obispo de los Charcas" to "muy reverendo y muy magnifico señor," (probably the viceroy), undated (probably 1552, making the author Fray Tomás de San Martín), 2 ff.

35 Cieza de León, *Crónica del Perú, Primera Parte*, 272–23 [cap. 99]: "si no fuera mediante ello, las más de las gentes de su señorío . . . biuieran con gran necessidad, como antes que por ellos fueron señoreados . . . Aunque en todo el Collao no se coge ni siembra mayz, no les falta a los señores naturales dél, ni a los que lo quieran procurar con la orden ya dicha: porque nunca dexan de traer cargas de mayz, coca, y fructas de todo género, y cantidad de miel."

36 Castro and Ortega, "Relación y declaración del modo que este valle de Chincha y sus comarcanos se gobernaban. . . ." [1558], 245–26.

37 Espinoza Soriano, "Migraciones internas en el Reino Colla."

38 Assadourian, "Exchange in the Ethnic Territories between 1530 and 1567," 119; Regalado de Hurtado, "La percepción colonial de los mitmaqkuna."

39 The most important sources for licenciado Polo Ondegardo's life include: Hampe, "Un letrado exitoso"; González Pujana, *Polo de Ondegardo*; Presta, *Encomienda, familia y negocios en Charcas colonial (Bolivia)*; Honores, "El licenciado Polo y su informe al licenciado Briviesca de Muñatones." Scholars used to think his name was Juan Polo de Ondegardo, but it was simply Polo Ondegardo, and his contemporaries referred to him as licenciado Polo. (Renzo Honores, personal communication.) He served the king in the wars against Gonzalo Pizarro in 1547–48 and against Francisco Hernández Girón in 1554, receiving his leg wound in the latter war.

40 Polo, "Informe" and "Relación de los fundamentos."

41 Polo, "Informe," 176–78: "ay muy pocas tierras, o ninguna en la sierra, que los indios puedan pasar sin yr a otras por lo necezario," 176; "sería quitalles su orden, que entienden, . . . y no dalles otra ninguna," 178.

42 Ibid.: "era tanta la orden que tuvieron estos indios, que a mi paresçer, avnque mucho se piense en ello, sería dificultoso mejorarla, conosçida su condiçión y costumbres . . .", 148. Inca resettlements: ibid., 134. As we have seen, in some areas the effect of Inca rule was exactly the opposite of what Polo believed, leading to a *more* dispersed pattern of settlement.

43 Ibid.: "si mucho se pensare en ello, no se hallará mejor camino ni medio que el que está dado," 177.

44 On early encomienda grants, see Puente, *Encomienda y encomenderos en el Perú*, 30–37. Because the sequence of conquest and encomienda grants proceeded from west to east, highland communities were much more likely to lose control of their mitimas in the west than in the east: Saignes, "The Ethnic Groups in the Valleys of Larecaja," 321.

45 Polo, "Informe," 177–78. He had obtained his goal in the case of Chucuito, compensating affected encomenderos with other communities, and in 1561 called for doing the same in the province of Carangas. "Provisión del Virrey don Hurtado de Mendoza a petición de los caciques de Chuquito," Lima, 20 Feb. 1557, in Barriga, ed., *Documentos para la Historia de Arequipa*, 3:299–301. See Trelles Aréstegui, *Lucas Martínez Vegazo*, 142–65. The decision apparently was recognized as a precedent in the Spanish court: see Real Cédula, Madrid, 12 Feb. 1569, in AGI Charcas 418, L 1, ff 139v–140r.

46 AGI Indiferente 737, no. 66. Consulta del Consejo de Indias, "Sobre dejar a los indios de las provincias del Collao en libertad para explotar sus minas, dando un tributo a su majestad y no permitiendo que viva entre ellos ningun cristiano," [1555]. The Consejo and king decided to ask the viceroy's opinion on this proposal, but it is unclear if there was a response.

47 Valverde to king, Cuzco, 20 March 1539, in *Colección de documentos inéditos*, first series, 3:92–137: "segun su manera dellos," 112.

3. The Grid

1 Parry, *The Spanish Seaborne Empire*, 193–94.

2 Freedman, *Images of the Medieval Peasant*, pt. 3.

3 Nirenberg, "Muslims in Christian Iberia, 1000–1526," 61; Burns, *Islam Under the Crusaders*, 10–11, 157 216, 187–8; Harvey, *Islamic Spain, 1250–1500*, 65; Graubart, "De qadis y caciques." Aragonese Valencia was admittedly an extreme example of colonial pluralism, but the medieval Castilian king Alfonso VI likewise styled himself, in Arabic, "ruler of two religions" (Burns, *Islam Under the Crusaders*, 186). Much of medieval Iberian law was determined by the religion, region or municipality to which one belonged. Benton, *Law and Colonial Cultures*, chap. 2.

4 The forced conversion of Muslims in Castile (including Granada) was a gradual process extending from 1499 to 1502. Aragon followed Castile's example in 1526. Domínguez Ortiz and Vincent, *Historia de los moriscos*, 18 and chap. 1.

5 Domínguez Ortiz and Vincent, *Historia de los moriscos*, 28–33.

6 Reales cédulas to Santo Domingo, Alcalá de Henares, 20 March 1503, and Zaragoza, 29 March 1503, in Solano, ed., *Normas y leyes de la ciudad hispanoamericana*, 1:24–26: " . . . es necesario que los indios se repartan en pueblos en que vivan juntamente y que los unos no estén ni anden apartados de los otros por los montes. . . ." The monarchs repeated the order in 1509: ibid., 1:34.

7 Leyes de Burgos, 27 Dec. 1512, in Konetzke, ed., *Colección de documentos para la historia de la formación social de Hispanoamérica (1493–1810)*, 1:38–57, see 38–41; Real Instrucción, 13 Sept. 1516, in Solano, ed., *Normas y leyes*, 1:47–51.

8 Royal order, Valladolid, 26 June 1523, in Konetzke, *Colección*, 1:74: "los dichos indios tienen manera y razón para vivir política y ordenadamente en sus pueblos que ellos tienen, [pero] habéis de trabajar, . . . poniéndolos en buenas costumbres y toda buena orden de vivir. . . ."

9 Gibson, "Spanish-Indian Institutions and Colonial Urbanism in New Spain," 233.

10 "Real cédula para que se pongan en policía los indios," Valladolid, 23 Aug. 1538, in Konetzke, *Colección*, 1:186–87: "Yo he sido informado que para que nuestra santa fe católica sea ampliada entre los indios, . . . sería necesario ponerlos en policía humana para que sea camino y medio de darles a conocer la divina, y que para esto se debría dar orden como viviesen juntos en sus calles y plazas concertadamente. . . ."

11 Zucker, *Town and Square*, 132–35; Torres Balbás, *Ciudades hispanomusulmanas*, 10–12; Kostof, *The City Shaped*, 48–50.

12 Durston, "Un régimen urbanístico en la América hispana colonial," 63.

13 Kubler, *Mexican Architecture*, 1:76; Gakenheimer, "Decisions of Cabildo on Urban Physical Structure."

14 Urban grids in prehispanic America tended to have rectangular blocks, not the rigidly square ones found in most colonial Spanish cities.

15 Cervantes de Salazar, *Life in the Imperial and Loyal City of Mexico in New Spain*, 260: "Nec censeo, in utroque orbe aequale inveniri posse, bone Deus quam & planum & capax est, quam hilare, . . . si porticus illi, quae nunc contra nos sunt, e medio tolerentur, integrum exercitum capere potuisset."

16 For this paragraph and the next, see Kubler, *Mexican Architecture*, 1:68–102; Solano, *Ciudades hispanoamericanas y pueblos de indios*; Kostof, *The City Shaped*, chap. 2; Gutiérrez, "Las reducciones indígenas en el urbanismo colonial"; Durston, "Un régimen urbanístico"; Sullivan, "La congregación como tecnología disciplinaria en el siglo XVI," 45; Low, *On the Plaza*, chap. 4; Escobar, *The Plaza Mayor*; Cummins, "Forms of Andean Colonial Towns, Free Will, and Marriage"; Rose-Redwood, "Genealogies of the Grid."

17 Lefebvre, *The Production of Space*, 151–52; Fraser, *The Architecture of Conquest*, 7, 147.

18 Sánchez-Concha, "La tradición política y el concepto del 'cuerpo de república' en el Virreinato," 110; Mörner, *La Corona Española y los foráneos en los pueblos de indios*; Martínez, *Genealogical Fictions*. In later colonial Mexico, the phrase *república de indios* often referred to an individual community; in Peru it usually meant indigenous society generally.

19 Covarrubias, *Tesoro de la lengua castellana o española*, s.v. *reduzir*; Real Academia Española, *Diccionario de Autoridades*, s.v. *reducciones*; Cummins, "Forms of Andean Colonial Towns, Free Will, and Marriage," 202–3. Hanks, *Converting Words*, 4.

20 See Real Cédula to Guatemala, Madrid, 10 June 1540, in Solano, ed., *Normas y leyes*, 1:135.

21 Kubler, *Mexican Architecture*, 1:87.

22 The Franciscan Toribio de Motolinía wrote that the resettlement policy had been controversial for its possible harm to Indian communities, but that successful experiments in Guatemala had disproven the dangers. Motolinía to king, Mexico City, 15 May 1550, ibid., 1:76.

23 Congregación de prelados, Mexico, 1546, quoted in Real Cédula, Madrid, 15 Feb. 1567, in *Colección de documentos inéditos*, first series, 18:514–15: " . . . porque para ser verdaderamente cristanos y politicos, como hombres racionales que

son, es nescessario estar congregados y reducidos en pueblos, y no vivan deramados y dispersos por las sierras y montes."

24 "Por la . . . mas blanda y amorosa vía." Reales cédulas, Valladolid, 9 Oct. 1549. Peru version printed in Málaga Medina, *Reducciones toledanas en Arequipa*, 217–18; Mexico version in Konetzke, *Colección*, 1:260–61; New Granada version in Friede, ed., *Documentos inéditos para la historia de Colombia*, 9:305.

25 Sullivan, "Un diálogo sobre la congregación en Tlaxcala," 39.

26 Fray Tomás de Cárdenas and Fray Juan de Torres to king, 6 Dec. 1555, quoted in Lovell, "Mayans, Missionaries, Evidence and Truth," 281–82.

27 Mexico Audiencia oidor Vasco de Puga to crown, 1564, quoted in Gerhard, "Congregaciones de indios en la Nueva España en 1570," 352.

28 On resettlement in Guatemala, , see Antonio de Remesal, "Historia general," excerpted in Solano, ed., *Normas y leyes*, 1:143–47; Saenz, "La 'reducción a poblados' en el siglo XVI en Guatemala"; Lovell, " Mayans, Missionaries, Evidence and Truth"; on the Yucatan (where resettlement was vigorous and well-documented following the intervention of Tomás López Medel in 1552), Farriss, "Nucleation versus Dispersal"; Bracamonte y Sosa and Solis Robleda, *Espacios mayas de autonomía*, 69–73; Hanks, *Converting Words*, chaps. 2–3; on central Mexico, Simpson, "The Civil Congregation"; Gerhard, " Congregaciones de indios en la Nueva España en 1570"; Lockhart, *The Nahuas After the Conquest*, 44; Hoekstra, *Two Worlds Merging*, 68–70; on Florida, see Bushnell, "The Sacramental Imperative."

29 AGI Patronato 187, ramo 14, "Ordenanzas promulgadas por la Audiencia de Lima para que los indios se junten en pueblos," Lima, 20 Oct. 1550.

30 Reales cédulas, Madrid, 17 Dec. 1551, printed in Málaga, *Reducciones toledanas en Arequipa*, 219–20, and 21 March 1552, ibid., 40. See also Real Provisión to the Audiencia of Panamá, Cigales, 21 March 1551, in Konetzke, *Colección*, 1:283–85. Early modern Castilian legislation was relatively informal, in that kings promulgated a steady stream of laws that did not distinguish clearly between major policies and minor instructions, were not well catalogued or indexed at court (let alone outside of it), often repeated and sometimes contradicted each other. Pedro de la Gasca, governor of Peru, urged Andean resettlement in his memorial to his successor on 25 Jan. 1550: Pérez de Tudela, ed., *Documentos relativos a don Pedro de la Gasca y a Gonzalo Pizarro*, 299–300.

31 Vargas Ugarte, ed., *Concilios limenses (1551–1772)*, 1:33. "Porque comúnmente en esta tierra los indios están divididos en muchos poblezuelos y sería gran perjuicio y pesadumbre si se obieren de juntar todos. . . ."

32 Gerónimo de Loayza, archbishop of Lima, conspicuously ignored the topic in his "Instrucción sobre la doctrina . . ." Lima, 14 Feb. 1549, in Lisson Chávez, *La iglesia*, 1:135–45.

33 For the anti-Indian view, see Juan de Matienzo, discussed below. For the pro-Indian view, see Santillán, "Relación del origin, descendencia política y gobierno de los Incas" [1563], 106; "Relación hecha al Obispo Fray Bartolomé de Las

Casas por el Padre Fray Domingo de Santo Tomás," in Vargas, *Fray Domingo de Santo Tomás*, 87–108, see 107–8.

34 Bandera, "Relacion general de la disposición y calidad de la provincia de Guamanga," Guamanga, 26 Aug. 1557, in Jiménez de la Espada, ed., *Relaciones geográficas de Indias*, 1:176–80 (also discussed in chapter 2); Niles, *The Shape of Inca History*, 124. On Cañete's Lima resettlement, see Málaga Medina, *Reducciones toledanas en Arequipa*, 25; on Polo's Cuzco resettlement, see Montesinos, *Anales del Perú*, 1:258.

35 Instructions to inspectors, Lima, 22 Dec. 1561, in Ortiz de Zúñiga, *Visita de la provincia de Leon de Huánuco en 1562*, 1:8–16, see 15. This instruction, given to Ortiz de Zúñiga for his inspection of Huánuco, appears to have been standard for the inspectors: for comparison see AGI Patronato 188, ramo 28, "Instrucciones otorgadas por la Audiencia de Lima a los visitadores."

36 Ramírez, *The World Upside Down*, 30–31, 73–74; Klaus, "Out of Light Came Darkness," 319.

37 Loayza to king, Lima, 2 Aug. 1564, in Lisson Chávez, *La iglesia*, 2:272–82.

38 Conde de Nieva to king, Lima, 4 May 1562, in *Gobernantes*, 1:395–472: "como esta poblada la tierra los yngas la asentaron y dexaron assy[;] es de creer a lo menos de sospechar siendo a lo que se entiende tan buen govierno en lo [mundano] el suyo si oviera comodidad los redugera a mayores poblaciones . . . ," 428.

39 Ibid.: "esto se dize porque algunos caciques an venido a hablar sobre este articulo de reduzillos a mayores poblaciones diziendo que se les haria agravio como quiera que esto sea asi es bien tratallo . . . ," 428–29.

40 Nieva took Indian resettlement off the top of his agenda, although he did not give up entirely on it: Conde de Nieva to king, Lima, 26 Dec. 1562, ibid, 1:486–504, see 503.

4. Lords

1 AGI Justicia 434, no. 2, ramo 1, pieza 2, f. 6v. Testimony by Francisco Hernández about an offer made by Cuzco-area caciques, 1561: " . . . avian savido quel Rey lo hazia constrenido de nescesydad e que muchos dellos heran Ricos e poderosos e que le querian hazer algun servi. de dineros para suplir pte. de su nescesydad, e que no los hiziese perpetuos en sus amos." The account is secondhand: Hernández, *escribano*, is reporting what he learned from Pedro Pacheco, *corregidor* of the city of Cuzco.

2 Marvin Goldwert, "La lucha por la perpetuidad de las encomiendas en el Perú virreinal, 1550–1600"; Assadourian, *Transiciones hacia el Sistema Colonial Andino*, 209–92; Abercrombie, "La perpetuidad traducida"; Mumford, "Aristocracy on the Auction Block."

3 Fernández de Palencia, *Primera y segunda parte de la historia del Perú*, pt. 2, bk. 2, chaps. 28–58.

4 The proposal had appeared before, at the urging of Mexican encomenderos in earlier decades, but never gone beyond idle discussion: Muro Orejón, "Las Leyes Nuevas de Indias," 607–8.

5 Puente Brunke, *Encomienda y encomenderos.*

6 Abercrombie, "La perpetuidad traducida," 92.

7 Mercado de Peñalosa to King, Lima, 25 Feb. 1558 in Levillier, ed., *Audiencia de Lima,* 1:198–201.

8 Mendiburu, *Diccionario histórico-biográfico del Perú,* 378–79.

9 Goldwert, "La lucha por la perpetuidad de las encomiendas en el Perú virreinal, 1550–1600," 351. In 1553–54, Castile's debt had risen from 3.1 to 4.3 million ducats. (Rodríguez Salgado, *The Changing Face of Empire,* 4–5.) If Ribera meant his offer in *pesos ensayados,* as is likely, it amounted to 8.6 million ducats. (The two coins at this time were worth 425 and 375 maravedises, respectively: Luengo Múñoz, "Sumaria noción de las monedas de Castilla e Indias en el siglo XVI.") A pernil was worth seven *tomines,* or 0.93 *pesos ensayados;* a pair of *ojotas* was 2.5 *tomines,* or 0.33 *pesos ensayados.* Around this time in Spain, a hunting falcon was worth 5.51 *pesos de a ocho,* or 3.52 *pesos ensayados.* (Lee and Bromley, eds., *Libros de cabildos de Lima,* 4:656; Lohmann Villena, *El corregidor de indios en el Perú bajo los Austrias,* 58; www.castillodeniebla.com/ingles/body_visita4.htm.)

10 Philip II to Consejo de Indias, London, 17 Feb. 1555, in Konetzke, ed., *Colección de documentos para la historia de la formación social de Hispanoamérica (1493–1810),* 1:326–28.

11 "Memorial-sumario a Felipe II" [1556], in Las Casas, *Obras escogidas,* 455.

12 Pereña Vicente, "La pretensión a la perpetuidad de las encomiendas del Perú," 428–29.

13 Instruction to commissioners, Brussels, 15 March 1559, in Zabálburu and Rayon, eds., *Nueva colección de documentos inéditos para la historia de España y sus Indias,* 6:191–93.

14 Power of attorney, Lima, 19 July 1559, in Hanke, "Un festón de documentos lascasianos."

15 Las Casas and Santo Tomás, Memorial, c. 1560, in Las Casas, *Obras escogidas,* 5:467.

16 *Kuraka* was the most common of several Andean words for a native lord. Almost universally in colonial discourse, however, they were called caciques, a word borrowed from Caribbean languages and used all over the Americas. Within the large literature on caciques, see especially Díaz Rementería, *El cacique en el virreinato del Perú;* Pease, *Curacas, Reciprocidad y Riqueza;* Guevara Gil, "Los caciques y el señorío natural en los Andes coloniales (Perú, siglo XVI)"; Ramírez, *To Feed and Be Fed.*

17 Santillán, "Relación del origin, descendencia política y gobierno de los Incas"; Damián de la Bandera, "Relacion general de la disposición y calidad de la provincia de Guamanga," Guamanga, 26 Aug. 1557, in Jiménez de la Espada, ed., *Relaciones geográficas de Indias,* 1:176–80, see 178.

18 Góngora, *El estado en el derecho indiano,* 216–7.

19 Espinoza Soriano, ed., "El memorial de Charcas" [1581], 132.

20 Lockhart, *Spanish Peru,* chap. 2.

21 Espinoza Soriano, "Los huancas, aliados de la conquista."

22 Garcilaso de la Vega, *Royal Commentaries of the Incas and General History of Peru*, 1:335.

23 D'Altroy, "Transitions in Power."

24 Garcilaso, *Royal Commentaries*, 1:334–36.

25 D'Altroy, "Transitions in Power."

26 Murra, "The Economic Organization of the Inca State," chap. 5.

27 Spalding, "The Crises and Transformations of Invaded Societies," 933–35.

28 Espinoza Soriano, "Los huancas"; Murra, "Litigation over the Rights of 'Natural Lords' in Early Colonial Courts in the Andes"; Pease, "Curacas," 154–58.

29 Andres de Vega, "La descripción que se hizo en la provincia de Xauxa," 1582, in Jiménez de la Espada, ed., *Relaciones geográficas de Indias*, 1:166–72: Lurinhuanca had twelve thousand tributaries (i.e., households) under the last Inca king and 3,500 in 1572; I am assuming four to five members in an average household.

30 Assadourian, *Transiciones hacia el Sistema Colonial Andino*, 19–62.

31 Espinoza Soriano, ed., "Los huancas," 226.

32 Huancas' pride in their service to the king in the war against Girón remained fresh for decades: Scott, *Contested Territory*, 61.

33 Las Casas to fray Bartolomé Carranza, Aug. 1555, in Las Casas, *Obras escogidas*, 5:430–50, see 444–45.

34 Undated *parecer*, Zabálburu and Rayon, *Nueva Colección*, 6:270–74.

35 King to Nieva and commissioners, Toledo, 7 Feb. 1561, in Jiménez de la Espada, ed., *Relaciones geográficas de Indias*, 1:40–41.

36 Goldwert, "La lucha por la perpetuidad de las encomiendas," 211.

37 AGI Justicia 434, no. 2, ramo 1, pieza 2, f. 6v.

38 Jiménez de la Espada, ed., *Relaciones geográficas de Indias*, 1:41 (citing Antonio León Pinelo). I thank Donato Amado Gonzales for telling me the two princes' names.

39 "Acuerdo y exhortación de los señores del Consejo a los órdenes sobre ciertos desórdenes," Lima, 17 Oct. 1561, in Olmedo Jiménez, *Jerónimo de Loaysa, O.P.*, 307–8.

40 AGI Justicia 434, no. 2, ramo 1, Cuenca contra Antón Ruiz, lengua, 1561–1563; Cuenca to king, Cuzco, 26 Jan. 1562, in Levillier, ed., *Audiencia de Lima*, 262–63. See Abercrombie, "La perpetuidad traducida."

41 On Santo Tomás's companions, see Lic. Monzón to king, Lima, 2 Jan. 1563, in Levillier, ed., *Audiencia de Lima*, 277–81, see 279. Although Monzón does not name them, it is likely that these were the same men previously deputized by the Cuzco caciques.

42 Santo Tomás et al. to king, Lima, 26 Feb. 1562, in Lissón Chaves, ed., *La iglesia de España en el Perú*, 2:232–33; Santo Tomás to Lima Consejo Real de Hacienda, Andahuaylas, 5 April 1562, ibid., 2:203–4. See also Goldwert, "La lucha," 214–15; Pereña, "La pretension a la perpetuidad de las encomiendas del Perú," 440; Murra, "Nos Hazen Mucha Ventaja," 82.

43 Santo Tomás to don Alonso Manuel de Anaya, Guamanga, 23 March 1562, in

Lissón Chaves, *La iglesia*, 2:202: "El señor lic. Polo les da a entender los grandes provechos que les vendra estando perpetuos en ellos con todo esto dizen que manacancho quieren perpetuidad."

44 AGI Indiferente General 1530, ff 615–43, power of attorney, Mama, 21 Jan. 1562.

45 Espinoza Soriano, ed., "Los huancas," 180–84.

46 Goldwert, "La lucha," 214.

47 King to commissioners, Madrid, 13 Feb. 1562, in *Colección de documentos inéditos*, first series, 18:25–27.

48 Conde de Nieva to king, Lima, 4 May 1562, in *Gobernantes*, 1:395–472.

49 Zabálburu and Rayon, *Nueva Colección*, 6:136–65.

50 Felipe de Segovia Briceño to Castro, received 5 Dec. 1564, in Odriozola, ed., *Documentos históricos del Perú en las épocas del coloniaje despues de la conquista y de la independencia hasta la presente*, 3:3–9, see 6–8.

51 Castro to king, Lima, 6 March 1565, in *Gobernantes*, 3:54–69: "con ser estos yndios de este valle los que siempre an acudido mas al servicio de VM que otros algunos . . . ," 59.

52 Ibid.: " . . . ellos dicen que las hacian [i.e., las picas] que si yo las hubiese menester para la jornada de chile . . . ," 59.

53 Probanza of don Gerónimo Guacrapaucar, in Espinoza Soriano, ed., "Los huancas," 225.

54 Since wood was relatively scarce in the central Andes, the Huancas' pikes may not have been as long as this, however.

55 McNeill, *The Pursuit of Power*, 66.

56 AGI Lima 121, loose file, f. 5, Castro to king, Lima 30 April 1566. Spanish officials had long debated whether caciques should be permitted to own arms and horses, and the king had banned it in 1551, but this had been ignored, as orders from court routinely were: Real Cédula, Madrid, 17 Dec. 1551, in Konetzke, *Colección*, 1:292–97. Castro's order was not fully effective either, as at least one document from 1568 shows a cacique in the northern coast who owned a horse: Zevallos Quiñones, "La visita del pueblo de Ferreñafe (Lambayeque) en 1568," 157–58.

57 Spalding, *Huarochirí*, 213.

58 See *Gobernantes* 3:59–60.

59 Lohmann Villena, *El corregidor de indios en el Perú bajo los Austrias*.

60 Castro to king, Lima, 30 April 1565, in *Gobernantes*, 3:78–85.

61 AGI Justicia 415, N1, R2, ff 12–13, Instructions to Nicolás Ruiz de Estrada, corregidor of Chucuito, Lima, 2 April 1565; AGI Lima 121, loose file, ff 24r–30v, Instructions to corregidores, Lima, 3 July 1565.

62 BNE, Ms 3043, ff 1–5, Instructions to Juan de Larreinaga, corregidor of Jauja, Lima, 27 June 1565.

63 Mendiburu, *Diccionario histórico-biógrafico*, 9:338.

64 AGI Lima 121, ff 45r–48r, Cabildo de Jauja, parcialidad Ananguancas, to king, Jatunjauja, 3 Jan. 1566; Espinoza Soriano, "Reducciones, pueblos, y ciudades."

65 AGI Lima 121, f. 51, fray López de la Fuente to Castro, Jauja, 14 Jan. 1566. The folio numbers here and below refer to a single series of papers, which itself is only one of several files in this *legajo* and is not otherwise identified.

66 Ibid., ff 57–58, Cabildo of Chongos to king, 8 Jan. 1566 [misdated 1565].

67 Ibid., ff 53, Francisco de Balboa to Castro, 12 Jan. 1566: "beviendo con los caciques y principales en la plaça donde hazen todos los dias del mundo cavildo." The letter is not fully legible, but Balboa seems to be corregidor of Yauyos.

68 Ibid., ff 13r–14r, Huarochirí and Yauyos caciques' petition to Castro, 18 July 1565.

69 Castro to Consejo, 12 Jan. 1566, in *Gobernantes*, 3:144–56; Charcas Audiencia to Castro, La Plata, 10 June 1566, in Levillier, ed., *Audiencia de Charcas*, 2:437–56.

70 AGI Lima 121, "Los caciques e yndios del Peru sobre que se quiten los corregidores que el lic. Castro proveyó para en los pueblos de yndios," 11 Oct. 1565–10 Jan. 1566.

71 Loayza to king, Lima, 1 March 1566, in Lissón Chaves, *La iglesia*, 2:310–18.

72 AGI Lima 121, ff 13r–14r, petition to Castro, 18 July 1565. Even Castro's allies agreed that the new tax was a miscalculation: AGI Lima 121, loose file, ff 49r–50, Cuenca to king, 26 Jan. 1566.

73 Ibid., Gerónimo de Silva to king, 28 Feb. 1566: " . . . pareciendole que hera cossa con que se podria descargar de tanta gente como a permitido pretendan pedir de comer[,] nonbro un genero de corregidores de los yndios[,] cosa nueva para toda la tierra. . . ."

74 Ibid., ff 11r, "Provision del presi. Castro sobre q los corregidores no cobren los dos tomines de salario de los ys," Lima, 11 Feb. 1566.

75 Ibid., ff 2r, Baltasar de Loaysa to king, 1 March 1566 [Date from accompanying document]: "[que sean] tratados con la libertad y justicia que los demas vros vasallos. . . ."

76 Cuenca, "Ordenanças de los Yndios," Jayanca, 29 Aug. 1566, in Rostworowski, "Algunos comentarios hechos a las Ordenanzas del doctor Cuenca."

77 Zevallos Quiñones, "La visita del pueblo de Ferreñafe," 157–58.

78 Ramírez, *The World Upside Down*, 176n52 and chap. 6. At least some Andean communities already had alguaciles when Cuenca arrived: Rostworowski, "Algunos comentarios," 134. On the early and severe population loss in the north coast, see Cook, *Demographic Collapse*, 143.

79 Lohmann Villena, *El corregidor de indios*, assumes there was continuity between Castro's officials and Toledo's; Julien, "Spanish Reform and Change in the Potosí Hinterland," argues that there was not.

80 See Toledo to king, 8 Feb. 1570, in *Gobernantes*, 3:341–79, see 342. Castro did, however, boast to the king that he had had more success in resettling Andeans than any governor before him, even claiming to have consolidated 573 hamlets into 40 pueblos in one unidentified province: Castro to king, Lima, 20 Dec. 1567, in *Gobernantes*, 3:270–86, see 277. His royal instructions did not explicitly mandate the reforms he carried out, and he wrote repeatedly to the king justify-

ing himself in the face of his critics; early in 1566 however, the king reaffirmed the resettlement policy and praised Castro's determination to carry it out. Instructions to Castro, Madrid, 16 Aug. 1563, in *Gobernantes*, 3:623–41; King to Castro, 16 Feb. 1566, in Málaga Medina, *Reducciones toledanas en Arequipa (pueblos tradicionales)*, 33.

81 Matienzo to king, La Plata, 20 Oct. 1561, in Levillier, ed., *Audiencia de Charcas*, 1:54–60.

82 Barnadas, ed., *Diccionario histórico de Bolivia*, s.v. "Matienzo, Juan de." Manfredi Merluzzi argues that Toledo read Matienzo's book before leaving Spain: *Politica e governo nel Nuovo Mondo*, 47.

83 Matienzo, *Gobierno del Perú*, chap. 14. "Ni pueden ser dotrinado ni ser hombres perpetuamente, no estando juntos en pueblos, y en esto no es menester dar más razones de las que todo el mundo sabe," 48. See discussions of Matienzo's town plan in MacCormack, *On the Wings of Time*, 119–21; Cummins, "Forms of Andean Colonial Towns, Free Will, and Marriage," 217.

84 Matienzo, *Gobierno del Perú*, 52, 83. Mulattoes, mestizos and black people, on the other hand, were to be banned from the reducción.

85 AGI Lima 121, loose file, f. 5, Castro to king, Lima, 30 April 1566.

86 Matienzo, *Gobierno del Perú*: "Los indios de este Reyno son tan hábiles, que ninguna cosa les enseñan que no aprendan muy bien, como no sean cosas que requiren prudencia. . . . que si esto no les faltara, no fueran de los que Aristóteles dice que nacieron de naturaleza siervos," 69.

87 The scholar was Juan Ginés de Sepúlveda. The best recent treatment of his debate with Las Casas is Adorno, *The Polemics of Possession in Spanish American Narrative*, chap. 4.

88 Matienzo, *Gobierno del Perú*: " . . . no tengo yo por servidumbre compeler a los que tan poco entendimiento tienen como estos, que creó Naturaleza para obedecir y servir . . . que hagan aquello que les está bien, aunque ellos quieren otra cosa," 87.

89 AGI Lima 121, loose file, f. 5. Castro to king, Lima, 30 April 1566: " . . me parescio que hera bien questos naturales tuvyesen el govierno que Guaynacava les havia puesto, para que no se le levantasen. . . ." While Matienzo discussed the office of tuquyriyoq, Castro referred to the larger Inca system of decimal administration.

90 Nader, *Liberty in Absolutist Spain*.

91 Guevara Gil, "Los caciques y el señorío natural en los Andes coloniales (Perú, siglo XVI)," 145. On continuity in the office of cacique, see Ramírez, *To Feed and Be Fed*, 115–54; Martínez Cereceda, *Autoridades en los Andes*.

92 The king reiterated the policy in 1565: Real cédula, Bosque de Segovia, 13 Sept. 1565, in Konetzke, *Colección*, 1:416.

5. "That So-Qualified Assembly"

1 Ramos Pérez, "La crisis indiana y la Junta Magna de 1568"; Poole, *Juan de Ovando*, chap. 7. "Aquella tan calificada junta": Toledo, preamble to tasa, c. 1573, in Romero, "Libro de la visita general del virrey don Francisco de Toledo, 1570–1575," 188.

2 Parker, *The Grand Strategy of Philip II*, 8.

3 For arguments that Toledo was simply carrying out decisions taken at court, see: Merluzzi, *Politica e governo nel Nuovo Mondo*, 64; Salles and Noejovich, *La Visita General y el Proyecto de Gobernabilidad del Virrey Toledo*, 14–15.

4 Bakewell, *Miners of the Red Mountain*, chaps. 1–2.

5 Juan de Ovando to king, undated, in Maúrtua, ed., *Antecedentes de la Recopilación de Indias*, 3–18: "La una, que en el Consejo no se tiene ni se puede tener noticia de las cosas de Indias. . . . La segunda, que ni en el Consejo ni en las Indias no se tiene noticia de las Leyes y Ordenanzas por donde se rigen y gobiernan todos aquellos estados."

6 Poole, *Juan de Ovando*. Much of the historiography on Philip's early and middle years has focused on the alleged rivalry between an "Open Spain" policy championed by the Prince of Eboli and a "Closed Spain" policy championed by the Duke of Alba. José Martínez Millán convincingly argues that the two factions were driven more by personal rivalry than ideology, whereas Cardinal Espinosa, who had ties to both factions, was ideologically consistent, prioritizing the goal of religious orthodoxy in political matters: "En busca de la ortodoxia."

7 Gómez Rivas, *El virrey del Perú don Francisco de Toledo*, chaps. 1–2. Contrary to its title, this book is primarily a well-documented study of Toledo's life *before* his appointment as viceroy.

8 The three main orders were Santiago, Calatrava, and Alcántara. Ruiz Rodríguez, "Las órdenes militares castellanas (siglos XVI y XVII)." The lifetime grants given in the military orders were called encomiendas, like those given in the New World.

9 Gómez Rivas, *El virrey del Perú*, 71–82. Roberto Levillier wrote that Philip passed him over for the position of comendador mayor in 1567, choosing another candidate although Toledo was the senior one: Levillier, *Don Francisco de Toledo*, 1:38–39. Gómez Rivas, on the other hand, implies that this appointment was not a possibility until 1573, when the comendador mayor Zúñiga died; Toledo's grievance, according to Gómez Rivas, was not being appointed even to the secondary post of *clavero* at the time of his appointment as viceroy. *El virrey del Perú*, 82.

10 Gómez Rivas, *El virrey del Perú*, chap. 5; Fernández Collado, "Felipe II y su mentalidad reformadora en el Concilio Provincial Toledano de 1565."

11 Seigneurial rule, or a lord's administration of quasi-governmental powers over his vassals, is distinct from feudalism, the medieval legal structure for delegating territory from kings to lords and from greater lords to lesser ones.

The extent of early modern Spanish lords' seigneurial power is controversial. Territorial lords and the military orders certainly claimed such powers, while acknowledging the overarching authority of the king. See Guilarte, *El régimen señorial en el siglo XVI*; López-Salazar Pérez, "El régimen local de los territorios de Órdenes Militares."

12 We don't know exactly what was in the Junta Magna's library. There survives a partial inventory, mostly focused on Mexico (see Mustapha, "Contribution a l'histoire de la Junta Magna de 1568 sur la perpetuitad des encomiendas"). But Ovando probably made available many or most of the reports that he had solicited in his visita of the Council of the Indies; Toledo's own broad knowledge of Peru, acquired in the Junta Magna, is evidence of this. The British Library contains a large collection of these reports (see Peña Cámara, "Nuevos datos sobre la visita de al Consejo de Indias [1567–1568]") and other reports on Peru that survive elsewhere indicate that they were written in response to Ovando's queries, including by Polo Ondegardo, Francisco de Falcón, Cristóbal Ramírez de Cartagena, Salazar de Villasante, and Francisco de Morales. See Poole, *Juan de Ovando*, 117–29.

13 "Memoria de don Francisco de Toledo," in Zabálburu and Rayon, eds., *Nueva colección de documentos inéditos para la historia de España y sus Indias*, 6:295–306: "de salvajes hombres y de bárbaros políticos," 302–3.

14 "Billete de don Francisco de Toledo," [1568], in Zabálburu and Rayon, *Nueva colección*, 6:294–95: "abrir un poco la materia del gobierno y justicia." Merluzzi, however, is skeptical of the suggestion that the Junta Magna did not intend to discuss these issues eventually: *Politica e governo nel Nuovo Mondo*, 60.

15 The four main sections of the Junta Magna's report treated the Church, royal income, commerce, and the question of making encomiendas perpetual, which were the same subjects Toledo listed as having been already resolved. The secretary of the Junta Magna, Mateo Vazquez de Leca, was also secretary to Cardinal Espinosa and later to the king himself.

16 The closest thing to a final report from the Junta Magna of which I know is a draft report in the Archivo del Ministerio de Justicia, Madrid, Ms 41 [wrongly numbered 51], ff 1–102, "Estos discursos y juntas se tuvieron para despachar al Virrey Francisco de Toledo," undated, probably 1568: "De lo que se ha tratado en los quatro puntos propuestos de la doctrina, hazienda, comercio y perpetuidad . . . ," f. 1r. The postscript, titled "gobierno," has these comments on Indian resettlement: "ha sido de antiguo muy encargada a los virreyes . . . y aunque esto y con la sucesión del tiempo se ha hecho mucho efecto, tiene el negocio en sí tanta dificultad y en algunas partes casi imposibilidad, que queda mucho por hacer, y asi ha parecido que esto se os debe de nuevo tornar a encargar para que hagais en ello suma diligencia. . . ."

17 Hanke, ed., *Los Virreyes españoles en América durante el gobierno de la Casa de Austria*, 1:94–117, see 108–10. The text on these subjects (taken from a fair copy of Toledo's instructions in AGI Indiferente General 2859) is almost identical to that

in the undated Junta Magna draft report in Archivo de Ministerio de Justicia cited above.

18 Borges Morán, "La Nunciatura indiana." In a lucid analysis of these events, Stafford Poole cautions against exaggerating the papal threat: Pius's advisors were generally pro-Spanish, and his efforts at expanding his influence were tentative. But Philip and his councilors believed that the pope was responding aggressively to friars' complaints of Spanish abuse. *Juan de Ovando*, 111–15.

19 Muldoon, *Popes, Lawyers, and Infidels*, 151; Pagden, *Spanish Imperialism and the Political Imagination*, 15.

20 Adorno, *The Polemics of Possession in Spanish American Narrative*, chaps. 3–4; Castro, *Another Face of Empire*. In the New Laws of 1542, Charles prohibited colonists from enslaving Indians outright, and tried to phase out the institution of encomienda (an attempt that failed in Peru in the face of massive resistance by the colonial elite), but he refused to go further than that.

21 García Jordán, "Las dudas del Emperador"; Castro, *Another Face of Empire*.

22 Bataillon, "Las 'doce dudas' peruanas resueltas por Las Casas."

23 Pérez Fernández, *Bartolomé de las Casas en el Perú*.

24 The claim that the king might go to hell (which royal officials called "scandalous and seditious") was made in 1566 by fray Alonso Maldonado de Buendía, OFM. See Assadourian, "Fray Alonso de Maldonado."

25 Luis Sánchez to Cardinal Espinosa, Madrid, 26 Aug. 1566, in Pereña Vicente and Baciero, eds., *Escuela de Salamanca*, 318–24; report submitted to the Junta Magna by the bishop of Cuenca, 1568, in Zabálburu and Rayon, *Nueva colección*, 6:260–67. Merluzzi contends that Sánchez's report made a deep impact on Espinosa: *Politica e governo nel Nuovo Mondo*, 36.

26 The Junta Magna was one of about 175 "ad hoc" government juntas or conferences that took place in Castile between 1484 and 1664. But most of them were theological and judicial in focus. Dolores M. Sánchez argues that the ad hoc juntas facilitated a "modern" form of efficient and flexible decision making: *El deber de consejo en el Estado moderno*, 23, 205–8. But her own evidence shows that most juntas' decisions were theoretical rather than directly linked to policy making; the Junta Magna was exceptional.

27 Philip's commitment to the discourse of "conscience" was real. Late in life he demanded approval for decisions of state from his private confessor, who wrote to him: "I, your majesty's confessor, cannot say more, nor does God oblige me to do so. . . . God *does* oblige me to deny your majesty all sacraments unless you do what I say." Quoted in Parker, *The World Is Not Enough*, 32–33.

28 Ramos Pérez, "La crisis indiana," 16, 22.

29 Unlike Toledo, most members of the Junta Magna apparently did not read many of the documents assembled for their benefit; Ovando, who helped bring about the Junta Magna, later complained that its members knew few specifics of the Spanish American situation. Ovando to king, 25 Nov. 1573, quoted in Poole, *Juan de Ovando*, 136–37.

30 Domínguez Ortiz and Vincent, *Historia de los moriscos*, 28–33. See Chap. 3, above; Pino Díaz, "De la Granada morisca a los Andes indianos."

31 In a landmark article, Carlos Sempat Assadourian showed that Indian forced labor was the elephant in the Junta Magna's chamber: "Acerca del cambio." It may seem paradoxical that Spanish theologians and jurists were profoundly concerned with Indian forced labor yet never doubted that it was legitimate to hold Africans as chattel slaves. The reason was that Spaniards (usually) purchased African people who had already been enslaved outside of Spanish jurisdiction, for causes presumed to have been just, and which it was not the legal burden of the Spanish purchaser to investigate. Indians, by contrast, were free at the time they came under Spanish jurisdiction and in most circumstances could not legally be enslaved.

32 This is especially true for Toledo's first *instrucción*, of which long sections are copied directly from the *instrucciones* given to the three previous governors. "Instrucción al Virrey Francisco de Toledo," Aranjuez, 30 Nov. 1568, in Hanke, *Los Virreyes*, 1:79–94.

33 Ibid., 79, 43, 160.

34 Ibid., 1:87, 83.

35 Ibid., 82; the original version is on page 46.

36 Philip II to Toledo, Madrid, 28 Sept. 1568, quoted in Assadourian, "Acerca del cambio en la naturaleza del dominio sobre las Indias," 30: " . . como quiera que está ordenado que no se les haga fuerza ni compulsion, por todos los medios justos y raciones [sean] atraídos para que en las dichas minas haya continuo el número necesario."

37 AGI Lima 578, Lib. 2, ff 238r–v. "Don Francisco de Toledo, visorrey del Peru, sobre que los indios bivan en pueblos y congregados," El Escorial, 4 Nov. 1568, incorporating text of Real Cédula issued in el Bosque de Segovia, 13 Sept. 1565, printed in Konetzke, ed. *Colección de documentos para la historia de la formación social de Hispanoamérica (1493–1810)*, 1:416. See Julien, "Spanish Reform and Change in the Potosí Hinterland," 19.

38 Borges Morán, "Nuevos datos sobre la comisión pontificia para las Indias de 1568," 239.

39 This raises the vexed question of "secret" viceregal instructions; see appendix.

40 In one letter to the king, Toledo refered enigmatically to secret instructions, but did not imply that they justified his own policies, which he was asking the king (in vain) to endorse. Toledo to king, Cuzco, 1 March 1572, in *Gobernantes*, 4:48–208, see 52.

41 "Puntos de la carta anterior y decretos puestos en ella," ibid., 4:209–51: "Que parece muy bien la reduction que dize . . . pero que sea con prudencia . . . de manera que lo que se haze por su bien no redunde en su detrimento," 225.

42 Parker, *The World Is Not Enough*, 19.

43 Karen Spalding, personal communication.

44 AGI Lima 29, no. 10, f 13–14, Real Cédula, Potosí, 27 Dec. 1572: "mandamos a to-

dos los visitadores corregidores y justicias mayores y menores de este reyno . . .
que guarden y cumplen las probisiones quel dicho nuestro visorrey obiere dado
o les diere para los efetos susodichos."

45 Toledo to king, Lima, 18 April 1578, in *Gobernantes*, 6:39–70, see 49–50.

6. The Viceroy

1 Toledo to Consejo de Indias, Chicacopi, 19 Oct. 1572, in *Gobernantes*, 4:488–97,
see 489; Toledo to king, Cuzco, 1 March 1572, ibid., 4:48–340, see 49. AGI Lima
29, no. 7, ff 1–13, Toledo to king, Cuzco, 1 March 1572: "a de ser muy extra-
hordinaria y continua la lumbre de dios para governar mundo tan extrahordi-
nario . . . ni es posible poder entender, por ynferencia de otros reynos presen-
tes," 1 (Toledo sent off a large number of letters on 1 March 1572; I have not
found a published version of this particular letter, which is in the Archivo General de Indias).

2 This is the number given in the list cited in the following note, subtracting replacement inspectors and ecclesiastical inspectors. Ecclesiastical inspectors
were not independent operators but members of a team headed by the secular
inspector. (A typical entry in this list is "Jerónimo de Silva, y en su compañía,
por visitador ecclesiástico, al licenciado Merlo. . . .") In what follows, the word
"inspector" by itself means secular inspector; ecclesiastical inspectors are
identified as such.

3 Toledo, "Instrucciones para los visitadores," Lima, undated [1569–70],
in Romero, "Libro de la visita general del virrey don Francisco de Toledo,
1570–1575," 129–72 (also published in Toledo, *Disposiciones gubernativas para el
Virreinato del Perú*, 1:1–39). The document was written at some point between
Toledo's arrival in November 1569 and an addendum to it dated 16 Oct. 1570;
it is a template for instructions given to individual inspectors, and specific,
dated copies of it addressed to individual inspectors also survive in archives.
The template is accompanied by a list of sixty-three inspectors, of whom forty-
eight were civil and fifteen ecclesiastical, and six (all secular inspectors) whom
he appointed to replace others who were reassigned or unable to complete the
job: ibid., 121–24. This list does not include an ecclesiastical inspector for every
secular inspector, but it is likely that the other ecclesiastical inspectors were
simply left off the list.

This list is not exhaustive. At least one inspector is not included on it: Pedro Ortiz de Zárate, who inspected the repartimientos of Chichas, Puna, and
Copacabana. For the last of these repartimientos (and possibly the first two as
well) he was a replacement for another inspectors. See ANB Expedientes Coloniales 1611–1608; Espinoza Soriano, "Copacabana del Collao," 6; "Normas para
la aplicación de la Provisión por la que se exoneraba a los naturales del pago del
tributo correspondiente al lapso empleado en . . . la reducción," Potosí, 21 May
1575, in Toledo, *Disposiciones gubernativas*, 47–58.

In most local records from the General Inspection, the secular inspector is listed as carrying out all the activities associated with the inspection, including resettlement. In at least one case, though, the ecclestical inspector appears as the agent of resettlement: the case of Luis Mexía in Condes, discussed in chapter 8.

4 The *tasa* lists approximately 440 repartimientos in the Audiencias of Lima and Charcas (a number of which were combinations of several smaller ones consolidated in one).

5 Toledo, "Instrucciones para los visitadores," in Romero, "Libro de la visita general," 131: "se reduzgan en pueblos donde vivan juntos y acompañados, unos con otros, como viven los xpstianos."

6 Ibid.

7 An amendment to Toledo's instructions acknowledged that neither the alguacil nor the notary was an ideal candidate for this position, and permitted appointing a local literate Spanish-speaking Andean (*indio ladino*) as curador: "Aclaraciones a la instrucción general," Cuzco, 16 June 1571, in Toledo, *Disposiciones gubernativas*, 1:117–20, see 117. In practice, inspectors sometimes appointed a local Spaniard to play this role, under the title of protector or curador: AHC EC 16, f 9, petition of don Hernando Ticona and don Martin Poma, Sipesipe, 17 July 1573.

8 Abercrombie, *Pathways of Memory and Power*, 237.

9 Toledo, "Instrucciones para los visitadores," in Romero, "Libro de la visita general," 163–71.

10 Málaga Medina, *Reducciones toledanas en Arequipa (pueblos tradicionales)*, 36–37. An early order for concentrating Lima's Andeans in a reducción is in AGI Patronato 187, ramo 14, "Ordenanzas promulgadas por la Aud. de Lima para que los indios se junten en pueblos," Lima, 20 Oct. 1550. On Castro's foundation, see Coello de la Rosa, "Resistencia e integración en la Lima colonial."

11 Cieza de León, *Crónica del Perú: Segunda parte*, cap. 20: " . . . echado por sierras tan agrias y espantosas que por algunas partes mirando aboxo se quita la vista," 40–41.

12 Acosta, *Historia natural*, L 3, cap. 9: "iba preparado lo mejor que pude conforme a los documentos que dan allá, los que llaman vaquianos o pláticos," 167.

13 Alejandre Coello de la Rosa estimates that sixty people accompanied Toledo from Lima, while Alejandro Málaga Medina estimated seventy, but the overall number is probably higher; these numbers are conservative. Toledo's companions from the outset included at least eighteen men prominent enough to appear regularly in the record: Francisco de Carabeo and Martín García de Loyola, captains of cavalry and foot soldiers; Toledo's *criados* Gerónimo Pacheco, Juan Soto, and Francisco de Barrasa y Cárdenas; his nephew don Gerónimo de Figueroa; his secretaries Alvaro Ruiz de Navamuel and Diego López de Herrera; *contadores* Antonio de Salazar and Pedro de Rivera; historian and *cosmógrafo* Pedro Sarmiento de Gamboa; naturalist Dr. Tomás Vázquez; physician Sánchez de Renedo; friars Pedro Gutiérrez Flórez and Fray García de Toledo; the Jesuit

Provincial Ruiz Portillo; and the interpreters Juan de Ynestrosa and Gonzalo Gómez Jiménez. Given the availability of Andean labor to elite Spaniards, each likely brought several servants and porters. See Levillier, *Don Francisco de Toledo, Supremo Organizador del Perú*, 205; Málaga Medina, *Reducciones toledanas en Arequipa*, 38; Coello de la Rosa, "Discourse and Political Culture in the Formation of the Peruvian Reducciones in the Spanish Colonial Empire (1533–1592)," 196.

14 "Carta que se escribio a su Magd por el Virrey Don Francisco de Toledo con relacion de los principales puntos y buenos effetos de su visita," [Cuzco?] 12 March 1571, in BNE, Ms 3044, no. 4 (ff 41–52): "Y aunque se dio a los visitadores la orden que devian tener para la reducion de los naturales por ser cosa en que han hecho siempre gran contradicion y repugnancia fue menester poner yo en ello la mano assi para que los visitadores la hallasen mas llana y ayudarlos en esto como por ser cosa muy necessaria para le brevedad de la visita general," f 44r. Toledo claimed to have personally selected sites and initiated resettlement in Huarochirí, Jauja, Yauyos, and the area around Guamanga.

15 Toledo, "Instrucción para los visitadores," in Romero, "Libro de la visita general," 166. After this "breve término" had elapsed, the inspectors had the option of appointing an outside person, presumably a Spaniard, to finish overseeing it at the Andeans' own cost.

16 Lima, 16 Oct. 1570, in Toledo, *Disposiciones gubernativas*, 1:43.

17 "Instruccion nueva para visitadores," Cuzco, 8 Sept. 1571, in Romero, "Libro de la visita general," 177–86, see 181.

18 "Instrucciones en lo de la reducción de los pueblos de yndios," unsigned and undated, believed Toledo, 1572, in Lissón Chaves, ed., *La iglesia de España en el Perú*, 2:618–20, see 619.

19 "Provisión con las normas para los reducidores de los indios," "Normas sobre promoción de la doctrina," and "Apuntamientos aclaratorios de la Instrucción General," Potosí, 6 March 1573, in Toledo, *Disposiciones gubernativas*, 1:245–70. Even in his initial instructions Toledo had raised the possibility of appointing reducidores if necessary, without going into any detail.

20 AGI Lima 29, no. 10, ff 2–11. Toledo to the *alcalde de corte* for the Lima Audiencia, 17 Aug. 1573.

21 "Provisión para llevar a la práctica las reducciones," Quilaquila, 7 Nov. 1573, in Toledo, *Disposiciones gubernativas*, 1:281–83.

22 Toledo, speech to caciques, Arequipa, 10 Sept. 1575, ibid., 1:91–95, see 91.

23 AGI Lima 29, no. 07, ff 75–79; 81–83. Toledo to king, La Plata, 8 Nov. 1574: " . . . entiendo questos negocios de tan grande ymportancia que no se hicieron por otros ministros no pueden dejar de ser mordidos en las circunstancias para descargarse dellos de no los aver hecho yo ando y he andado por todo este reyno viendo y adviertiendo a los visitadores. . . ."

24 "Apuntamientos aclaratorios de la Instrucción General," Potosí, 6 March 1573, in Toledo, *Disposiciones gubernativas*, 1:266. Toledo initially required An-

dean communities to give up lands more than one league from their reducción (instruction to inspectors, Romero, "Libro de la visita general," 165), but later allowed them to retain such lands if they could not trade them for others: "Instrucción a los jueces de naturales," La Plata, 20 Dec. 1574, in Toledo, ibid., 1:461–86, see 466.

25 "Ordenanzas para la vida común en los pueblos de indios," Arequipa, 6 Nov. 1575, ibid., 2:217–66, see 224–25.

26 Toledo, preamble to tasa, in Romero, "Libro de la visita general," 191.

27 Toledo to king, Lima, 8 Feb. 1570, in Gobernantes, 3:341–79: " . . . las mismas causas que dan los yndios para no reducirse son las que muestran lo que conviene reducirlo y mucho mas las que callan que es exercitar sus adoratorios y ydolatrias y borracheras . . . sin testigos en sus escondrijos," 342.

28 See, e.g., Fray Domingo de Santo Tomás to Bartolomé de Las Casas, c. 1562, in Vargas, Fray Domingo de Santo Tomás, 107–8; Archbishop Loayza to king, 2 Aug. 1564, in Lissón Chaves, La iglesia, 273.

29 Anonymous, "Parecer acerca de la perpetuidad y buen gobierno de los indios del Perú . . ." Undated, c. 1563, in Urteaga, ed., Informaciones, 147–66: "Las poblaciones que tienen, ordinariamente son . . . muy viles, y bajas, y estrechas, y tan sucias que perpetuamente nunca saben qué cosa es barrer . . . adonde comen, allí duermen y hacen todo lo demás," 148.

30 "Memorial dado por el racionero Villarreal al virrey Toledo," undated, in BPR, II/ 2846, no. 12, ff 291–315: " . . . tienen una casilla que mas parece de monejos que de hombres, alli les apetece la soledad y su mala inclinazion a continuos sacrificios al Diablo, y a vivir vestialmente, durmiendo con su madre y hijas," f 304v.

31 "Copia de una carta escrita a SM sobre los negocios de las Indias," in Zabálburu and Rayon, eds., Nueva colección de documentos inéditos para la historia de España y sus Indias, 6:218–59. Anonymous and undated, apparently by the royal treasurer in Potosí, before 1570.

> Es cuestión en todos estos reinos, tratada por muchos, si conviene que los pueblos de los indios se junten y . . . se hagan . . . pueblos grandes y políticos; los que dicen que no y que sería dar gran molestia a los indios . . . dan por causa principal ser mucha la cuantidad de los indios y la tierra estrecha de valles y lugares para sembrar y coger sus comidas, y que estando como están al presente 10 casas o 20 . . . y no estan mas de los que la tierra puede sustentar . . . ," 243–44.

32 Toledo to king, Lima, 8 Feb. 1570, in Gobernantes, 3:341–79: " . . . aunque vuestra magestad no uviera mandado tan encargadamente este punto, . . . aunque viese por experiençia algun daño particular por el grande y notable provecho que se le siguiese que quando por esta causa muriesen algunos de los naturales, . . . no avria porque parar en hazello aunque no quisiesen, . . . los que quedasen y sus descendientes quedaran utiles para el servicio de nuestro señor y de vuestra magestad y bien suyo," 342–43.

33 "Plantallos cerca de las lavores de las minas," ibid., 343.

34 Archbishop Loayza, Lima, 25 May 1572, in Lissón Chaves, La iglesia, 2:609–10.

35 Don Cristóbal Guacai to king, 26 April 1572, quoted in Wightman, Indigenous Migration and Social Change, 21.

36 Juan de Vera to Consejo de Indias, Cuzco, 9 April 1572, printed in Urbano, "Sexo, pintura de los Incas y Taqui Onqoy," 240.

37 AGI Lima 29, no. 06, contents of Toledo letter to king, 1573: "No ay negocio de govierno que el audiencia no lo probea con toda libertad . . . y en lo de las reducciones de los yndios cosa de grandisimo estorvo e ynconiniente para ellas . . . en aver mandado cesar la visita hasta que den fianças los visitadores aviendo mas de dos años y medio que estan entendiendo en ellas con que se comiença a desconponer todo y creo que esto es lo que se pretende . . . ," f. 8r.

38 Lima Audiencia to king, Lima, 27 Jan. 1573, in Gobernantes, 7:138–48, see 139.

39 Lima Audiencia to king, Lima, 15 March 1575, ibid., 7:244–48. Unfortunately for historians, few of these complaints have been found in archives.

40 Lima Audiencia to king, Lima, 27 Jan. 1573, ibid., 7:138–48: "la perdicion y menoscabo deste Reino," 138.

41 Toledo to king, Cuzco, 1 March 1572, ibid., 4:48–208, see 191–92. See discussion in chapter 8.

42 Toledo to king, Lima, 8 Feb. 1570, ibid., 3:341–79 see 342.

43 This was a major source of Spanish frustration with the reducciones in the seventeenth century: Scott, Contested Territory, 71–72.

44 Toledo ordered the Charcas inspectors to count the Andeans on haciendas but to leave the question of how to resettle them until he himself arrived. ANB CACh 11, Cuzco, 19 June 1572.

45 Toledo, "Instrucciones a los visitadores," 128; AGI Contaduría 1785, ff 5–8. "Relación sumaria de las quentas q van en este libro q se an tomado a algunos de los vesitadores q fueron proveydos pa la vesita general de los Reptims de yndios deste Reyno q se an Resvisto por mandado de su m. q son las sigtes," 22 March 1577. Pending a careful analysis of these accounts, the finances of the General Inspection remain obscure.

46 Real Cédula to Audiencia de Guatemala, Madrid, 10 June 1540, in Solano, ed., Normas y leyes de la ciudad hispanoamericana, 1:135–36; resolution of Mexican church council, 1546, excerpted in Colección de documentos inéditos, first series, 18:514–15; Real Cédula to Lima Audiencia, Madrid, 17 Dec. 1551, printed in Málaga Medina, Reducciones toledanas en Arequipa, 219–20; comment by unknown court official in margin of licenciado Castro's "instrucciones a los corregidores de indios, c. 1565," in Gobernantes, 3:117.

47 ANB Rück Mss 2.1, f. 453. Toledo order to inspectors for La Paz district, La Plata, 7 July 1573. On July 7, 1573, Toledo wrote that he had heard that aggressive attempts to collect tribute were slowing down the Resettlement and ordered that collection be delayed. On April 23, 1574, Juan Gómez Marrón, escribano for the inspector of Pacajes, wrote on the back of the sheet that he had not

embargoed any tribute except for the one-third portion which Toledo himself had ordered to pay for the Resettlement: " . . ny a fecho embargo alguno dellos mas de la tercia parte que su Exa manda pa pagar las reduciones." In 1575, with the resettlement dragging on longer than expected, he assigned a full half of the tribute for the previous year to the Resettlement budget and restored to the encomenderos their full income for the future: "Normas para la aplicación de la provisión por la que se exoneraba a los naturales del pago del tributo correspondiente al lapso empleado en . . . la reducción," Potosí, 4 March 1575 and 21 May 1575, in Toledo, *Disposiciones gubernativas*, 2:47–58.

48 AGI Lima 313. "Dudas que pregunta y propone su Xc. al presidente y oydores de la Rl. au. de la plata con el parecer del presidente a pie de cada una," 6 ff, and "Abreviando y sumando mas lo que se pregunta y pide Parecer por parte de su xa. a los letrados eclesiasticos," 2 ff. Both undated but apparently 30 Dec. 1574. All supported the principle of fining encomenderos for *faltas de doctrina*, except for Antonio Lopez de Haro, the archdean of the La Plata cathedral, and the fiscal of the Audiencia.

49 "Instrucción al Virrey Francisco de Toledo," Aranjuez, 30 Nov. 1568, in Hanke, ed. *Los Virreyes españoles en América durante el gobierno de la Casa de Austria*, 1:79–94, see 87.

50 See Assadourian, *Transiciones hacia el Sistema Colonial Andino*, 209–114.

51 AGI Lima 313. "Dudas que pregunta y propone," f 3v: " . . . resultaria mayor calamidad que antes a los naturales y menosprecio de los que les goviernan." The document refers to "justicia y executores," i.e., corregidores. Antonio Lopez de Haro alone refused to accept corregidors: ibid., f 5v.

52 Don Lope Diez de Armendariz to king, La Plata, 25 Sept. 1576, in Levillier, ed., *Audiencia de Charcas*, 1:331–85:

> los indios . . . no fueron tan atormentados ni aflijidos con todas las alteraciones y guerras pasadas porque a durado mas de 4 anos la persecucion destos visitadores y reduzidores que a costa de los yndios an comido con mucha gente y cavallos que cada uno traya y los an hecho poblar muchas vezes mudandolos de unas partes a otras y quemandoles las casas. . . . lo peor a sido que las reduciones o poblaciones muchas o las mas dellas las han herrado de manera que no pueden permanecer . . . porque tienen muy lexos las chacaras y tierras donde coxen sus comidas y para yr a cultivarlas an de pasar por vados rios caudalosos de gran peligro . . . y los yndios andan como atonitos y asonbrados, 373.

53 "Normas para la aplicación de la provisión por la que se exoneraba a los naturales del pago del tributo correspondiente al lapso empleado en . . . la reducción," Potosí, 4 March 1575 and 21 May 1575, in Toledo, *Disposiciones gubernativas*, 2:47–58, see 48.

54 See Julien, "Spanish Reform and Change in the Potosí Hinterland."

55 Spalding, *Huarochirí*, chaps. 5–6; Merluzzi, *Politica e governo nel Nuovo Mondo*, chap. 4.

56 Glave, "Tambos y caminos andinos en la formación del mercado interno colonial."

57 Toledo, ordenanzas on coca growing, Cuzco, 25 Feb. 1572 and 3 Oct. 1572 [misdated as 3 Nov.], in Toledo, *Disposiciones gubernativas*, 1:143–7 and 231–44; on the abuse of Andean porters, Cuzco, 26 Aug. 1572, ibid., 1:151–52.

58 Carlos Díaz Rementería printed, as an example, the title Toledo gave to the cacique principal of Guanoquite, Cuzco, 25 Jan. 1572: *El cacique en el virreinato del Perú*, 219.

59 Rostworowski, *Curacas y sucesiones*; Stern, *Peru's Indian Peoples and the Challenge of Spanish Conquest*, 133.

60 This and the following paragraphs are based on "Ordenanzas para la vida común en los pueblos de indios," Arequipa, 6 Nov. 1575, in Toledo, *Disposiciones gubernativas*, 2:217–66, and on Toledo's first instructions for the inspectors in 1569.

61 With the exception that one alcalde could be a principal.

62 Toledo's 1575 ordenanzas (ibid., 2:238) imply that reducción notaries will keep records exclusively in written form, not in quipus. But John Charles argues that Toledo intended them to preserve both kinds of records, and cites another order by Toledo that tributaries keep quipus recording what they owed. Charles, *Allies at Odds*, 92–3. See the discussions of Andean *escribanos de cabildo* in Burns, *Into the Archive*.

63 Toledo, *Disposiciones gubernativas*, 2:259; Toledo granted Gutierre Velázquez de Ovando the right to seize up to 20 "cimarrón" Indians as yanaconas: ANB Expedientes Coloniales 1605–04, ff 8v–10r, provisión, Lima, 18 Aug. 1577.

7. Tyrants

1 Levillier, *Don Francisco de Toledo, Supremo Organizador del Perú*, vol. 1, pt. 2; Valcárcel, "El Virrey Toledo, Gran Tirano del Peru." For portrayals similar to Levillier's, see: Málaga Medina, "El virrey don Francisco de Toledo y la reglamentacion del tributo en el virreinato del Peru"; Vargas Ugarte, *Historia general del Perú*, vol. 1, chap. 10; Zimmerman, *Francisco de Toledo, Fifth Viceroy of Peru, 1569–1581*.

2 See the useful discussion in Colajanni, "El Virrey Francisco de Toledo como 'primer antropólogo aplicado' de la edad moderna," 65–70.

3 Pease, *Las crónicas y los Andes*, 36; Porras Barrenechea, *Cronistas del Perú (1528–1650)*; Means, "Biblioteca Andina." The trend was only temporary; by the early seventeenth century, portrayals of the Incas in Spanish chronicles was once again very positive.

4 Brading, *The First America*, 138. Perhaps the first exponent of this view was Spalding, *Huarochirí*, 212–14. See also Colajanni, "El Virrey Francisco de Toledo"; Cook and Cook, *People of the Volcano*, chap. 4; Julien, "History and Art in Translation"; Wernke, "Negotiating Community and Landscape in the Peruvian Andes," 133. For an account balanced between the old and new views, see Merluzzi, *Politica e governo nel Nuovo Mondo*.

5 BNE Ms 3044, no. 4, ff 41–52, "Carta que se escribio a su Magd por el Virrey Don Francisco de Toledo con relacion de los principales puntos y buenos effetos de su visita," [Cuzco], 12 March 1571: "La lengua no me ha traydo oy ningun testigo para la ynformacion de la orden que se tenia en el govierno desta tierra, aunque se lo he dho, en el entretanto he sacado la memoria de la Visita General para la relacion que ha de ymbiar VE a su Mag la qual va con esta . . . ," f. 44r.

6 Cited in Julien, "Francisco de Toledo and His Campaign against the Incas," 262.

7 Thomas Aquinas, "De regimine principum," chap. 4; Bartolus, "De tyrannia," chap. 2. Cicero, Augustine, Gregory the Great and Isidore of Seville had also written about tyranny, but after its rediscovery Aristotle's *Politics* eclipsed these authorities. See Monahan, *From Personal Duties towards Personal Rights*, 166. Sara Castro-Klarén emphasizes Plato's *Republic* in grounding ideas of tyranny within Toledo's circle ("Historiography on the Ground," 154–57), but his influence was far less important than Aristotle's.

8 Most medieval and early modern political writers agreed that tyrannicide was theoretically legitimate but not to be undertaken lightly. See Coleman, *History of Political Thought*, 112–16.

9 Aristotle, *The Politics*, bk. 3, chap. 7; bk 5, chaps. 10–12.

10 Alonso IX, *Las Siete Partidas*, 2:1:10:

> Tyrano, tanto quiere dezir, como señor, q es apoderado, en algun reyno, o tierra por fuerça o por engaño, o por traycion. E estos atales, son de tal natura, q despues q son bien apoderados en la tierra, aman mas de fazer su pro, maguer sea daño de la tierra q la pro comunal de todos, porque siempre biuen a mala sospecha de la perder.

The text of the *Siete Partidas* varied slightly in early modern editions; this text is taken from the 1610 edition, as edited in 1555 by Gregorio López.

11 Ibid: " . . . usaron ellos de su poder siempre contra los del pueblo: en tres maneras de arteria. La primera es: que estos atales, punan siempre que los de su señorío, sean necios e medrosos, porque quando tales fuessen, non osarian leuantarse contra ellos, no contrastar sus voluntades. La segunda es, que los del pueblo ayan desamor, entre si, de guisa que non le fien unos de otros. . . . La tercera es, que punan de los fazer pobres: e de meterles a tan grandes fechos, que los nunca pueden acabar. . . . E sobre todo, esto siempre punaron los tyranos de estragar los poderosos, e de matar los sabidores . . . , e procuran todavia, de saber lo que se dize, o se faze en la tierra."

12 Duviols, "Revisionismo histórico y derecho colonial en el siglo XVI"; Millones, "De señores naturales a tiranos." Toledo's library also contained one of the most important contemporary studies of political science, which discussed the legitimacy of Spanish conquests: Domingo de Soto's *De iustitia et iure* (1553). See Hampe Martínez, "Las bibliotecas virreinales, en el Perú y la difusión del saber italiano," 546, 552. Interestingly, Soto drew on the work of Toledo's *bête noire*, Las Casas: Cárdenas Bunsen, *Escritura y Derecho Canónico en la obra de fray Bartolomé de las Casas*.

13 "Anónimo de Yucay," Chinèse, ed. The document is anonymous, identified in the manuscripts only by the date and place of completion: 16 March 1571, in the Yucay valley. It survives in three manuscripts; all contain the same primary text (which is the document I discuss in this chapter), but two include extra sections added later. With respect to the primary text, earlier historians proposed various candidates for its authorship, but Monique Mustapha convincingly argued in 1977 ("Encore le 'Parecer de Yucay'") that the author was fray García de Toledo. The only serious challenge to this attribution is that of Isacio Pérez Fernández, who in his 1995 edition of the Anónimo de Yucay, *El anónimo de Yucay frente a Bartolomé de Las Casas*, contends that the primary text (attributed by Mustapha to fray García de Toledo) actually had multiple authors, including Polo Ondegardo. Pérez Fernández's argument is quite speculative; I follow Mustapha's attribution.

14 This was a doctrine derived from Roman law, called *praescriptio longi temporis*. See Brundage, *Medieval Canon Law*, 159, citing Gratian; Brett, *Liberty, Right and Nature*, 186n, citing Fernando Vázquez de Menchaca, *De praescriptione* (1564).

15 "Y es cossa que pone admiracion la ignorancia destos quen casi mill años que comenzaron a tiranizar no supieron darse maña a ser ligítimos señores. Admira también la sabiduría de Dios en saver guardar estos Reynos . . . sin ligítimo título," "Anónimo de Yucay," 137.

16 "Esta es la ynformación y prouança que por mandado de su Excelencia se hizo del origen y decendencia de la tirania de los yngas deste rreyno y del hecho verdadero de como antes y despues desta tiranya no huuo señores naturales en esta tierra . . . ," Levillier, *Don Francisco de Toledo*, 2:14. The full text of this and the succeeding *informaciones* is in this volume. A new edition of the *informaciones*, edited by Catherine Julien, will be published by the Pontificia Universidad Católica del Perú.

17 Interrogatorio, Yucay, 2 June 1571, Levillier, *Don Francisco de Toledo*, 2:123–25.

18 "Dijeron cada uno de por sí y todos juntos que saben por cosa muy cierta que los indios de este reino es gente de tan poco entendimiento que han menester curador que los gobierne." Don Pedro Cayo Cuxi, cacique de Paucarpata, et al., Información, Yucay, 2 June 1571, ibid., 2:131.

19 Toledo to king, La Plata, 26 Dec. 1573, in *Gobernantes*, 5:310–14: "afirman principios falsos de los hechos de los yngas que perjudican mucho a los derechos que vuestra magestad tiene en estos Reynos . . . No nos a dado pequena esperiencia las obras que chiapa dejo escritas de las cosas de yndios para escarmentar de no creer a otros que tienen menos auturidad que el en letras y bida," 310–12. See Lohmann Villena, "Respuestas de solución de juristas y políticos en América," 652; MacCormack, *On the Wings of Time*, 84.

20 Agustín de Zárate's *Historia del descubrimiento y conquista del Perú*, cited in Lohmann Villena, "Respuestas de solución," 653. Zárate added the phrase, "sin guardar orden legítima de sucesión, sino por via de tyrania y violencia."

21 On Sarmiento, see Brian Bauer and Jean-Jacques DeCoster, "Introduction"; Julien, "History and Art in Translation"; Mumford, "The Inca Legend in Colonial Peru."

22 Sarmiento, letter to king, 4 March 1572, in Sarmiento, *Historia de los Incas*, 17–25.

23 Ibid., 172: "Ite procul scioli, uobis non locus in istis! / Rex indos noster nam tenet innocue." In context, "rightfully" seems the best translation for *innocue*. *Sciolus*, the late Latin diminutive of the adjective *scius* ("knowledgeable") means "one who speaks with spotty or superficial knowledge."

24 Luis Millones Figueroa and Eric Vaccarella, among the most recent and insightful scholars to examine the subject, have analyzed how Sarmiento deployed the category of tyranny (as well as Renaissance theories of knowledge) to define the Incas, but have treated tyranny as a fairly uncomplicated term of condemnation: Millones, "De señores naturales a tiranos"; Vaccarella, "Fábulas, letras, and razones historiales fidedignas." See also Castro-Klarén, "Historiography on the Ground." For a different, highly original interpretation of Sarmiento, see Julien, *Reading Inca History*, chap. 4.

25 Sarmiento, *Historia de los Incas*: "Todas las ordenanzas que hizo de pueblo fueron encaminadas a tiranía y particular interés," 126, chap. 47. See Millones, "De señores naturales," 94.

26 Sarmiento, *Historia de los Incas*, chaps. 30, 32, 39, 43, 45. Sarmiento's Incas were even physically impressive: the dynasty's twelve generations extended to 968 years, due, Sarmiento explained, to their good health and habit of marrying late and preserving their vital juices into old age.

27 Ibid., chap. 17.

28 "Fue franco, piadoso en la paz y cruel en la guerra y castigos, favorecedor de pobres, animoso y varón de mucha industria, edificador. Fue el mayor tirano de todos los Incas," ibid., 137, chap. 54.

29 Millones points out that personally visiting one's kingdom, to see conditions with one's own eyes and hear complaints, was a standard recommendation in sixteenth-century treatises addressed to kings: "De señores naturales," 74–75.

30 If any such record existed, it has not survived.

31 Sarmiento, *Historia de los Incas*, chaps. 30, 45, 46, 52.

32 Ibid., 110, chap. 39. On the Andean practice of making three-dimensional landform maps, largely but not entirely lost after the Spanish conquest, see Kagan and Marías, *Urban Images of the Hispanic World, 1493–1793*, 47.

33 "La mayor tiranía que él hizo, aunque colorada con especie de largueza . . . ," Sarmiento, *Historia de los Incas*, 110, chap. 39.

34 "Redujo muchos de los indios a pueblos y casas; porque antes vivían en cuevas y cerros y a las riberas de los ríos, cada uno por sí," ibid., 134, chap. 52. See MacCormack, "The Incas and Rome," 16.

35 Polo Ondegardo, "Relación de los fundamentos acerca del notable daño que resulta de no guardar a los indios sus fueros," 16: "lo primero que hicieron fue rreduçir los yndios á pueblos y mandarles que viviesen en comunydad porque hasta entonçes vivian muy divididos é apartados."

36 Toledo to king, Cuzco, 1 March 1572, in *Gobernantes*, 3:542–44: "la pulicia que halcançaron en su tiempo de trajes e instrumentos belicos y cultos de religion

de sus ydolatrias, . . . para entretener y admirar a qualquiera príncipe que vi-
niese a la corte de vuestra magestad . . ." 543–44. See Cummins, "Allí vallen,
aquí también." See also Julien, "History and Art in Translation."

37 Toledo to king, Cuzco, 1 March 1572, in Gobernantes, 4:48–208: "no ha sido
menester poca maña para desengañarlos," 132–33. See Lohmann Villena, "Respuestas de solución de juristas y políticos en América," 650; Urbano, "Sexo,
pintura de los Incas y Taqui Onqoy," 239–41. On rebels' heads: Toledo to king,
Cuzco, 1 March 1572, in Gobernantes, 4:321–32, see 328.

38 Garrett, Shadows of Empire, chap. 1.

39 Julien's "Francisco de Toledo" is the best analysis of this episode. See also
Nowack, "Las provisiones de Titu Cusi Yupangui" and "Las mercedes que pedía
para su salida."

40 In any case they had never endorsed the Vilcabamba Incas' claim to power, arguing that Manco Inca and his sons should have been excluded from the succession, as he was descended from a non-Inca wife of Huayna Capac. Garrett,
Shadows of Empire, 22.

41 Nowack and Julien, "La campaña de Toledo contra los señores naturales
andinos."

42 Toledo to king, Cuzco, 8 May 1572, Gobernantes, 4:363–69: " . . . se hiziese por ra-
zon de su culpa lo que sus yngas hazian con estos naturales cada dia por asegu-
rar su tirania que era hazellos mitimaes pasandolos de vnas provincias a otras
. . . diuidillos esparcidamente en las prouincias abajo donde son aborrecidos y
que . . . se consumiese esta semilla de yngas en este reyno," 366. See also Toledo
to king, Cuzco, 30 April 1572, ibid., 4:355; MacCormack, On the Wings of Time,
222–23.

43 Aristotle, Politics, 225–27, bk. 5, chap. 11; Bartolus, "De tyrannia" [c. 1350],
142–44; Siete Partidas 2:1:10, with López's gloss.

44 "Anónimo de Yucay": "el mayor tributo que jamás llevó tirano," 138–39.

45 Toledo to king, 1 March 1572, printed in Levillier, Don Francisco de Toledo, 2:3–13:
" . . . cuando no auia cossas utiles los hazian trabajar en cossas ynutiles como
hera en echar rrios por unas partes y por otras y hazer paredes muy largas de
una parte y de otra por por los caminos y scaleras de piedras de que no auia
neçesidad y questo lo hazian por que les parecia cossa muy conuiniente tenerlos
siempre ocupados," 9.

46 Aristotle, Politics, 225–26, bk. 5, chap. 11; Siete Partidas 2:1:10: " . . . meterles a tan
grandes fechos, q los nunca pueden acabar. . . ." See MacCormack, On the Wings
of Time, 57–58 and chap. 7; Lupher, Romans in a New World.

47 Testimony of Juan de Pancorbo, Cuzco, 22 Feb. 1572, in Levillier, Don Francisco
de Toledo, 2:198: " . . . quando mas seguro estaua el yndio en su casa le mudaua
de su naturaleza por fuerça y le ponia en otra muy lejos. . . ." See Bartolus, "De
tyrannia," 144.

48 Siete Partidas 2:1:10: " . . . saber lo q se dize, o se faze en la tierra. . . ."

49 As early as February 1570 he wrote that his predecessor Vaca de Castro's orde-

nances "seemed good to those of that time because many of them were very similar to those of the Inca[s]," including his endorsement of Indian forced labor. Toledo's stance here was ambiguous, leaving it unclear whether he agreed or disagreed with Vaca de Castro's position. Later Toledo himself invoked Inca precedent for Spanish authoritarianism. Toledo to king, Lima, 8 Feb. 1570, in *Gobernantes*, 3:304–21: "hizo ordenanças las quales pareçieron bien a los de aquel tiempo por ser muchas dellas muy semejantes a las del ynga, como fueron las de las permisiones de serviçios y cargas de yndios," 305.

50 Toledo to king, 1 March 1572, printed in Levillier, *Don Francisco de Toledo*, 2:3–13: ". . . aunque las contradigan y parezcan contra su libertad, como veria [seria?] quitarles que no esten ociosos y ocuparlos en cossas que a ellos les esten bien," 12.

51 Ibid.: "Prueuase que estos naturales es gente que ha menester curador para los negocios graves que se les ofrecen ansi de sus almas como de sus haziendas," 9.

52 Toledo to Juan de Ovando, Chicacopi, 19 Oct. 1572, in *Gobernantes*, 4:488–97: ". . . entender la naturaleza de esta gente y lo que an menester temer para ser gouernados," 491.

53 Toledo, preamble to *tasa*, undated but after 1573, in Romero, "Libro de la visita general del virrey don Francisco de Toledo, 1570–1575": parents and children, 201; "tan mansos y . . . hechos a no poseer cosa propia," 187; "no consentillos holgar . . . y tener cuenta con la vida de cada uno en particular," 190.

54 Aristotle, *Politics*, 136, bk. 3, chap. 14. To barbarian kings, quasi-tyrannical yet legitimate, Aristotle applied the term "despot."

55 Pedro de Moya y Contreras to king, 1579, cited in Martin, *Los vagabundos en la Nueva España, siglo XVI*, 162: "en tiempo de Moctezuma que mandaua a sus governadores y tequitatos, que tuuiesen quenta particular de la ocupacion de cada uno, compeliendoles a trauajar."

56 Murra, *Formaciones económicas y políticas del mundo andino*, 75; Saignes, "Lobos y ovejas," 107–8; Loza, " 'Tyrannie' des Incas et 'naturalisation' des Indiens." See the useful discussion in Durston, "El proceso reduccional en el sur andino," 76.

57 Toledo, Instructions for inspectors, Lima, undated, in Romero, "Libro de la visita general": "se guarde la costumbre del tiempo del Inga y se les restituya lo que se les hubiere quitado," 149.

58 The original instructions said: "Aunque los tengan en diferentes pueblos, en la visita han de ir asentados toda la dicha parcialidad junta." Ibid., 133–34. The "aclaraciones" of 16 June 1571 added that it was unnecessary to wait for tributaries absent in Potosí and Porco, but to count them based on the testimony of their caciques; ibid., 173.

59 "Instruccion nueva para los inspectors," Cuzco, 8 Sept. 1571, ibid., 185.

60 See the example of Macha, discussed in Jurado, "Las reducciones toledanas a pueblos de indios."

61 Loza, " 'Tyrannie' des Incas," interprets this ten-year rule as a process of "naturalization" for the mitimas, but it is clear from context that it refers not to miti-

mas but to the people the Spanish called *forasteros*, who lived away from home by their own choice. Loza's paper examines Toledo's policy toward mitimas in the Yucay valley, where he did indeed try to naturalize mitimas; but the demography of this valley, the site of Inca royal estates, was unique in the Andes, and Toledo's policy there was different from in the General Resettlement as a whole.

62 Roads, bridges, tambos, storehouses: Toledo, Instructions for inspectors [1569–1570], in Romero, "Libro de la visita general," 154–55. Distribution of land and water,148; craft specialists (*cumbicamayos* or skilled weavers), 149; cotton agriculture, 151.

63 Toledo to king, Cuzco, 1 March 1572, in *Gobernantes*, 4:48–251, see 162ff and 239–41. The king and Consejo de Indias dismissed the suggestion: ibid., 238, and AGI Patronato 192, no. 2, ramo 2, f 4r.

64 Durston, "El proceso reduccional," 81; Cook and Cook, *People of the Volcano*, 106–7.

65 Toledo, ordenances on coca, Cuzco, 3 Oct. 1572, in Toledo, *Disposiciones gubernativas para el Virreinato del Perú*, 1:231–44.

66 Toledo, Instructions for inspectors [1569–1570], in Romero, "Libro de la visita general," 147: " . . . comer en las pampas, . . . por el beneficio que se sigue a los indios pobres." See Cook and Cook, *People of the Volcano*, 113.

67 Cuenca claimed to have drafted the instructions himself: Cuenca to king, Lima, 6 Feb. 1571, in *Gobernantes*, 7:9–18. Another early source says that Cuenca, Loayza, and Pedro Sánchez de Paredes helped Toledo draft them: "De Virreyes y Gobernadores del Pirú," in *Colección de documentos inéditos*, first series, 8:212–93.

68 Loayza to king, Lima, 2 Aug. 1564, in Lissón Chaves, ed., *La iglesia de España en el Perú*, 2:272–82, see 273.

69 Hampe Martínez, *Don Pedro de la Gasca*, 131–38, 502.

70 Loayza at the beginning judged Toledo good at listening but slow to make up his mind: Gerónimo de Loayza, Lima, 9 Aug. 1570, in Lissón Chaves, *La iglesia*, vol. 2, 467–48. It is, however, hard to establish definitely Loayza's influence on Toledo, who was suspicious of Loayza from early on: Toledo to king, 8 Feb. 1570, in *Gobernantes*, 3:341–79, see 374. On Toledo's relationships to his various advisors, see Lohmann Villena, "Juan de Matienzo, Autor del 'Gobierno del Perú' "; Brading, *The First America*, 139; Murra, "Nos Hazen Mucha Ventaja"; Murra, "Litigation over the Rights of 'Natural Lords' "; Merluzzi, *Politica e governo nel Nuovo Mondo*, 84–88.

71 Polo, "Relación de los fundamentos," 16. I base my translation of *fundamentos* as "arguments" on Covarrubias, *Tesoro*, s.v. "fundar": "Fundamento, . . . la causa y razón que se da para apoyar nuestra opinión o nuestra acción." The word *fuero* meant local or customary law, different from but as important as the more formal *ley*. Spanish cities' municipal *fueros* were the subject of study, commentary, and litigation, and Spanish judges theoretically recognized indigenous customary law: *Siete Partidas*, pt. 1, tit. 2, ley 7; Tau Anzoátegui, *El poder de la costumbre*;

Honores, "Una sociedad legalista," 8; Mumford, "Litigation as Ethnography in Sixteenth-Century Peru."

72 Polo, "Relación de los fundamentos,": "asperisyma y fuerte," "mejor maña y mayor entendimiento," "muy mejor orden en lo que toca a la vida humana que todos los demas," 12–13.

73 Polo Ondegardo, "Informe . . . al Licenciado Briviesca de Muñatones sobre la perpetuidad de las encomiendas en el Perú," 177.

74 Polo, "Relación de los fundamentos," 46–47. See also Hampe Martínez, "El Licdo. Polo de Ondegardo," 515; Merluzzi, *Politica e governo nel Nuovo Mondo*, 195; Coello de la Rosa, "Discourse and Political Culture in the Formation of the Peruvian Reducciones in the Spanish Colonial Empire (1533–1592)," 217. For reasons of his own, Polo chose not to call the people of these enclaves mitimas, but other writers and they themselves called them by that name. See Mumford, "Litigation as Ethnography."

75 On this episode, see ibid.

76 Toledo to Oropesa corregidor Cap Francisco de Hinojosa, Arequipa, 14 Aug. 1575, in Morales, ed., *Repartimiento de tierras por el Inca Huayna Cápac (testimonio de un documento de 1556)*, 27–31.

77 Cook, ed., *Tasa de la visita general de Francisco de Toledo*, 16.

78 BNE Ms 3044, no. 4 (ff 41–52), "Carta que se escribio a su Magd por el Virrey Don Francisco de Toledo con relacion de los principales puntos y buenos effetos de su visita," [Cuzco,] 12 March 1571. " . . . mandadoles que hiziesen las pinturas y descriptiones de los pueblos que avia en cada repartimiento y donde se podrian reducir aviendolas visto con acuerdo de todos se hizo la reducion dellos en los assientos y partes que parescio que mas convenia," 45v.

79 Mundy, "Relaciones Geográficas," in Pillsbury, ed., *Guide to Documentary Sources for Andean Studies, 1530–1900*, 1:144–62; Barrera-Osorio, *Experiencing Nature*, chap. 4.

80 Sarmiento, *Historia de los Incas*, 110, chap. 39.

8. On the Ground

1 Toledo to king, 8 Feb. 1570, in *Gobernantes*, 3:341–79: "La primera parte y mas principal y sin la qual ningun efecto bueno se puede hazer con ellos que es el reduçillos y congregallos en poblaçiones," 341–42.

2 Toledo, instructions to inspectors, Lima, 1569–1570, in Romero, "Libro de la visita general del virrey don Francisco de Toledo, 1570–1575," 164–71.

3 Toledo, "Instrucciones en lo de la reducion de los pueblos de yndios" [unsigned and undated, probably 1572], in Lissón Chaves, ed., *La iglesia de España en el Perú*, 618–20.

4 Also, Andeans who lived in valleys east and west of the altiplano were often mitimas from highland communities: Platt et al., *Qaraqara-Charka*, 523.

5 Wightman, *Indigenous Migration and Social Change*, 11, 15; Gade and Escobar, "Village Settlement and the Colonial Legacy in Southern Peru," 434; Fraser, *The Ar-*

chitecture of Conquest, 78. But there may also have been a countervailing tendency to move Andean settlements closer to mines.

6 The cacique of Picacuri negotiated with Toledo in La Plata about the location of a reducción: Río, "Estrategias andinas de supervivencia," 61; Platt et al., *Qaraqara-Charka*, 518.

7 Toledo, "Provisión para llevar a la práctica las reducciones," Quilaquila, 7 Nov. 1573, in Toledo, *Disposiciones gubernativas para el Virreinato del Perú*, 1:281–83: "donde tienen sus idolatrías y entierros de sus pasados . . . ," 281–82.

8 Toledo to king, Cuzco, 25 March 1571, in *Gobernantes*, 3:490–523: "en la reduzion se ua teniendo consideracion a elegir el mejor sitio a donde comunmente ay yglesia," 508. See Wernke, "Analogy or Erasure?"; Gose, *Invaders as Ancestors*.

9 Platt et al., *Qaraqara-Charka*, 516–18.

10 The reducción's location might reflect complex relationships among a repartimiento's ayllus and factions. Gary Urton brilliantly analyzed this process via toponyms in Pacarictambo, near Cuzco: *The History of a Myth*, 88–93.

11 Gade and Escobar, "Village Settlement," 448.

12 Abercrombie, *Pathways of Memory and Power*, 255. This example is discussed below.

13 This was San Marcos de Miraflores in the repartimiento of Macha: Platt: "Pensamiento político Aymara," 372–81.

14 When one inspector moved families of repartimiento Conima away from land they owned, while moving families of repartimiento Guaycho closer to them, he gave Conima a document formally guaranteeing their land rights. ANB Expedientes Coloniales 1586–03, ff 5–6. Cap. Francisco de Cáceres, *mandamiento*, Villa de Cáceres de Achacache, 18 Jan. 1574.

15 AGI Contaduría 1785, "Pliego y comision para tomar las quentas a Juan de Yturrieta de lo que fue a su cargo de la rreçeptoria general . . ," 26 March 1576.

16 As we have seen, Toledo convinced church leaders to assign to the inspectors any fines imposed on encomenderos for failure to provide priests to Andean communities. The other major source of funding for the General Inspection was from Andean tribute. The king had ordered that native communities should receive a remission of one third of the tribute they owed during the time it took them to move to reducciones. Toledo amended this rule to state that this money be collected and paid to the inspector: AGI Contaduría 1785, ff 276–77, Toledo, model *titulo de receptor*, undated but some time after 2 Oct. 1570 (the date of the Lima junta to which it refers): " . . . a todos los dhos yndios a alcançado beneff. y aumento en esta Visita es justo les alcançe tanbien parte de la paga. . . ." If tribute payments had in fact been redirected for the full time it took to settle the reducciones, we would know how long that was. But Toledo, concerned that the process would deny the Crown its full tribute for an open-ended period, later capped the amount of tribute held back at half a year.

17 "Provisión con las normas para los reducidores de los indios," Potosí, 6 March 1573, in Toledo, *Disposiciones gubernativas*, 1:245–49.

18 AGI Contaduría 1785, 242r–v.

19 Matienzo to king, La Plata, 21 Jan. 1573, in Levillier, ed., *Audiencia de Charcas* 2:465–90: "con las manos en la masa," 465.

20 Ibid., f 143r. In Matienzo's report to the king, however, he reported paying three hundred pesos (or 17 percent of his own salary) to "a man whom I left there to execute" the two reducciones of Moromoro and Caracara. Levillier, ed., *Audiencia de Charcas* 2:468. Theoretically, reducidores were to receive two pesos per day: Toledo, "Apuntamientos aclaratorios de la Instrucción General," Potosí, 6 March 1573, in Toledo, *Disposiciones gubernativas*, 2:259–70, see 268.

21 Ibid., 266.

22 AGI Contaduría 1785, no. 1, ff 138–47.

23 Lima Aud to king, Lima, 27 Jan. 1573, in *Gobernantes*, 7:138–48: " . . . no tienen de que se sustentar sino es desta bisita y yr probeidos a costa de culpados para ellos remediar su necessidad es forçoso hallar culpas y buscarlas tan antiguas que parece muy feo tratar dellas . . . ," 139.

24 AGI Contaduría 1785, no. 1, f 6r. (7,375 pesos is the sum given by the royal accountants but the actual list of transactions comes to 6,427 pesos ensayados.)

25 Matienzo to king, 21 Jan. 1573, in Levillier, ed., *Audiencia de Charcas* 2:465–90, 466. Matienzo counted 204 tributaries, a number that very roughly maps to the number of households. By the time Toledo's formal tasa was drawn up, more people had apparently been added, since the tasa lists 279 tributaries: Cook, ed., *Tasa de la Visita General de Francisco de Toledo*, 33.

26 Levillier, ed., *Audiencia de Charcas* 2:466.

27 Matienzo, *Gobierno del Perú*, 83.

28 Levillier, ed., *Audiencia de Charcas* 2:473–74.

29 Ibid., 475.

30 Juan de Hoces, auto de reducción, Chérrepe, 23 Oct. 1572, edited and analyzed in Ramírez, "Chérrepe en 1572," 119–21.

31 Rama, *The Lettered City*. Of course, many peasant municipalities in Castile likewise generated very little surviving documentation: Nader, *Liberty in Absolutist Spain*, 17–18, 23.

32 Ramírez, "Chérrepe en 1572," 119–21.

33 In Mexico the larger towns were called cabeceras and the smaller ones *sujetos, anejos* or *visitas*. See, e.g., Hoekstra, *Two Worlds Merging*, 65.

34 Toledo did indicate that one reducción would be "la cabeza del repartimiento," for the purpose of keeping repartimiento documents: "Ordenanzas para la Ciudad de Guamanga," Guamanga, Jan. 1571, in *Disposiciones gubernativas*, 1:105–12, see 111.

35 Referring to Guadalupe as "the pueblo of the farming Indians which is being gathered and built," Hoces wrote: "Let them build their pueblo there, formed with its streets and plaza in a grid, with each farmer building his home there in the house-lot they choose" ("Alli agan su pueblo formado con sus calles y plaça en quadra haziendo cada yo labrador en el su morada y bibienda con el solar

que quisieren . . . el pueblo q se junta y edifica de los naturales labradores"). In the case of Chérrepe, by contrast, he wrote of the Andeans "squaring the said pueblo by its streets and plaza so that it is not scattered as it [now] is" (" . . . quadrando el dho pueblo por sus calles y plaza de modo que no este como esta desparramado"). Ramírez, "Chérrepe en 1572," 119.

36 Noquique's population was apparently thirty to forty-five tributaries out of about 290 in the repartimiento as a whole: ibid., 86.

37 Ibid., 119.

38 Ibid., 80–81, 93–94; Ramírez, The World Upside Down, 30–31, 71–72. Ramírez, however, finds it plausible that Noquique was the community's ritual center (personal communication).

39 "El un s. or. de yndios pescadores y el otro de labradores," Ramírez, "Chérrepe en 1572," 120.

40 The various manuscripts of Toledo's tasa, however, contain different kinds of information for different regions: see appendix.

41 The analysis that follows is my own, using data drawn from Julien, Condesuyo. The document, in AGI Charcas 142, was published in Ulloa, "Documentos del Virrey Toledo." Most records of the General Resettlement name the secular inspector as making all important decisions; when the ecclesiastical inspector appears at all, he seems to be in the background. In this case, on the other hand, the ecclesiastical inspector took the lead, not the secular inspector he was assigned to accompany, Gómez Hernández.

42 AGI Contaduría 1785, no. 1, ff 9–16.

43 The encomienda of Recuay in Ancash is another example of smooth variation. It was divided among fourteen reducciones, varying in size from fifty-six to three hundred tributaries. Five had fewer than one hundred tributaries, five had between one and two hundred and three had over two hundred. By contrast, the neighboring twin encomienda of Ichoc Huaraz and Allauca Guaraz was concentrated into a single reducción with about 660 tributaries. Zuloaga Rada, "La organización política," 153, citing a 1593 ecclesiastical inspection by Archbishop Toribio de Mogrovejo.

44 Julien, Condesuyo, 129.

45 Apart from those cited below, some of the project's findings are in: Pease, ed., Collaguas I; Cook, People of the Colca Valley.

46 Wernke, "An Archaeo-history of Andean Community and Landscape," 99; Wernke, "Negotiating Community and Landscape in the Peruvian Andes," 136–37.

47 In two sites, Uyu-Uyu and San Antonio, early Franciscan chapels appear across the Inca plaza from the kallanka.

48 Wernke discusses the logic behind the Franciscan founding of Coporaque: "Negotiating Community and Landscape," 139; Wernke, "Analogy or Erasure?" 165.

49 Wernke drew on a visita of Yanquecollaguas Hanansaya from 1615–17. What follows is a simplified account of a complicated argument. Furthermore, I am leaving out Wernke's analysis of the different pattern of landholdings for Yan-

quecollaguas Hurinsaya, and the possible reasons why the community's two sayas showed such different patterns; it is the Hanansaya pattern that is relevant to the location of the reducción.

50 More precisely, these toponyms referred to clusters of fields sharing the same primary irrigation canal.

51 Wernke, "Negotiating Community and Landscape," 139.

52 Weighting the distribution by size of landholdings, he was able to represent each ayllu's scattered lands as an ellipse, showing in simplified form the core area and center of the ayllu's property.

53 Ibid., 143–44.

54 Málaga Medina, "Los Collaguas en la historia de Arequipa," 99–101; Treacy, *Las chacras de Coporaque*, 135–37.

55 Cook and Cook, *People of the Volcano*, 94–95; Cook, "The Corregidores of the Colca Valley, Peru" 423–25. As part of his archaeological survey, Wernke identified the home village of the Checas as the site of Uyu Uyu, one of the large secondary Inka administrative centers of the central valley that also houses a small chapel. It is most likely one of the early Franciscan doctrinas established between the 1540s and 1560s, and was subsequently abandoned during the Resettlement. Wernke, "Analogy or Erasure?" 173.

56 ANB Expedientes Coloniales 1611–08. The inspector who assigned the mitimas a block of houses (*cuadra*) was Pedro de Zárate, the cacique was Juan Colque Guarache, and the mitimas were Asanaques living and working on a potato and oca field near the village of Tacobamba, near Potosí, in order to feed the Asanaque Indians who came to work in Potosí. The witness Luis Condori testified in 1610: Zárate "les mando que acudiessen a Tacobamba donde les senalo sitio pa que asistiessen en ello y acudiessen desde las dhas tierras como parescia por el dho amparo y *repartimiento* de la dha quadra a que se refiere," f 26r. See Abercrombie, *Pathways of Memory and Power*, 255, and Platt et al., *Qaraqara-Charka*, 526.

57 ANB Expedientes Coloniales 1611–02, "Los caciques e indios de Millerta [sic] del Collao, sobre que los reduzca al pueblo de Guancané," 1609–1611, 104. This case is discussed briefly in Murra, "Los olleros del Inka," and extensively, with an archaeological analysis, in Spurling, "The Organization of Craft Production in the Inka State." The interpretation here, however, is based on my own reading.

58 These outsiders were from Chiquicache. For the boundaries and organization of this and other regions in the Titicaca zone, see Julien, "Finding a Fit," 190–99.

59 Ibid., f 34v: Moho cacique and Omasuyo gobernador don Pedro Condori testified in 1583 that when the Spaniards came, Chucuito cacique Cari told the mitimas: "hermanos ya no es tiempo del Ynga agora y os podeis volver a vra tierra cada uno." However Condori, who was about fifty, could not have witnessed this for himself.

60 Intriguingly, about a third of the colonists were single women. It may be that women were traditionally potters, or that it was a way for widows or single women without land to support themselves.

61 Zimmerman, *Francisco de Toledo, Fifth Viceroy of Peru, 1569–1581*, 229, 250–51; Gómez Rivas, *El virrey del Perú don Francisco de Toledo*, 147–48; Bauer and DeCoster, "Introduction"; Vaccarella, "Fábulas, letras, and razones historiales fidedignas," 96–97.

62 Zimmerman, *Francisco de Toledo*, 198–99; Gómez Rivas, *El virrey del Perú*, 151–54. Toledo's requests for recall were many; see, among others: Toledo to Consejo de Indias, Cuzco, 1 March 1572, in *Gobernantes*, 3:536–40; Toledo to king, Lima, 17 April 1578, ibid., 7:407–18; Toledo to king, undated [probably December 1579], in *Colección de documentos inéditos para la historia de España*, 13:558–66. In requesting the position of comendador mayor of Alcántara, Toledo pointed out that Nicolás de Ovando, viceroy of Santo Domingo, had received it in 1509 on his return from governing "that island alone." Toledo to king, undated, in Hanke, ed., *Los Virreyes españoles en América durante el gobierno de la Casa de Austria*, 1:122–28, see 128. Insultingly, Philip instead appointed Toledo to the lesser position of clavero of the Order of Alcántara: Gómez Rivas, *El virrey del Perú*, 82.

63 Garcilaso de le Vega and Guaman Poma independently told versions of this story, so it was clearly in circulation early, but the documentary evidence shows only that Toledo was accused of misappropriation of funds—a common situation for returning governors, and one that was resolved only years later, to the detriment of his heirs. See Julien, "Garcilaso y el caso de la mala muerte del Virrey Toledo."

64 "Relación general de las poblaciones espanolas del Perú hecha por el licenciado Salazar de Villasante" [c. 1568], in Jiménez de la Espada, ed., *Relaciones geográficas de Indias*, 1:121–46: "Son tan frescos los lugares, que la gente de la ciudad se van con sus mugeres las fiestas a comer y merendar allá . . . ," 135.

65 Toledo to king, Cuzco, 1 March 1572, in *Gobernantes*, 4:48–208, see 191–92.

66 Newson, *Life and Death in Early Colonial Ecuador*, 219–21, 161. Licenciado Francisco de Cárdenas submitted accounts showing fines that he had charged, though the circumstances are somewhat unclear: AGI Contaduría 1785, 5–8, "Relación sumaria de las quentas," Francisco de Cardenas, 22 March 1577.

67 This was the pueblo of Pintag, in the outskirts of the city of Quito. Its cacique and principales wrote to the king in 1580, asserting that the town was founded by Gerónimo de Cepeda at the king's command. Kris Lane dates the founding to 1575: *Quito 1599*, 83.

68 "Carta del sinodo de Quito a SM el Rey," Quito, 15 May 1572, in Pereña Vicente and Baciero, eds., *Escuela de Salamanca*, 189–202, see 190. The bishop of Quito, however, expressed anxiety that forced resettlement would undermine the legitimate authority of the caciques: Ortiz Crespo and Terán Najas, "La reducción de indios en la zona interandina de la Real Audiencia de Quito," 210.

69 Salcedo Salcedo, "Los pueblos de indios en el Nuevo Reino de Granada y Popayán," 187–90.

70 Calero, *Chiefdoms under Siege*, 64–66.

71 Salcedo Salcedo, "Los pueblos de indios en el Nuevo Reino," 182–83.

72 Ibid., 186.

73 Bartolomé Gil Naranjo founded the town of Mucuchies, 29 March 1586; the traza of 1619 established an eighty-eight-meter-wide plaza and streets between five and eight meters wide. Calderón Trejo, "Antecedentes históricos de algunos pueblos de indios de los Andes venezolanos," 80–81. See also: Fals Borda, "Indian Congregaciones in the New Kingdom of Granada, 1595–1850"; López Rodríguez, *Tiempos para rezar y tiempos para trabajar*.

74 "Tasa y ordenanza para los indios hecha por Martín Ruiz de Gamboa," 1580, cited in Durston, "Un régimen urbanístico en la América hispana colonial."

75 Nicolini, "Pueblos de indios en el noroeste argentino"; Viñuales, "Los poblados de indios del centro y del litoral argentinos"; Farberman and Gil Montero, eds., *Los pueblos de indios del Tucumán colonial*; Farberman, "Curacas, mandones, alcaldes y curas."

76 While Treacy found that the preresettlement hamlets closest to the reducción of Coporaque were dismantled, there is no evidence that this happened during the General Resettlement. *Las chacras de Coporaque*, 135–36.

77 Maldonado Buendía to king, Lima, 25 March 1575, printed in Málaga Medina, *Reducciones toledanas en Arequipa (pueblos tradicionales)*, 229–30.

78 "Relación de la Provincia de los Pacajes," in Jiménez de la Espada, ed., *Relaciones geográficas*, 1:334–41, see 335.

79 See, e.g., AGI Lima 314, Probanza del Bachiller Moreno Vellido, 1576; AGI Charcas 142, Probanza del Bachiller Juan Martinez Altamirano, Chucuito, 24 Jan. 1580; AGI Charcas 42, Probanza de Damián de la Bandera, 6 May 1586; AGI Escribanía 500A, ff 75r–83r, Probanza de Juan de Salas Valdes, 1593. Neither Juan de Matienzo's cumulative report to the king on his own achievements, La Plata, 14 Oct. 1576, nor the probanza, which his son prepared after his death, dated 19 Jan. 1580, mention his work in the resettlement project: Levillier, ed., *Audiencia de Charcas*, 1:400–5 and 2:517–49. On the other hand, the 1584 probanza of Cristóbal de Albornoz referred to his work as ecclesastical inspector in Chinchaysuyo, albeit briefly: Albornoz "las hizo reducir, y puso dotrina en ellas y las visitó con mucha rectitud . . ." Millones, ed., *El retorno de las huacas*, 204.

80 AHC Expedientes Coloniales 30, ff 580–671, "Don Juan Uno, cacique de Tapacari, contra Gerónimo Chiriguana, cacique de Tapacari, sobre tierras de Moyapampa, 1584": testimony of Alonso Yucra about the reducción of Hormire, 26 Aug. 1585, f668r.

81 Alvarez, *De las costumbres y conversión de los indios del Perú*, 11, quoted in Gose, *Invaders as Ancestors*, 136.

82 Procurador, convent of San Francisco (Lima), to viceroy, 9 Jan. 1600, quoted in Gutiérrez, "Las reducciones indígenas en el urbanismo colonial," 28: "[El

pueblo de Pocsi] se comenzó a edificar, algunas casas estan acabadas otras a medio hacer y otras empezadas . . . y los indios en los antiguos poblezuelos y quebradas de tan ruines caseríos que no es posible entrar a ellos."

9. In and Out of the Reducciones

1 Guaman Poma, *Nueva corónica y buen gobierno*, 606: "Como quereys vuestra magestad que no ausente yndios?" (I follow the pagination of Guaman Poma's original text, as corrected by Murra and Adorno in their edition.)

2 The primary modern authority on Guaman Poma's life and book is Rolena Adorno. See, among others: *Guaman Poma*; "The Genesis of Felipe Guaman Poma de Ayala's *Nueva corónica* y buen gobierno"; *The Polemics of Possession*, chap. 2. The Nueva corónica is available online in facsimile, along with Murra's and Adorno's transcription: http://www.kb.dk/permalink/2006/info/es/frontpage .htm.

3 By licenciado, Guaman Poma may have referred to a credential in prehispanic Peru analogous to a university degree in Spain, but more likely he simply meant a well-educated person.

4 Ibid., 591; "hizo rreducir y poblar a los yndios, algunos en buena parte, algunos en mala parte, como la suerte cayó," 447; " . . . se ua acauando los yndios deste rreyno . . . porque se apartaron los yndios de unos pueblos que tenian escogidos citios, rincones por sus principales sauios y dotores, lesenciados, filosofos y aprouado de los primeros Yngas los tenples y tierras y agua para multiplicar la gente . . . [Los nuevos] citios causa en partes tierra umida y pistilenciales . . . hedor . . . pestilencia," 965.

5 ANB Expedientes Coloniales 1584–05. "Juicio seguido por Juan Laime Huanca, cacique de Pucarani, sobre tierras." This was not a typical reducción but a small settlement for Pucarani Indians serving in the city of La Paz. The final outcome does not appear in the record.

6 Luis de Monzon, "Descripción de la tierra del repartimiento de los Rucanas Antamarcas de la corona real, jurisdición de la ciudad de Guamanga," 1586, in Jiménez de la Espada, ed., *Relaciones geográficas de Indias*, 1:237–48, see 238–39.

7 Wernke, "Negotiating Community and Landscape in the Peruvian Andes."

8 Guaman Poma, *Nueva corónica*, 447. *Querencia* was applied to people and animals.

9 *Amparo* given to don Sebastián de Guara Mitimac, cacique of Pipo, San Lorenzo, 4 April 1587, in Konetzke, ed., *Colección de documentos para la historia de la formación social de Hispanoamérica (1493–1810)*, 1:579.

10 ANB Expedientes Coloniales 1579–06. "Juicio entre los indios de Macha y Alonso Diaz sobre las tierras de Casibamba [sic]," 1578–1579, 104 ff. For the Macha settlement at Carasibamba before and after the Resettlement, see ff 50, 83, 89, 123; for the fighting, see ff 14–15, 21. The document is published in Platt et al., *Qaraqara-Charka*, 541–70.

11 ANB Expedientes Coloniales 1593–19. "Composición de tierras de Guaranga en el repartimiento de Macha, en favor de Luis Frías," 1592, 34 ff: "los pedazos los

que estos yndios siembran es mas pa ympidir con ella que españoles no se les metan," ff 24–25.

12 In the region of Arequipa in 1575, Diego Guaquilla of the reducción of Quilca sold ten to twelve fanagadas of land in the Pachaqui valley, six leagues from the reducción, to Diego Hernandez de Alarcon for 250 pesos corrientes, a mare and some corn; six weeks later the buyer's father lent 100 pesos to Guaqilla's encomendero. See Galdos Rodríguez, "Concentraciones andinas y 'reducciones de yndios a pueblos'," 64–65.

13 Guaman Poma, *Nueva corónica*, 807–19.

14 Ibid., 450.

15 AHC Expedientes Coloniales 12, ff 445–447. "Causa ejecutiva seguido por Martín Pongo del pueblo de Santiago de Hurmire (Tapacarí) contra Estéban Calla de Sipesipe y Francisco Canoma," 1580–1586.

16 ANB Expedientes Coloniales 1617–08, "Los indios de Achacache contra Alonso de León, sobre las tierras de Tintilaya y Guacangache," f 47v. More precisely, the spokesman was Achacache's segunda persona.

17 This is not to say that Spanish inspectors and corregidors did not interact with alcaldes. A 1592 case showed both caciques and alcaldes formally receiving a document respecting tambo service: ANB Expedientes Coloniales 1762–16, ff 23–24. More often, though, the alcaldes were absent from official interactions between Spanish officials and caciques. See, e.g., ANB Expedientes Coloniales 1584–07, ff 21–59, "Visita de Sicasica," 1583–1584; ANB Expedientes Coloniales 1586–03, "Juicio entre los indios de Conima y Guaycho, sobre unas tierras de Cojota," 1585.

18 Guaman Poma, *Nueva corónica* 497, 811.

19 Ibid., 505, 600, 620, 872.

20 Ibid., 508 (". . . tanbien los rreligiosos andan a la rronda toda la noche . . . ; estando dormiendo las donzellas, abren la frezada y se la mira la guerguenza"), 588–89.

21 Ávila, *The Huarochirí Manuscript*.

22 Guaman Poma, *Nueva corónica*, 606, 686, 637, 920.

23 AGI Charcas 17, ramo 2, no. 16. "Memoria de los caciques de Chucuito," 5 Feb. 1591: "ques lastima belle de la manera que vive. . . ."

24 Guaman Poma, *Nueva corónica*, 522, 781–83, 787, 870–77.

25 Ibid., 448. See Sánchez-Concha Barrios, "La tradición política y el concepto del 'cuerpo de república' en el Virreinato." Toledo himself rejected the terminology of "two republics," and was ambivalent on the principle that no Spaniards should live in reducciones: Toledo to king, 1 March 1572, in Levillier, *Gobernantes* 4: 48–208, see 128–29; "Instrucción de los jueces de naturales," La Plata, 20 Dec. 1574, in Toledo, *Disposiciones gubernativas para el Virreinato del Perú*, 1:461–86, see 461, 471.

26 Guaman Poma, *Nueva corónica*, 662–63.

27 Ibid., 522. In a more serious case, Guaman Poma asked an Andean commoner

to store his clothing for him, but the reducción's priest seized it and sold the clothes for his own profit; ibid., 921.

28 Ibid., 568, 795. Guaman Poma's attitude toward traditional Andean song and dance was complex and usually positive, but he believed that it was sometimes an expression of idolatry.

29 Ibid., 957.

30 Ibid., 601, 871; Wightman, *Indigenous Migration and Social Change*, 50; Bakewell, *Miners of the Red Mountain*, 98, 101, 105; Choque Canqui, "El problema de género entre los mitayos"; Premo, "From the Pockets of Women."

31 Guaman Poma, *Nueva corónica*, 546.

32 Ibid., 696.

33 Información de Ysidro Sánchez, cited in Gose, *Invaders as Ancestors*, 132–35. See Ramírez, *To Feed and Be Fed*.

34 Examples from Cochabamba, Tacobamba and Tarija, respectively: AHC Expedientes Coloniales 10, ff 193–95, "Don Agustin Chinche contra don Pedro Velez," 1586; ANB Expedientes Coloniales 1611–08, ff 9v–10r, Asanaque petition to Potosi corregidor, 12 Aug. 1592; ANB Expedientes Coloniales 1605–04, dispute between Gutierre Velázquez de Ovando and Manuel de Pereyra, Tarija vecinos, over Chucuito yanacona, 1602–1605. As we have seen, some Spaniards carried a special license from Toledo or a later viceroy to seize up to a given number of Andeans. ANB Expedientes Coloniales 1605–04, f 8v, Toledo to Gutierre Velázquez de Ovando, Lima, 18 Aug. 1577. The license granted Velázquez, as one of the first settlers in San Bernardo de la Frontera, Tarija, the right to seize up to twenty Andeans as laborers from among the "cimarrones y fugitivos" who had escaped being enrolled in a reducción, and were not under the tutelage of a priest; Velázquez was to give them whatever was the customary wage of a yanacona in Tarija.

35 Guaman Poma, *Nueva corónica*, 454, 986–87.

36 Ibid., 467, 592, 986.

37 Ibid., 592.

38 AAL, Papeles Importantes, 3:13. The Andeans of the annex complained that that they received "notable discouragement, since they had build the said church . . . at their own cost, and adorned it according to their abilities" ("notable desconsuelo por aver hecho la dicha yglesia de Cayaguaya a su costa y adornadola segun su pusible"), 8r.

39 Enríquez to king, Lima, 22 Sept. 1581, in *Gobernantes*, 9:44–53: "de muchas partes ay quexas de yndios y no puede ser menos habiendo sido negocio tan atropellado," 51; Licenciado Cepeda to king, La Plata, 10 Feb. 1588, in Levillier, ed., *Audiencia de Charcas*, 368–80, see 368. See Spalding, *Huarochirí*, 225.

40 Pedro de Ribera and Antonio de Chaves y de Guevara, "Relación de la ciudad de Guamanga y sus terminos," 22 Feb. 1586, in Jiménez de Espada, ed., *Relaciones geográficas de Indias*, 1:181–201 see 184–85; Diego Cabeza de Vaca et al., "Descripción y relación de la ciudad de La Paz," 8 March 1586, ibid., 1:342–51, see 344.

(Cabeza de Vaca, unlike Ribera and Chaves, wrote that the locations of the reducciones were healthy.)

41 López de Velasco, *Geografía y descripción universal de las Indias*: "no estan del todo reducidos a pueblos, aunque se ha procurado, porque ellos no están en ellos de buena voluntad," 234.

42 Velasco to successor, 28 Nov. 1604, in Hanke, ed., *Los Virreyes españoles en América durante el gobierno de la Casa de Austria Virreyes*, 2:46–66: "Las Reducciones que hizo el señor D. Francisco de Toledo están algo desbaratadas en las provincias de arriba a causa de haberse muerto muchos indios y de otros que se han huido por evadirse de las mitas y de los servicios personales que están repartidos y de las vejaciones y malos tratamientos que reciben de sus corregidores y ministros de doctrina que son muy grandes y de los caciques que son los que peor los tratan y otros por haberse recogido a chacaras donde los retienen sus dueños a titulo de yanaconas," 52. The last clause of the sentence, referring to Andeans' flight to Spaniards' haciendas, will be discussed in the following chapter.

10. Four Hundred Years

1 Escobedo Mansilla, *Las comunidades indígenas y la economía colonial peruana*, 60. While relatively few researchers have examined the Resettlement campaign itself, many have studied the history of Andean society in the ensuing centuries; even so, reliable generalizations about settlement patterns are elusive. For accessible surveys, see Saignes, "The Colonial Condition in the Quechua-Aymara Heartland (1570–1780)"; and the historiographical survey in Zagalsky, "El concepto de 'comunidad' en su dimensión espacial." To a remarkable extent, Karen Spalding's monograph, *Huarochirí*, sketched out the narrative and themes that scholars have elaborated upon since then.

2 Spalding, *Huarochirí*, 179, 225; Saignes, "Lobos y ovejas." The area of greatest cultural survival was the Aymara territories of the Audiencia of Charcas.

3 Scholars have debated when the exodus from the reducciones began. Alejandro Málaga Medina accepts the official complaints that Andeans were abandoning the reducciones by the 1590s: "Las reducciones en el virreinato del Perú (1532–1580)," 41. Going further, Thierry Saignes speculates that in some areas most reducciones were empty from the beginning: "Las etnías de Charcas frente al sistema colonial," 72; *Ambana, tierra y hombres (Provincia de Camacho, Departamento de La Paz—Bolivia)*, 20. Catherine Julien is more cautious: "The reduction towns endured, but whether the people who were reduced in these towns remained there cannot be assessed." *Condesuyo*, 123.

4 Sánchez-Albornoz, "Mita, migraciones y pueblos"; Cook, "Patrones de migración en el virreinato del Perú"; Wightman, *Indigenous Migration and Social Change*; Powers, *Andean Journeys*, 11; Charney, *Indian Society in the Valley of Lima, Peru, 1532–1824*; Escobari de Querejazu, *Caciques, yanaconas y extravagantes*; Brock-

ington, *Blacks, Indians, and Spaniards in the Eastern Andes*, 220. In the introduction to a new edition of his classic *Demographic Collapse*, however, Noble David Cook warns against exaggerating the role of migration in falling census numbers, arguing that Spanish administrators placed forasteros on the tribute rolls more successfully than Sánchez-Albornoz believed, and that absolute population continued to fall in the early seventeenth century: *La catástrophe demográfica*, 24–27.

5 Huertas Vallejo, "El proceso de concentración social en el espacio andino, siglos XVI, XVII y XVIII," 805. Viceroy Cañete wrote to the king in 1592 that the epidemics of 1588–1590 had caused many to flee the reducciones: Gose, *Invaders as Ancestors*, 136.

6 Cook, "Patrones de migración," 143; Stavig, "Continuing the Bleeding of These Pueblos Will Shortly Make Them Cadavers." The Audiencia of Quito was unusual in that censuses recorded a rise in Indian population between 1590 and 1660; Karen Powers argues that in this region, migration was initially *toward* population centers, before reversing itself and moving into the haciendas in the later seventeenth century: *Andean Journeys*, 7–10.

7 Sánchez-Albornoz, *Indios y tributes en el Alto Perú*. Beginning in the 1620s, new laws enabled caciques to incorporate some forasteros as tributaries or as personal retainers: Saignes, "The Colonial Condition," 91.

8 Cook, "Patrones de migración," 136–41; Escobari de Querejazu, "Poblados de indios dentro de poblados españoles." The pattern of mitayos staying at Potosí after completing the term of their mita service preceded the General Resettlement: Mangan, *Trading Roles*, 34.

9 For example, Cochabamba saw a systematic census of yanaconas on Spanish chacaras in 1630: AHC Expedientes Coloniales 15, ff 908–1011.

10 Wightman, *Indigenous Migration and Social Change*, 150; Powers, *Andean Journeys*, 7–10.

11 Saignes, *Los Andes orientales*; Scott, *Contested Territory*, 126–27.

12 Spalding, *Huarochirí*, 225. See Thierry Saignes, "Las etnías de Charcas."

13 Monsalve, *Reducion universal de todo el Piru y de mas Indias, con otros muchos auisos, para el bien de los naturales dellas, y en aumento de las reales rentas.*

14 Gose, *Invaders as Ancestors*, 195–96.

15 Choque Canqui, *Sociedad y economía colonial en el sur andino*, 51.

16 AGI Lima 302. Archbishop Gonzalo de Campo to king, Lima, 15 Oct. 1626: "que es el estilo que aca se tiene quando no se quiere hazer nada."

17 Don Luis de Oznayo, corregidor of Guamanga, 25 April 1620, quoted in Scott, *Contested Territory*, 72.

18 Gose, *Invaders as Ancestors*, 190–91.

19 Lima archbishop Hernando Arias Ugarte, writing in the 1630s, wrote that previous viceroys had "liberally [given] permission to the Indians to return to their old towns at the request of their badly informed protectores;" ibid., 194.

20 Pedro Ramírez del Aguila, *Noticias políticas de Indias*, cited in Saignes, "The Colo-

nial Condition," 102. More precisely, the writer referred to *doctrinas* rather than reducciones, but in practice the two were usually synonymous at this time.

21 Spalding, *Huarochirí*, 226. The seventeen original reducciones had begun with a mean population of 1500, and the 49 villages in the eighteenth century had a mean population of 160. One of the original reducciones had begun with a remaining population of twenty while another was entirely deserted.

22 Ibid., 180.

23 Alejandro Málaga Medina finds that all seventy-four reducciones in the province of Arequipa eventually became functioning towns: *Reducciones toledanas en Arequipa (pueblos tradicionales)*, 126.

24 "Las poblaciones de los que estan poblados son en el comedio de los alto y bajo de los montes, en tierra antes fria que caliente, de donde gozan de dos extremos, de la fria para ganados y caza, y de la caliente para sementeras," López de Velasco, *Geografía y descripción universal de las Indias*, 234.

25 Ramírez, *The World Upside Down*, 73–74; Klaus, "Out of Light Came Darkness," 319.

26 Non-Andeans "gradually, illegally, but permanently moved into the reducciones—the corregidor or his representative, the owners of estates or textile mills (obrajes), tradespeople, and mestizos." Saignes, "The Colonial Condition," 83. The process was fastest for reducciones located on the main roads.

27 *Recopilación de leyes de los reynos de las Indias*, Parte 6, título 3, ley 21.

28 Mörner, *La Corona Española y los foráneos en los pueblos de indios*, 175–78, 196–99. Visitas by oidores, in theory every one to three years but in fact less frequent, were one vehicle for sporadic enforcement of the segregation policy; ibid., 185–87.

29 AHN Inq 1:1647:15, Juan de Pineda, 1643–8, criollo, natural de La Paz, por bigamia.

30 Mörner, *La Corona Española y los foráneos*, 179–80.

31 Bastien, *Mountain of the Condor*, 25–28.

32 Cabanaconde Anansaya's population consisted of 489 Andeans, 23 mestizos, and 122 Spaniards: Gelles, *Water and Power in Highland Peru*, 32.

33 Ramírez, "Don Clemente Anto, procurador del común del pueblo de Lambayeque."

34 This process was called *composición de tierras*. There was a major one in the 1590s; see ANB Expedientes Coloniales 1593–19, "Composición de tierras de Guaranga en el repartimiento de Macha, en favor de Luis Frías," 1592.

35 Andean community property financed Spanish enterprises in two ways: by lending funds in the *caja de comunidad* at low interest, and by leasing fields for low rent. In 1610 the assets of Visisa were invested in a mercury company and in an estancia outside the community's borders: Zagalsky, "El concepto de 'comunidad' en su dimensión espacial," 80.

36 Glave, "Trajines"; Acosta Rodríguez, "Los clérigos doctrineros y le economía colonial (1600–1630)"; Cook and Cook, *People of the Volcano*, 137. Among any

number of such cases documented in judicial records, see ANB Minas 122, no. 5, 1592; AHC ECM 9, ff 383–406, "El cap Gomez Yañez de Amaya, diligencias sobre que los indios de su encomienda sean bueltos a su reducion," 1603.

37 Spalding, Huarochirí, chap. 7.

38 Ramírez, To Feed and Be Fed, chap. 4. The two religious traditions could coexist without necessarily harmonizing. Kenneth Mills writes of local leaders asking permission from the mummified ancestors to celebrate a Christian saint's day: An Evil Lost to View?, 64.

39 Gose, Invaders as Ancestors, 149–60. See Cook and Cook, People of the Volcano, 204. Haagen Klaus has documented archaeologically the changing practices of burial and exhumation in a reducción church: "Out of Light Came Darkness," chap. 9.

40 Cummins, "Forms of Andean Colonial Towns, Free Will, and Marriage," 209, 213.

41 Durston, "El proceso reduccional en el sur andino," 93–97; Abercrombie, Pathways of Memory and Power, 255–56.

42 Ibid., 9ff, 282–91.

43 Ramírez, To Feed and Be Fed, 116.

44 Mills, Idolatry and Its Enemies.

45 Scott, Contested Territory, 102–7.

46 Abercrombie, Pathways of Memory and Power; Cook and Cook, People of the Volcano, 101–12. The administrative term for saya was parcialidad. Some new ayllus were based on occupation, as some Andeans left farming for specialized work within the colonial economy.

47 Thomson, We Alone Will Rule, 44–54 (on the La Paz area); Serulnikov, Subverting Colonial Authority, 25 (on Chayanta).

48 Powers, Andean Journeys; Saignes, "The Colonial Condition," 71, 83; Serulnikov, Subverting Colonial Authority, 26; Garrett, Shadows of Empire, 102–8.

49 Penry, "The Rey Común"; Thomson, We Alone Will Rule; Serulnikov, Subverting Colonial Authority, 20–21.

50 Penry, "Transformations in Indigenous Authority and Identity in Resettlement Towns of Colonial Charcas (Alto Perú)," 47–54; and The People Are King.

51 A cacique lineage was still prominent in Huaquirca in the mid-twentieth century, but such cases were rare. Gose, Deathly Waters and Hungry Mountains, 37.

52 O'Phelan, Kurakas sin sucesiones. Ironically, in some areas the title of cacique mutated to become one of the rotating offices within the reducción. Rasnake, Domination and Cultural Resistance, 138–65.

53 Much of the population of Condocondo, for instance, lived in three villages outside the reducción: Penry, "Transformations in Indigenous Authority," 28.

54 The conflation of secular and sacred offices reflected the growing importance of the church as an instantiation of the Andean community's collective identity, through the cofradías or religious brotherhoods, each charged with devotion to a particular saint or other focus of Catholic worship. It also reflected the influence of the village priests who, though often rapacious and corrupt, frequently

allied with their flock against the caciques. Saignes speculated that alliances with priests promoted both the influence of the cabildo and the development of the cargo career: "The Colonial Condition," 84, 105.

55 Dictatorial Decrees, Cuzco, 4 July 1825, in Bolívar, El Libertador, 187–90. Bolívar reversed himself and restored tribute in his decree of 15 Oct. 1828: ibid., 191–96.

56 Thurner, From Two Republics to One Divided.

57 Platt, "Liberalism and Ethnocide in the Southern Andes," 8. Monique Nuijten and Davíd Lorenzo Rodríguez write: "the semi-autonomous juridical, productive and political sphere of the indigenous communities remained the fiscal basis of the Peruvian state" after independence: "Peasant Community and Territorial Strategies in the Andean Highlands of Peru," 34. The same can be said of Bolivia and Ecuador.

58 Peru abolished Indian tribute in 1854, Ecuador in 1857, and Bolivia in 1874: Larson, "Andean Highland Peasants and the Trials of Nation Making During the Nineteenth Century," 560.

59 Ibid., 601–5.

60 In Peru, the Civil Code of 1852 made Indians' land alienable and Indian citizens' contracts legally enforceable: ibid., 623–25. In Bolivia, the 1874 Ley de Ex-vinculación liquidated Indian corporate communities and required Indian citizens to buy title to the land they occupied, now defined as belonging to the state, while also taxing those lands: Platt, La persistencia de los ayllus en el norte de Potosí, 38–40. In Ecuador, Indian land was not legally disentailed until 1908, partly because haciendas already controlled much of the country's land by Independence: Albó, "Andean People in the Twentieth Century," 784–85. Hacendados often took Indian land less for its value than to convert its Indian owners into landless laborers: Nuijten and Rodríguez, "Peasant Community," 34.

61 Platt, La persistencia de los ayllus, 34; Larson, "Andean Highland Peasants," 567; Albó, "Andean People in the Twentieth Century," 769–70; Platt et al., Qaraqara-Charka.

62 There is a vivid fictional portrayal of such a town in the early twentieth century in the novel Yawar fiesta by José Maria Arguedas.

63 Albó, "Andean People in the Twentieth Century." See also Clark and Becker, "Indigenous People and State Formation." Along with historical studies, mid-twentieth-century ethnographies—typically in communities chosen because they were especially "traditional"—although superseded by later anthropologists, document community organization in the early and mid-twentieth century. See Parsons, Peguche; La Barre, The Aymara Indians of the Lake Titicaca Plateau, Bolivia; Keller, "Finca Ingavi—A Medieval Survival on the Bolivian Altiplano."

64 Gelles, Water and Power in Highland Peru, 23–25.

65 Gascón, "Compadrazgo y cambio en el altiplano peruano."

66 Rasnake, Domination and Cultural Resistance, 40–44. In Huaquirca in the 1970s, "local notions of race serve[d] to essentialize sociocultural distinctions that [were] in other respects quite fluid." Gose, Deathly Waters, xii.

67 Tschopik, *The Aymara of Chucuito*, 152; Rasnake, *Domination and Cultural Resistance*, 30–32; Gade and Escobar, "Village Settlement and the Colonial Legacy in Southern Peru," 442, 446.

68 Nash, *We Eat the Mines and the Mines Eat Us*; Albó, "Andean People in the Twentieth Century"; Klein, *A Concise History of Bolivia*, chap. 8; Waters, "Indigenous Communities, Landlords, and the State"; Becker, *Indians and Leftists in the Making of Ecuador's Modern Indigenous Movements*. In Bolivia, the 1952 revolution was followed by a social revolution in the hacienda-dominated regions, especially the areas of Cochabamba and La Paz, where Andean families and communities seized and kept land. In Peru, the military government of the 1960s transformed many haciendas into cooperative enterprises, theoretically owned by their workers but often controlled by government appointees who might be as abusive as the hacendados they replaced; even so, the reform reflected and stimulated the farmers' politicization and rising expectations for further reform; see Skar, *The Warm Valley People*, chap. 2. In Ecuador, a gradual process of modernization throughout the twentieth century prompted many hacendados to break up and sell off their haciendas.

69 Rivera Cusicanqui, "Liberal Democracy and Ayllu Democracy in Bolivia"; Albó, "Ethnic Identity and Politics in the Central Andes"; Van Cott, *From Movements to Parties in Latin America*; García, *The Making of Indigenous Citizens*; Clark and Becker, "Indigenous People and State Formation." Integrating the language of ethnicity into the larger currents of twenty-first-century politics has not been easy; see Lucero, "Representing 'Real Indians.'"

70 Taller de Historia Oral Andina, *Ayllu*; Fernández Osco, *La ley del ayllu*.

71 The *movimientos sociales* are not sharply defined; they are centered in highland indigenous organizations but extend beyond them.

72 Albó, "Ethnic Identity and Politics." Toledo emphasized his Andean ethnicity during his electoral campaign, but did not prioritize Indian ethnic interests as president: García, *The Making of Indigenous Citizens*, 55–56.

73 Albó, *Pueblos indios en la política*; Van Cott, *Radical Democracy in the Andes*.

74 Ibid., 183, 202–3.

75 Platt, *La persistencia de los ayllus en el norte de Potosí*, 34–36; Barragán, "Entre polleras, ñañacas y lliqllas"; McNeish, "Globalization and the Reinvention of Andean Tradition."

76 Matos Mar, "Taquileños, Quechuas del Lago Titicaca, en Lima"; Lazar, *El Alto, Rebel City*; Montoya Rojas, *Destinies of the Quechua Culture in Peru*. In the 1980s Lima's already rapid growth accelerated due to the Maoist insurgency and civil war that terrorized highland Peru in the 1980s.

77 Meisch, *Andean Entrepreneurs*; Avila Molero, "Worshipping the Señor de Qoyllur Ritti in New York."

78 Gelles, *Water and Power in Highland Peru*, 15, 25.

Epilogue

1 Cervantes, *Don Quijote*, 2:4 ("Yo he tomado el pulso a mí mismo y me hallo con salud para regir reinos y gobernar ínsulas") and 1:10 ("Por grande que sea, yo me siento con fuerzas de saberla gobernar tal y tan bien como otro que haya gobernado ínsulas en el mundo").

2 Cervantes's petition for a government job in Upper Peru is in AGI Patronato 253, ramo 1.

3 AGI Lima 29, no. 5, ff 16v, 32r, Toledo to king, Potosí, 20 March 1573. He described Aymara as "more obscure than other languages" and Puquina as too difficult for priests to learn. In the early colonial period Aymara was the dominant language in the region between Cuzco and Potosí, coexisting (often in a single community) with Quechua, Puquina, and several other languages. Puquina (extinct today) may have belonged to a local group subjugated by inmigrating Aymara-speakers at some point before the mid-fifteenth century, creating a situation similar to other conquest cultures in which the indigenous language was used mainly in the home and by women, the invaders' language in public life and by men. Quechua entered the region following fifteenth-century Inca conquests (it was widely used in Inca administration, and Spaniards assumed it was the official Inca language, although in fact the Inca royal family may have spoken a dialect of Aymara among themselves), but remained a minority language there. All of these languages, furthermore, had many dialects; sixteenth-century Andean language use remains poorly understood. See Torero, *Idiomas de los Andes*; Cerrón-Palomino, "Aimara as the Official Inca Language"; Durston, *Pastoral Quechua*, 41, 123; Charles, *Allies at Odds*, 49–50.

4 Ellinghaus, "Indigenous Assimilation and Absorption in the United States and Australia."

5 Apart from Espinosa's brutal and failed policy with the moriscos, this was an idea quite alien to the realities of royal rule in Spain: Suárez Fernández, *Nobleza y monarquía*; Owens, 'By My Absolute Royal Authority.'

6 Scott, *Seeing Like a State*, 231, 235, 238.

7 Ibid., 234–46.

8 Ibid., 203.

9 Clavero, "Institución política y derecho." On the political culture of the composite state of Castile and Aragon, and other western European monarchies, see Sarfatti, *Spanish Bureaucratic-Patrimonialism in America*; Ertman, *Birth of the Leviathan*.

10 Michel Foucault, "Omnes et Singulatim"; Foucault, "Governmentality."

11 *Polizei* and *police*, in their various cognates, passed through a series of meanings: proper conduct, the administrative science of instilling it, legislation about citizens' conduct as opposed to actual crime (known as police powers jurisprudence), and finally the people in charge of citizens' conduct on the ground, policemen and -women. Foucault, "Omnes et Singulatim," 243; Axtmann, "'Police' and the Formation of the Modern State."

12 Spanish theologians played a major role in one disseminator of notions of governmentality, the Council of Trent (1545–1563), in which Catholic prelates encouraged rulers to keep close track of their subjects and conform their lives to normative standards: Châtellier, *The Religion of the Poor*, 13; Poska, *Regulating the People*; Rico Callado, "Las misiones interiores en la España postridentina." See Foucault, "The Confession of the Flesh."

13 In its long development, governmentality has taken both authoritarian and liberal forms. The study of colonial governmentality has emphasized its more liberal form, based in nineteenth-century utilitarianism, and the subtle "capillary" influence of hegemonic ideologies, paying less attention to the brutal campaigns chronicled by James Scott. See D. Scott, "Colonial Governmentality," 200–3, 211–14; Comaroff, "Reflections on the Colonial State, in South Africa and Elsewhere"; Dean, *Governmentality*, 95; Cooper, *Colonialism in Question*, 146.

14 One of the few scholars who has explored this is Sara Castro-Klarén, who writes that sixteenth-century Peru exhibited "a level of repression which Europe was spared until later, when the combination of the pastoral model and reason of state would produce the totalitarian regimes of this century": "Historiography on the Ground," 164.

15 This idea, too, went back to Aristotle; see chapter 7, note 54.

16 Serrano Gassent, *Vasco de Quiroga*, 35.

17 D. Scott, "Colonial Governmentality."

18 Cooper, *Colonialism in Question*, 143.

19 Pels and Salemink, eds., *Colonial Subjects*, 22; Dirks, *Castes of Mind*, 6.

20 Mantena, *Alibis of Empire*, 3, 14–15.

21 Ibid., 9.

22 Ibid., 172–76; Steinmetz, "The Devil's Handwriting"; Trumbull, "An Empire of Facts"; Wilder, *The French Imperial Nation-State*.

23 Comaroff, "Reflections on the Colonial State."

24 Mumford, "Litigation as Ethnography in Sixteenth-Century Peru."

25 Did colonial ethnographers, in the sixteenth or the nineteenth century, discover the indigenous cultures they described, or invent them? That question has prompted intense debate among historians of modern empires, especially British India. Dirks and others, writing in the tradition of Edward Said's *Orientalism*, have portrayed ethnographic accounts as shaped by observers' preconceptions and the dynamic of colonialism; indeed, British misinterpretations (of, for instance, caste) *became* social realities through the force of colonial policy. Others have responded that this narrative removes agency from Indians, turning the conquerors into the creators of indigenous society, and argued that British accounts were fairly accurate precisely because they drew on Indians' knowledge of their own culture. (On this debate, see Bayly, *Empire and Information*, 366–74; Dirks, *Castes of Mind*, 309; Spear, "Neo-Traditionalism and the Limits of Invention in British Colonial Africa"; Guha, "The Politics of Identity

and Enumeration in India c. 1600–1990," 149–51.) For my purpose, in the context of sixteenth-century Peru, the question is not of central importance. The Spanish image of the archipelago model of settlement had aspects that were correct, in modern scholars' judgment, while their understanding of Inca rule was highly distorted. What is significant is that ethnographic discourse was multivalent, and contributed both to governmentality and to indirect rule.

26 Anderson, *Imagined Communities*, 50; Cañizares-Esguerra, *How to Write the History of the New World*.

Appendix

1 This number is approximate because in a few cases, several very small repartimientos are grouped together in the tasa and not individually named.

2 Cook, "Introducción," in *Tasa de la visita general de Francisco de Toledo*, ix–xxvii, see xiii–xiv.

3 See Noble David Cook, "Visitas, Censuses," in Pillsbury, ed., *Guide to Documentary Sources for Andean Studies, 1530–1900*, 1:129–43.

4 Toledo, Instruction for inspectors, Lima, 1569–1570, in Romero, "Libro de la visita general del virrey don Francisco de Toledo, 1570–1575," 164, 170, 174. See also Toledo to king, 8 Feb. 1570, in *Gobernantes*, 3:341–79, see 341–42.

5 More detailed information available from the author on request.

6 *Colección de documentos inéditos para la historia de España*, 94:344–46

7 Rodríguez Salgado, *The Changing Face of Empire*, 21–22.

8 Ramos Pérez, "La crisis indiana y la Junta Magna de 1568," 44.

9 [Antonio Bautista de Salazar], "De los Virreyes y Gobernadores del Pirú," in *Colección de documentos inéditos*, first series, 8:212–93, see 219.

10 Julien, "Spanish Reform and Change in the Potosí Hinterland," appendix.

11 AGI Lima 578, libro 2, ff 264v–71v, Aranjuez, 30 Nov. 1568, published in *Gobernantes*, 3:646–657. Also "Poder general al virrey," Madrid, 19 Dec. 1568, AGI Lima 578, libro 2, f 392v, unpublished.

12 Respectively: AGI Lima 578, libro 2, ff 279–93v, Aranjuez, 30 Nov. 1568, and AGI Indiferente 2859, no. 2, Madrid, 28 Dec. 1568, both published in Hanke, ed., *Los Virreyes españoles en América durante el gobierno de la Casa de Austria*, 1:74–117.

13 AGI Lima 578, libro 2, ff 238, 271v–79, 294–424, variously dated: El Escorial, 4 Nov. 1568; Aranjuez, 30 Nov. 1568; Madrid, 9 Dec. 1568; Madrid, 19 Dec. 1568; Madrid, 2 Jan. 1569; Madrid, 15 Jan. 1569. All unpublished.

14 Toledo to king, Lima, 18 April 1578, in *Gobernantes*, 6:39–70, see 51.

GLOSSARY

(A): Andean (Quechua, Aymara, or both)

(S): Spanish

(C): Caribbean (words the Spanish borrowed from Taino and used throughout the Americas)

alcalde (S). Official in Spanish and colonial Indian municipalities who presided over the cabildo and combined the functions of mayor and judge. A municipality typically had two alcaldes serving together, selected annually by lot or election. (The alcalde, also known as *alcalde ordinario*, was distinct from the *alcalde mayor*, an appointed official who oversaw a larger area, often with military powers.)

alguacil or *alguacil mayor* (S). Municipal constable who held a place on the cabildo. The inspectors (visitadores) in the Visita General were accompanied by alguaciles.

altiplano (S). Arid high plateau in the south-central Andes.

anejo (S). Annex village, typically founded as a satellite and dependency of an existing reducción that was designated its *cabecera*.

aqlla (A). Chosen woman. The *aqllakuna* (plural) were selected by the Inca regime to live in communal houses, serving the state and the official religious cults.

Audiencia (S). 1. Colonial high court; 2. Administrative district governed by that court. A viceroyalty had several Audiencias, each composed of a *presidente* (presiding judge), several *oidores* (judges), and other officials.

ayllu (A). The basic unit of Andean social structure, a kinship group sharing a common ancestor (real or mythical), which held land in common.

cabecera (S). Head town. Over time, many of the reducciones became cabeceras surrounded by a circle of anejos.

cabildo (S). Municipal council.

cacique (C). Indigenous lord, usually hereditary, though not through premogeniture. The Spanish used the word cacique throughout the Americas for indigenous leaders, and it was the colonial term for various Andean leadership categories including *kuraka*, *jilaqata*, and others. It was, however, distinguished in colonial usage from the lower office of *principal*, usually the leader of an ayllu. The *cacique principal* was the leader of a repartimiento, assisted by a *segunda persona*. Sometimes the two officials were also the respective leaders of the repartimiento's upper and lower *sayas*; in other cases, each saya had both a cacique and a segunda persona.

cargo (S). Political or religious position undertaken by a community member.

cédula or *real cédula* (S). Royal edict.

chácara (A). Field or group of fields.

chicha (C). Indigenous fermented drink, usually made from maize.

comunero (S). Community member with access to shared resources such as irrigation water and grazing lands, and the responsibility to contribute to quotas of tribute and labor.

corregidor (S). Governor and judge appointed by the crown. A *corregidor de indios* administered a territory called a *corregimiento*, composed of several *repartimientos*; a *corregidor de españoles* administered a Spanish city. When the word "corregidor" appears by itself in this book, I am generally using it to mean corregidor de indios.

Consejo de Indias (S). Council of the Indies, one of several advisory councils within the Hapsburg government, and the highest body charged with colonial policy making. Located in Spain, it was the final court of appeals for colonial litigation.

encomendero (S). Spanish holder of a grant, or *encomienda*, conferring the privilege of receiving tribute from one or more repartimientos. In the early colonial period, viceroys typically granted an encomienda for two lives, that of the recipient (based on his service to the crown) and his heir.

escribano (S). Notary and reporter of legal proceedings.

forastero (S). Outsider, foreigner; an Indian living in an indigenous community not his or her own. Forasteros usually were free from paying tribute or paid it at a lower level than comuneros, and lacked most community privileges.

hacienda (S). Spanish commercial farm or ranch; often also called *chácara*.

huaca (A). Andean sacred object or place. A huaca could be (among other things) a hill, a stone, a river, a mummy, or a carved object, and was often identified with a community's mythical ancester. Many were the object of secret devotion during the colonial period.

kuraka (A). See *cacique*.

lengua (S). Interpreter.

letrado (S). Member of the class of university-educated men, an increasingly important group in sixteenth-century Spanish government. Letrados held university titles such as *bachiller, licenciado,* and *doctor.*

licenciado (S). See *letrado.*

mestizo (S). Person of mixed descent, usually Spanish and Indian.

mita / *mit'a* (A). System of compulsary Indian rotational labor; corvée. Adapting the pre-conquest institution of mit'a, or "turn," the colonial mita drew fixed numbers of families from each of a community's ayllus for work in mines, *tambos,* cities, and *obrajes,* assigning laborers to Spanish employers for a low fixed wage.

mitima / *mitmaq* (A). Person removed from his or her community by the Inca state to settle as a colonist in another location, usually to labor for the state, while remaining ethnically and sometimes politically affiliated to the home community. After the conquest, the word referred to the descendants of these Inca colonists as well as Andeans who lived at a distance from their communities' core territory and shared products with it, as part of the vertical archipelago—two groups who blurred together in the colonial period.

morisco (S). Iberian Muslim convert to Christianity, or descendant of converts.

obraje (S). Manufacturing workshop, usually for textiles, with a Spanish owner and Andean laborers.

padrón (S). Census.

panaca (A). Kinship group among the Inca aristocracy in Cuzco.

parcialidad (S). See *saya.*

peso (S). Unit of currency. There were various kinds of pesos with different values, including the *peso corriente,* used for most transactions, and the more valuable *peso ensayado,* used for calculating tribute. Coins were defined in terms of a unit of account called a *maravedí;* in 1570, pesos corrientes and pesos ensayados were equivalent to 272 and 425 maravedís, respectively: see Luengo Múñoz, "Sumaria noción de las monedas."

picota or *rollo* (S). Pillar standing on the *plaza mayor,* at which criminals were whipped or executed.

policía (S). Civilized communal life, according to a Spanish Mediterranean model of community.

principal (S). See *cacique.*

quipu / khipu (A). Artifact composed of wool or cotton colored yarn, in which multiple strings hung from a primary string, carrying knots that conveyed information, usually quantitative information such as population figures and inventories of goods.

reducción (S). Indian village or town founded by Spanish authorities; also, the act of resettlement itself. Reducción was the word used in the Andes; in Mexico and Central America the equivalent was *congregación*.

reducidor (S). Spanish official appointed by an inspector to facilitate resettlement in a given locality.

regidor (S). Municipal councilor. A cabildo usually had from four to six regidores.

repartimiento (S). Community of Indians granted in encomienda to a Spaniard. It was usually but not always a preexisting ethnic or political unit, answering to a cacique principal, and became the primary unit of colonial Andean populations.

saya (A) / *parcialidad* (S). Upper or lower moiety of an Andean community. Andean population divisions, were often divided into *hanansaya* or upper half and *hurinsaya* or lower half.

solar (S). House lot.

tambo (A). Lodging house staffed by Andean mita laborers, which provided food, lodging, and freight carrying to Spanish travelers at fixed prices. The colonial institution was based on the Inca *tamp'u*, though it functioned differently.

tasa (S). Document laying out the tribute due from every repartimiento.

tributario (S). Tribute-paying adult male in a repartimiento.

ushnu (A). Platform in the plaza of an Inca state complex, from which an Inca official presided over state festivities.

vecino (S). Property-owning, male citizen of a municipality.

visita (S). 1. Administrative inspection; 2. Report produced in such an inspection. The visita was a basic tool in all branches of Spanish government. The crown sent inspectors (*visitadores*) to dioceses, courts, and councils to investigate charges of corruption, audit fiscal accounts, and compile reports. In Peru, there were frequent visitas to Indian repartimientos to compile a census, judge disputes, recommend tribute levels, and (often) found reducciones. A simultaneous inspection by various visitadores of all the repartimientos in a given jurisdiction was called a *Visita General* (General Inspection), of which the most famous was the one ordered and led by Francisco de Toledo, and which carried out the General Resettlement.

yanacona (A). Unfree Andean laborer working for a Spanish master. The word was derived from the Quechua plural of *yana*, the personal retainer of a preconquest Inca or ethnic lord.

BIBLIOGRAPHY

Abbreviations

AAL: Archivo Arzobispal de Lima, Lima, Peru
AGI: Archivo General de Indias, Seville, Spain
AHC: Archivo Histórico de Cochabamba, Cochabamba, Bolivia
AHN: Archivo Histórico de la Nación, Madrid, Spain
AMJ: Archivo del Ministerio de la Justicia, Madrid, Spain
ANB: Archivo Nacional de Bolivia, Sucre, Bolivia
AGNA: Archivo General de la Nación, Buenos Aires, Argentina
BNE: Biblioteca Nacional de España, Madrid, Spain
BPR: Biblioteca del Palacio Real, Madrid, Spain
Colección de documentos inéditos, first series: Colección de documentos inéditos relativos al descubrimiento, conquista y colonización de las posesiones españolas en América y Oceanía, sacados en su mayor parte del Real Archivo de Indias. 42 vols. Madrid: Imprenta Española, 1864–1889.
Gobernantes: Levillier, Roberto, ed. Gobernantes del Perú: Cartas y papeles, siglo XVI. Documentos del Archivo de Indias. 14 vols. Madrid: Sucesores de Rivadeneyra, 1921–1926.

Printed primary sources

Acosta, José de. Historia natural y moral de las Indias. Edited by J. Alcina Franch. Madrid: Dastín, 1986 [1590].
Alvarez, Bartolomé. De las costumbres y conversión de los indios del Perú: Memorial a Felipe II. Edited by María del Carmen Martín Rubio, Juan José R. Villarías Robles, and Fermín del Pino. Madrid, 1998 [1588].
"Anónimo de Yucay. Dominio de los Yngas en el Perú y del que su Magestad tiene en dichos reynos" [1571]. Edited by Josyane Chinèse. Historia y Cultura [Lima] 4 (1970): 97–152.

Aquinas, Thomas. "De regimine principum" [c. 1268]. In R.W. Dyson, ed., *Political Writings*, 5–51. Cambridge: Cambridge University Press, 2002.

Aristotle. *The Politics*. Translated by T. A. Sinclair. New York: Penguin, 1962.

Avila, Francisco de. *The Huarochirí Manuscript: A Testament of Ancient and Colonial Andean Religion*. Translated and edited by Frank Salomon and George Urioste. Austin: University of Texas Press, 1991 [c. 1609].

Barriga, Victor M., ed. *Documentos para la Historia de Arequipa*. Arequipa: Editorial Colmena, 1939–1955.

Bartolus of Saxoferrato. "De tyrannia" [c. 1350]. In Ephraim Emerton, ed., *Humanism and Tyranny: Studies in the Italian Trecento*, 126–54. Cambridge: Harvard University Press, 1925.

Betanzos, Juan de. *Suma y narración de los Incas*. Edited by M. del Carmen Martín Rubio. Madrid: Atlas, 1987 [1551].

Bolívar, Simón. *El Libertador: Writings of Simon Bolivar*. Edited by David Bushnell. Translated by Fred Fornoff. New York: Oxford University Press, 2003.

Castro, Cristóbal de, and Diego de Ortega Morejón. "Relación y declaración del modo que este valle de Chincha y sus comarcanos se gobernaban. . . ." [1558]. In Hermann Trimborn, ed., *Quellen zur Kulturgeschichte des präkolumbischen Amerika*, 217–57. Stettgart: Strecker und Schröder, 1936.

Cervantes de Salazar, Francisco. *Life in the Imperial and Loyal City of Mexico in New Spain*. Edited by Carlos Eduardo Castañeda. Translated by Minnie Lee Barrett Shepard. Austin: University of Texas Press, 1953 [1554].

Cervantes, Miguel de. *Don Quijote de la Mancha*. Edited by John Jay Allen. 2 vols. Madrid: Cátedra, 1998 [1615].

———. *Entremeses*. Edited by Eugenio Asensio. Madrid: Clásicos Castalia, 1970 [1615].

Cieza de León, Pedro de. *Crónica del Perú: Primera Parte*. Edited by Franklin Pease and Miguel Maticorea. Lima: PUCP, 1984.

———. *Crónica del Perú: Segunda Parte*. Edited by Francesca Cantú. Lima: PUCP, 1996.

Colección de documentos inéditos para la historia de España. 113 vols. Madrid: Impr. de la viuda de Calero, 1842–1895.

Cook, David Noble, ed. *Tasa de la visita general de Francisco de Toledo*. Lima: UNMSM, 1975.

Covarrubias Orozco, Sebastián de. *Tesoro de la lengua castellana o española*. Edited by Felipe C. R. Maldonado and Manuel Camarero. Madrid: Castalia, 1995 [1611].

Espinoza Soriano, Waldemar. "El primer informe etnológico sobre Cajamarca, año de 1540." *Revista Peruana de Cultura* 11/12 (1967): 5–41.

———. "El memorial de Charcas: 'Crónica' inédita de 1582." *Cantuta* (1969): 117–52.

———. "Copacabana del Collao: Un documento de 1548 para la etnohistoria andina." *Bulletin de l'Institut Français d'Etudes Andines* 1, no. 1 (1972): 1–16.

———. "Los huancas, aliados de la conquista: Tres informaciones inéditas sobre la participación indígena en la conquista del Perú." *Anales Científicos de la Universidad Nacional del Centro del Perú* 1 (1972), 5–407.

Espinoza Soriano, Waldemar. "Ichoc-Huánuco y el senorío del curaca huanca en el Reino de Huánuco, siglos XV y XVI: Una visita inédita para la etnohistoria andina." *Anales Científicos de la Universidad del Centro del Perú (Huancayo)* 4 (1975): 5–70.

———. "Migraciones internas en el Reino Colla: Tejedores, plumeros, y alfareros del Estado Imperial Inca." *Revista Histórica* 36 (1987–9): 209–305.

Estete, Miguel de. "La relación del viaje que hizo el senor Capitán Hernando Pizarro" [1533]. In Francisco de Xerez, *Verdadera relación de la conquista del Perú*, 130–48. Edited by Concepción Bravo. Madrid: Historia 16, 1985.

——— [presumed]. "Noticia del Perú" [1540s]. In Horacio Urteaga, ed., *Historia de los incas y conquista del Perú*, 3–71. Lima: Sanmartí, 1924.

Fernández de Palencia, Diego. *Primera y segunda parte de la historia del Perú*. Edited by Juan Pérez de Tudela Bueso. Madrid: BAE, 1963 [1571].

Friede, Juan, ed. *Documentos inéditos para la historia de Colombia*. Bogotá: Academia Colombiana de Historia, 1955–60.

Garcilaso de la Vega, El Inca. *Comentarios Reales y La Florida del Inca*. Edited by Mercedes Lopez-Baralt. Madrid: Espasa, 2003.

Gasca, Pedro de la. *Descripción del Perú*. Edited by Josep M. Barnadas. Cusco: Centro de Estudios Regionales Andinos Bartolomé de las Casas, 1998 [1551–1553].

González Holguín, Diego. *Vocabulario de la lengua general de todo el Perú llamada Lengua Qquichua o del Inca*. Edited by Raúl Porras Barrenechea. Lima: Imprenta Santa María, 1952 [1608].

Guaman Poma de Ayala, Felipe. *Nueva corónica y buen gobierno*. Edited by John Murra and Rolena Adorno. 3 vols. Mexico City: Siglo Veintiuno, 1980 [1615].

Hanke, Lewis. "Un festón de documentos lascasianos." *Revista Cubana* 16 (1941): 150–211.

———, ed. *Los Virreyes españoles en América durante el gobierno de la Casa de Austria: Perú*. Madrid: Atlas, 1978–1980.

Jiménez de la Espada, Marcos, ed. *Relaciones geográficas de Indias: Perú*. Madrid: Ministerio de Fomento, 1965.

Konetzke, Richard, ed. *Colección de documentos para la historia de la formación social de Hispanoamérica (1493–1810)*. 4 vols. Madrid: CSIC, 1953.

Las Casas, Bartolomé de. *Obras escogidas*. Edited by Juan Pérez de Tudela. 5 vols. Madrid: Biblioteca de Autores Españoles, 1957–1958.

Lee, Beltram T., and Juan Bromley, eds. *Libros de cabildos de Lima*. 20 vols. Lima: Torres Aguirre, 1935–1961.

Levillier, Roberto, ed. *Audiencia de Charcas: Correspondencia de presidentes y oidores*. Madrid: Biblioteca del Congreso Argentino, 1918–1922.

———, ed. *Audiencia de Lima: Correspondencia de presidentes y oidores, 1549–1564*. Madrid: Biblioteca del Congreso Argentino, 1922.

Lissón Chaves, Emilio, ed. *La iglesia de España en el Perú. Colección de documentos para la historia de la iglesia en el Perú*. 5 vols. Seville: Editorial Católica Española, 1943–1947.

López de Velasco, Juan. *Geografía y descripción universal de las Indias.* Edited by Marco Jiménez de Espada. Madrid: Atlas, 1971.

Matienzo, Juan de. *Gobierno del Perú.* Edited by Guillermo Lohmann Villena. Lima-Paris: Institut Francais d'Etudes Andines, 1967 [1567].

Maúrtua, Victor M., ed. *Antecedentes de la Recopilación de Indias.* Madrid: Imprenta de B. Rodríguez, 1906.

———, ed. *Juicio de límites entre el Perú y Bolivia: memoria de observaciones y tachas a la prueba de Bolivia, presentada a la Comisión asesora del gobierno argentino.* Buenos Aires: Compañía sud-americana de billetes de banco, 1907.

Millones, Luis, ed. *El retorno de las huacas: Estudios y documentos sobre el Taki Onqoy, Siglo XVI.* Lima: IEP, 1990.

Monsalve, Miguel de. *Reducion universal de todo el Piru, y de mas Indias, con otros muchos auisos, para el bien de los naturales dellas, y en aumento de las reales rentas.* Boston: Massachusetts Historical Society, 1925 [1604].

Montesinos, Fernando. *Anales del Perú.* Edited by Victor Maúrtua. 2 vols. Madrid: Imp. de Gabriel L. y del Horno, 1906 [1642–44].

Morales, Adolfo de, ed. *Repartimiento de tierras por el Inca Huayna Cápac (testimonio de un documento de 1556).* Cochabamba: Universidad de San Simón, 1977.

Odriozola, Manuel de, ed. *Documentos históricos del Perú en las épocas del coloniaje despues de la conquista y de la independencia hasta la presente.* Lima: Tip. de A. Alfaro, 1863–1877.

Ortiz de Zúñiga, Iñigo. *Visita de la provincia de Leon de Huanuco en 1562.* Edited by John Murra. 2 vols. Huánuco, Perú: Universidad Nacional Hermilio Valdizán, 1967–1972.

Pereña Vicente, Luciano, and Carlos Baciero, eds. *Escuela de Salamanca: Carta magna de los indios. Fuentes constitucionales, 1534–1609.* Madrid: CSIC, 1988.

Pérez Fernández, Isacio. *El anónimo de Yucay frente a Bartolomé de Las Casas: Estudios y edición crítica del Parecer de Yucay, anónimo.* Cusco: Centro de Estudios Regionales Andinos Bartolomé de las Casas, 1995.

Pérez de Tudela Bueso, Juan, ed. *Documentos relativos a don Pedro de la Gasca y a Gonzalo Pizarro.* Madrid: Real Academia de la Historia, 1964.

Pizarro, Francisco. *Testimonio: Documentos oficiales, cartas y escritos varios.* Edited by Guillermo Lohmann Villena. Madrid: CSIC, 1986.

Pizarro, Pedro. "Relación del descubrimiento y conquista de los reinos del Perú" [1571]. In *Las relaciones de la conquista del Perú.* Edited by Horacio Urteaga and Carlos Romero. Lima: Sanmartí, 1917.

Platt, Tristan, Thérèse Bouysse-Cassagne, Olivia Harris, con el aliento de Thierry Saignes. *Qaraqara-Charka: Mallku, inka y rey en la provincia de Charcas, siglos XV–XVII. Historia antropológica de una confederación aymara. Edición documental y ensayos interpretativos.* La Paz: IFEA, 2006.

Pogo, Alexander, ed. "The Anonymous 'La Conquista del Perú' (Seville, April 1534) and the Libro Vltimo del Svmmario delle Indie Occidentali (Venice, October 1534)." *Proceedings of the American Academy of Arts and Sciences* 64, no. 8 (1930): 177–286.

Polo Ondegardo. "Relación de los fundamentos acerca del notable daño que resulta de no guardar a los indios sus fueros" [1571]. In *Colección de documentos inéditos*, first series, 17, 5–177. Madrid: Imprenta Española, 1872.

———. "Informe . . . al Licenciado Briviesca de Muñatones sobre la perpetuidad de las encomiendas en el Perú" [1561]. *Revista Histórica* 13 (1940): 125–96.

Porras Barrenechea, Raul, ed. *Cartas del Perú (1524–1543)*. Lima: Sociedad de Bibliofilos Peruanos, 1959.

Real Academia Española. *Diccionario de Autoridades. Edición Facsímil*. 3 vols. Madrid: Editorial Gredos, 1969 [1737].

Recopilación de leyes de los reynos de las Indias. 4 vols. Madrid: Iulian de Paredes, 1681.

Romero, Carlos A. "Libro de la visita general del virrey don Francisco de Toledo, 1570–1575." *Revista Histórica* 7 (1924): 113–216.

Rowe, John Howland. "Un memorial del gobierno de los Incas del año 1551." *Revista Peruana de Cultura* 9–10 (1966): 27–39.

Ruiz de Arce, Juan. "Una nueva relación de la conquista" [1543]. *Boletín de la Academia Nacional de Historia* 35, no. 102 (1955): 179–200.

Salles, Estela Cristina, and Héctor Omar Noejovich, eds. *La Visita General y el Proyecto de Gobernabilidad del Virrey Toledo*. Lima: Universidad de San Martín de Porres, 2008.

Sancho de la Hoz, Pedro. *An Account of the Conquest of Peru*. Translated by P. A. Means. New York: Cortes Society, 1917 [1534].

Santillán, Hernando de. "Relación del origen, descendencia política y gobierno de los Incas" [c. 1563]. In Marcos Jiménez de la Espada, ed., *Tres Relaciones de Antigüedades Peruanas*, 33–131. Madrid: Ministerio de Fomento, 1879.

Sarmiento de Gamboa, Pedro. *Historia de los Incas*. Edited by Ramón Alba. Madrid: Miraguano, 2001 [1572].

Siete Partidas. Las siete partidas del sabio rey Don Alonso el Nono nuevamente glosadas, por el licenciado Gregorio Lopez, del Consejo real de Indias de Su Magestad. Con un Repertorio muy copioso, assi del testo como de la glossa. Madrid: I. Hasrey, 1610–1611.

Solano, Francisco de, ed. *Normas y leyes de la ciudad hispanoamericana*. Madrid: CSIC, 1996.

Sullivan, John. "Un diálogo sobre la congregación en Tlaxcala." *Colonial Latin American Review* 8, no. 1 (1999): 35–59.

Toledo, Francisco de. *Disposiciones gubernativas para el Virreinato del Perú*. Edited by Maria Justina Sarabia Viejo and Guillermo Lohmann Villena. 2 vols. Seville: CSIC, 1986–1989.

———. *Las Informaciones del virrey Francisco de Toledo y su campaña contra los señores naturales andinos*. Edited by Catherine J. Julien. Lima: PUCP, in press.

Ulloa, Luis. "Documentos del Virrey Toledo." *Revista Histórica* 3 (1908): 315–47.

Urteaga, Horacio, ed. *Informaciones sobre el antiguo Perú*. Lima: Sanmartí, 1920.

———. *Relación del sitio del Cusco*. Lima: Sanmartí, 1934 [1539].

Vaca de Castro, Antonio. "Ordenanzas de tambos: distancias de unos a otros, modo de cargar los indios y obligaciones de las justicias respectivas hechas en la ciudad del Cuzco en 31 de mayo de 1543." *Revista Histórica* 3 (1909): 427–92.

Vargas Ugarte, Rubén, ed. *Concilios limenses (1551–1772)*. Lima: Compañía de Impresiones y Publicidad, 1951.

Xérez, Francisco de. *Verdadera relación de la conquista del Perú*. Edited by Concepción Bravo. Madrid: Historia 16, 1985 [1534].

Zabálburu, Francisco de, and José Sancho Rayon, eds. *Nueva colección de documentos inéditos para la historia de España y sus Indias*. 6 vols. Madrid: Hijos de M.G. Herñandez, 1894–1896.

Zevallos Quiñones, Jorge. "La visita del pueblo de Ferreñafe (Lambayeque) en 1568." *Historia y Cultura* 9 (1975): 155–78.

Secondary sources

Abercrombie, Thomas. *Pathways of Memory and Power: Ethnography and History among an Andean People*. Madison: University of Wisconsin Press, 1998.

———. "La perpetuidad traducida: Del 'debate' de la perpetuidad a Taqui Oncoy y un movimiento comunero peruano." In Jean-Jacques Decoster, ed., *Incas e indios cristianos*, 79–120. Cuzco: IFEA, 2002.

Acosta Rodríguez, Antonio. "Los clérigos doctrineros y le economía colonial (1600–1630)." *Allpanchis* 16, no. 1 (1987): 117–49.

Adorno, Rolena. *Guaman Poma: Writing and Resistance in Colonial Peru*. Austin: University of Texas Press, 1986.

———. "The Genesis of Felipe Guaman Poma de Ayala's Nueva corónica y buen gobierno." *Colonial Latin American Review* 2, no. 1 (1993): 53–92.

———. *The Polemics of Possession: Another Face of Empire*. New Haven: Yale University Press, 2007.

Albó, Xavier. "Andean People in the Twentieth Century." In Frank Salomon and Stuart B. Schwartz, eds., *The Cambridge History of the Native Peoples of the Americas*. Vol. 3: *South America*, 765–871. New York: Cambridge University Press, 1999.

———. *Pueblos indios en la política*. La Paz: CIPCA, 2002.

———. "Ethnic Identity and Politics in the Central Andes: The Cases of Bolivia, Ecuador and Peru." In Jo-Marie Burt and Philip Mauceri, eds., *Politics in the Andes: Identity, Conflict, and Reform*, 17–37. Pittsburgh: University of Pittsburg Press, 2004.

Anderson, Benedict. *Imagined Communities: Reflections on the Origins and Spread of Nationalism*. 2nd ed. London: Verso, 1991.

Angelis-Harmening, Kristina. *'Cada uno tiene en la puna su gente': Intercambio y verticalidad en el siglo XVI en los yungas de La Paz*. Bonn: University of Bonn, 2000.

Arguedas, José María. *Yawar fiesta*. Lima: Editorial Horizonte, 1988 [1941].

Assadourian, Carlos Sempat. "Acerca del cambio en la naturaleza del dominio sobre las Indias: La mita minera del virrey Toledo." *Anuario de Estudios Americanos* 46 (1989): 3–70.

———. "Fray Alonso de Maldonado: La política indiana, el estado de damnación del Rey Católico y la Inquisición." *Historia Mexicana* 38, no. 4 (1989): 623–61.

———. *Transiciones hacia el Sistema Colonial Andino*. Lima: IEP, 1994.

———. "Exchange in the Ethnic Territories between 1530 and 1567." In Brooke Larson, Olivia Harris and Enrique Tandeter, eds., *Ethnicity, Markets, and Migration in the Andes*, 101–34. Durham: Duke University Press, 1995.

Avila Molero, Javier, and Erica Oshier. "Worshipping the Señor de Qoyllur Ritti in New York: A Transnational Andean Ethnography." *Latin American Perspectives* 32, no. 1 (2005): 174–92.

Axtmann, Roland. " 'Police' and the Formation of the Modern State: Legal and Ideological Assumptions on State Capacity in the Austrian Lands of the Habsburg Empire, 1500–1800." *German History* 10, no. 1 (1992): 39–61.

Bakewell, Peter. *Miners of the Red Mountain: Indian Labor in Potosi, 1545–1650.* Albuquerque: University of New Mexico Press, 1984.

Barnadas, Josep M. *Charcas: Orígenes históricos de una sociedad colonial.* La Paz: CIPC, 1973.

———, ed. *Diccionario histórico de Bolivia.* Sucre: Grupo de estudios históricos, 2002.

Barragán, Rossana. "Entre polleras, ñañacas y lliqllas: Los mestizos y cholas en la conformación de la 'Tercera Republica'." In Henrique Urbano, ed., *Tradición y modernidad en los Andes*, 43–74. Cusco: Centro de Estudios Regionales Andinos Bartolomé de las Casas, 1992.

Barrera-Osorio, Antonio. *Experiencing Nature: The Spanish American Empire and the Early Scientific Revolution.* Austin: University of Texas Press, 2006.

Bastien, Joseph W. *Mountain of the Condor: Metaphor and Ritual in an Andean Ayllu.* St. Paul: West Publishing, 1978.

Bataillon, Marcel. "Las 'doce dudas' peruanas resueltas por Las Casas." In *Estudios sobre Bartolomé de las Casas*, 301–14. Barcelona: Peninsula, 1976.

Bauer, Brian S. *Ancient Cuzco: Heartland of the Inca.* Austin: University of Texas Press, 2004.

Bauer, Brian S., and Jean-Jacques DeCoster. "Introduction: Sarmiento and the History of the Incas." In Pedro Sarmiento de Gamboa, *The History of the Incas*, 1–34. Austin: University of Texas Press, 2007.

Bayly, C. A. *Empire and Information: Intelligence Gathering and Social Communication in India, 1780–1870.* Cambridge: Cambridge University Press, 1996.

Becker, Marc. *Indians and Leftists in the Making of Ecuador's Modern Indigenous Movements.* Durham: Duke University Press, 2008.

Benton, Lauren. *Law and Colonial Cultures: Legal Regimes in World History, 1400–1900.* New York: Cambridge University Press, 2002.

Billman, Brian R., and Gary M. Feinman, eds. *Settlement Pattern Studies in the Americas: Fifty Years since Virú.* Washington, D.C.: Smithsonian Institution, 1999.

Boixadós, Roxana. "Los pueblos de indios de La Rioja colonial." In Judith Farberman and Raquel Gil Montero, eds., *Los pueblos de indios del Tucumán colonial*, 15–58. Buenos Aires: Ediunju, 2002.

Borges Morán, Pedro. "Nuevos datos sobre la comisión pontificia para las Indias de 1568." *Missionalia Hispánica* 16 (1959): 213–43.

————. "La Nunciatura indiana: Un intento pontificio de intervención directa en Indias bajo Felipe II (1566–68)." *Missionalia Hispánica* 19 (1962): 169–227.

Bracamonte y Sosa, Pedro, and Gabriela Solis Robleda. *Espacios mayas de autonomía: El pacto colonial en Yucatán.* Mérida: Universidad Autónoma de Yucatán, 1996.

Brading, David A. *The First America: The Spanish Monarchy, Creole Patriots, and the Liberal State, 1492–1867.* Cambridge: Cambridge University Press, 1991.

Braudel, Fernand. *The Mediterranean and the Mediterranean World in the Age of Philip II.* Translated by Siân Reynolds. New York: Harper and Row, 1972 [1949].

Bray, Tamara L. "Inka Pottery as Culinary Equipment: Food, Feasting, and Gender in Imperial State Design." *Latin American Antiquity* 14, no. 1 (2003): 3–28.

Brett, Annabel S. *Liberty, Right and Nature: Individual Rights in Later Scholastic Thought.* Cambridge: Cambridge University Press, 1997.

Brockington, Lolita Gutiérrez. *Blacks, Indians, and Spaniards in the Eastern Andes: Reclaiming the Forgotten in Colonial Mizque, 1550–1782.* Lincoln: University of Nebraska Press, 2006.

Brokaw, Galen. *A History of the Khipu.* Cambridge: Cambridge University Press, 2010.

Brundage, James A. *Medieval Canon Law:* London: Longman, 1995.

Burns, Kathryn. *Into the Archive: Writing and Power in Colonial Peru.* Durham: Duke University Press, 2010.

Burns, Robert I. *Islam under the Crusaders: Colonial Survival in the Thirteenth-Century Kingdom of Valencia.* Princeton: Princeton University Press, 1973.

Bushnell, Amy Turner. "The Sacramental Imperative: Catholic Ritual and Indian Sedentism in the Provinces of Florida." In David Hurst Thomas, ed., *Columbian Consequences,* 475–490. Washington, D.C.: Smithsonian Institution, 1990.

Calderón Trejo, Eligia. "Antecedentes históricos de algunos pueblos de indios de los Andes venezolanos." In Ramón Gutiérrez, ed., *Pueblos de indios: Otro urbanismo en la región andina,* 65–108. Quito: Abya-Yala, 1993.

Calero, Luis Fernando. *Chiefdoms under Siege: Spain's Rule and Native Adaptation in the Southern Colombian Andes, 1535–1700.* Albuquerque: University of New Mexico Press, 1997.

Cañedo-Argüelles Fábrega, Teresa. "Las reducciones indígenas en el sur andino." *Revista Complutense de Historia de America* 21 (1995): 123–40.

Cañizares-Esguerra, Jorge. *How to Write the History of the New World: Histories, Epistemologies, and Identities in the Eighteenth-Century Atlantic World.* Stanford: Stanford University Press, 2001.

Cárdenas Bunsen, José Alejandro. *Escritura y Derecho Canónico en la obra de fray Bartolomé de las Casas.* Madrid: Iberoamericana, 2011.

Carzolio, María Inés. "En los orígenes de la ciudadanía en Castilla." *Hispania* 62, no. 211 (2002): 637–92.

Castro, Daniel. *Another Face of Empire: Bartolomé de Las Casas, Indigenous Rights, and Ecclesiastical Imperialism.* Durham: Duke University Press, 2007.

Castro-Klarén, Sara. "Historiography on the Ground: The Toledo Circle and Guaman Poma." In Ileana Rodríguez, ed., *The Latin American Subaltern Studies Reader,* 143–71. Durham: Duke University Press, 2001.

Charles, John. *Allies at Odds: The Andean Church and Its Indigenous Agents, 1583–1671.* Albuquerque: University of New Mexico Press, 2010.

Charney, Paul. *Indian Society in the Valley of Lima, Peru, 1532–1824.* Lanham, Md.: University Press of America, 2001.

Châtellier, Louis. *The Religion of the Poor: Rural Missions in Europe and the Formation of Modern Catholicism, c. 1500–c.1800.* Translated by Brian Pearce. Cambridge: Cambridge University Press, 1997.

Choque Canqui, Roberto. *Sociedad y economía colonial en el sur andino.* La Paz: HISBOL, 1993.

———. "El problema de género entre los mitayos." *Historia y Cultura* 26 (2000): 39–44.

Clark, A. Kim, and Marc Becker. "Indigenous People and State Formation in Modern Ecuador." In *Highland Indians and the State in Modern Ecuador*, 1–21. University of Pittsburgh Press: Pittsburgh, 2007.

Clavero, Bartolome. "Institución política y derecho." *Revista de Estudios Politicos* 19 (1981): 43–57.

Coello de la Rosa, Alexandre. "Discourse and Political Culture in the Formation of the Peruvian Reducciones in the Spanish Colonial Empire (1533–1592)." PhD diss., SUNY: Stony Brook, 2001.

———. "Resistencia e integración en la Lima colonial: el caso la reducción de indios de El Cercado de Lima (1564–1567)." *Revista Andina* 35 (2002): 111–28.

Colajanni, Antonino. "El Virrey Francisco de Toledo como 'primer antropólogo aplicado' de la edad moderna." In Laura Laurencich Minelli and Paulina Numhauser, eds., *El silencio protagonista: El primer siglo Jesuita en el Virreinato del Perú 1567–1667*, 51–94. Quito: Abya Yala, 2004.

Coleman, Janet. *A History of Political Thought: From the Middle Ages to the Renaissance.* Oxford: Blackwell, 2000.

Comaroff, John. "Reflections on the Colonial State, in South Africa and Elsewhere: Factions, Fragments, Facts and Fictions." *Social Identities* 4, no. 3 (1998): 321–62.

Cook, David Noble. "La visita de los Conchucos por Cristóbal Ponce de León, 1543." *Historia y Cultura* 10 (1976–7): 23–45.

———. *Demographic Collapse: Indian Peru, 1520–1620.* Cambridge: Cambridge University Press, 1981.

———. "Patrones de migración en el virreinato del Perú: Mitayos, mingas y forasteros." *Histórica* 13, no. 2 (1989): 125–52.

———. "The Corregidores of the Colca Valley, Peru: Imperial Administration in an Andean Region." *Anuario de Estudios Americanos* 60, no. 2 (2003): 413–39.

———. *La catástrofe demográfica andina. Perú 1520–1620.* Translated by Javier Flores Espinoza. Lima: PUCP, 2011.

Cook, Noble David, and Alexandra Parma Cook. *People of the Volcano: Andean Counterpoint in the Colca Valley of Peru.* Durham: Duke University Press, 2007.

Cooper, Frederick. *Colonialism in Question: Theory, Knowledge, History.* Berkeley: University of California Press, 2005.

Corradine Angulo, Alberto. "Urbanismo español en Colombia. Los pueblos de indios." In Ramón Gutiérrez, ed., *Pueblos de indios. Otro urbanismo en la región andina*, 157–78.Quito: Abya-Yala, 1993.

Cummins, Thomas B. F. "Forms of Andean Colonial Towns, Free Will, and Marriage." In Claire L. Lyons and John K. Papadopoulos, eds., *The Archaeology of Colonialism*, 199–240. Los Angeles: Getty Publications, 2002.

———. *Toasts with the Inca: Andean Abstraction and Colonial Images on Quero Vessels*. Ann Arbor: University of Michigan Press, 2002.

———. "Allí Valen, Aquí También: Philip II and Gifts from America." Unpublished manuscript.

D'Altroy, Terence. "Transitions in Power: Centralization of Wanka Political Organization under Inka Rule." *Ethnohistory* 34, no. 1 (1987): 78–102.

———. *The Incas*. Oxford: Blackwell, 2002.

———. "Remaking the Social Landscape: Colonization in the Inka Empire." In Gil Stein, ed., *The Archaeology of Colonial Encounters*, 263–95. Albuquerque: SAR Press, 2005.

D'Altroy, Terence, and Timothy K. Earle. "Staple Finance, Wealth Finance, and Storage in the Inka Political Economy." *Current Anthropology* 26, no. 2 (1985): 187–206.

Dean, Carolyn S. "Creating a Ruin in Colonial Cusco: Sacsahuaman and What Was Made of It." *Andean Past* 5 (1998): 161–84.

Dean, Mitchell. *Governmentality: Power and Rule in Modern Society*. London: Sage, 1999.

Díaz Rementería, Carlos. *El cacique en el virreinato del Perú: Estudio histórico-jurídico*. Seville: Universidad de Sevilla, 1977.

Dirks, Nicholas B. *Castes of Mind: Colonialism and the Making of Modern India*. Princeton: Princeton University Press, 2001.

Domínguez Ortiz, Antonio, and Bernard Vincent. *Historia de los moriscos: Vida y tragedia de una minoría*. Madrid: Revista de Occidente, 1978.

Durston, Alan. "Un régimen urbanístico en la América hispana colonial: El trazado en damero durante los siglos XVI y XVII." *Historia* 28 (1994): 59–115.

———. "El proceso reduccional en el sur andino: Confrontación y síntesis de sistemas espaciales." *Revista de Historia Indígena* 4 (1999/2000): 75–101.

———. *Pastoral Quechua: The History of Christian Translation in Peru, 1550–1650*. Notre Dame: University of Notre Dame Press, 2007.

———. "Native-Language Literacy in Colonial Peru: The Question of Mundane Quechua Writing Revisited." *Hispanic American Historical Review* 88, no. 1 (2008): 41–70.

Duviols, Pierre. "Revisionismo histórico y derecho colonial en el siglo XVI: El tema de la tiranía de los Incas." In *Indianidad, etnocidio, indigenismo en América Latina*, 25–39. Mexico: Instituto Indigenista Interamericano, 1988.

Eagle, Marc. "Beard-Pulling and Furniture-Rearranging: Conflict Within the Seventeenth-Century Audiencia of Santo Domingo." *The Americas* 68, no. 4 (2012): 467–94.

Earle, Timothy, Terence D'Altroy, C.J. LeBlanc, Christine Hastorf, and Terry Y.

LeVine. "Changing Settlement Patterns in the Upper Mantaro Valley, Peru." *Journal of New World Archaeology* 4 (1980): 1–49.

Ellinghaus, Katherine. "Indigenous Assimilation and Absorption in the United States and Australia." *Pacific Historical Review* 75, no. 4 (2006): 563–85.

Ertman, Thomas. *Birth of the Leviathan: Building States and Regimes in Medieval and Early Modern Europe*. New York: Cambridge University Press, 1997.

Escobar, Jesús R. *The Plaza Mayor and the Shaping of Baroque Madrid*. New York: Cambridge University Press, 2003.

Escobari de Querejazu, Laura. "Poblados de indios dentro de poblados espanoles: El caso de La Paz y Potosí." In Ramón Gutiérrez, ed., *Pueblos de indios: Otro urbanismo en la región andina*, 317–80. Quito: Abya-Yala, 1993.

———. *Caciques, yanaconas y extravagantes: La sociedad colonial en Charcas, s. XVI–XVIII*. La Paz: Plural, 2001.

Escobedo Mansilla, Ronald. *Las comunidades indígenas y la economía colonial peruana*. Bilbao: Universidad del País Vasco, 1997.

———. "Pervivencias prehispánicas en el derecho criollo peruano." In *XI Congreso del Instituto Internacional de Historia del Derecho Indiano*, 2:119–43. Buenos Aires: IIHD, 1997.

Espinoza Soriano, Waldemar. "Reducciones, pueblos, y ciudades." In Duccio Bonavia and Rogger Ravines, eds., *Pueblos y culturas de la Sierra Central del Perú*, 100–13. Lima: Cerro de Pasco Corp., 1972.

Fals Borda, Orlando. "Indian Congregaciones in the New Kingdom of Granada, 1595–1850." *The Americas* 13 (1957): 331–51.

Farberman, Judith. "Curacas, mandones, alcaldes y curas." *Colonial Latin American Historical Review* 13, no. 4 (2004), 367–398.

Farberman, Judith, and Raquel Gil Montero, eds. *Los pueblos de indios del Tucumán colonial. Pervivencia y desestructuración*. Buenos Aires: Ediunju, 2002.

Farriss, Nancy M. "Nucleation versus Dispersal: The Dynamics of Population Movement in Colonial Yucatan." *Hispanic American Historical Review* 58, no. 2 (1978): 187–216.

Fernández Collado, Angel. "Felipe II y su mentalidad reformadora en el Concilio Provincial Toledano de 1565." *Hispania Sacra* 50, no. 102 (1998): 447–66.

Fernández Osco, Marcelo. *La ley del ayllu: Práctica de jach'a justicia y jisk'a justicia (justicia mayor y justicia menor) en la comunidades aymaras*. La Paz: Programa de Investigación Estratégica en Bolivia, 2000.

Foucault, Michel. "The Confession of the Flesh." In *Power/Knowledge: Selected Interviews and Other Writings 1972–1977*, 194–228. Edited by Colin Gordon. London: Harvester Wheatsheaf, 1980.

———. "Omnes et Singulatim: Towards a Criticism of 'Political Reason'." In *The Tanner Lectures on Human Values*, 2, 223–55. Cambridge: Cambridge University Press, 2011 [1981].

———. "Governmentality" [1978]. In *The Foucault Effect: Studies in Governmentality*, 87–104. Edited by Graham Burchell, Colin Gordon, and Peter Miller. London: Harvester Wheatsheaf, 1991.

Fraser, Valerie. *The Architecture of Conquest: Building in the Viceroyalty of Peru 1535–1635*. New York: Cambridge University Press, 1990.

Freedman, Paul. *Images of the Medieval Peasant*: Stanford: Stanford University Press, 1999.

Gade, Daniel, and Mario Escobar. "Village Settlement and the Colonial Legacy in Southern Peru." *Geographical Review* 72, no. 4 (1982): 430–49.

Gakenheimer, Ralph A. "Decisions of Cabildo on Urban Physical Structure." In Jorge E. Hardoy, and R. P. Schaedel, eds., *El proceso de la urbanización en América*, 241–60. Buenos Aires: Editorial del Instituto, 1969.

Galdos Rodríguez, Guillermo. "Concentraciones andinas y 'reducciones de yndios a pueblos'." In *Reflexiones y confrontaciones etnohistóricas*, 27–65.Arequipa: UNSA, 1995.

García, María Elena. *The Making of Indigenous Citizens: Identity, Development, and Multicultural Activism in Peru*. Stanford: Stanford University Press, 2005.

Garrett, David. *Shadows of Empire: The Indian Nobility of Cusco, 1750–1825*. New York: Cambridge University Press, 2005.

Gascón, Jorge. "Compadrazgo y cambio en el altiplano peruano." *Revista Española de Antropología Americana* 35 (2005): 191–206.

Gasparini, Graziano, and Luise Margolies. *Arquitectura Inka*. Caracas: Universidad Central de Venezuela, 1977.

Gelles, Paul H. *Water and Power in Highland Peru: The Cultural Politics of Irrigation and Development*. New Brunswick, N.J: Rutgers University Press, 2000.

Gerhard, Peter. "Congregaciones de indios en la Nueva España en 1570." *Historia Mexicana* 26, no. 103 (1977): 347–95.

Gibson, Charles. "Spanish-Indian Institutions and Colonial Urbanism in New Spain." In Jorge E. Hardoy and R. P. Schaedel, eds., *El proceso de la urbanización en América*, 225–39. Buenos Aires, 1969.

Glave, Luis Miguel. "Trajines: Un capítulo en la formación del mercado interno colonial." *Revista andina* 1 (1983): 9–75.

———. "Tambos y caminos andinos en la formación del mercado interno colonial." *Anuario de Estudios Americanos* 45 (1988): 83–138.

Goldstein, Paul S. "Communities without Borders: The Vertical Archipelago and Diaspora Communities in the Southern Andes." In Marcello A. Canuto and Jason Yaeger, eds., *The Archaeology of Communities: A New World Perspective*, 182–209. New York: Routledge, 2000.

Goldwert, Marvin. "La lucha por la perpetuidad de las encomiendas en el Perú virreinal, 1550–1600." *Revista Histórica* 22, 23 (1955–1956, 1958–1959): 350–60, 207–20.

Gómez Rivas, León. *El virrey del Perú don Francisco de Toledo*. Madrid: Instituto Provincial de Investigaciones, 1994.

Góngora, Mario. *El estado en el derecho indiano: Época de fundación (1492–1570)*. Santiago: Universidad de Chile, 1951.

González Pujana, Laura. *Polo de Ondegardo: Un cronista vallisoletano en el Perú*. Valladolid: Universidad de Valladolid, 1999.

Gose, Peter. *Deathly Waters and Hungry Mountains: Agrarian Ritual and Class Formation in an Andean Town.* Toronto: University of Toronto Press, 1994.

———. "Oracles, Divine Kingship, and Political Representation in the Inka State." *Ethnohistory* 43, no. 1 (1996): 1–32.

———. "The State as a Chosen Woman: Brideservice and the Feeding of Tributaries in the Inka Empire." *American Anthropologist* 102, no. 1 (2000): 84–97.

———. *Invaders as Ancestors: On the Intercultural Making and Unmaking of Spanish Colonialism in the Andes.* Toronto: University of Toronto Press, 2008.

Graubart, Karen B. "Indecent Living: Indigenous Women and the Politics of Representation in Early Colonial Peru." *Colonial Latin American Review* (2000): 213–35.

———. "De qadis y caciques." *Bulletin del Institut Français d'Etudes Andines* 37, no. 1 (2008): 83–95.

Guevara Gil, Armando. "Los caciques y el señorío natural en los Andes coloniales (Perú, siglo XVI)." In *XIII Congreso del Instituto Internacional de Historia del Derecho Indiano,* 2, 137–58. San Juan: Asamblea Legislativa de Puerto Rico, 2003.

Guevara Gil, Jorge Armando, and Frank Salomon. "A 'Personal Visit': Colonial Political Ritual and the Making of Indians in the Andes." *Colonial Latin American Review* 3, no. 1–2 (1994): 3–36.

Guilarte, A. M. *El régimen señorial en el siglo XVI.* Valladolid: Universidad de Valladolid, 1962.

Gutiérrez, Ramón. "Las reducciones indígenas en el urbanismo colonial: Integración cultural y persistencias." In Ramón Gutiérrez, ed., *Pueblos de indios: Otro urbanismo en la región andina,* 11–63. Quito: Abya-Yala, 1993.

Hampe Martínez, Teodoro. *Don Pedro de la Gasca: Su obra política en Espana y America.* Lima: PUCP, 1989.

———. "El Licdo: Polo de Ondegardo, encomendero, burócrata y conocedor del mundo andino (ca. 1520–1575)." *Anuario del Archivo y Biblioteca Nacionales de Bolivia* 5 (1999): 487–530.

———. "Un letrado exitoso en los andes coloniales. La carrera de Polo Ondegardo como político, negociante y etnógrafo (siglo XVI)." *Ambiente Jurídico* 9 (2007): 122–50.

———. "Las bibliotecas virreinales en el Perú y la difusión del saber italiano: El caso del virrey Toledo (1582)." In Francesca Cantù, ed., *Las cortes virreinales de la Monarquía española,* 537–54. Rome: Università di Roma Tre, 2008.

Hanks, William F. *Converting Words: Maya in the Age of the Cross.* Berkeley: University of California Press, 2010.

Haring, Clarence. *The Spanish Empire in America.* New York: Oxford University Press, 1947.

Hartmann, Roswith. "Mercados y ferias prehipánicos en el área andina." *Boletín de la Academia Nacional de Historia* 54, no. 118 (1971): 214–35.

Harvey, L. P. *Islamic Spain, 1250–1500.* Chicago: University of Chicago Press, 1990.

Hemming, John. *The Conquest of the Incas.* New York: HBJ, 1970.

Herzog, Tamar. *Defining Nations: Immigrants and Citizens in Early Modern Spain and Spanish America*. New Haven: Yale University Press, 2003.

———. "Early Modern Spanish Citizenship in the Old and the New World." In John Smolenski and Thomas J. Humphrey, eds., *New World Orders*, 205–25. Philadelphia: University of Pennsylvania Press, 2005.

Himmerich y Valencia, Robert. "The 1536 Siege of Cuzco: An Analysis of Inca and Spanish Warfare." *Colonial Latin American Historical Review* 7, no. 4 (1998): 387–418.

Hoekstra, Rik. *Two Worlds Merging: The Transformation of Society in the Valley of Puebla, 1570–1640*. Amsterdam: CEDLA, 1993.

Honores, Renzo. "El licenciado Polo y su informe al licenciado Briviesca de Muñatones." In Ignacio Arellano and Fermín del Pino Díaz, eds., *Lecturas y ediciones de crónicas de Indias*, 387–407. Madrid: CSIC, 2004.

———. "Una sociedad legalista: Abogados, procuradores de causas y la creacíon de una cultura legal colonial en Lima y Potosí, 1540–1670." PhD diss., Florida International University, 2007.

Huertas Vallejo, Lorenzo. "El proceso de concentración social en el espacio andino, siglos XVI, XVII y XVIII." In Javier Flores Espinoza and Rafael Varón Gabai, eds., *El hombre y los Andes: Homenaje a Franklin Pease G. Y.*, 2, 805–16. Lima: IFEA, 2002.

Hyslop, John. *The Inka Road System*. New York: Academic Press, 1984.

———. *Inka Settlement Planning*. Austin: University of Texas Press, 1990.

Isbell, William H. *Mummies and Mortuary Monuments: A Postprocessual Prehistory of Central Andean Social Organization*. Austin: University of Texas Press, 1997.

Julien, Catherine J. *Condesuyo: The Political Division of Territory under Inca and Spanish Rule*. Bonn: University of Bonn, 1991.

———. "Finding a Fit: Archaeology and Ethnohistory of the Incas." In Michael A. Malpass, ed., *Provincial Inca*, 177–233. Iowa City: University of Iowa Press, 1993.

———. "History and Art in Translation: The Paños and Other Objects Collected by Francisco de Toledo." *Colonial Latin American Review* 8, no. 1 (1999): 61–89.

———. *Reading Inca History*. Iowa City: University of Iowa Press, 2000.

———. "Francisco de Toledo and His Campaign against the Incas." *Colonial Latin American Review* 16, no. 2 (2007): 243–72.

———. "Spanish Reform and Change in the Potosí Hinterland." Unpublished manuscript.

———. "Garcilaso y el caso de la mala muerte del Virrey Toledo." Unpublished manuscript.

Jurado, Carolina. "Las reducciones toledanas a pueblos de indios: aproximación a un conflicto. El repartimiento de Macha (Charcas), siglo XVI." *Cahiers des Amériques Latines* 47 (2004): 123–37.

Kagan, Richard L., and Fernando Marías. *Urban Images of the Hispanic World, 1493–1793*. New Haven: Yale University Press, 2000.

Keller, Frank L. "Finca Ingavi—A Medieval Survival on the Bolivian Altiplano." *Economic Geography* 26, no. 1 (1950): 37–50.

Klaus, Haagen D. "Out of Light Came Darkness: Bioarchaeology of Mortuary Ritual, Health, and Ethnogenesis in the Lambayeque Valley Complex, North Coast Peru (AD 900–1750)." PhD diss., Ohio State University, 2008.

Klein, Herbert. *A Concise History of Bolivia.* New York: Cambridge University Press, 2003.

Kostof, Spiro. *The City Shaped: Urban Patterns and Meanings Through History.* London: Thames and Hudson, 1991.

Kubler, George. *Mexican Architecture of the Sixteenth Century.* 2 vols. New Haven: Yale University Press, 1948.

La Barre, Weston. *The Aymara Indians of the Lake Titicaca Plateau, Bolivia.* Washington, D.C.: American Anthropological Association, 1948.

La Lone, Darrell E. "The Inca as a Nonmarket Economy: Supply on Command versus Supply and Demand." In Jonathan E. Ericson and Timothy K. Earle, eds., *Contexts for Prehistoric Exchange,* 291–316. New York: Academic Press, 1982.

Lamana, Gonzalo. *Domination without Dominance: Inca-Spanish Encounters in Early Colonial Peru.* Durham: Duke University Press, 2008.

Lane, Kris. *Quito 1599: City and Colony in Transition.* Albuquerque: University of New Mexico Press, 2002.

Larson, Brooke. "Andean Highland Peasants and the Trials of Nation Making During the Nineteenth Century." In Frank Salomon and Stuart B. Schwartz, eds., *The Cambridge History of the Native Peoples of the Americas. Vol. 3: South America, 2,* 558–703. New York: Cambridge University Press, 1999.

Lazar, Sian. *El Alto, Rebel City: Self and Citizenship in Andean Bolivia:* Durham: Duke University Press, 2008.

Lechner, Juan. "El concepto de policía y su presencia en la obra de los primeros historiadores de las Indias." *Revista de Indias* 41, no. 165–66 (1989): 395–409.

Lefebvre, Henri. *The Production of Space.* Translated by Donald Nicholson-Smith. Oxford: Oxford University Press, 1991.

Levillier, Roberto. *Don Francisco de Toledo, Supremo Organizador del Perú: Su vida, su obra (1515–1582).* 3 vols. Madrid: Espasa-Calpe, 1935–1940.

Lockhart, James. *Spanish Peru, 1532–1556.* Madison: University of Wisconsin Press, 1968.

————. *The Men of Cajamarca: A Social and Biographical Study of the First Conquerors of Peru.* Austin: University of Texas Press, 1972.

————. *The Nahuas After the Conquest: A Social and Cultural History of the Indians of Central Mexico, Sixteenth Through Eighteenth Centuries.* Stanford: Stanford University Press, 1992.

Lohmann Villena, Guillermo. *El corregidor de indios en el Perú bajo los Austrias.* Lima: PUCP, 2001 [1957].

————. "Juan de Matienzo, Autor del 'Gobierno del Perú': Su personalidad y su obra." *Anuario de Estudios Americanos* 22 (1966): 767–886.

————. "Respuestas de solución de juristas y políticos en América." In Demetrio Ramos Pérez, ed., *La ética en la conquista de America,* 631–58. Madrid: CSIC, 1984.

López Rodríguez, Mercedes. *Tiempos para rezar y tiempos para trabajar.* Bogotá: Instituto Colombiano de Antropología e Historia, 2001.

López-Salazar Pérez, Jeronimo. "El régimen local de los territorios de Órdenes Militares: Siglos XVI y XVII." In José Manuel de Bernardo Ares and Enrique Martínez Ruiz, eds., El Municipio en la España Moderna, 249–304. Córdoba: Universidad de Córdoba, 1996.

Lorandi, Ana María, and Lorena Rodríguez. "Yanas y mitimaes: Alteraciones incaicas en el mapa étnico andino." In Ana María Lorandi, ed., Los Andes, cincuenta años después, 1953–2003: Homenaje a John Murra, 129–70. Lima: PUCP, 2003.

Lovell, W. George. "Mayans, Missionaries, Evidence and Truth: The Polemics of Native Resettlement in Sixteenth-Century Guatemala." Journal of Historical Geography 16, no. 3 (1990): 277–94.

Low, Setha M. On the Plaza: The Politics of Public Space and Culture. Austin: University of Texas Press, 2000.

Loza, Carmen Beatriz. " 'Tyrannie' des Incas et 'naturalisation' des Indiens: La politique de Francisco de Toledo, vice-roi du Pérou (1571–1628)." Annales ESC 57, no. 2 (2002): 375–405.

Lucero, Jose Antonio. "Representing 'Real Indians': The Challenges of Indigenous Authenticity and Strategic Constructivism in Ecuador and Bolivia." Latin American Research Review 41, no. 2 (2006): 31–56.

Luengo Múñoz, Manuel. "Sumaria noción de las monedas de Castilla e Indias en el siglo XVI." Anuario de Estudios Americanos 7 (1950): 326–66.

Lupher, David A. Romans in a New World: Classical Models in Sixteenth-Century Spanish America. Ann Arbor: University of Michigan Press, 2003.

MacCormack, Sabine. "The Incas and Rome." In José Anadon, ed., Garcilaso Inca de la Vega, 8–31. Notre Dame: University of Notre Dame Press, 1998.

———. "History, Historical Record, and Ceremonial Action: Incas and Spaniards in Cuzco." Comparative Studies in Society and History 43, no. 2 (2001): 329–63.

———. On the Wings of Time: Rome, the Incas, Spain, and Peru. Princeton: Princeton University Press, 2006.

Málaga Medina, Alejandro. "El virrey don Francisco de Toledo y la reglamentación del tributo en el virreinato del Perú." Anuario de Estudios Americanos 29 (1972): 597–624.

———. "Las reducciones en el virreinato del Perú (1532–1580)." Revista de Historia de América 80 (1975): 8–45.

———. "Los Collaguas en la historia de Arequipa en el siglo XVI." In Franklin Pease, ed., Collaguas I, 93–130. Lima: PUCP, 1977.

———. Reducciones toledanas en Arequipa (pueblos tradicionales). Arequipa: UNSA, 1989.

Mangan, Jane E. Trading Roles: Gender, Ethnicity, and the Urban Economy in Colonial Potosí. Durham: Duke University Press, 2005.

Mantena, Karuna. Alibis of Empire: Henry Maine and the Ends of Liberal Imperialism. Princeton: Princeton University Press, 2010.

Martin, Norman. Los vagabundos en la Nueva España, siglo XVI. Mexico City: Editorial JUS., 1957.

Martínez Cereceda, José L. Autoridades en los Andes: Los atributos del señor. Lima: PUCP, 1995.

Martínez, Maria Elena. *Genealogical Fictions: Limpieza de Sangre, Religion, and Gender in Colonial Mexico*. Stanford: Stanford University Press, 2008.

Martínez Millán, José. "En busca de la ortodoxia: El Inquisidor General Diego de Espinosa." In José Martínez Millán, ed., *La corte de Felipe II*, 189–228. Madrid: Alianza, 1994.

Matos Mar, José. "Taquileños, Quechuas del Lago Titicaca, en Lima." *América Indígena* 51, no. 2–3 (1991): 107–66.

McNeill, William H. *The Pursuit of Power: Technology, Armed Force, and Society since A.D. 1000*. Chicago: University of Chicago Press, 1982.

McNeish, John. "Globalization and the Reinvention of Andean Tradition: The Politics of Community and Ethnicity in Highland Bolivia." *Journal of Peasant Studies* 29, no. 3–4 (2002): 228–69.

Means, Philip Ainsworth. "Biblioteca Andina. Part One. The Chroniclers." *Transactions of the Connecticut Academy of Arts and Sciences* 29 (1928): 271–525.

Meisch, Lynn A. *Andean Entrepreneurs: Otavalo Merchants and Musicians in the Global Arena*. Austin: University of Texas Press, 2002.

Mendiburu, Manuel de. *Diccionario histórico-biográfico del Perú*. 12 vols. 2nd ed. Lima, 1931–1935 [1874–1880].

Merluzzi, Manfredi. *Politica e governo nel Nuovo Mondo: Francisco de Toledo, viceré del Perù (1569–1581)*. Rome: Carocci, 2003.

Millones Figueroa, Luis. "De señores naturales a tiranos: el concepto político de los Incas y sus cronistas en el siglo XVI." *Latin American Literary Review* 26 (1998): 72–99.

Mills, Kenneth. *An Evil Lost to View? An Investigation of Post-Evangelisation Andean Religion in Mid-Colonial Peru*. Liverpool: University of Liverpool, 1994.

———. *Idolatry and Its Enemies: Colonial Andean Religion and Extirpation, 1640–1750*. Princeton: Princeton University Press, 1997.

Monahan, Arthur P. *From Personal Duties towards Personal Rights: Late Medieval and Early Modern Political Thought, 1300–1600*. Toronto: McGill-Queen's University Press, 1994.

Montoya Rojas, Rodrigo. *Destinies of the Quechua Culture in Peru: The Outlook in Lima, Villa El Salvador, and Puquio*. Sussex: Academic Press, 2011.

Moore, Jerry D. "The Archaeology of Plazas and the Proxemics of Ritual: Three Andean Traditions." *American Anthropologist* 98, no. 4 (1996): 789–802.

Mörner, Magnus. *La Corona Española y los foráneos en los pueblos de indios*. 2nd ed. Madrid: Agencia Española de Cooperación Internacional, 1999.

Morris, Craig. "The Infrastructure of Inka Control in the Peruvian Central Highlands." In George A. Collier, et al., eds., *The Inca and Aztec States, 1400–1800*, 153–71. New York: Academic Press, 1982.

———. "Storage, Supply, and Redistribution in the Economy of the Inka State." In John Murra, Nathan Wachtel, and Jacques Revel, eds., *Anthropological History of Andean Polities*, 56–68. Cambridge: Cambridge University Press, 1986.

Morris, Craig, and Donald E. Thompson. *Huánuco Pampa: An Inca City and Its Hinterland*. London: Thames and Hudson, 1985.

Muldoon, James. *Popes, Lawyers and Infidels*. Philadelphia: University of Pennsylvania Press, 1979.

Mumford, Jeremy Ravi. "The Inca Legend in Colonial Peru." *Colonial Latin American Review* 17, no. 1 (2008): 125–41.

———. "Litigation as Ethnography in Sixteenth-Century Peru: Polo de Ondegardo and the Mitimaes." *Hispanic American Historical Review* 88, no. 1 (2008): 5–40.

———. "Aristocracy on the Auction Block: Race, Lords, and the Perpetuity Controversy of Sixteenth-Century Peru." In Matthew D. O'Hara and Andrew B. Fisher, eds., *Imperial Subjects: Race and Identity in Colonial Latin America*, 39–59. Durham: Duke University Press, 2009.

Muro Orejón, Antonio. "Las Leyes Nuevas de Indias." *Anuario de Estudios Americanistas* 16 (1959): 561–619.

Murra, John V. "The Economic Organization of the Inca State." PhD diss., University of Chicago, 1956.

———. "Rite and Crop in the Inca State." In *Culture in History: Essays in Honor of Paul Radin*. Edited by Stanley Diamond, 393–407. New York: Columbia University Press, 1960.

———. "Cloth and Its Functions in the Inca State." *American Anthropologist* 64 (1962): 710–28.

———. *Formaciones económicas y políticas del mundo andino*. Lima: IEP, 1975.

———. "Los olleros del Inka: Hacia una historia y arqueología del Qollasuyu." In *Historia, problema y promesa: Homenaje a Jorge Basadre*, 1, 415–23. Lima: PUCP, 1979.

———. "Andean Societies Before 1532." In Leslie Bethell, ed., *Cambridge History of Latin America*, 1, 90. Cambridge: Cambridge University Press, 1984.

———. Murra, John V. "Le débat sur l'avenir des Andes en 1562." In Raquel Thiercelin, ed., *Cultures et sociétés: Andes et Méso-Amérique: mélanges en hommage à Pierre Duviols*, 2, 625–32. Aix en Provence: Université de Provence, 1991.

———. " 'Nos Hazen Mucha Ventaja': The Early European Perception of Andean Achievement." In Kenneth J. Andrien and Rolena Adorno, eds., *Transatlantic Encounters: Europeans and Andeans in the Sixteenth Century.*, 79–83. Berkeley: University of California Press, 1991.

———. "Litigation over the Rights of 'Natural Lords' in Early Colonial Courts in the Andes." In Elizabeth Hill Boone and Tom Cummins, eds,. *Native Traditions in the Postconquest World*, 55–62. Washington, D.C.: Dumbarton Oaks, 1998.

Mustapha, Monique. "Encore le 'Parecer de Yucay': Essai d'attribution." *Ibero-Amerikanishes Archiv* 3, no. 2 (1977): 215–29.

———. "Contribution a l'histoire de la Junta Magna de 1568 sur la perpetuitad des encomiendas." *Annales de la Faculté des Lettres et Sciences Humaines de Nice* 30 (1978): 81–100.

Nader, Helen. *Liberty in Absolutist Spain: The Habsburg Sale of Towns, 1516–1700*. Baltimore: Johns Hopkins University Press, 1990.

Nair, Stella. "Witnessing the In-visibility of Inca Architecture in Colonial Peru." *Buildings and Landscapes* 14 (2007): 50–65.

Nash, June C. *We Eat the Mines and the Mines Eat Us: Dependency and Exploitation in Bolivian Tin Mines.* 2nd ed. New York: Columbia University Press, 1993.

Newson, Linda A. *Life and Death in Early Colonial Ecuador.* Norman: University of Oklahoma Press, 1995.

Nicolini, Alberto. "Pueblos de indios en el noroeste argentino." In Ramón Gutiérrez, ed., *Pueblos de indios: Otro urbanismo en la región andina,* 381–448. Quito: Abya-Yala, 1993.

Niles, Susan. *The Shape of Inca History: Narrative and Architecture in an Andean Empire.* Iowa City: University of Iowa Press, 1999.

Nirenberg, David. "Muslims in Christian Iberia, 1000–1526: Varieties of Mudejar Experience." In Peter Linehan and Janet Nelson, eds., *The Medieval World,* 60–76. New York: Routledge, 2000.

Nowack, Kerstin. "Las provisiones de Titu Cusi Yupangui." *Revista Andina* 38 (2004): 139–79.

———. "Las mercedes que pedía para su salida: The Vilcabamba Inca and the Spanish state, 1539–1572." In David Cahill and Blanca Tovías, eds., *New World, First Nations,* 57–91. Brighton: Sussex Academic Press, 2006.

Nowack, Kerstin, and Catherine Julien. "La campaña de Toledo contra los señores naturales andinos." *Historia y Cultura* 23 (1999): 15–81.

Nuijten, Monique, and Davíd Lorenzo Rodríguez. "Peasant Community and Territorial Strategies in the Andean Highlands of Peru." In Franz von Benda-Beckmann, Keebet von Benda-Beckmann, and Anne Griffiths, eds., *Spatializing Law: An Anthropological Geography of Law in Society,* 31–56. Farnham, UK: Ashgate, 2009.

Olmedo Jiménez, Manuel. *Jerónimo de Loaysa, O.P.: Pacificador de Españoles y protector de Indios.* Granada: Universidad de Granada, 1990.

O'Phelan Godoy, Scarlett. *Kurakas sin sucesiones: Del cacique al alcalde de indios (Perú y Bolivia 1750–1835).* Cusco: Centro de Estudios Regionales Andinos Bartolomé de las Casas, 1997.

Ortiz Crespo, Alfonso, and Rosemarie Terán Najas. "La reducción de indios en la zona interandina de la Real Audiencia de Quito." In Ramón Gutiérrez, ed., *Pueblos de indios: Otro urbanismo en la región andina,* 205–61. Quito: Abya-Yala, 1993.

Ots Capdequí, José María. "Apuntes para la historia del municipio hispano-americano durante el período colonial." *Anuario de Historia del Derecho Español* 1, no. 93–126 (1924).

Owens, J. B. *'By My Absolute Royal Authority': Justice and the Castilian Commonwealth at the Beginning of the First Global Age.* Rochester: University of Rochester Press, 2005.

Pagden, Anthony. *Spanish Imperialism and the Political Imagination.* New Haven: Yale University Press, 1990.

———. *Lords of All the World: Ideologies of Empire in Spain, Britain and France c. 1500–c. 1850.* New Haven: Yale University Press, 1995.

Parker, Geoffrey. *The Grand Strategy of Philip II.* New Haven: Yale University Press, 1998.

————. *The World Is Not Enough: The Imperial Vision of Philip II of Spain*. Waco, Tex: Markham Press Fund, 2001.

Parry, J. H. *The Spanish Seaborne Empire*. New York: Harper and Row, 1966.

Parsons, Elsie C. *Peguche: Canton of Otavalo, Privince of Imbabura, Ecuador: A Study of Andean Indians*. Chicago: University of Chicago Press, 1945.

Pease, Franklin. *Curacas, Reciprocidad y Riqueza*. Lima: PUCP, 1992.

————. *Las crónicas y los Andes*. Lima: PUCP, 1995.

Pease, Franklin, ed. *Collaguas I*. Lima: PUCP, 1977.

Pels, Peter, and O. Salemink, eds. *Colonial Subjects: Essays on the Practical History of Anthropology*. Ann Arbor: University of Michigan Press, 1999.

Peña Cámara, Jose Maria de la. "Nuevos datos sobre la visita de al Consejo de Indias (1567–1568)." *Anuario de Historia del Derecho Espanol* 12 (1935): 425–38.

Penry, S. Elizabeth. "Transformations in Indigenous Authority and Identity in Resettlement Towns of Colonial Charcas (Alto Perú)." PhD diss., University of Miami, 1996.

————. "The Rey Común: Indigenous Political Discourse in Eighteenth-Century Alto Perú." In Luis Roniger and Tamar Herzog, eds., *The Collective and the Public in Latin America: Cultural Identities and Political Order*, 219–37. Sussex: Academic Press, 2000.

————. *The People Are King: The Making of an Andean Indigenous Politics*. New York: Oxford University Press, forthcoming.

Pereña Vicente, Luciano. "La pretensión a la perpetuidad de las encomiendas del Perú." In *Estudios sobre política indigenista española en América* 2, 427–67. Valladolid: Universidad de Valladolid, 1976.

Pérez Fernández, Isacio. *Bartolomé de las Casas en el Perú: El espíritu lascasiano en la primera evangelización del Imperio Incaico, 1531–1573*. Cusco: Centro de Estudios Regionales Andinos Bartolomé de las Casas, 1988.

Pillsbury, Joanne, ed. *Guide to Documentary Sources for Andean Studies, 1530–1900*. 3 vols. Norman: University of Oklahoma Press, 2008.

Pino Díaz, Fermín del. "De la Granada morisca a los Andes indianos." In Isadora de Norden, ed., *Influencia y legado español en las culturas tradicionales de los Andes tradicionales*, 27–40. Bogotá: Dupligráficas Limitada, 2003.

Platt, Tristan. "Liberalism and Ethnocide in the Southern Andes." *History Workshop* 17 (1984): 3–18.

————. "Pensamiento político Aymara." In Xavier Albó, ed., *Raíces de América: el mundo Aymara*, 365–450. Madrid: Alianza, 1988.

————. *La persistencia de los ayllus en el norte de Potosí*. La Paz: Fundación Diálogo, 1999.

Poole, Stafford. *Juan de Ovando: Governing The Spanish Empire in the Reign of Philip II*. Austin: University of Texas Press, 2004.

Porras Barrenechea, Raul. *Cronistas del Perú (1528–1650)*. Lima: Sociedad de Bibliofilos Peruanos, 1962.

Powers, Karen Vieira. *Andean Journeys: Migration, Ethnogenesis, and the State in Colonial Quito*. Albuquerque: University of New Mexico Press, 1995.

Premo, Bianca. "From the Pockets of Women: The Gendering of the Mita Tribute in Colonial Chucuito, Peru." *The Americas* 57, no. 1 (2000): 63–94.

Presta, Ana Maria. *Encomienda, familia y negocios en Charcas colonial (Bolivia): Los encomenderos de La Plata, 1550–1600*. Lima: IEP, 2000.

Protzen, Jean-Pierre, and John Howland Rowe. "Hawkaypata: The Terrace of Leisure." In Zeynep Çelik, Diane Favro, and Richard Ingersoll, eds., *Streets: Critical Perspectives on Public Spaces*, 235–46. Berkeley: University of California Press, 1994.

Puente Brunke, José de la. *Encomienda y encomenderos en el Perú. Estudio social y political de una institución colonial*. Seville: Diputación Provincial de Sevilla, 1992.

———. "Codicia y bien público: los ministros de la Audiencia en la Lima seiscentista." *Revista de Indias* 66, no. 236 (2006): 133–48.

Quirós, C. Bernaldo de. *La picota: Crímenes y castigos en el país castellano en los tiempos medios*. Madrid: Victoriano Suárez, 1907.

Rama, Angel. *The Lettered City*. Translated by John C. Chasteen. Durham: Duke University Press, 1996 [1984].

Ramírez, Susan. "Chérrepe en 1572: Un análisis de la visita general del Virrey Francisco de Toledo." *Historia y Cultura* 11 (1978): 79–122.

———. *The World Upside Down: Cross-Cultural Contact and Conflict in Sixteenth-Century Peru*. Stanford: Stanford University Press, 1996.

———. "Don Clemente Anto, procurador del común del pueblo de Lambayeque." In Javier Flores Espinoza and Rafael Varón Gabai, eds., *El hombre y los Andes: Homenaje a Franklin Pease G. Y*, 831–40. Lima: IFEA, 2002.

———. *To Feed and Be Fed: The Cosmological Bases of Authority and Identity in the Andes*. Stanford: Stanford University Press, 2005.

Ramos Pérez, Demetrio. "La crisis indiana y la Junta Magna de 1568." *Jahrbuch fur Geschichte von Staat, Wirtschaft und Gesellschaft Lateinamerikas* 23 (1986): 1–63.

Rasnake, Roger Neil. *Domination and Cultural Resistance: Authority and Power among an Andean People*. Durham: Duke University Press, 1988.

Regalado de Hurtado, Liliana. "La percepción colonial de los mitmaqkuna." A paper delivered at the 53 Congreso Internacional de Americanistas, Mexico City, July 20 2009.

Rico Callado, Francisco Luis. "Las misiones interiores en la España postridentina." *Hispania Sacra* 55, no. 111 (2003): 109–29.

Río, Mercedes del. "Estrategias andinas de supervivencia: El control de recursos en Chaqui [1989]." In Ana Maria Presta, ed., *Espacio, Etnías, Frontera. Atenuaciones políticas en el sur del Tawantinsuyu, siglos XV–XVIII*, 49–78. Sucre: Imprenta Tupac Katari, 1995.

———. *Etnicidad, territorialidad y colonialismo en los Andes: Tradición y cambio entre los Soras de los siglos XVI y XVII (Bolivia)*. Lima: IFEA, 2005.

Rivera Cusicanqui, Silvia. "Liberal Democracy and Ayllu Democracy in Bolivia: The Case of Northern Potosí." *Journal of Development Studies* 26, no. 4 (1991): 97–121.

Rodríguez Salgado, Maria-José. *The Changing Face of Empire: Charles V, Philip II and Habsburg Authority, 1551–1559*. New York: Cambridge University Press, 1988.

Romero, Carlos A. "La fundación española del Cuzco." *Revista Histórica* 14 (1941): 123–55.

Rose-Redwood, Reuben S. "Genealogies of the Grid: Revisiting Stanislawski's Search for the Origin of the Grid-Pattern Town." *Geographical Review* 98, no. 1 (2008): 42–58.

Rostworowski de Diez Canseco, María. *Curacas y sucesiones: Costa Norte*. Lima: IEP, 1961.

———. "Algunos comentarios hechos a las Ordenanzas del doctor Cuenca." *Historia y Cultura* 9 (1975): 119–54.

———. *Etnía y sociedad: Costa peruana prehispánica*. Lima: IEP, 1977.

———. *Estructuras andinas del poder: Ideología religiosa y política*. Lima: IEP, 1983.

———. *Doña Francisca Pizarro: Una ilustre mestiza 1534–1598*. 3rd ed. Lima: IEP, 2005.

Rostworowski de Diez Canseco, María, and Craig Morris. "The Fourfold Domain: Inka Power and Its Social Foundations." In Frank Salomon and Stuart B. Schwartz, eds., *The Cambridge History of the Native Peoples of the Americas. Vol. 3: South America*, 1, 769–863. New York: Cambridge University Press, 1999.

Ruiz Rodríguez, Jose Ignacio. "Las órdenes militares castellanas (siglos XVI y XVII): Dinámica política, estancamiento económico y freno social." *Hispania* 54, no. 188 (1994): 897–916.

Sáenz de Santa María, Carmelo. "La 'reducción a poblados' en el siglo XVI en Guatemala." *Anuario de Estudios Americanos* 29 (1972): 187–228.

Saignes, Thiérry. *Ambana, tierra y hombres (Provincia de Camacho, Departamento de La Paz—Bolivia)*. Lima: IFEA, 1980.

———. "Las etnías de Charcas frente al sistema colonial: Ausentismo y fugas en el debate sobre la mano de obra indígena (1595–1665)." *Jahrbuch für Geschichte von Staat, Wirtschaft und Gesellschaft Lateinamerikas* 21 (1984): 27–75.

———. *Los Andes orientales: Historia de un olvido*. Cochabamba: IFEA, 1985.

———. "The Ethnic Groups in the Valleys of Larecaja: From Descent to Residence." In John Murra, Nathan Wachtel, and Jacques Revel, eds., *Anthropological History of Andean Polities*, 311–41. Cambridge: Cambridge University Press, 1986 [1978].

———. "Lobos y ovejas: Formación y desarrollo de los pueblos y comunidades en el sur andino (siglos XVI–XX)." In Segundo Moreno Y. and Frank Salomon, eds., *Reproducción y transformación de las sociedades andinas, siglos XVI–XX*, 1, 91–135. Quito: Abya-Yala, 1991.

———. "The Colonial Condition in the Quechua-Aymara Heartland (1570–1780)." In Frank Salomon and Stuart B. Schwartz, eds., *The Cambridge History of the Native Peoples of the Americas. vol. 3: South America*, 2, 59–137. New York: Cambridge University Press, 1999.

Salcedo Salcedo, Jaime. "Los pueblos de indios en el Nuevo Reino de Granada y

Popayán." In Ramón Gutiérrez, ed., *Pueblos de indios: Otro urbanismo en la región andina*, 179–203. Quito: Abya-Yala, 1993.

Sánchez Bella, Ismael. *Las visitas generales en la América española (Siglos XVI y XVII)*. Pamplona: Universidad de Pamplona, 1992.

Sánchez, Dolores M. *El deber de consejo en el Estado moderno: Las Juntas 'ad hoc' en España (1471–1665)*. Madrid: Polifemo, 1993.

Sánchez-Albornoz, Nicolás. *Indios y tributos en el Alto Perú*. Lima: IEP, 1978.

———. "Mita, migraciones y pueblos: Variaciones en el espacio y en el tiempo. Alto Perú, 1573–1692." *Historia Boliviana* 3, no. 1 (1983): 31–59.

Sánchez-Concha Barrios, Rafael. "La tradición política y el concepto del 'cuerpo de república' en el Virreinato." In Teodoro Hampe Martinez, ed., *La tradición clásica en el Perú virreinal*, 101–14. Lima: UNMSM, 1999.

Sarfatti, Magali. *Spanish Bureaucratic-Patrimonialism in America*: Berkeley: University of California Press, 1966.

Scott, David. "Colonial Governmentality." *Social Text* 43 (1995): 191–220.

Scott, Heidi V. *Contested Territory: Mapping Peru in the Sixteenth and Seventeenth Centuries*. Notre Dame: University of Notre Dame Press, 2009.

Scott, James C. *Seeing Like a State: How Certain Schemes to Improve the Human Condition Have Failed*. New Haven: Yale University Press, 1998.

Serrano Gassent, Paz. *Vasco de Quiroga: Utopía y derecho en la conquista de América*. Madrid: Fondo de Cultura de España, 2001.

Serulnikov, Sergio. *Subverting Colonial Authority: Challenges to Spanish Rule in Eighteenth-Century Southern Andes*. Durham: Duke University Press, 2003.

Sherbondy, Jeanette. "Panaca Lands: Re-invented Communities." *Journal of the Steward Anthropological Society* 24, no. 1–2 (1996): 173–210.

Simpson, Leslie Byrd. "The Civil Congregation." In *Studies in the Administration of the Indians in New Spain*, 31–129. Berkeley: University of California Press, 1934.

Skar, Harald. *The Warm Valley People: Duality and Land Reform among the Quechua Indians of Highland Peru*. New York: Columbia University Press, 1982.

Solano, Francisco de, ed. *Ciudades hispanoamericanas y pueblos de indios*. Madrid: CSIC, 1990.

Spalding, Karen. *Huarochirí: An Andean Society Under Inca and Spanish Rule*. Stanford: Stanford University Press, 1984.

———. "The Crises and Transformations of Invaded Societies: Andean Area (1500–1580)." In Frank Salomon and Stuart B. Schwartz, eds., *The Cambridge History of the Native Peoples of the Americas. vol. 3: South America*, 1, 904–72. New York: Cambridge University Press, 1999.

Spear, Thomas. "Neo-Traditionalism and the Limits of Invention in British Colonial Africa." *Journal of African History* 44, no. 1 (2003): 3–27.

Spurling, Geoffrey Eugene. "The Organization of Craft Production in the Inka State: The Potters and Weavers of Milliraya (Peru)." PhD diss., Cornell University, 1992.

Stavig, Ward. "Continuing the Bleeding of These Pueblos Will Shortly Make Them Cadavers: The Potosi Mita, Cultural Identity, and Communal Survival in Colonial Peru." *The Americas* 56, no. 4 (2000): 529–62.

Steinmetz, George. "The Devil's Handwriting: Precolonial Discourse, Ethnographic Acuity, and Cross-Identification in German Colonialism." *Comparative Studies in Society and History* 45, no. 1 (2003): 41–95.

Stern, Steve. *Peru's Indian Peoples and the Challenge of Spanish Conquest: Huamanga to 1640.* Madison: University of Wisconsin Press, 1982.

Suárez Fernández, Luis. *Nobleza y monarquía: entendimiento y rivalidad. El proceso de construcción de la corona española.* Madrid: Esfera de los Libros, 2003.

Sullivan, John. "La congregación como tecnología disciplinaria en el siglo XVI." *Estudios de Historia Novohispana* 16 (1996): 33–55.

Taller de Historia Oral Andina. *Ayllu: Pasado y futuro de los pueblos originarios.* La Paz: Aruwiyiri, 1995.

Tau Anzoátegui, Víctor. *El poder de la costumbre: estudios sobre el derecho consuetudinario en América hispana hasta la emancipación.* Buenos Aires: IIHD, 2001.

Thomson, Sinclair. *We Alone Will Rule: Native Andean Politics in the Age of Insurgency.* Madison: University of Wisconsin Press, 2002.

Thurner, Mark. *From Two Republics to One Divided: Contradictions of Postcolonial Nation-making in Andean Peru.* Durham: Duke University Press, 1997.

Torres Balbás, Leopoldo. *Ciudades hispanomusulmanas.* 2 vols. Madrid: Ministerio de Asuntos Exteriores, 1970.

Treacy, John M. *Las chacras de Coporaque: Andenería y riego en el Valle de Colca.* Lima: IEP, 1994.

Trelles Aréstegui, Efraín. *Lucas Martínez Vegazo: funcionamiento de una encomienda peruana inicial.* Lima: PUCP, 1982.

Trumbull, George Rea, IV. "An Empire of Facts: Ethnography and the Politics of Cultural Knowledge in French Algeria, 1871–1914." PhD diss., Yale University, 2005.

Tschopik, Harry, Jr. *The Aymara of Chucuito, Peru: 1. Magic.* New York: American Museum of Natural History, 1951.

Urbano, Henrique. "Sexo, pintura de los Incas y Taqui Onqoy: Escenas de la vida cotidiana en el Cuzco del siglo XVI." *Revista Andina* 15 (1997): 207–41.

Urton, Gary. *The History of a Myth: Pacariqtambo and the Origin of the Inkas.* Austin: University of Texas Press, 1990.

———. *Signs of the Inka Khipu: Binary Coding in the Andean Knotted-String Records.* Austin: University of Texas Press, 2003.

Vaccarella, Eric. "Fábulas, letras, and razones historiales fidedignas: The Praxis of Renaissance Historiography in Pedro Sarmiento de Gamboa's Historia de los Incas." *Colonial Latin American Review* 16, no. 1 (2007): 93–107.

Valcárcel, Luis E. "El Virrey Toledo, Gran Tirano del Peru: Una revisión histórica." *Revista del Museo Nacional* 9, no. 2 (1940): 153–74, 277–309.

Van Buren, Mary. "Rethinking the Vertical Archipelago: Ethnicity, Exchange, and

History in the South Central Andes." *American Anthropologist* 98, no. 2 (1996): 338–51.

Van Cott, Donna Lee. *From Movements to Parties in Latin America: The Evolution of Ethnic Politics.* New York: Cambridge University Press, 2005.

———. *Radical Democracy in the Andes.* New York: Cambridge University Press, 2008.

VanValkenburgh, Parker. "Out of Urbs, Civitas: Landscapes of Colonial Forced Resettlement in the Zaña and Chamán Valleys, Perú." PhD diss., Harvard University, in progress.

Vargas, José María. *Fray Domingo de Santo Tomás: Defensor y apóstol de los indios del Perú.* Quito: Editorial Santo Domingo, 1937.

Vargas Ugarte, Rubén. *Historia general del Perú.* 10 vols. Lima: EditorialMilla Batres, 1966–1971.

Vassberg, David. *Land and Society in Golden-Age Castile:* Cambridge: Cambridge University Press, 1984.

Viñuales, Graciela María. "Los poblados de indios del centro y del litoral argentinos." In Ramón Gutiérrez, ed., *Pueblos de indios: Otro urbanismo en la región andina,* 449–514. Quito: Abya-Yala, 1993.

Von Hagen, Adriana, and Craig Morris. *The Cities of the Ancient Andes.* London: Thames and Hudson, 1998.

Waters, William F. "Indigenous Communities, Landlords, and the State: Land and Labor in Highland Ecuador, 1950–1975." In A. Kim Clark and Marc Becker, eds., *Highland Indians and the State in Modern Ecuador,* 120–38. Pittsburgh: University of Pittsburgh Press, 2007.

Wernke, Steven A. "An Archaeo-history of Andean Community and Landscape: The Late Pre-Hispanic and Early Colonial Colca Valley, Peru." PhD diss., University of Wisconsin, 2003.

———. "Analogy or Erasure? Dialectics of Religious Transformation in the Early Doctrinas of the Colca Valley, Peru." *International Journal of Historical Archaeology* 11, no. 2 (2007), 152–82.

———. "Negotiating Community and Landscape in the Peruvian Andes: A Transconquest View." *American Anthropologist* 109, no. 1 (2007): 130–52.

Wightman, Ann M. *Indigenous Migration and Social Change: The Forasteros of Cuzco, 1570–1720.* Durham: Duke University Press, 1990.

Wilder, Gary. *The French Imperial Nation-State: Negritude and Colonial Humanism between the Two World Wars:* Chicago, University of Chicago Press, 2005.

Yaranga Valderrama, Abdón. "Las 'reducciones,' uno de los instrumentos del etnocidio." *Revista Complutense de Historia de América* 21 (1995): 241–62.

Zagalsky, Paula. "El concepto de 'comunidad' en su dimensión espacial: Una historización de su semántica en el contexto colonial andino (siglos XVI–XVII)." *Revista Andina* 48 (2009): 57–90.

Zavala, Silvio A. *La encomienda indiana.* 2nd ed. Mexico: Ed. Porrua, 1973.

Zimmerman, Arthur F. *Francisco de Toledo, Fifth Viceroy of Peru, 1569–1581.* Caldwell, Idaho: Caxton, 1938.

Zucker, Paul. *Town and Square: From the Agora to the Village Green.* New York: Columbia University Press, 1959.

Zuidema, R. Tom. "El ushnu." *Revista de la Universidad Complutense* 28, no. 117 (1980): 317–61.

Zuloaga Rada, Marina. "La organización política india bajo el poder español en el Perú. Las guarangas y las autoridades locales en Huaylas (1532–1610)." PhD diss., Colegio de Mexico, 2008.

INDEX

cabildos: defined, 22; Andean, before General Resettlement, 65–71; Andean, in General Resettlement, 87, 97, 124, 126, 138; Andean, after General Resettlement, 146–51, 157, 163, 167, 169, 249n54; Andean *alcalde* as judge in, 148; Mesoamerican Indian, 45, 48–9; Spanish, 18–9, 31, 41, 64, 144–5, 202n38; today, 172–3. *See also alguaciles; pregoneros*

caciques: defined, 20, 28–30, 56–7, 96; and acculturation, 68–71, 164; and *cabildos*, 45, 66–70, 71, 97, 121, 152; and *corregidores de indios*, 64–8, 71, 95; and *encomenderos*, 28–32, 57–61, 68, 89; and Incas, 25, 56–8, 63, 101–4; and *mitimas*, 31–7, 112, 116, 120, 133–4; and General Resettlement, 7–9, 51, 86–97, 112–3, 116, 120, 126–9, 133, 139, 144, 164, 185, 190; after General Resettlement, 145, 148, 150–66, 181, 184; as natural lords, 57, 59, 70; in Mesoamerica, 45, 48; succession of, 96, 110, 166, 181. *See also encomienda; perpetuity controversy; repartimientos*

Cajamarca, 14–17, 23, 27, 30, 130, 207n23

canals, 105, 109, 132, 239n50

Cañaris, 20, 31

Cañete, Marquis of, Andrés Hurtado de Mendoza, Viceroy of Peru (1556–1560), 50–1, 62

Carangas, 115–6, 209n45

Cárdenas, licenciado Francisco de, 136, 240n66

cargos and cargo careers, 167

Caribbean Islands, 1, 7, 20, 28, 42, 44–5, 175, 213n16

Casas, Bartolomé de las, 21, 55–6, 59, 70, 80–1, 99–105, 114, 217n87, 229n12

casta. See segregation policy

Castilian language, 43, 50, 68, 179

Castro, licenciado Lope Garcia de, governor of Peru (1564–9), 62–71, 83, 87, 93

censuses, 5, 30, 33, 58, 65–7, 86–7, 112,

122, 128, 131, 138, 148, 158–9, 165, 179, 181–2, 188. *See also visitas*

Cercado, El, 87

Cervantes, Miguel de. *See Don Quixote*

chacaras, 145–6, 159

Charcas, Audiencia of, 5–6, 69, 86, 92–4, 122, 124, 151, 156, 161, 187

Charles V and I, Holy Roman Emperor and King of Spain (1516–1555), 21, 32, 45, 49, 55, 77, 80, 86

Chérrepe, 125–7

chicha, 14, 23–5, 97–8, 126, 134, 154, 172, 174

Chile, Audiencia of, 5, 62, 137, 151

Chimba, La, 193

Chiriguanos, 99, 135

Chucuito, 114, 150, 170, 209n45, 215n61, 239n59, 243n23, 244n34

Church: administration and politics, 77–81, 99, 194; calendar and festivals, 98, 153, 157; Councils, 49, 50, 78. *See also* churches; friars; Inquisition; priests in Andean communities

churches: in Spanish cities, x, 23, 46; in Indian villages before General Resettlement, 48, 58, 120, 130, 145; in *reducciones*, 1, 26, 69, 87, 98, 124, 125, 132–3, 138–9, 146, 154, 156, 157, 164; in annexes, 156, 167

Cieza de León, Pedro de, 36, 105, 109, 206n14, 208n35, 223n11

cities and towns: as ceremonial centers, 8, 23–6, 204n54; foundation ceremonies for, 18, 125; and ideology of urbanism, 2, 21–3, 46–7; juridical status of (*ciudad, villa* and *aldea*), 22; Mesoamerican, 45; Spanish colonial, 31, 46, 60, 93, 95, 159. *See also* Inca; plazas; *policía; reducciones*; urban grid

citizenship, universal, 167–8, 171–2

civil wars of Peru, 27, 37, 50, 54–5, 58–9, 76, 102, 107

civilization, idea of, 14, 21, 34, 47, 109, 182. *See also policía*

classicism, 4, 14, 34, 109, 111, 178

cloth and clothing, 174, 98, 146, 244n27;

establishment of, 14, 21, 57–8, 103–4, 130–1; feasting and reciprocity, 13–14, 24–5, 58; government institutions, 70–1, 105, 154; memory today, 171–2; and *mitimas*, 28, 31–9, 106, 108–9, 114–5, 133, 180–1; palaces, 13, 17–20; resettlements, 36, 106; Spanish admiration for, 3–4, 9–10, 21, 26, 36–9, 51, 70, 104–5, 109, 113–4, 179–80, 184; storage, 15, 21, 23, 27, 36; as tyrants, 99–117, 134. *See also aqlla*; Cuzco; *panacas*; roads; *tamp'u*

incest, 2, 70, 98. *See also* sexual intercourse

India, 182–3

inns within *reducciones*, 49, 69. *See also* segregation policy; *tambos*

Inquisition, 37, 77, 81, 99, 104, 135, 162, 194

inspectors. *See* General Resettlement of Indians; *visitas*

Isabella and Ferdinand, monarchs of Castile and Aragon, 43–4

Isidore of Seville, 22, 229n7

jails, 49, 69, 81, 87, 97, 124, 135, 159

Jauja, 27, 35, 54, 57–68, 199n5, 203n53, 224n14

Jesuits, 88, 99, 135

Jews, 42–3

juego de cañas, 70

Julien, Catherine, 128, 194, 230n16, 245n3

Junta Magna, 7, 75–83, 101

justicia. See gobierno and *justicia*

keys and locks, 97, 144, 174

La Paz, 95, 144, 159, 173, 189, 242n5, 250n68

La Plata, 6, 35, 36, 69, 85, 93, 122, 189, 194–5. *See also* Charcas

Lake Titicaca, 133, 175, 193

Lambayeque, 163

languages. *See under names of specific languages*

Larecaja, 163, 208n44

Latin language, 48, 101, 104–5

law and laws, 30, 34, 37, 97, 134, 179, 180; after Independence, 167–8; Andean, 42–3, 59, 105, 112–4; customary, and legal pluralism, 181–3, 209n3, 234n71; medieval, 101, 105; natural or universal, 80, 82, 99–101; *ordenanzas*, 68, 69, 85–6, 96, 119, 145, 163; *reales cédulas*, 49, 77, 93, 95, 162, 196, 202n37, 211n30. *See also gobierno* and *justicia*

lawsuits: by Andeans, 60, 67, 93, 115, 133, 143–6, 150, 158, 166; by encomenderos, 33–4; and General Resettlement, 123, 125, 133–4, 138–9; as historical source, 133–4; *interrogatorios* in, 103–4; revenue from, 93, 123, 138, 145; slowness of, 145, 161–3; within *reducciones*, 148. *See also gobierno* and *justicia*

lawyers and jurists, 23, 37, 69, 80, 82, 93, 145

letrados, 62, 77. *See also* lawyers and jurists

Lima, Audiencia of, 5–6, 50, 62, 86, 89, 92–3, 96, 136, 156, 187; city of, 50, 59, 60–1, 66, 80, 85, 87–8, 108, 135, 139, 159, 173–4

literacy, 21, 97, 125, 148, 150. *See also quipus*

llamas and alpacas, 3, 14, 21, 25, 33, 35, 114, 121, 123, 148, 173

Loarte, doctor Gabriel de, 100, 103

Loayza, fray Gerónimo de, 113–4, 211n32, 212n37, 216n71, 225n28, 226n34

López de Velasco, Juan, 161

Macha, 145–6, 189, 194–5, 223n60, 236n13

Machaca la Grande, and Jesús de Machaca, 173, 193

maize, 3, 23, 27, 35–6, 115. *See also chicha*

mallqui. See mummies

resettlement. *See* General Resettlement of Indians; *reducciones*

Ribera, don Antonio de, 54–66

roads: Inca, 14, 17, 105; after Independence, 168, 172; and labor draft, 25, 97, 113; need for, 66, 176; Spanish admiration for, 14, 36, 88, 109–10, 180. *See also* tambos; *tamp'u*

Roman Empire. *See* classicism

Sacsayhuaman, 17, 20–1

Sahagún, fray Bernardino de, 35

saints, in Andean village devotion, 156, 167, 174, 248n38, 248n54

Santa Fe, Audiencia of, 137

Santa Fe, Spain, 47

Santillán, Hernando de, 211n33, 213n17

Santo Domingo, Audiencia of, 199n3, 209n6, 240n62; city of, 46. *See also* Caribbean islands

Santo Tomás, fray Domingo de, 35, 39, 56, 60–1, 225n28

Sarmiento de Gamboa, Pedro, 104–7, 110, 116, 130, 135, 223n13

saya, 29, 113, 131, 165, 188, 206n20. *See also ayllus; repartimientos*

Scott, James, 176–9

segregation policy excluding non-Andeans from *reducciones*, 124, 152, 162–3, 217n84

Seville, 18, 77, 81, 122, 194

sexual intercourse, 2, 70, 87, 98, 149

Siete Partidas, 101–3, 108–9

slavery, 23, 109, 155; African, 20, 221n31; Indian, 44; "natural," 69–70

Soto, Domingo de, 229n12

Soviet Union, 1, 117–8

Spanish language. *See* Castilian language

Suazo, Lope de, 130–2

Tacobamba, 189, 194, 239n56, 244n34

Taino. *See* Caribbean Islands

tambos (Spanish), 95–7, 113, 124, 153, 204n59; inns within *reducciones*, 49, 69.

tamp'u (Inca), 14–5, 25, 36, 95, 105, 180; defined, 204n59.

Tanzania, 1, 176–8

Tarija, 244n34

tasa. See General Inspection

Tawantinsuyu. *See* Inca

Tenochtitlán, 46, 201n34. *See also* Mexico City

theology, 35, 65, 80–2, 101, 104, 252n12

Titu Cusi, 107–8

Toledo, Alejandro, 172

Toledo, don Francisco de, Viceroy of Peru (1569–81): and caciques, 89–90, 95–6, 120, 164, 181; career of, 75–80, 135–6; and *corregidores*, 93–4, 216n79; entourage of, 88, 100, 223n13; historiography of, 8–9, 76, 99–100; and Incas, 96, 99–112, 179; legislation by, 94–8; memory of, 154–6; and *mitimas*, 112–6; opposition to, 92–4, 135–6; royal instructions to, 78, 80–3, 108, 194–6, 122, 198n5. *See also* General Inspection; General Resettlement of Indians; *reducciones*

Toledo, fray García de, 102–4, 109

Topa Inca Yupanqui, 105–6

trade and markets, 23, 49, 163, 169, 174; absence of, in prehispanic Peru, 21, 23–4, 37, 203n53; Andeans in colonial, 115, 153; in Atlantic economy, 81, 194. *See also* wage labor

traza. See urban grid

tributaries, 30, 93, 128, 131, 181, 187–93, 228n62. *See also* General Inspection

tribute. *See encomienda; repartimientos*

Tucumán, 5, 137

tyrants: Aristotle's definition of, 7, 101, 105; caciques as, 102, 166; conquistadors as, 102; Incas as, 99–117, 134, 179–80; in Siete Partidas, 101–3; Toledo as, 99–100

urban grid: in Inca cities, 14, 46; in colonial Spanish cities, 18–19, 46–7; in *reducciones*, 1, 8, 48, 87, 125–6, 160, 165. *See also* cities and towns; plazas

Jeremy Ravi Mumford is a visiting assistant professor of history at
Brown University.

Library of Congress Cataloging-in-Publication Data
Mumford, Jeremy Ravi.
Vertical empire : the General Resettlement of Indians in the
colonial Andes / Jeremy Ravi Mumford.
p. cm.
Includes bibliographical references and index.
ISBN 978-0-8223-5296-9 (cloth : alk. paper)
ISBN 978-0-8223-5310-2 (pbk. : alk. paper)
1. Indians of South America—Andes Region—Government
relations.   2. Spain—Colonies—America—Administration.
3. Andes Region—History—16th century.   I. Title.
F2230.1.G68M86 2012
980—dc23 2012011597